Martyrdom, Self-Sacrifice, and Self-Immolation

Martyrdom, Self-Sacrifice, and Self-Immolation

Religious Perspectives on Suicide

Edited by
MARGO KITTS

OXFORD
UNIVERSITY PRESS

OXFORD
UNIVERSITY PRESS

Oxford University Press is a department of the University of Oxford. It furthers the University's objective of excellence in research, scholarship, and education by publishing worldwide. Oxford is a registered trade mark of Oxford University Press in the UK and certain other countries.

Published in the United States of America by Oxford University Press
198 Madison Avenue, New York, NY 10016, United States of America.

CIP data is on file at the Library of Congress
ISBN 978-0-19-065649-2 (pbk.)
ISBN 978-0-19-065648-5 (hbk.)

Contents

List of Contributors

Asma Afsaruddin is Professor of Islamic Studies in the School of Global and International Studies at Indiana University. A Carnegie Scholar, she is the author and editor of seven books, including *Striving in the Path of God: Jihad and Martyrdom in Islamic Thought* (Oxford University Press, 2013).

David Brick is Senior Lecturer of Sanskrit at Yale University. His publications include *Brahmanical Theories of the Gift: A Critical Edition and Annotated Translation of the Dānakāṇḍa of the Kṛtyakalpataru* (Harvard Oriental Series, 2015); "The Dharmaśāstric Debate on Widow-Burning" (JAOS, 2010); "The Widow-Ascetic Under Hindu Law" (IIJ, 2014); "Bhoḥ as a Linguistic Marker of Brahmanical Identity" (JAOS, 2016).

Louis E. Fenech, a native of Toronto, Canada, has been involved in the study of the Sikh tradition throughout his entire academic career. He is the author of a number of monographs and articles on the tradition as well as co-editor, with Pashaura Singh, of the *Oxford Handbook of Sikh Studies* (Oxford University Press, 2014).

Mohammed M. Hafez is Associate Professor of National Security Affairs at the Naval Postgraduate School in Monterey, California. A specialist in Islamist violence, he is the author of *Why Muslims Rebel: Repression and Resistance in the Islamic World* (Lynne Rienner, 2003), among other works. Dr. Hafez earned his PhD from the London School of Economics in 2000.

Najam Haider is an Associate Professor of Religion at Barnard College of Columbia University. His most recent book is *Shīʿī Islam: An Introduction* (Cambridge University Press, 2014). His research interests include identity formation and historical memory in the premodern Muslim world. His current project focuses on the link between Late Antique and Early Muslim historiography.

Margo Kitts is Professor and Coordinator of Religious Studies and East-West Classical Studies at Hawai'i Pacific University. She is the author or editor of six books and over thirty articles dealing with ancient literature and/or religion and violence. Her most recent book is *Elements of Ritual and Violence* (Cambridge University Press, 2018). She edits the *Journal of Religion and Violence* and co-edits the series, Cambridge Elements of Religion and Violence.

Reiko Ohnuma is Professor of Religion, Asian and Middle Eastern Studies, and Women's, Gender, and Sexuality Studies at Dartmouth College. She specializes in the Buddhist traditions of South Asia. She is the author of *Head, Eyes, Flesh, and Blood: Giving Away the Body in Indian Buddhist Literature* (Columbia University Press, 2007).

Benjamin Schonthal is Senior Lecturer in Buddhism and Asian Religions at the University of Otago, in New Zealand. Ben's research examines the intersections of religion, law, and politics in late-colonial and contemporary Southern Asia. He is the author of *Buddhism, Politics and the Limits of Law: The Pyrrhic Constitutionalism of Sri Lanka* (Cambridge University Press, 2016).

Shmuel Shepkaru is the Schusterman Professor of Jewish Intellectual and Religious History at the University of Oklahoma. He has published on the topic of martyrdom, Jewish-Christian relations, and Israeli culture. One of his publications is *Jewish Martyrs in the Pagan and Jewish Worlds* (Cambridge University Press, 2006).

Jacqueline I. Stone teaches Buddhism and Japanese Religions in the Religion Department at Princeton University. She has co-edited two volumes of essays on death and dying in Buddhist cultures. Her most recent study is *Right Thoughts at the Last Moment: Buddhism and Deathbed Practices in Early Medieval Japan* (University of Hawai'i Press, 2016).

Mary Storm has an MA in East Asian Studies from Stanford University and a PhD in South Asian Art History from the University of California, Los Angeles. She is the author *of Head and Heart: Valour and Self-Sacrifice in the Art of India* (Routledge, 2013). In search of art-historical adventures, she has travelled from Ladakh to Tamil Nadu and Rajasthan to Orissa. She lives and works in Galle, Sri Lanka.

Gail P. Streete is Professor Emerita of Religious Studies at Rhodes College. She is the author of numerous articles on women in antiquity, asceticism, and

Christian martyrdom, as well as four books, the latest of which, *Redeemed Bodies* (Westminster/John Knox, 1997), discusses the connection between gender and martyrdom in early Christianity.

Anne Vallely is Associate Professor of Religious Studies at the University of Ottawa since 2004. She is an anthropologist of South Asian religion whose research centers on asceticism, devotional practices, animals, human/non-human boundaries, and death and mourning rituals in India, especially among the Jaina community.

Catherine Wessinger is Rev. H. James Yamauchi, S.J. Professor of the History of Religions at Loyola University New Orleans. She is author of *How the Millennium Comes Violently: From Jonestown to Heaven's Gate* (Seven Bridges Press, 2000); editor of *Millennialism, Persecution, and Violence: Historical Cases* (Syracuse University Press, 2000), and *The Oxford Handbook of Millennialism* (Oxford University Press, 2011).

Jimmy Yu is Associate Professor at Florida State University, where he teaches courses on Buddhism and East Asian religions. His research interests include the history of the body in Chinese religions, Buddhist material culture, Chan/Zen Buddhisms, and popular religious movements within the broader context of fifteenth- to seventeenth-century China. He is the author of *Sanctity and Self-Inflicted Violence in Chinese Religions, 1500–1700* (Oxford University Press, 2012).

Martyrdom, Self-Sacrifice, and Self-Immolation

I

Introduction

ON DEATH, RELIGION, AND RUBRICS FOR SUICIDE

Margo Kitts

HOWEVER BROADLY OR narrowly one conceives the sphere of religious imagination, death is one element at its core. Analysts from Sigmund Freud to Giorgio Agamben have pondered religion's fascination with death, and religious art is saturated with death-related spectacles: not only hells and Armageddons, but also tortures and mutilations—that is, images of suffering unto death. But, as this volume shows, religious fascination with death extends beyond speculation about suffering, punishments, and end times to the notion of elective death, its desirable or baleful circumstances, the virtue or scandal of those who perform it, and how best to commemorate it.

This volume's chapters address the legendary foundations for those elective deaths which might be framed as religiously sanctioned suicides. With the exceptions of three contemporary perspectives often ascribed classical roots (those of two Christian apocalyptic groups [Wessinger], contemporary Salafist Islamists [Hafez], and some Tamils [Schonthal]), most perspectives herein focus on originary visions which lie at the heart of classical religious traditions and which continue to shape the imaginations of adherents. This introduction sketches some underlying themes in those visions by reflecting on the title's terms: suicide, religion, martyrdom, self-sacrifice, and self-immolation.

Suicide

"Suicide" is perhaps the most contested of these terms. Broadly condemned as cowardice across the world's moral codes, suicide under different rubrics—such as martyrdom, self-sacrifice, or self-immolation—is conferred a dynamic quality in a number of religious legends, some tragic and others uplifting. Audiences respond to such legends presumably because choosing death in certain circumstances is seen as heroic and often as catalyzing redemption, for the individuals who die, for their communities, or for humanity. It is obvious that envisioning suicide as virtuous clashes with popular conceptions of suicide as weak, immoral, and even criminal, but that is precisely the point. Suicide as elective death (hereinafter so named), its heroic connotations, and its redemptive framings are legendary, and they continue to resonate in both religious and nationalist lore.[1]

Compelling lore about elective death might be surmised too as behind the contemporary profusion of terroristic self-killings enacted under religious banners. Despite the focus on origins in these chapters (with the aforementioned exceptions), we would be remiss here to ignore this pressing reality and some of the analyses typically offered to explain it. Since at least the 1970s, historians of religion have been forced to confront the violence in inspirational religious texts, whether that violence is meant as actual or symbolic, and whether perceptions of its origins are historically apt. Over the last five decades we have been immersed in a robust and often bombastic discourse on religion and its destructive effects.[2] Despite this discourse, many analysts of suicide terrorism downplay religious inspirations in favor of, say, regional tensions and their complex historical contingencies, ethnic humiliation and the degrading impact of colonialism, disenchantment with Western mores (fanned by social media), or the strategic aims of asymmetrical warfare; occasionally, they treat charismatic leadership and the cultural construction of altruism. These last two factors implicitly relate to the power of religious

1. Elective death due to despair or insurmountable difficulty is also not lacking in early sources, of course. The despair of Job is nearly lethal (Job 3); Jocasta's despair is indeed lethal (*Oedipus Rex* 1369); Saul has no way out (1 Sam. 31.1–10); and nor does Samson, who, at least on the surface of the text (Judg. 16), is lauded for simultaneously inflicting mass casualties as he dies.

2. Important resources for exploring the theoretical dimensions include the *Oxford Handbook of Religion and Violence, Princeton Readings in Religion and Violence, Blackwell Companion to Religion and Violence*, all issues of the *Journal of Religion and Violence*, and special issues of other journals, such as the *Asian Journal of Social Sciences* vol. 38, no. 3 (2010).

modeling,[3] even as interwoven with many other motivations, all of which are not easy to disentangle.

But it would be foolish to deny that some individuals who choose to perform terroristic self-killings may do so based on seemingly sincere religious motivations, however bewildering those motivations may seem to most of us. To so deny would be to ignore the hagiographies and martyr videos that celebrate them as pious heroes who exude extraordinary selflessness and dedication, both to otherworldly goals and to eliminating suffering for their own communities. The cosmic war scenario and the thrill of individual participation in it have been well described by Mark Juergensmeyer,[4] while the valorization of selflessness is conspicuous in artifacts such as the last will and testament of Muhammad Hazza al-Ghoul: "We do not sing songs of death, but recite the hymns of life . . . We die so that future generations may live."[5] Strategic end goals aside, it is undeniable that elective death here is lionized, as it is in a variety of the traditions discussed in this volume. Not only in the West but in Asia, personal motivations do matter for evaluating elective death, which is why the study of felt religious triggers, however slippery to analytical grasp, also matters.

As a point of comparison, it would be inconceivable to eliminate religious triggers in analyzing elective deaths in ancient Christianity, which, albeit, lacked the dimension of suicide terrorism. Yet elective deaths as represented by early Christians were not short on militaristic trope and spectacular suffering, which they saw as intrinsically religious. Hence Tertullian: "We [Christians] want to suffer, just as a soldier wants to fight," "[Christians are] a race ready for death," and "If he is denounced, he glories in it . . . when he is condemned, he renders thanks."[6] And, Clement of Alexandria: "Be of good courage like the man in the arena . . . [who] nobly confronts toils rendering thanks to God." And, Cyprian: "In the battle line the soldier is tested." And, Justin: "Although we are beheaded and crucified, and exposed to wild beasts

---

3. On which see, e.g., Hassan; Hafez, "Alchemy"; Somasundaram; Bloom, *Dying*; Tosini.

4. N.b., Juergensmeyer's *Terror*, "Performance Violence," and "Cosmic War."

5. Quoted in Hafez, "Rationality" 176. See also the glorification of young death in this poetic refrain from the Last Instructions of 9/11:

> "Smiling towards the face of the perished one (dead): O youth
> You are coming to the Gardens of Eternity" (Kitts, *"Last Night"* 297).

6. ad mart.4. Discussed so well in Bowersock 59–74.

and chains and flames, and every other means of torture, it is evident that we will not retract our profession of faith; the more we are persecuted, the more do others in ever increasing numbers embrace the faith and become worshipers of God through the name of Jesus."[7] There is an agonistic tone to this "rhetoric of resistance," as Gail Streete points out in Chapter 3.

Just as it is today, one target of that agonistic rhetoric was those who were prone to resist its logic. Christian apologists adeptly exploited the tropes of warrior, athlete, and victory with an astute ear for Roman sensibilities, which they sought both to defy and to reshape. Yet, the flamboyant suffering of Christians caused some Romans to recoil. For example, the marriage of religious ardor with bloody torture in the arena scandalized Marcus Aurelius, a Stoic who approved autothanasia, but was repulsed by the contumacious displays of victimhood by Christians.[8] Epictetus, Lucian, and their contemporaries were just as appalled, not only at the theatricality, but at Christians' devout desire for death, as illustrated in Ignatius's petition to die gruesomely and with joy[9]:

> Suffer me to be eaten by the beasts, through whom I can attain to God. I am God's wheat and I am ground by the teeth of wild beasts that I may be found the pure bread of Christ . . . Then shall I be truly a disciple of Jesus Christ, when the world shall not see my body . . . If I suffer I shall be Jesus Christ's freedman. (*Ad Romanos* 4.1– 3)[10]

While not self-effacing, as Marcus would have preferred, such sufferings must at least have piqued the curiosity of Roman spectators weaned on Greek legends of Iphigenia, Polyxena, Menoeceus, and acts of *devotio* by Roman generals such as Decius.[11] Those patriotic and selfless deaths helped to set the stage for the reception of early Christian suffering, with the startling difference, per Tertullian, Clement, and others, that Christians sought glory in the next life, not for themselves or their brethren in this one.[12]

---

7. See perceptive studies by Perkins; Bowersock; Shaw; de Ste. Croix; Castelli; Coleman; as well as Streete, *Redeemed Bodies* and Chapter 3 within, showing that the comparison of Christians, both male and female, to warriors was shrewdly manipulated by Church fathers.

8. Discussed in detail by Perkins 15–40, 173–99; and in passing by Bowersock and van Hooff.

9. Discussed by Perkins 104–23; de Ste.Croix 186–89, 192–93.

10. See Castelli 79; and Streete, Chapter 3.

11. See the evidence in van Henten and Avemarie.

12. Hence, Clement of Alexandria: "Forsake our sojourning in this world and . . . do the will of him who called." (Lake 1917: II; Clement 5.1; in Perkins 24.)

Similar valor but also controversies inform virtually every tradition treated in this volume. Under the same Roman halo as the Christians, Philo and Josephus eloquently ascribed heroism to the Jews who embraced death during the Roman siege at Masada, although the two denied the virtue of elective death elsewhere (see Shepkaru, Chapter 2). The earliest Islamic discourses unambiguously disparaged elective death, and heavenly rewards were not predicated on struggle. Yet the merit attributed to those embracing death in battle shifted in some later hadiths (Afsaruddin, *Striving*, "Martyrdom," and Chapter 5). Shīʿī Imāms, nearly all of them, are adored for having stood for justice while murdered, but their heroism is complicated by a presumed foreknowledge of their imminent murders, in tension with the general Islamic prohibition on suicide: in other words, if they were prescient, why didn't they avoid their impending deaths (Haider, Chapter 6)? On the Sikhs, Lou Fenech notes (Chapter 11) the essential role of the martyrologist in constructing the famed soldier-saint; reverence for the self-sacrificing śahīdī rose in waves from the late eighteenth century up to the last decades of the twentieth, retrojected back onto the earliest gurus via increasingly glorifying poetry and prose. In the case of the Liberation Tigers of Tamil Eelam (hereinafter LTTE), Ben Schonthal points out (in Chapter 12) that speeches commemorating the self-killing Black Tigers were restrained in tone, and judiciously ambiguous, lest the subject of their elective deaths offend religious tastes. Note that, while a tenor of righteous struggle pervades some of these memorializations, it is often attenuated by theological caution.

Some other elective deaths might appear comparatively pristine, but there are ambiguities in virtually all cases. In the Jain tradition, for example, greatly revered are deaths by sallekhanā, wherein fasting to death is meant to minimize one's burden on other living beings, but also to enable one's self-actualization (see Vallely, Chapter 10). So how altruistic is it? Across the panorama of Buddhist traditions too, there is a fine irony in giving one's life selflessly to help other beings, but then benefitting from it by accruing spiritual merit (as noted by Ohnuma, Yu, and Stone, in Chapters 13, 14, and 15, respectively). The altruism ascribed to the Hindu sati, or self-immolating widow, is applauded for certain castes in early law texts, but there are disputes about the widow's proper role: is winning heaven for herself and her husband the most desirable goal, or should she instead strive for liberation from the cycle of rebirth through ascetic celibacy (see Brick, Chapter 9)? The early Indian sannyāsin and sadhu, thought to have burned off secular ties to the self, were lauded for ascetic practices that led to their personal extinguishments, even though some texts condemned elective death (see Storm, Chapter 8). The cultivation of emptiness in some Jain, Buddhist, and Hindu traditions certainly mandates a different lens for viewing selfless acts, particularly if there is no felt self. Assuming, with Durkheim for a moment, that practitioners of religious asceticism may feel engulfed in something they regard as their true essence, it would be difficult to apply a cost-benefit analysis to acts of selflessness which are rooted in a sublime sense of self that transcends corporeal life.

Religion

What could be such a sublime sense of self that transcends corporeal life? The religious dimension to all this is also contested, as is conspicuous in the case of the LTTE, some of whom deny the relevance of religion altogether (Schonthal, Chapter 12). It is indisputable that scholarship on the nature of religion is in the throes of a thorough refashioning. No longer do we assume that religion must address *logoi* about *theoi* (as in "theologies"); instead, awareness of global diversity—e.g., the varying Asian sensibilities mentioned above—has forced us to question the lenses through which we historically have viewed religion. One emergent lens is imagination, particularly narrative imagination, which happens to correlate well with the study of the textual traditions explored herein. Another lens is visceral perception, and a third, related to the others, is the generative capacity of ritual. We can barely scratch the vast surface of religious studies in this introduction, but we can reference briefly some scholarly insights stemming from these emerging foci.

First, a focus on narrative imagination allows a study not only of heroes and antiheroes, but of aesthetics, ethnic receptions, and figurative language, along with those category-bending perceptions that may be elicited by poetic turns of phrase. Arguably, poetic turns of phrase are the stuff of religious imagination because, as Aristotle understood, they can evoke heightened or skewed perceptions and bring subliminal discernments to consciousness.[13] Metaphor, catachresis, and poetic extension are well-known tools for such evocations, but more central to our discourse these days are the existential layers of perception that those tools attempt to evoke. No longer do we accept that all categories of experience simply are socially imposed; rather, since the existential phenomenologists and the perceptive theorists who harvested their thoughts,[14] some of us seek

13. Aristotle, *Poetics* 22. Black and Ricoeur famously add to this discussion.

14. Notable among these are Vasquez; Csordas; Bryan Turner, 31–121; Johnson; and Friedson, *Dancing Prophets* and *Remains of Ritual*.

to explore those visceral dimensions to experience that seem to elude discursive signification. Instead of pointing up to the transcendent, astute religious scholars now look deep into perception to ponder both how certain perceptions are aroused and the cultural vessels through which they are communicated. So, for instance, under the topical umbrella of religion and violence we have, on the one hand, a thriving study of occult practices and the ritualized manufacture of visceral terror,[15] and, on the other, the study of the somatic dimension to comprehension and the subtle reach of visceral terror into thought and expression.[16] We are fascinated by, among other things, those somatic comprehensions that do not quite make it to the level of thought and yet are felt (variously characterized as the eerie, the uncanny, chilling fear, etc.).

Next, at the broader level of collective narratives, we must reckon with the shared and shifting imaginaries that support and respond to elective death. Since at least the work of Charles Taylor, we have distinguished an imagination from an imaginary by the way the latter manifests in practice; it is "that largely unstructured and inarticulate understanding of our whole situation, within which particular features of our world become evident" and for which "practice largely carries the understanding" (107). As is well studied, contemporary imaginaries, barely tethered to cosmologies, perpetually expand, shift, and mutate, birthing the conceivable from the inconceivable, the normative from the liminoid (as Victor Turner used the term). Yet they don't simply pop out of nowhere. Imaginaries have roots in traditional understandings, however bent into contemporary formations. Elsewhere I correlated the ways these bent formations are recognized with Goran Aijmer's iconic dimension of the violent imaginary, wherein "symbolic displays of strong expressive force . . . make manifest people's intuitive cognizance as to what ultimately conditions social and personal experience" (3).[17] As touched upon ahead under self-immolation, representations of elective deaths, as "symbolic displays of strong expressive force," may pierce complacency and disturb received worlds, all the while seeded in those worlds. With its shifting nature

15. See generally Kitts, "Evil and Terror," and *Ritual.* On assault sorcery and shamanic terror see Whitehead, Stewart and Strathern, *Violence;* Strathern and Stewart; and Behrend.

16. E.g., Innis; Kapferer; Friedson, *Remains*; and Kitts, *Ritual.* Cf the cognitive evolutionists, whose limits of imagination are captured well by Laidlaw and by Stewart and Strathern, *Ritual,* 109, 111, 114–16. Related to the vivid sway of icons on perception, see the study of corporeal imagination by Cox Miller. On the physicality of demons as perceived in late antiquity, see Smith.

17. Kitts, "Literary Perspectives," "Discursive, Iconic," and *Elements.*

and simultaneously deep roots, the imaginary has become a rivet for a generation of scholars of religion, sociology, and anthropology.

Last, because the imaginary is manifested and carried through practice, a related and thriving discourse addresses the generative capacity of ritual. Scholars from Freud and Jensen through Girard and Burkert have fixated on the inducement of epiphanies through ritualized violence, and some subject areas, such as the ancient Near East, are awash with studies of ritualized menace, as in debasing corpses (Olyan, Noegel) and dancing with disembodied heads (Collon). Less macabre but no less significant are the ritual purifications that precede some elective but murderous deaths which are staged, figuratively speaking, under religious shrouds. The "godly asceticism" of LTTE self-immolators (Schalk) and the prayer, bathing, and expectorating of religious verses into clothing by the 9/11 bombers (Kitts, "Last Night") are but a few sensational illustrations of ritual practices which seem expected somehow to lift elective deaths (if not their murderous repercussions) to a sublime sphere.

In sum, the study of religion, in all its complexity, now leans toward the sensuous and the imagined. The study of elective death too correlates a sensuous dimension of comprehension, such as grasping what it means to suffer, with an imagination, however fluid and ritually enhanced, of what it means to die.

Martyrdom

A person who dies nobly in the face of religious persecution is generally accepted as a martyr, but the history of the word "martyr" is far more complex. Despite the notion's longstanding allure in the West, martyrdom's deepest roots are surprisingly overlooked. The Greek word "martyr" originates in Homeric epic in the call for divine witnesses to oath-making rituals, wherein Zeus and other gods are invoked as *martyroi* to "punish men, whosoever should swear a false oath" (e.g., Il. 3.276–80; 19.259–60).[18] By ritual analogy,

18. Beekes and Beek observe that the tu-r suffix of "martyr" indicates its non-Indo-European origin, and that speculation about its Sanskrit root in *smer ("remember") cannot be correct. Against the usual reconstruction from Sanskrit *smarati* (as a derivative of Greek *mermana*, care, making *martys* remembrance), it is pointed out that a reconstruction smr-tu would give instead *βρατυ-. They conclude, therefore, that the word *martys* is not Indo-European but rather a loan, which is confirmed by the non-Indo-European suffix tu-s or tu-r (909). Thus, Homeric *martys* must be seen as the first such reference in any Indo-European language. There is quite a different history and trajectory for other terms in the Homeric oath-making lexicon, such as *homnumi* ("I swear an oath, take a vow"), *homoklē* ("a threatening cry, a reprimand"), and *tamnō* ("I cut [an oath]"), all of which do bear Indo-European roots. *Sphazdō*

punishments range from spilling brains to slitting throats, with human witnesses, along with the gods, swearing to impose these retributions on oath-violators (Il. 3.297–301). The death of the oath-victim at the heart of the ritual not only mirrors the punishment due oath-violators, but also seals into finality the commitments sworn (Kitts, *Sanctified Violence*). The twin notions of witnessing and commitment extend throughout classical literature into the Gospels, where the legal context for the martyr seems to persist. Given the scholarly fascination with Christian martyrdom, it is surprising that so few scholars actually ponder the transformation of martyr from a witness (*martys*) invited to punish oath-violators and to call divine punishment upon them, to someone who suffers mortally in witnessing to religious conviction.[19]

Because of the word's semantic flip and the notion's bloody legacy, it is worth attempting to capture this moment of transformation. The shift in meaning does not begin with Hesiod, who continues to use *martyra* to refer to a witness who offers a fence against duplicity (*Works and Days* 370–72). It is not with Greek tragedy, where *martyromai* can denote witnessing to speech acts, with the implication of punishment for deceit (n.b., Euripides, *Medea* 619). It is not quite with the classical sphere of law, where *martyrein* denotes testifying (Demosthenes 29.15–16, 20; 45.60[20]). The legal sense of the word persists into Matthew 26.59, where *pseudomartyrian* denotes giving false witness; into Acts 7.58, where the stoners of Stephen are designated legal witnesses (*hoi martyres*) to the punishment; and even into Revelation 3.14 which, as I read it, denotes a faithful witness to the truth—*ho martys ho pistos kai alēthinos*—describing the Lord (hence *Amēn* just before it), quite on a par with Homeric usage. Bowersock notes the conceivable inception of Christian martyrdom with Revelation 2.13, which refers to Antipas, "my faithful witness [martyr] who was killed among you" (*ho martys mou, ho pistos mou, hos apektanthē par hymin*), and that the passage is ambiguous: was Antipas a witness who happened to be slain, or was he slain because he was a witness? But Gail Streete points out (Chapter 3) that Luke has Jesus equate testimony (*martyrion*) on his behalf with persecution (*diōxousin*) for his followers (Luke 21:12–13), and that imitation of Christ is an outstanding theme in the death of Stephen in Luke-Acts, with earlier hints in the letters of Paul. Given

("I slaughter, cut the throat"), a verb used in commensal sacrifices, also is original with Homer (Beekes and Beek).

19. Bowersock does ponder exactly the transformation from the legal context, although I hope to have enriched his analysis.

20. Sommerstein, Bayliss, and James 89, n.98.

that the time frame for Revelation (90–95 CE) roughly matches that for Luke (ca. 90 CE) and fits inside that surmised for 1 Peter 4:12–19 (80–110 CE)—another text which full-throatedly extols Christian suffering—and given that both Revelation and Luke anticipate the aforementioned writing of Ignatius (d. 98–117 CE), who craved being rent by beasts, it is likely that the Greek understanding of "martyr" makes its shift just before the turn of the second century CE. In any case, it isn't until the death of Polycarp (155 CE) that the term "martyr" clearly is launched into Christian vernacular to denote one who suffers and dies as a witness to religious conviction, rather than one who punishes oath-violators.[21]

If persecution, suffering, and death are the markers of martyrdom, however, we need not begin or stop with Christians. Typically, death both zealously welcomed and zealously inflicted characterizes Maccabean legends of triumphal sufferings at the hands of the Seleucids and the apparent civil war and ethnic cleansing that followed, in second-century BCE Judea. Assmann, along with van Henten and Avemarie, correlates the defiant sufferings of Eleazar, Hannah, and her seven sons, as rendered in 2 and 4 Maccabees, with the roughly contemporaneous book of Daniel, because of the sufferings by fire withstood by the three Judeans in Daniel 3.[22] However, Shmuel Shepkaru shows in Chapter 2 that the Maccabean tales are inconsistent: While 1 Maccabees 2:39–41 exhorts militant resistance rather than passive martyrdom (a theme which picks up in 2 Maccabees 8), 2 Maccabees 6 and 7, stylistically different and likely composed later, are notable for marrying mortal suffering with devotional fervor. Some literary representations up to and including the deaths at Masada follow suit. One cannot rule out the influence of Roman *devotio* traditions on these later Jewish conceptualizations of noncombatant martyrdom.

Of course, martyrdom has a tremendous arc beyond biblical religions into others around the world. As alluded already, Islamic uses of the word shahid are controversial and vary from the Qur'an to the commentators; initially, "those slain in the path of God" were figured not necessarily as victims of battle, but as victims of drownings, pestilence, childbirth, and anyone who endured great trials for faith (Afsaruddin, *Striving,* "Martyrdom," and Chapter 5). The link of martyrdom with suicide is vigorously disputed in Shīʿī discourse, but yet contentious, given the Imāms' purported prescience of their deaths,

21. Van Henten and Avemarie note this first use of the term, but unfortunately ignore its long history and transformation (1–8).

22. Assmann correlates as well burgeoning apocalyptic themes and the notion of immortality.

combined with the aforementioned fact that most of them were murdered (Haider, Chapter 6). Nonetheless, the Imāms are venerated. Jihadi-salafi discourse since the beginning of the twenty-first century has been riddled with contradictions viz. the longing to embrace conservative theological mores, which in fact condemn killings of self and noncombatants, and to embrace the tactical advantages to terror. Yet, perhaps surprisingly, the more notorious Jihadi groups are not particularly concerned about the contradiction at all (Hafez, Chapter 7). The notion of martyrdom has appeal beyond Abrahamic traditions into the Sikhs and some Hindu Tamils, considering the gifting of the lives of their legendary heroes (Fenech and Schonthal, Chapters 11 and 12, respectively). Needless to say, in popular culture martyrdom is all bound up with the language of sacrifice.

Sacrifice and Self-Sacrifice

Just as overlooked as martyrdom's origins are the origins of sacrifice. While the Latin etymology of the term breaks down to "making or doing sacred," now famous theorists have pointed to an additional lethal dimension in early religions, wherein cutting the throats of victims on religious altars reputedly riveted spectators and educed a profound confrontation with death. We are told that lethal sacrifice was the route to the sacred ("Religion is perpetrated in the arena of death," [Burkert 438]) or at least to an epiphany of it ("violence . . . the signifier of cherished being, the signifier of divinity," [Girard 151]). If one accepts these premises, sacrifice is felt as far more than the much-touted notion of gift, despite self-gifting innuendos in, say, the Song of the Suffering Servant (Isa. 53) and early Christian discourse.[23] Because of the violent connotations in some contemporary theories, understanding ritual sacrifice is now a historical challenge.

Notably, for our oldest sources in the West, the very notion of sacrifice must be acknowledged as anachronistic and the presumption of its violence as problematic. Ancient Near Eastern sources do not universally support the conflation of ritual offering with ritual killing, nor even the religious justification for ritual killing, although some mythic killings indeed are deemed foundational for the cosmic order—the killing of Tiamat, for instance.[24] Biblical

23. For a short sketch of sacrificial theories in Western discourse, see Kitts, *Princeton*. For a critical summary of sacrificial theories in relation to biblical materials, see Klawans.

24. Difficulties well discussed by, among others, Schwartz, and Pongratz-Leisten, "Ritual Killing."

"sacrifice" is rich in terminology, ritual procedure, reputed aetiology,[25] and represented differently in ritual prescriptions than in their origination-stories, which often feature considerably more violence than the rituals themselves, as if the storied violence were tacked on to ritual practice (Watts). In our oldest surviving poem in alphabetic Greek, the two primary "sacrifice" conventions, *thysia* (commensal sacrifices) and *horkia* (oath-sacrifices), could not be more different in phraseology, behavior, and proclaimed motivation for killing victims; *thysia* rituals are represented so nonviolently that the death of the animals (one hundred of them in Iliad Book 1) is entirely muted, whereas for the *horkos* ritual in Iliad Book 3, the painful death of oath-victims is staged so as to send a shudder of recognition down the spine of anyone even contemplating violating an oath (Kitts, *Sanctified*, and "Anthropology"). In Roman traditions, sacrifice as divine offering is not confused with ritual killing—the latter a practice confirmed by archaeological as well as written records (Schultz)—although in royal representation divine offering and wartime killing sometimes were juxtaposed artistically to make a dramatic point (Nasrallah). In Hellenistic Egypt, where animals were killed for some ritual purposes, the violence in *thysia*-representations was peripheral at best, and often camouflaged entirely by the end product of, say, mummification or food-preparation (Frankfurter).[26] Early Christians did use the word *thysia* to denote both divine offering and dying, but their use of the word was unstable: *thysia* was deployed in a war of rhetoric against pagan blood offerings thought not possibly to please any god (e.g., Matt. 9.13; Or. *mart.* 45[27]); yet the same term was deployed to depict Jesus and those who chose to die like him (e.g., Rom. 12.1; Heb. 7.27, 9.12–14, 9:26), as self-sacrifices.

Just the above sketch illustrates the reckless imprecision in forcing varied ritual and mythic phenomena into the single category of sacrifice. And of course, this is a sketch only for the West, where self-sacrifice now conjures a host of nationalist and religious sentiments that we quite take for granted.

Historical origins aside, though, the notion of self-sacrifice today has powerful appeal in both the West and Asia. For the West the appeal is based partly

25. Discussion in Janzen. On the reliability of sacrificial ritual prescriptions, McClymond demonstrates the fixation on formal procedure when there was no more temple for the procedure, in an instructive analysis of ritual fastidiousness and fiction in the Mishnah (245–46).

26. But cf the deliberate exploitation of the trope of sacrifice in ritualized human slayings by Senusret I, millennia earlier (Muhlestein "Sacred Violence," "Execration Ritual").

27. Cited in Smith.

on the allegorical understanding of Christ as a willing victim who suffered vicariously on behalf of the faithful and whose death mitigated a cosmic stain. Despite a variety of pre-existing Near Eastern ritual schematics—expiation, purification, appeasement, redemption, intercession, restoration of cosmic order and the like (Pongratz-Leisten, "Sacrifice")—it is the gifting of one-self, particularly of one's body, that has captured imaginations and invited countless imitations (Streete, *Redeemed Bodies,* and Chapter 3). Beyond the martyrs and into the desert ascetics, the deprived body—pierced, starved, and ravaged—was attributed a beneficent glow, conceived as an angelic fullness or as signaling a restoration of Adam-like original perfection, in some early Christian discourse (Cox-Miller, "Desert Asceticism"; Streete, Chapter 3). The notion is residual in Western art.

Asian lore is equally rich in spectacular bodily deprivations. Bodily slicing, starvation, drowning, and spontaneous combustions are alleged in the Chinese context to have invited biocosmic response in the form of rain, communal well-being, auspicious flights of birds and extravagant rays of color (Yu, Chapter 14; Benn). The disfigured bodies of self-sacrificing bodhisattvas are lauded for transcendent beauty in Indian Buddhist lore; effects are like the "elephant whose tusks emit six-colored rays of light, or the king whose body emits a powerful halo 'like rays from the disk of the moon'" (Ohnuma, Chapter 13). In Japanese Pure Land traditions, bodhisattva auto-cremations educe purple clouds, mysterious fragrance, and divine music (Stone, Chapter 15). In some tantric traditions, representations of devotional acts include self-mutilation and self-decapitation, to please the goddess (Storm, Chapter 8). Less graphic, but still striking, is the Jain forfeiture of immediate life to mitigate harm for other beings, in the ritual form of a fasting death (Vallely, Chapter 10). Thus, in Asian contexts too, the sacrificed body is loaded with significance, sometimes conceived as healing and as a gift.

Self-sacrifice is not always perceived as healing, of course, particularly as represented in art and ceremonies which depict wartime brutality and violent death. As they have for millennia and across civilizations, shrines, cemeteries, songs, poems, and passion plays continue to commemorate those perceived as willing sacrificial victims, often attributing them saint-like status. A fertile mix of religious and nationalist themes is conspicuous in the case of the LTTE: Great Hero cemeteries, hagiographies, and holiday celebrations highlight self-sacrifice in a complicated religio-nationalist register (Schonthal, Chapter 12). The same urge for commemoration may be seen in some Shīʿī performances and pilgrimages (Haider), as well as in Sikh martyrologies (Fenech, Chapter 11). As discussed ahead under self-immolation, such performances evince not only sympathy for suffering and loss, but reflections on the causes for which life is given.

Besides signaling gratitude and regret, such commemorations also witness to the forceful violence which made the victims dead. Memorial tributes to the violently dead—not only in classical religious art, but in holocaust shrines, murals of martyrs, walls of names, and piles of eyeglasses, skulls, and bones—seem designed to arouse not only gratitude, but public horror, revulsion, and also visual captivation (the proverbial "lust of the eye"). These may not be specifically religious sentiments but, as Achille Mbembé mused about piles of skulls and bones and the presence of living but mutilated victims, such visible after-effects of war preserve a tension between placid material facts and a stubborn will to mean something (35). Some critics rue our inurement to spectacles of suffering and painful death,[28] but Susan Sontag noted that for the religious, such spectacles continue to resonate. Representations of the martyrdom and beheading of Hussein still stir some Shīʿa; portrayals of crucifixion have not lost salience for devoted Christians; and staged performances of Buddhist-themed war tales still educe tears from Japanese audiences: "They weep, in part, because they have seen it many times. People want to weep. Pathos, in the form of a narrative, does not wear out" (65).

Self-Immolation

The vivid nature of such representations is inescapable. As noted at the start of this chapter, religious imagination is fascinated by spectacles of death, and this includes death by self-immolation. Typically, self-immolation, conceived as auto-cremation or as bodily annihilation by other means, is treated as a form of self-sacrifice. Yet it seems undeniable that self-immolation in the forms of, say, ascetic deprivation, auto-cremation, or suicide bombing, do not all arouse the same kind of response. One can imagine responses ranging from thoughts about higher consciousness, altruism, gift, pain, political cause, to the essence of life and death. Some political scientists decry any second-order semiosis in the face of self-annihilating spectacles (see Michelsen on auto-cremating Tibetan monks), while other critics notice our ineluctable, multi-tiered responses, at least two of which are shock and implicit self-identification with the mutilated corpse (see Bell on the severed torso of a beautiful Chechen suicide bomber in 2003). It is hard to avoid what have been called the haptic

28. E.g., Crane; Giroux; Baudrillard.

dimensions of our responses to spectacles of self-immolation (Morgan); that is, we grasp self-immolating spectacles not only conceptually but sensuously, by extending our virtual selves into them.

The most striking feature of self-immolation, then, is its sensational display, at least when reported or seen. In Indian lore, venerable traditions report yogic deaths by jumping off cliffs, drowning at sacred fords, self-immolation by fire, and starvation by subsisting only on air. Mythic piety in bhakti traditions was represented by feats such as offering one's eyes, one's hair, one's child, or one's life to various gods, especially to Śiva or Durga. However private the spiritual elevation ascribed to these yogis and bhaktas, the manner of public exhibition is provocative, at least as portrayed in art (Storm, Chapter 8). The same may be said for Jain sallekhanā, or "properly thinning or scratching out" (of passions and body) by fasting to death, lauded as the ultimate act of nonviolence by the Jain conqueror (Sanskrit "Jinā") of passions (Vallely, Chapter 10). Devotees of the medieval Japanese Buddhist Pure Land tradition reportedly self-immolated by burning, drowning, fasting, leaping from cliffs, performing disembowelment (also known as seppuku), and setting sail in sealed, rudderless boats (Stone, Chapter 15). While Theravada Buddhism overall enjoins the gentler Middle Way, jātaka tales of the Buddha's former lives report him rending his body to save others: gouging out his eyes to help a blind man see, feeding his body to a hungry tigress to deter her from devouring her cubs, and hurling himself as a hare into a fire to feed a wandering mendicant (Ohnuma, Chapter 13; Yu, Chapter 14). Such acts of elective death and maiming clearly rely on a special perception of human life and also of bodies, conceivably canvases on which is drawn corporeal disgust, but also, in some cases, a kind of transcendent beauty (Ohnuma, Chapter 13; Yu, Chapter 14). The aspiration to self-immolate is significant in part because of its distance from Daoist and other traditions' insistence that the body be intact in order to gain heavenly liberation (discussed by Yu, Chapter 14). In all of these cases, understandings of the body—whether mutilated, annihilated, intact, or even in the process of metamorphosing—are enmeshed in complex webs of cultural aesthetics and special metaphysical understandings of the self.

Self-immolations are perhaps most shocking when they are collective. The spectacular deaths *en masse* of the Branch Davidians and the followers of Heaven's Gate remain unfathomable for most of us in part because of the members' willingness to die all as one—although death by FBI and ATF arms was not precisely the "baptism by fire" initially sought by the Branch Davidians (see Wessinger, Chapter 4). Astonishing yearnings are said to have triggered the final moments for both groups. The perception of a Satanic foe ("a two-horned beast"), an end-times prophecy, and hope for resurrection into Christ's army of the "200 million martyrs of all the ages" (based on Rev. 9:16[29]) colored the metaphysics behind Branch Davidian expectations, whereas members of Heaven's Gate anticipated grafting onto Do (Marshall Applewhite, the reputed Second Christ), in order to transform into eternal, extraterrestrial bodies suited for the Kingdom of Heaven. Against the exhilaration of participating in such a cosmic and collective event, the appeal of individual life on earth apparently paled. Yet that thrill only partly explains these willing and collective deaths, as Catherine Wessinger shows in Chapter 4. It should be noted that, aside from the technical capacity to accomplish mass deaths simultaneously, the rejection of earthly life among these fragile millennial groups (Wessinger's coinage) is not so different from that of the early Christians or, for that matter, of early Jewish and some contemporary Jihadi groups in response to what is perceived as a world gone awry.[30]

As already suggested, despair alone is not enough to explain these choices. The element toughest for most intellectuals to grasp is the religious ardor of individuals choosing to destroy their bodies utterly. The petition of Ignatius to be "ground by the teeth of wild beasts that I may be found the pure bread of Christ" may have disturbed Romans, but clearly he basked in devotion. The devotional aspect is striking too among Jews during the Inquisition who, as Shmuel Shepkaru has shown, embraced the psalm: "Yet for your sake we face death all day long/ we are considered as sheep to be slaughtered" (Ps. 44.23 (NIV trans); "Martyr's Heaven," 339). Confronting overwhelming persecution, Sikh solider-saints embraced the "game of love" and offered "their heads" for the "truth that is God" (Fenech, Chapter 11). It was multi-tiered devotion that reportedly drove Palestinian suicide bombers in the late twentieth century: they longed to fight persecution in the shadow of the Prophet, to redeem their people in a situation of impossible malaise—but alongside that, they wanted to be able to intercede on behalf of loved ones once in heaven (Hafez, "Rationality," 175–76; on the theme of heavenly intercession see too Afsaruddin, Chapter 5, and Brick, Chapter 9). Against such fervent hopes, materialist analyses, by themselves, are unpersuasive.

---

29. There angelic troops are discharged to kill a third of humans: "The number of the mounted troops was twice ten thousand times ten thousand. I heard their number" (NIV translation).

30. Assmann; Boyarin, *Dying*. On the broad theme, see Wessinger's excellent *Oxford Handbook of Millennialism*.

Concluding Thoughts

We end where we started, pondering the appeal of spectacles of death. As Vikki Bell noted about the beautiful upper torso of the Chechen suicide bomber in Moscow, anyone viewing her severed corpse afresh, without political context, might feel a distinct and personalized foreboding, lodged somehow in the viewer's own body. There is a fleeting recognition of a common vitality, alongside a startling awareness of life's corporeal puniness—so easily snuffed out. This is not a political observation. The conundrum of comprehension transcends political dynamics and extends arguably into art. Art historians point out that representations of suffering and death yank at our somatic comprehensions, which can elude articulation in words.[31] Yet Susan Sontag articulated one aspect succinctly: representations of the pain of others motivate engagement with sufferers and the dead, but they also refresh the pleasure of survival for those who did not die (69).

31. n.b., Morgan 111–126; Siebers.

2

To Die For

THE EVOLUTION OF EARLY JEWISH MARTYRDOM

Shmuel Shepkaru

RABBINIC LAW (*HALAKHAH*) distinguishes between negative and positive forms of voluntary death. Voluntary deaths that are ascribed to a *meabed a'tzmo lada'at* (that is, one who intentionally and consciously destroys himself) are considered self-murder and thus sinful (*Semahot* 2:3–5). Generally, the act refers to self-killings motivated by non-religious reasons. Suicide roughly corresponds with this Hebrew phrase (Rosner; Hankoff; Goldstein; Kaplan and Schwartz). In contrast, voluntary death labeled *Kiddush ha-Shem* (or, sanctifying the Divine Name) is commended and commemorated. The term refers to the act of voluntarily submitting to death in order to avoid religious transgressions. *Kiddush ha-Shem* is loosely identified with martyrdom. Rabbinic literature borrowed the phrase *Kiddush ha-Shem* from the Bible (Lev. 22:32; Num.20:12; Ezek. 36:22–23), even though the biblical meaning differs entirely from its rabbinic designation. In the Bible, it is God who sanctifies the Name when He miraculously delivers Israel and the nations are moved to acknowledge Him. Conversely, when Israel transgresses against God, they profane the Name (Ezek. 20:39; Lev. 19:12, 22:2). But as we shall see in this chapter, the rabbinic distinction between the two types of self-inflicted death was hardly clearcut. And, each category in itself presented constant moral and religious challenges to individuals and communities. Complicating the issue of definition is the existence of voluntary death in Jewish accounts that long preceded the *halakhic* rulings on the subject.

The Hebrew Bible

Reports of voluntary death appear already in the Hebrew Bible, although there are only six cases of such death. Except for the self-killing of King Saul's anonymous armor-bearer (1 Sam. 31:5), the other five cases revolve around powerful men: the judges Abimelech and Samson, King Saul, Ahithophel (King David's advisor), and King Zimri. These individuals destroyed themselves in various ways.

Abimelech was killed by his armor-bearer at the battle for the city of Thebez. A millstone dropped from a tower by a woman broke Abimelech's skull. Fearing that men might say, "a woman slew him," Abimelech ordered his armor-bearer to thrust him through with his sword, and he complied with the order (Judg. 9:50–57).

The others died by their own hands. Samson brought the Palace of Dagon on himself and the Philistines (Judg. 16:23–31). The fatally wounded King Saul fell on his sword to avoid capture and humiliation by the Philistines (1 Sam. 31).[1] Ahithophel hanged himself when realizing that the coup d'etat attempt he had supported against King David was doomed to fail (2 Sam.16, 17). Zimri, the king of northern Israel, burned the palace over him once defeat in battle became imminent (1 Kgs 16).

Missing in these biblical accounts is a standard noun for voluntary death. Instead, only descriptions of the self-killings are provided. Moreover, no moral or legal guidelines supplement these accounts; the Hebrew Bible does not condemn nor condone these voluntary deaths. No special sanction against these individuals followed their demise. Samson and Ahithophel were buried in their fathers' tombs. Ahithophel set his house in order and his last wishes were respected. King Saul received proper burial together with his sons who were slain in battle (2 Sam. 21:12–14). The Bible makes no distinction between the self-killings of the king and his armor-bearer and the slaying of Saul's sons and soldiers by the Philistines. A seven-day mourning period followed the burial of Saul and his sons (1 Sam. 31:13). Upon hearing the news, David rent his cloth and eulogized Saul and his sons, praising their bravery without mentioning Saul's suicide (2 Sam. 1).

But these five individuals are certainly not role models, either. Excluding Saul's armor-bearer, the five share a crucial trait: all had sinned directly or indirectly against God, and so their deaths were predetermined punishments.

---

1. According to 2 Sam. 1:1–16, an Amalekite young man killed the gravely wounded Saul at his request. The version in 1 Chron. 10 follows 1 Sam. 31.

In Saul's case, the spirit of the prophet Samuel informed him of his tragic fate on the eve of his last battle (1 Sam. 28:19). In accordance with the general view of the Bible, these premature violent deaths signify a divine punishment for sinful behaviors. The voluntary deaths themselves are not under discussion; at issue, rather, is the question of why, rather than how, these individuals died. Their deaths merely indicate desperation and divine intervention—God willed it that they should die. Neither "suicide" nor "martyrdom" per se is discussed in these stories, and this conclusion applies to the rest of the Bible as well. Indeed, attempts have been made to associate other biblical stories with martyrdom, especially the story of Isaac's *Akkedah* (the Binding of Isaac), his near sacrifice in Genesis 22, and the stories in Daniel 3 and 6 of Daniel's friends in the fiery furnace and Daniel in the lions' den (Droge and Tabor 53–72; van Henten and Avemarie 42–45, 51–62). Suffice here to say that none of these individuals suffered or died. The hero in Genesis 22 is Abraham, not Isaac; not much can be inferred from Isaac's only line (v. 7), "Behold the fire and the wood; but where is the lamb for a burnt-offering?" In Daniel's case, he urges his three friends to pray to God that they "should not perish" (2:18). The book also indicates that the kings knew that God would miraculously save Daniel and his three friends. In short, the Hebrew Bible does not discuss the concepts of suicide and martyrdom (Brettler; Shepkaru 6–11).

Early Apocrypha

Additional references to voluntary death exist in the apocryphal literature. For example, 1 and 2 Maccabees set their examples of voluntary death against the background of King Antiochus Epiphanies' anti-Jewish decrees and the Maccabean revolt (167–160 BCE), which forced one thousand Jews to flee into the wilderness. The king's supporters discovered them on a Sabbath day and demanded compliance with the king's orders so "you will live." But the refugees "did not answer them or hurl a stone at them or block up their hiding places, for they said, 'Let us all die in our innocence; heaven and earth testify for us that you are killing us unjustly.' So they attacked them on the Sabbath, and they died, with their wives and children and livestock, to the number of a thousand persons" (1 Macc. 2:34–38).

A much shorter version is provided by 2 Maccabees 6:11. In this version, Jews gathered in a cave to observe the Sabbath secretly. Unlike the parallel version, these Jews were not offered a choice between life and death. When discovered, they were immediately "burned together, because their piety kept them from defending themselves, in view of their regard for that most holy day."

Of the two versions, it is 1 Maccabees that offers a more comprehensive martyrological account. A choice between life and death was given, and these Jews choose the latter. At first glance, it appears that the refugees' refusal to save themselves by violating the Sabbath was at issue. The author's intention, however, was not to promote such passive behavior; indeed, the leader of the Jewish revolt, Mattathias, and his followers mourned for the fatalities deeply. Yet they never praised them either. Mattathias and his friends found no practical or religious value in the refugees' behavior. Mattathias viewed passive behavior as both sacrilegious and dangerous, because "If we all do as our kindred have done and refuse to fight with the Gentiles for our lives and for our ordinances, they will quickly destroy us from the earth. So they made this decision that day: 'Let us fight against anyone who comes to attack us on the Sabbath day; let us not all die as our kindred died in their hiding places'" (1 Macc. 2:39–41). The story of the thousand escapees served to denounce the very passive behavior it describes. Fighting against the enemies constitutes a central theme in the Maccabean books. To demonstrate the importance of active resistance, the story of the refugees instructs that fighting takes precedence even over keeping the Sabbath (Mantel 102–07; Kampen 78–80).

Mattathias's view prevailed. Following his denunciation, "all who became fugitives to escape their troubles joined them and reinforced them" (v. 43). Mattathias's final speech continued to promote the combative option. To support his call, Mattathias provided biblical examples of divine deliverance to those who put their trust in God. It is important to note that among his models were Abraham (rather than Isaac), Daniel, and his three friends. Together with other combative heroes like David and Joshua, Mattathias viewed them as resistance protagonists, rather than martyrs. His approach to persecution was to fight "for our lives and for our ordinances." He called on the people of Israel to unite around this concept. Dying passively without a fight "in hiding places" implied the absence of conviction and courage. Maccabean ideology followed the biblical model of holy war (see Firestone, Chapter 1).

Second Maccabees 6 and 7 appear to offer an alternative option. Chapter 6 opens with a list of King Antiochus's anti-Jewish decrees. Jews who "did not choose to change over to Greek customs," were to be put to death. Next follows the specific example of the elderly Eleazar the Scribe, who endured torture and death to avoid eating pork sacrificed to idols. He would not save himself even by pretending to eat the idolatrous sacrifice (while actually eating permissible food prepared by him). Eleazar went "at once" to the rack, "leaving in his death an example of nobility and a memorial of courage, not only to the young but to the great body of his nation" (6:31).

In Chapter 7, Antiochus himself oversaw the brutal executions of seven anonymous brothers in the presence of their mother (Duran, "The Martyr"; van Henten, *The Maccabeans*; Himmelfarb, "Judaism"; Rajak, *The Jewish Dialogue*). The seven chose death rather than violate their ancestral laws. Their mother was not forced to transgress, but she encouraged "each of them in the language of their ancestors" to die nobly. Given the generally belligerent tone of 2 Maccabees, Eleazar and the seven sons stand as exceptional examples. They are noncombatant ordinary people who chose a passive death. This is in contrast to the pattern in 2 Maccabees of celebrating famed "noble warriors" and their victory (Berthelot 45–60). The two models of reaction to persecutions differ sharply. The biblical model of holy war runs throughout the book. In contrast, the deaths of Eleazar and the brothers resemble the death that Christian martyrs embraced in later years (Joslyn-Siemiatkoski, *Christian Memories*). How can this contradiction be explained?

It has been long established that stories of martyrdom are a legendary creation, rather than based in any historical event. Scholars have questioned the relationship between the two martyrological stories and the rest of 2 Maccabees (Habicht 171–77, 233; Hengel 2:65 n. 299; Bowersock 7–8, 28; Shepkaru, Chapter 1; Himmelfarb, "Judaism," 31–33; cf. Rajak, *The Jewish Dialogue*, 104). The dating of 2 Maccabees from the middle of the second century BCE to the middle of the first century CE further complicates this question (van Henten, *The Maccabees* 51). Here are only some of the reasons that open the door to the possibility that the stories are an addition of a later provenance. Chapter seven is stylistically and thematically different. The martyrs never mentioned the Temple—the absence of the Temple is uncharacteristic for a book dubbed "Temple propaganda" (Duran, *Temple Propaganda*; Zsengellér 181–95). In contrast to the victorious tone of the book, the martyrological reports correspond with a *histoire pathétique* style. The sons pray for divine intervention, but God remains silent (as also in the story of Eleazar). In contrast, God answered the combatants' prayers immediately in 2 Maccabees 8. He was satisfied with their choice of action: "As soon as Judas Maccabeus got his army organized, the Gentiles could not withstand him, for the wrath of the Lord had turned to mercy" (2 Macc. 8:5). Accounts of divine intervention on behalf of the warriors follow thereafter. Additionally, the stories of Eleazar and the sons interrupt the account about Judas organizing his army that starts in chapter 5 and resumes thereafter in chapter 8 with his military victories. These are some of the reasons that raise the possibility of an interpolation.

In short, 1 and 2 Maccabees elevated the bellicose option to a divine commandment as in biblical times. Beyond the questionable stories of the martyrs, 2 Maccabees did not promote the doctrine of noncombatant martyrdom (Bowersock 26–27). But 1 Maccabees went a step further, explicitly denouncing such behavior, for it could not prevent the "very great wrath [that] came upon Israel" (1 Macc. 1:64). More importantly, there are no indications that the two stories of sacrifice produce a Jewish doctrine of martyrdom in the Hellenistic period. As we are about to discuss, only when the stories of Eleazar and the mother with her seven sons re/emerged late in the second century CE, did a Jewish doctrine of martyrdom start to crystalize.

Roman-Period Accounts

Jewish accounts of the Roman period reveal a dramatic increase not only in reports of voluntary death, but also in ethical and theological discussions regarding the act (Droge and Tabor 85–97). Two factors in particular accounted for this development: 1) the escalation in the Jewish-Roman conflict; and 2) the influence of the Roman concept of noble death on Jewish authors and society. The Roman conquest familiarized the Jews not only with Roman might, but also with Rome's penchant for heroic death. Known as *devotio*, ritualistic self-sacrifices of Roman soldiers were believed to appease the gods and guarantee victory in battle. In imperial times, the technical term *devotio* was extended to acts of self-sacrifices committed on behalf of the *patria* and the emperor. In the same spirit of *devotio*, the Romans considered death as a noble delivery from slavery, defeat, and dishonor in general (Edwards, Chapter 1).

Jewish familiarity with Greco-Roman ideas is evident in a plethora of Jewish accounts. The discussion in this section relies on non-religious accounts that date from the early first century to possibly the late second century. The earliest extant accounts in this category are by Philo of Alexandria (25 BCE–45 CE). Well-versed in both Jewish religion and Greek philosophy, Philo synthesized these two traditions in his philosophical works. Philo's admiration for Greco-Roman ideas is evident in his *Every Good Man Is Free*, in which he praises the "wise [who] would most gladly choose death rather than slavery" (135). This Stoic principle was not followed by philosophers and soldiers alone. Ordinary men, and "even" women, and lads whom nature endowed "with little sense," would eagerly seek death for the love of liberty (117). Philo states the precise culture that inspired such altruism. Anyone who has "taken even a slight hold of [Greco-Roman] culture" knows that freedom is honorable and slavery a disgrace (136); and "anyone" would include the subjugated Jewish population as well.

According to Philo, not only did Jews display Roman altruism, they surpassed Roman adherence to it. For this reason, reported Philo, General Petronius found alarming Emperor Caligula's wishes to install a statue of himself in the Jewish Temple in Jerusalem. Caligula's order violated both the status quo and Jewish law. Caligula and Petronius expected the Jews to fight for their Temple, but Petronius believed that, more than any other nation, the "Jews would willingly endure to die not once but a thousand times, if it were possible, rather than allow any of the prohibited actions to be committed" (*The Embassy To Gaius* 209–10, 216–17). In Rome, the Judean king, Herod Agrippa, also made a disturbing prediction. He cautioned Caligula that the Jews "would slaughter their whole families, women and children alike, and finally immolate themselves upon the corpses of their kin" in defense of their Temple. Agrippa displayed a similar altruistic tendency. Aware of the consequences of questioning Caligula's orders, Agrippa asked the emperor not to punish him. Instead he asked, "bid me take myself out of the way forthwith" (308, 329). But because Caligula considered Agrippa his friend, he pardoned him (330–33).

Agrippa's and Petronius's warnings nearly came to pass. A multitude of Jewish protestors descended on Petronius and his troops. But instead of fighting, as Petronius feared, they resolved to submit to death peacefully. They even offered to take their own lives:

> Ourselves will conduct the sacrifices, priests of a noble order, wives will be brought to the altar by wife-slayers, brothers and sisters by fratricides, boys and girls in the innocence of their years by child-murderers . . . Then standing in the midst of our kinsfolk after bathing ourselves in their blood, the right bathing for those who would go to Hades clean, we will mingle our blood with theirs by the crowning slaughter of ourselves. When we are dead let the prescript be carried out; not God himself could blame us who had a twofold motive, respectful fear of the emperor and loyalty to the consecrated laws. (*The Embassy* 234–36)

Philo was not an eyewitness to these events, so the exact nature of what transpired between Petronius and the protestors is difficult to ascertain. But the mixed metaphors in the Jewish declarations expose Philo's discomfort with the proposed act of murder-suicide. He designates the protestors as sacrifices and slayers, noble priests and murderers, guiltless and guilty. These incompatible terms mirror a clash between the Jewish tradition that valued life and the Roman affinity for noble death. The self-blame that the Jews expressed could have stemmed from the Torah's commandment against slaughter (Exod. 20:13; Deut. 5:17). Any deliberate killing unrelated to war is considered murder punishable by death (Num. 35). Perhaps because of these dictates in the Torah, Philo, who admired the Stoic idea of noble death, declined to designate as noble the proposed acts of murder-suicide—yet he also declined to explicitly condemn the proposed drastic acts. After all, not even the Giver of the law could blame those ready to commit murder-suicide on His behalf. Philo labored to reconcile the biblical teachings with the Greco-Roman ideal of self-sacrifice.

Philo's attempt at ideological reconciliation was not just a philosophical exercise. Like Agrippa, Philo expressed a similar willingness to sacrifice his own life for Jewish law, the protection of his community, and the Temple. When anti-Jewish riots broke out in his hometown of Alexandria in the year 38, Philo led an embassy to meet with Caligula in order to plead for protection. This very attempt could have been perceived as an act of defiance punishable by death, so Philo prepared himself for a "glorious death."

> And even if we were allowed to approach him unmolested, what have we to expect but death against which there is no appeal? Well so be it, we will die and be no more, for the truly glorious death, met in defense of laws. (*The Embassy* 191–92)

Philo and the rest of the delegation survived because Caligula dismissed them, "not because we clung to life and cringed from death" (369). In Judea, the Jewish protesters escaped death because Caligula had been assassinated. Regardless of the outcome, Agrippa, Philo, and the Jewish protestors agreed to suffer a Roman-like death in order to uphold and embody Jewish law.

The Jewish historian Josephus Flavius (37–100 CE) also recounted the incident with Petronius among his numerous reports on voluntary death (Newel, "The Suicide Accounts," "The Forms"; Klawans, especially 92–136). Unlike Philo, Josephus did not mention the Jewish threats to commit murder-suicide. At Ptolemais (modern Acre), the Jews declared unambiguously their refusal to fight Petronius. They preferred to be killed rather than see the statue erected. At Tiberias, Petronius heard similar declarations. The Jews threw themselves face down, and stretched out their throats, saying they were ready to be slain (*Jewish Antiquities* 18.271). Josephus provided additional details in his *Jewish War*: the Galilean Jews forewarned Petronius that he would need to "sacrifice the entire Jewish nation" and that they, their wives, and children were ready for the slaughter. The statements allegedly impressed Petronius so much that he decided to postpone Caligula's orders at the risk of losing his own life. Petronius was "ready on behalf of the lives of so many to surrender" his own (*Jewish War* 2.192–98). Josephus put here Jewish ultraism on a par with the Roman values of honorable death. Readers may get the impression that the Jewish reaction inspired Petronius's altruism; this would be consistent with Josephus' general view of voluntary death.

Josephus claimed that the idea of dying nobly originated with the Jews, who exceeded the Greeks and Romans in bravery. His commentary on the story of the *Akkedah* (Isaac's near-sacrifice in Genesis 22) contends that already the twenty-five-year-old Isaac had agreed to be sacrificed on the altar to obey both his father and God (*Jewish Antiquities* 1.223–36). Jews differed from the Greeks, who would not suffer even the "smallest personal injury" for their laws and books. Unlike other nations, Jewish heroism is not "that easiest of deaths, on the battlefield, but death accompanied by physical torture, which is thought to be the hardest of all" (*Against Apion* 2.232–34). Since Isaac's act, self-sacrifice had become an innate Jewish trait:

> It is an instinct with every Jew, from the day of his birth, to regard them [the scriptures] as the decrees of God, to abide by them, and, if need be, cheerfully to die for them. Time and again ere now the sight has been witnessed of prisoners enduring torture and death in every form in the theaters rather than utter a single word against the laws and the allied documents. (*Against Apion* 1.42–48)

Such claims of origin and originality intended to distinguish Jewish self-sacrifice from that of the Romans, but Josephus's attempts at establishing his claims are evidence to the contrary. Assertions that Jews would prefer "to die if they could not live as free men" (*Jewish Antiquities* 12.315), and that passion for liberty motivated Jews to "think little of submitting to death in unusual forms" (*Jewish Antiquities* 18.23), echo the same Roman values (Weitzman 230–45). The same Roman code shapes the report on the rebellion against King Herod. According to Josephus, love of liberty motivated the Jewish rebels to fight to the death. He offers the memorable example of an old man among the rebels, hiding in the caves of Arbel in the lower Galilee with his seven children and wife. Against their will, he slaughtered them one by one before taking his own life, "thus submitting to death rather than to slavery" (*Jewish Antiquities* 14:429–30; *Jewish War* 1:312–13). Although love of liberty motivated the old man, Josephus neither absolved nor condemned his actions.

In other cases, however, Josephus showed grudging support for elective death. In his account of Merius, and Josephus son of Dalaeus, Josephus offers mild appreciation for suicide. Having the choice of saving their lives, these "two persons of distinction" preferred to plunge into the fire that destroyed the Temple in 70 CE (*Jewish War* 6.279–80). In other places, however, Josephus clearly expressed his disdain for the options of self-killing, and especially of murder-suicide. In his report of Pompey's invasion of the Temple in 63 BCE, Josephus praised the priests who "were butchered in the act of pouring libations and burning incense, putting the worship of the Deity above their own preservation." In contrast, he considered those who perished in the fire they had set, "driven mad by their hopeless plight" (*Jewish War* 1:150–51).

Not surprisingly, Josephus explained why he considered suicide an act of madness when his own life was on the line. Before becoming a historian, Josephus served as the general of the Galilean rebels during the Jewish revolt. After failing to defend the town of Yodefat (67 CE), Josephus and forty other men hid from the Romans in a cave (*Jewish War* 3.330). The men decided to commit suicide, but Josephus disagreed, so they gave him a choice: die willingly as a Jewish general, or be killed unwillingly as a traitor. Josephus found the characterizations of the two options inappropriate. Indeed, he argued, it is "honorable to die in war," but only by the hand of the enemy. It is "honorable to die for liberty . . . but on condition that one dies fighting, by the hands of those who would rob us of it." But it was not "noble to destroy oneself." Josephus viewed self-killing an act "against God our Creator" who alone has the power to give and take life. Josephus based his rejection of suicide on Jewish law. "Our most wise legislator," Josephus believed, condemned self-killing. Those who have laid "mad hands upon themselves" send their souls to the darker regions of the nether world. God also "visits upon their posterity the outrageous acts of the parents. That is why this crime, so hateful to God, is punished also by the sagest of legislators." Additionally, argued Josephus, the Romans' promise to spare the lives of the men in the cave further exacerbated the crime of self-killing (*Jewish War* 3.355–82). Josephus considered voluntary death noble when death by the enemy's hands for reasons of religion and freedom was inevitable. Josephus employed Jewish theology to modify the Roman philosophy of noble death. In his view, surrendering was not always ignoble, nor self-destruction always noble.

Josephus came out of this ordeal alive. He tricked his comrades into taking each other's lives, until only he and one other were left. He then convinced the man to surrender, and the Romans to spare him. For surviving in a dishonorable way, Josephus's compatriots rendered him a traitor.

In contrast to his explicit rejection of suicide at Yodefat, Josephus presents a seemingly ambivalent view in his account of the Roman siege of Masada in the year 73 (Cohen 385–405). Before the Romans breached Masada's walls, the beseeched Sicarii rebels had chosen ten men who would assume the responsibility of killing all of the rebels, as well as themselves, at the end. At first glance, Josephus seems to express both reservation and admiration for the 960 Jewish men, women, and children who perished at Masada. But the decision to self-destruct did not come easily. The Sicarii's leader, Eleazar ben Yair, had to deliver two speeches to convince his fellow insurgents to commit his proposed acts of familial suicide and homicide (Stern 367–98). In his speech, Eleazar employed two sets of arguments to justify his proposal.

His first argument echoes Roman thinking. God granted the besieged the favor of dying "nobly and in freedom—a privilege denied to others who have met with unexpected defeat" (*Jewish War* 7. 324–30). Self-destruction was intended to prevent dishonor and preserve liberty. In his second argument, Eleazar emphasized Jewish religion and tradition:

> For from of old, since the first dawn of intelligence we have been continually taught by those precepts, ancestral and divine—confirmed by the deeds and noble spirit of our forefathers—that life, not death, is man's misfortune. For it is death which gives liberty to the soul and permits it to depart to its own pure abode, there to be free from all calamity.

Eleazar presents a dubious religious argument.[2] His rationale still sounds more Roman than Jewish. "From old," tradition did not teach that life was a

---

2. As recently as the late twentieth century, scholars still debated if the occupants at Masada acted in keeping with halakhah, and if they met the definition of Jewish martyrdom. Shubert Spero calls them "completely holy" ("In Defense of the Defenders of Masada." *Tradition: A Journal of Orthodox Jewish Thought*, Vol. 11, No. 1, 1970, pp. 31–43; see also Louis Rabinowitz, "The Masada Martyrs According to the Halakhah." *Tradition: A Journal of Orthodox Jewish Thought*, Vol. 11, No. 3, 1970, pp. 31–37; and Dov I. Frimer, "Masada: In the Light of Halakhah." *Tradition: A Journal of Orthodox Jewish Thought*, Vol. 12, No. 1 (1971), pp. 27–43. Sidney B. Hoenig is correct to reject halakhic connections and the title of "martyr" in his "Historic Masada and the Halakhah." *Tradition: A Journal of Orthodox Jewish Thought*, Vol. 13, No. 2, 1972, pp. 100–15. In any case, we should be careful not to treat Eleazar's speech as historical.

calamity and death a benefit. His argument that life is misfortune and death liberates the soul to its pure abode is very Greek. Biblical teachings view premature and violent death a curse and long peaceful life a blessing.

Ultimately, Eleazar's misrepresentation of Judaism failed to achieve its goal:

> Yet, even had we from the first been schooled in the opposite doctrine and taught that man's highest blessing is life and that death is a calamity, still the crisis is one that calls upon us to bear it with a stout heart, since it is by God's will and of necessity that we are to die. For long since, so it seems, God passed this decree against the whole Jewish race in common, that we must quit this life if we would not use it aright. (*Jewish War* 7.358–66)

The "opposite doctrine" corresponds more accurately with the traditional Jewish view that violent death is a tragedy and a punishment for personal failings.

Eventually, Josephus fused the conflicting Jewish and Roman traditions. Josephus considered the Sicarii to be criminals for launching the revolt and committing murderous acts along the way. For example, in the nearby town of En Geddi, the Sicarii had slaughtered seven hundred women and children. The Sicariis' demise, therefore, was seen as a divine punishment. Even Eleazar allegedly admitted that voluntary death would be a fitting punishment. For Josephus, the acts of murder-suicide were not just a punishment and an acknowledgment of guilt; they were sins in and of themselves. Based on his anti-suicide speech at Yodefat, Josephus would have granted the Sicarii some respect had they died fighting. But, the only people who did respect the Sicarii were the Romans: when the Roman soldiers discovered what transpired within the walls, "instead of exulting as over enemies, they admired the nobility of their resolve and the contempt of death displayed by so many in carrying it, unwavering, into execution" (*Jewish War* 7.402–10). According to Josephus, the Sicariis' murder-suicide practices gained reverence from Romans and repudiation from Jews.

What actually transpired within the walls of Masada is extremely difficult to determine. Josephus was not there. No less doubtful is the report about Yodefat, even though Josephus was there. Josephus was a complex man who wrote a complicated history. His work, however, mirrors not only the multifaceted characteristics of his personality, but also of the cultural ambiance in which he lived. The life-and-death dilemmas he wrote about were not only his own; a whole nation in crisis faced similar moral and religious quandaries. The pros and cons in his accounts bear the moral and religious perplexities that the adoption of the Roman noble-death idea presented to Jewish society.

Such dilemmas are less discernible in the *Testament of Moses*, which dates to the late first or early second century. This pseudepigraphic work survived only in Latin and is believed to be of a Palestinian provenance (Licht 95–105; Nickelsburg; Tromp 109–11; Droge and Tabor 72; Van Henten and Avemarie 79–80; Loftus 212–23; Whitters 718–31). Unlike Philo and Josephus, the anonymous author did not debate the legitimacy of voluntary death; rather, he viewed self-sacrifice as a traditional Jewish response. Set against a background reminiscent of the persecutions under Antiochus Epiphanes, Chapter 9 tells the story of Taxo and his seven sons:

> There will be a man of the tribe of Levi whose name will be Taxo, who, having seven sons, will speak to them, exhorting them: "Observe my sons, behold a second visitation has come upon the people, and a punishment merciless and far exceeding the first. For what nation or what region or what people of those who are impious toward the Lord, who have done many abominations, have suffered as great calamities as have befallen us? Now therefore my sons, hear me: for observe and know that neither did our fathers nor their forefathers tempt God, so as to transgress his commands. And ye know that this is our strength and thus we will do. Let us fast for the space of three days and on the fourth let us go into a cave which is in the field and let us die rather than transgress the commands of the Lord of Lords, the God of our fathers. For if we do this and die, our blood will be avenged before the Lord. (*The Assumption of Moses* 9:1–7)

Taxo and his sons did not face an immediate ultimatum. Taxo proposed a preventive measure in anticipation of religious coercion. The proposal had an additional function: Taxo assigned their deaths redemptive powers. He and his sons would become vicarious sacrifices for the redemption of Israel—but how Taxo and his sons expected to perish is unclear. Self-starvation is a possibility. The language that describes their potential death is telling: rather than using a phrase for suicide (*morten sibi consciscere*, for example), the author preferred "let us die" (*moriamur*). The phraseology exposes perhaps the author's hesitation to designate Taxo's proposal "self-killing." Yet, the redemptive power of voluntary death betrays the advancement of martyrdom to a cultic status.

Of all the accounts examined so far, 4 Maccabees, which dates to the second century (Bickerman 266–71; Anderson 2:531–564; *cf.*, Rajak, 104–05), is the only account devoted entirely to the value of voluntary death. Four Maccabees narrates only the ordeals of Eleazar, the seven brothers, and their mother. Eleazar and the family serve to deliver the book's main philosophical tenet. The nine demonstrated that devout reason could govern desires and emotions even to the point of overcoming the fear of death (Renehan; DeSilva; van Henten, *The Maccabean Martyrs* 305–06; Rajak, *The Jewish Dialogue* Chapter 6). Antiochus's inhuman decrees became "an opportunity to show" the human race their "noble sufferings" for the law (11:12). Dying in defense of Judaism was not "madness" (8:5), as King Antiochus argued, but a rational religious act. Thus, 4 Maccabees reconciles stoic philosophy and Jewish theology.

Evoking the language of Roman gladiatorial contests, the seven sons hastened to death "as though running the course toward immortality" (14:5). The fifth son came to Antiochus of his own accord. More thirst for death was shown by the seventh son and the mother. He "flung himself into the braziers and so ended his life" (12:19). She hurled herself into the flames, "so that no one might touch her body." Thanks to "devout reason," she proved to be "more noble than males in steadfastness, and more manly than men in endurance" (17:1; 15:23–30; Young 67–81; Moore and Anderson 249–73; van Hooff 21–26; Cobb 60–61, 78, 103, 115; Weigold 197–210; Rajak, "The Mother's Role," 111–28).

Despite its strongly Stoic flavor, 4 Maccabees presents all of these types of voluntary death as a traditional Jewish attribute. Like Josephus, the book traces this tradition back to Isaac. When Abraham wielded the sword to offer his son as a burnt offering, Isaac "did not cower" (16:20). Isaac willingly participated in his near-sacrifice. His bravery inspired both Eleazar and the sons. The mother drew her inspiration from Abraham. "She was of the same mind as Abraham . . . as the daughter of God-fearing Abraham she remembered his fortitude" (4 Macc. 14:20; 15:28).

The Book of Daniel offered additional inspiration. The mother of Maccabees urged her sons to show the "the same faith in God" that Daniel and his three friends had displayed when put to the test by foreign kings. For "the sake of the law," the seven wished to "imitate the three youths in Assyria who despised the same ordeal of the furnace" (13:9; 16:3–4, 21).

These biblical stories served not only to underscore the Jewish origin of dying nobly, but also to rationalize the sons' passive and active forms of voluntary death. While accusing Antiochus of committing homicide and treating the sons as if they were murderers, 4 Maccabees still praises the self-killings of the mother and the youngest son. But traces of the religious and moral anxieties that are apparent in Philo's and Josephus' works are still present in 4 Maccabees, if only for the sake of argument. Had the seven sons elected to live, they could have justified their choice by the following arguments:

> [17] "O wretches that we are and so senseless! Since the king has summoned and exhorted us to accept kind treatment if we obey him, [18] Why do we take pleasure in vain resolves and venture upon a disobedience that brings death? [19] O men and brothers, should we not fear the instruments of torture and consider the threats of torments, and give up this vain opinion and this arrogance that threatens to destroy us? [20] Let us take pity on our youth and have compassion on our mother's age; [21] and let us seriously consider that if we disobey we are dead! [22] Also, *divine justice will excuse* us for fearing the king when we are under compulsion. [23] Why do we banish ourselves from this most pleasant life and deprive ourselves of this delightful world? [24] Let us not struggle against compulsion nor take hollow pride in being put to the rack. [25] *Not even the law itself would arbitrarily slay* us for fearing the instruments of torture. [26] Why does such contentiousness excite us and such a fatal stubbornness please us, when we can live in peace if we obey the king?" [27] But the youths, though about to be tortured, neither said any of these things nor even seriously considered them.

Instead of following this rationale, the sons defeated Antiochus with their "own philosophy . . . and bright reasoning." But "their own philosophy . . . and reasoning" reflect more accurately the Roman philosophy of the time. The arguments that were made by "not" making them, resonate more with the Jewish tradition of old. "Their philosophy" dismissed even the significant arguments that Jewish law did not require them to die to avoid transgressions. Divine justice would have forgiven the brothers had they elected to live (verses 22, 25). These counterarguments evoke the statements made by the Jewish protestors in Philo's *The Embassy* ("not God himself could blame us," 234–36). This parallel is significant because the two statements are independent of one other.[3] Both Philo and 4 Maccabees reflect the religious anxiety and

3. Both Philo and Josephus were unfamiliar with the stories of Eleazar and the mother with seven sons. Mason observes that words like: "torture," "test," and "torment," in 4 Maccabees appear also in Josephus. This (the parallels) "seems to highlight Josephus' debt to" 4 Maccabees

dilemma that come with the decision to die for the law that did not require self-sacrifice. But in contrast to the sentiments expressed by Philo and Josephus, 4 Maccabees is content with both passive and active forms of voluntary death. The victory of the sons' "own philosophy . . . and right reasoning" over the pro-life defense demonstrates that the Roman idea of the noble death earned a legitimate place in some second-century Jewish communities. The general scholarly consensus is that 4 Maccabees represents a diasporic view of martyrdom. The Palestinian provenance of the *Assumption of Moses* would suggest that the Jews of Roman Palestine also adopted martyrological views.

Rabbinic Text

Unlike Philo, Josephus, and 4 Maccabees, rabbinic literature is unconcerned with the question of the origin of noble death and the tension with Roman altruism. Halakhic discussions present the conception of Jewish martyrdom in the context of Emperor Hadrian's anti-Jewish decrees (*gezerot Hadrianus*). Rabbinic literature dubbed the period "the generation of persecution" (*dor ha-shemad*) for the first generation of rabbis, the *Tannaim* (first- and second-century rabbis).

Against the background of persecution, a second-century rabbinic council is said to have met in an attic in the Judean town of Lod to determine the circumstances that would require Jews to submit to death rather than to violate the law. The council concluded that if a person is "commanded: 'transgress and suffer not death,' he may transgress and not suffer death, excepting idolatry, illicit sex (*gilui arayot*, literally incest), and murder (*shfichut damim*, bloodshed)" (BT *Sanehdrin* 74a; JT *Sevi'it* 4.2a). The council rejected Rabbi Ishmael's view that permitted idolatrous acts in order to save life. Based on Leviticus 18:5 ("Ye shall therefore keep My statutes, and Mine ordinances, which if a man do, he shall live by them"), Ishmael argued that the commandments were given to live by them, not die for them. The majority vote disagreed and prohibited idolatrous acts in "public" (in the presence of

---

(Steve Mason, *Flavius Josephus: Translation and Commentary, Judean War, Vol. 1b*. Brill, 2008, 2, 122 n. 931). Following Mason's suggestion, Klawans implies that Josephus was familiar with the Maccabean stories of martyrdom (273 n. 102). Both claims are speculative and unconvincing. It is not unusual to find these words in the accounts of the time. If Josephus had known the Maccabean stories of martyrdom, he would have mentioned them explicitly. The stories would have served well his (and Philo's) repeated attempts to establish an ancient Jewish tradition of voluntary death for the law. Loftus sees no relation between the Maccabean stories and Josephus (222–23).

at least ten Jews), because "Scripture says (Lev. 22:32), 'And ye shall not profane my holy name'" (BT *Avodah Zarah* 27b; BT *Sanhedrin* 74a).

Another rabbinic version narrowed Ishmael's dilemma to transgressions in private or public. This version, too, banned idolatry in public (*Sifra*, "Ahare Mot" 13). Reflected in these discussions are the attempts to strike a balance between the core rabbinic principle that emphasizes the importance of life and the commitment to Jewish law.

The late second-century *Tosefta Shabbat* 16:14 continued the quest for equilibrium between "dying for" and "living by" the law:

> Behold, the commandments were only given to Israel that they might live by them, as it is written "Which a man shall perform and live by them" - he shall live by them, and not die by them. Nothing takes precedence over saving a life (*pikuah nefesh*), save idolatry, sexual sins, and murder. In which circumstances are these things said? When it is not a time of persecution. But, when it is a time of persecution, even when it comes to the smallest of small commandments, a person should die for it, as it is written: "Do not profane my holy name" (Leviticus 22) and "the Lord made everything for his own sake." (Proverbs 16).

This account presents a stricter opinion. Despite the rabbinic rule of *pikuah nefesh* (which dictates that the preservation of human life takes precedence over any other religious requirement), this text required Jews to submit to death in a time of persecution even for the most trivial commandments. Sterner yet was the view ascribed to Rabbi Yohanan. Even if persecutions were not officially decreed, one still "should let himself be killed rather than transgress publically even a minor commandment" (BT *Sanhedrin* 74a–b). An *Amoraic* report (dating to the third to fifth century) recalled that the Jews of the Land of Israel indeed gave themselves up in time of persecution to avoid more than just the three offenses listed by the council of Lod (*Mekhilta de-Rabbi Ishmael*, "*Behodesh*" 6; BT *Shabbat* 130a).

Attention must be given to the language employed in these discussions. The *Tannaim* did not utilize in their halakhic formulations the present term for martyrdom, *kiddush ha-Shem*. Late-second-century (and later) rabbis still recalled stories of martyrdom from the generation of the persecution without employing the phrase *kiddush ha-Shem*.[4] When *kiddush ha-Shem* does appear

4. For example, R. Shimon b. Elazar, BT *Shabbat* 130a; R. Joshua b. Korha, *Sanhedrin* 110b. In BT *Pesahim* 53b *kiddush ha-Shem* does appear in the context of martyrdom: "Hananiah,

in the Talmud, the phrase usually indicates virtuous behaviors unrelated to martyrdom, or refers to God performing miracles among the nations.[5] This absence of a standard noun or verb for acts of voluntary death may suggest that the rabbinic doctrine of martyrdom was still in its infancy in the late second century (Boyarin, "Martyrdom").

Rabbinic literature compensated for the absence of a martyrological term by employing the phrase "be killed rather than transgress." This choice of words is telling. Phrasing the rule in the passive voice implies that martyrdom should not be self-inflicted. It is also important to point out that the halakhic formulation did not discuss voluntary martyrdom. *Bereshit Rabbah* "*Vayyishlach*" 82:8 (an early aggadic/halakhic midrash of the Land of Israel with later additions dating to 300–500 CE) explains that one should not volunteer for death even in time of persecution because "it is not the way of man to deliberately and consciously destroy himself (*leabed et a'tzmo lada'at*)." In the post-Talmudic tractate *Semahot,* the phrase has the negative connotation of suicide. In short, the halakhic discussions convey that Jews should not present themselves for martyrdom, nor should they take their own life when the need for martyrdom presents itself.

Numerous talmudic tales of martyrdom adhere to these principles. Suffice here to mention the examples of two paradigmatic martyrs. The Romans arrested Rabbi Akiva for teaching Torah and, more likely, for supporting the Bar Kokhva revolt. Several stories tell that Akiva avoided taking unnecessary risks. Rabbi Simeon ben Yohai is said to have asked Akiva to teach him Torah, while visiting him in prison. Akiva refused because it was too risky (BT *Pesahim* 112a).

On a different occasion, Rabbi Meir recalled:

> One time we were sitting in the *Bet Midrash* (Study Hall) in front of Rabbi Akiva and we were reading the *Shema*, but we were not saying it loud enough to be able to hear ourselves, because of a *quaesdor* who was standing by the door. (*Tosefta Berakhot* 2:13)

Mishael, and Azariah . . . deliver themselves to the fiery furnace for sanctification of the name of God." But the phrase "sanctification of the name" is a late addition, which does not appear in the main manuscripts (see Grunewald; Safrai, "*Kiddush ha-Shem* in the Teachings of the Tannaim" [Hebrew], *Zion* (1979), 28–42, especially, 31–2 with reference to *Sifra*, "Ahare Mot," 13.

5. *Kiddush ha-Shem* is a miracle in *Sifrie* "hazinu" (Venice 1864), 55. Significantly, even the would-be martyr Rabbi Akiva used *kiddush ha-Shem* in a non-martyrological sense in BT *Baba Kamma*, 113a.

Part of the *Shema* prayer is the loud recitation "Hear (*shema*), Israel, the Lord is our God, the Lord is One" (Deuteronomy 6:4). The Hadrianic decrees forbade reciting it. Since a Roman informer (*quaesdor*) was listening in, the group did not recite the *Shema* loudly. As in the previous example, Akiva refused to put himself and his colleagues at risk.

Death caught up with Akiva when the time came to recite the *Shema* (it is recited twice a day, morning and night).

> When they took Rabbi Akiva out to be executed, it was time for the recitation of *Shema*. And they were raking his flesh with iron combs, and he was (reciting *Shema*, thereby) accepting upon himself the yoke of Heaven. His students said to him: Our teacher, even now (as you suffer, you recite *Shema*)? He said to them: All my days I have been troubled by the verse: With all your soul (Deut. 6:5) (meaning): Even if God takes your soul. I said (to myself): When will the opportunity be afforded me to fulfill this (verse)? Now that it has been afforded me, shall I not fulfill it? He prolonged (his uttering of the word): One, until his soul left (his body as he uttered his final word): One. A voice descended (from heaven) and said: Happy are you, Rabbi Akiva, that your soul left (your body as you uttered): One. (BT *Berakhot* 61b)

Death gave meaning to Akiva's life and the *Shema*. Loving God with all your soul was the heart of being Jewish, and dying with the *Shema* on one's lips the essence of Jewish martyrdom. The *Shema* thus became the Jews' ultimate martyrological cry (Boyarin, *Dying* 96, 105–14; *Martyrdom* 609). In this context, the story in *Tosefta Berakhot* 2:13 is noteworthy: Akiva and his friends did not recite the important *Shema* audibly to avoid possible execution—but he did recite the verse happily when death found him.

The story of Rabbi Hananiah ben Teradyon offers another example of commitment to passive martyrdom. The Romans set Teradyon on fire because he provocatively taught Torah in public and gathered assemblies. The executioner wrapped him in Torah scrolls, placed on his heart woolen sponges soaked in water to prolong his agony, and set him on fire. Terrified by the horrible scene, his student asked: "Why do you not open your mouth so that the flames will enter into you and put an end to your suffering?" Teradyon replied, "better that He who gave me my soul should take it, than that I should destroy myself" (BT *Avodah Zarah* 18a). Even for the most provocative of martyred rabbi, life remained an absolute value. Teradyon refused to actively contribute to his own destruction even by the trivial act of opening his mouth, despite the inevitability of his end.

Not all Talmudic stories of martyrdom were passive, however. BT *Gittin* 57b tells the story of four hundred boys and girls who drowned themselves in the sea before they could be sold as slaves in brothels. Their decision to quit life could be justified in halakhic terms, but their act of suicide could not. Nevertheless, the story endorses their self-destruction. BT *Gittin* 57b does not seem to perceive their drowning as a full-fledged active suicide. The Talmud applies to the story of the four hundred boys and girls in Psalm 44:23: "[F]or Your sake *we are killed* all the day long; we are reckoned as sheep for the slaughter." A commentary by Rav Yehudah (a late third-century *amora*) immediately follows. He preferred to apply the verse to the woman and her seven sons. Here as in parallel rabbinic versions, the Maccabean story is set in a time of Roman persecutions. Quoting biblical verses, the seven sons explain to an anonymous emperor why they will not worship idols. Their explanations are in line with the rabbinic teachings, rather than with the arguments found in the Maccabean accounts. This is especially true with respect to the philosophical 4 Maccabees. Unlike 4 Maccabees, the youngest son and the mother do not kill themselves in BT *Gittin* 57B. The son was taken "to be killed." After losing her sons, "she went up to the roof, and fell (*naphelah*), and died. A Divine Voice emerged and said: 'A joyful mother of children'" (Ps. 113:9).

The story of the mother with her seven sons gained prominence in rabbinic texts.[6] But "Rabbi Akiva and his colleagues" who were executed during the "great persecution" remain at the center of early rabbinic martyrology (BT *Rosh ha-Shanah* 23a; BT *Sanhedrin* 110b). Their stories of sacrifice for the nation, Torah, and God served to establish their emerging authority in Jewish society following the Bar Kokhva revolt. Tales about the *Tannaim's* sacrifices intended also to support their own teachings. Their sacrifices sanctified their doctrine.

Post-Talmudic traditions amalgamated the individual stories of rabbis into the famous legend of *Aseret Harugei Malkhut* ("Ten who were Killed

---

6. The version in *Lamentations Rabbah* 1:16, 50 tells that the mother, now named Miriam bat Tanhum, went out of her mind and jumped to her death. This midrash does not castigate the mother for her suicide; she is still the hero of the story. The post-Talmudic tractate *Semahot* 2:3 considers a suicide only an act committed by one who kills himself deliberately and "in a sound mind" (*be-da'at*). On the folkloric aspect of this midrash, see Rokem 114–29; Himmelfarb, "The Mother." Later versions are in *Pesikta Rabbati* 43; see *Lamentaion Zuta* 21, as here the mother fell to her death as in BT *Gittin* 57b. See also Gershon D. Cohen; Doran; Elisheva Baumgarten and Rella Kushelevsky; Joslyn-Siemiatkoski, "The Mother."

by the Empire"), often translated as "The Ten Martyrs" (Krauss; Finkelstein; Zeitlin; Reeg; Stern 143–65). *Aseret Harugei Malkhut* developed into a mystical story that has no sound foundation in the Talmudic tradition (Dan, *The Hebrew Story* 62–68; "Hekhalot Rabbati"; Boustan). The legend depicts a Roman emperor executing ten pious rabbis in a single day. In the different versions, the names of the martyrs vary slightly, and it is not always clear how some of these individuals lost their lives. General statements like, "Rabbi Shimon and Rabbi Ishmael are slated for the sword, and their colleagues for killing" (BT *Sotah* 48b), sufficed for some authors to include these two rabbis among the ten martyrs (Lieberman 213–45), even though they were not contemporaneous with Rabbi Akiva and his colleagues. Dramatic effects served a far more important purpose than historical exactness. The story credits the rabbis' vicarious sacrifices not only for the survival of Israel in Roman times, but in every generation. The story was transmitted also through the emotional *piyyut* (liturgical hymn) *Eleh Ezkera* ("These I Remember"). Its appearance in several versions attests to the popularity it gained during the years. *Eleh Ezkera* is among the lamentations (*kinnot*) recited in the synagogue on *Tisha be-Av* (Ninth of Av), the commemoration day of the destructions of the two Temples, and the *selihot* (penitential) prayers of *Yom Kippur* (Day of Atonement), the holiest day in the Jewish calendar. It is thanks to these post-Talmudic liturgical and legendary martyrologies that the deaths of "Rabbi Akiva and his colleagues" stayed alive in Jewish collective memory. The other martyrology that enjoyed such longevity is that of the mother and her seven sons. The story of the family, too, is among the *kinnot* recited on *Tisha be-Av* in some Jewish communities (Tzabar; Avishur). Together with "Rabbi Akiva and his colleagues," their collective memories inspired generations of Jewish martyrs and martyrologists (Chazan; Jeremy Cohen; Shepkaru; Goldin).

Conclusions

The earliest known Jewish accounts of martyrdom appear in 2 Maccabees 6 and 7. While a minority of scholars considers the stories to be of a later provenance than the book, the scholarly consensus is that the stories are a second-century BCE, martyr text. Be that as it may, a martyr text alone is hardly indicative of a martyrological doctrine or a cultural phenomenon. The crucial question that needs to be asked is, how did these stories impact the development of Jewish martyrdom in the short run and in the long run? These two isolated tales did not change the overall militant thrust of 2 Maccabees, let alone the dominant Jewish thinking of the time. The components that make up a martyrological doctrine are missing. Hellenistic Judaism did not codify these two stories of martyrdom in their beliefs, incorporate them in a teaching system, present the martyrs as inspiration for others, develop the two narratives into a martyrological genre, nor utilize the stories to solidify or modify religious laws. In short, Hellenistic Judaism did not embrace martyrdom.

The earliest Jewish accounts that combined martyrological components come from the Roman period. The numerous reports of potential and actual cases of voluntary death signaled a new cultural development in Jewish society. This new trend aroused fresh religious and philosophical dilemmas regarding the "Jewishness" of the act of elective, voluntary death and its legitimacy. In addition to reporting cases of voluntary death, Jewish accounts attempted to affirm the Jewish (rather than pagan) origin of voluntary death, to legitimize the act in light of (or in spite of) biblical laws, its proper performance (active or passive), and the circumstances that would warrant such drastic actions. What accounted for these ideological and cultural developments was not a Hellenistic tradition. By the time the Maccabean martyrs emerged in the late first- or early second-century text, 4 Maccabees, Jewish writings had already employed the idea of voluntary death for at least a century, without any apparent knowledge of these martyrs. What accounted for the cultural and behavioral shifts was the Jewish exposure to the Roman idea of noble death. During desperate times of intense tension and violence, Jews from all walks of life (rebels, priests, aristocrats, peaceful ordinary families) considered this Roman idea a reasonable solution. In its Jewish garb, the Roman code of dying honorably for the emperor and the *patria* spread throughout native and diasporic Jewries as the idea of dying piously for God and his law.

By the time rabbinic literature discussed voluntary death, the question was no longer if, but rather when, Jews should submit to death. Rabbinic literature answers the question in the context of the Hadrianic persecutions. But the *halakha* of *kiddush ha-Shem* developed throughout the late antique period. The end result was a rabbinic genre of martyrdom that portrays a peaceful, passive, and pious martyr dying to sanctify God's name. In most cases, the martyr was a rabbi. Thus, the martyr became the embodiment of the rabbi's passionate relationship with the divine and, by extension, of the personality of Rabbinic Judaism.

3

Performing Christian Martyrdoms

Gail P. Streete

CHRISTIAN MARTYRDOM—MUCH like ascetic behavior, the counterpart that accompanied and eventually succeeded it—might well be described as a performance, using the body as an instrument and an arena in which to portray a message about ideal Christian behavior in opposition to the "world."[1] Each martyr enacts a sacrificial death, modeled on the willed death of Jesus as described in the New Testament, notably in the three so-called Passion Predictions in the earliest of the gospels, Mark: "Then he began to teach them that the Son of Man must undergo great suffering, and be rejected by the elders, the chief priests, and the scribes, and be killed, and after three days rise again" (Mk. 8:31).[2] Jesus also encourages his followers to "deny themselves, and take up their cross and follow me. For those who want to save their life will lose it, and those who lose their life for my sake and for the gospel, will save it" (Mk. 34b–35). Even more harsh and absolute is a saying in the gospel of Luke: "Whoever comes to me and does not hate father and mother, wife and children, brothers and sisters, yes, and even life itself, cannot be my disciple. Whoever does not carry the cross and follow me cannot be my disciple" (Lk. 14:26–27). Drawing upon Greco-Roman antecedents of the hero myth and the Stoic noble death, as well as Hellenistic Jewish narratives of death in obedience to God's law, Christian martyrologists constructed a

1. I have used the plural form "martyrdoms" because, like "Christianities," all martyrdoms are not alike, although they share important characteristics. The martyrdoms of men and women, for example, are arguably different.

2. Unless otherwise noted, biblical translation is that of the New Revised Standard Version (NRSV).

"master narrative" of martyrdom so compelling that, as Christian traditions recount, all twelve of Jesus's disciples, as well as the apostle Paul, died martyrs' deaths. Although at least "seventy authentic *passiones* [martyr-tales] survive,"[3] martyrologies share several salient characteristics. In this chapter, I will use some of the best-known and influential martyr stories to illustrate them: the death of Stephen in Acts 7, together with Gregory of Nyssa's two homilies on his feast day; Ignatius of Antioch's (martyred in 110) letter, *To the Romans*; the *Martyrdom of Polycarp* (while the martyrdom occurred in the second century, the dating of the text is dubious); *The Letter of the Churches of Vienne and Lyons to the Churches of Asia and Phrygia*, otherwise known as the *Martyrs of Lyons and Vienne*, contained in Eusebius's fourth-century *History of the Church* (*Historia Ecclesiae*) 5.1; the early third-century *Martyrdom of Perpetua and Felicitas*; and the second-century *Acts of Paul and Thecla*.

Christian writers were aware of, and ambivalent toward, the connection of voluntary death and suicide. The second-century apologist Justin Martyr explains that Christians prefer to face prosecution and possible death at the hands of others, rather than simply to commit suicide and "pass even now to God," because they may use the opportunity of martyrdom's public spectacle to instruct others (*martyrein*):

> If, then, we all kill ourselves we shall become the cause, as far as in us lies, why no one should be... instructed in the divine doctrines.... But when we are examined, we make no denial, because we are not conscious of any evil, but count it impious not to speak the truth in all things, which also we know is pleasing to God. (Justin Martyr, *Second Apology*)

And yet another late second-century apologist, Tertullian, famously advocated the necessity of the martyrs' deaths in propagating Christianity: "The oftener we are mown down by you, the more in number we grow; *the blood of Christians is seed*" (*Apology* 50).

Jesus's own death was modeled on that of the righteous martyrs of 2 and especially 4 Maccabees,[4] the latter of which deliberately and apologetically incorporated Stoic traditions of the noble death. Josephus's description of the speech of Eleazar ben Yair before the mass suicide of the defenders of Masada, however, seems also to incorporate but subtly alter that tradition by attributing the opportunity for a "noble death" to God: "I think it is God that

3. Elliott 25.

4. See especially Williams 245.

has given us the privilege that we can die nobly and as free men" (Josephus, *Jewish War* 7, 8:6). Jan Willem van Henten and Friedrich Avemarie have observed such alterations, in that these early Hellenistic Jewish, and later nascent Christian, martyr traditions incorporate elements that Greco-Roman traditions of the noble death do not have: specifically, an emphasis on religious fidelity that overrides obedience to any other authority, with death as the vehicle to an everlasting glory superior to that won on earth, in combat, battle, or the civic arena.[5]

There seems also to have been a development in Christian writing about martyrdom that carefully distinguished it from noble suicide. Tertullian encouraged the martyrs, who were "called to the army (*militiam*) of the living God" (*To the Martyrs* 3.1), by citing classic Greco-Roman examples of courage and noble death, including that of Lucretia, who, shamed by having been raped, killed herself "in the sight of her relatives," thereby winning "glory for her chastity" (4.4). Centuries later, however, in addressing the rape of chaste women and consecrated virgins in the sack of Rome in 410, Augustine condemned the example of Lucretia, who committed a greater crime than that of her rapist by killing, in killing herself, "a chaste, innocent woman" (*City of God* 19). Some Christians, like those identified as Gnostics, "advocated [martyrdom]; others repudiated it on principle," while others, like the followers of Valentinus, supported a middle position.[6] In the *Coptic Apocalypse of Peter*, for example, Jesus appears to accuse orthodox Christian bishops of being "dry canals" for urging martyrdom on their congregations, the "little ones," whom they mislead to death (VI 79, 22–31), thinking they are imitating a crucified Jesus, when the "living Savior" is "glad and laughing on the tree."

Christian writers constructed their propaganda of martyrdom through a rhetoric of resistance, both spoken and enacted, linked to elite concepts of Roman virtue, and transformed them by applying them to a despised minority that consisted, at least as far as Roman imperial suspicions went, largely of women, members of the artisan class, and slaves. All of these populations were regarded as ignorant or deluded, as expressed in the writings of the Greek philosopher, Celsus, in his *True Word* of 177, which Origen quotes only to refute:

> We see, indeed, in private houses workers in wool and leather, and fullers, and persons of the most uninstructed and rustic character,

5. Van Henten and Avemarie 1.

6. Pagels 90; cited in Tite 30, n.11. Tite's article is a nuanced discussion of the prevailing view that Gnostics, especially in the *Gospel of Judas*, repudiated martyrdom.

> not venturing to utter a word in the presence of their elders and wiser masters; but when they get hold of the children privately, and certain women as ignorant as themselves, they pour forth wonderful statements, to the effect that they ought not to give heed to their father and to their teachers, but should obey them. (Origen, *Against Celsus* III.55)

The virtues praised by the elite included the prerogative of free or open public speech (*parrhēsia*); courage, particularly in battle or other combat *(andreia)*; self-control (*sophrosynē*) and self-mastery (*enkrateia*); and chastity and modesty—the latter two particularly praised when applied to elite married women. Yet martyr-narratives also exalted the virtues of slaves (humility, obedience) that were considered inappropriate or shameful for elites, into models for Christian behavior. Conquest was achieved, not through military might, combat, or even armed resistance, but, paradoxically, through surrender. As Tertullian writes:

> It is our battle to be summoned to your tribunals that there, under fear of execution, we may battle for the truth. But the day is won when the object of the struggle is gained. This victory of ours gives us the glory of pleasing God, and the spoil of life eternal. But we are overcome. Yes, when we have obtained our wishes. Therefore we conquer in dying; we go forth victorious at the very time we are subdued. (*Apology* 50)

Their model, in turn, was Jesus himself; as the hymn in Paul's letter to the Philippians expresses it,

> Let the same mind be in you that was in Christ Jesus,/ who, though he was in the form/of God, did not regard equality with God /as something to be exploited,/but emptied himself,/taking the form of a slave . . ./he humbled himself/and became obedient to the point of death -- /even death on a cross./Therefore God also highly/exalted him,/and gave him the name./that is above every name. (Phil. 2:5–9)

Although Paul is the first to use the language of imitation in speaking of suffering in obedience to Christ (for example, in 2 Cor. 4:8–10: "We are . . . always carrying in the body the death of Jesus, so that the life of Jesus may be made visible in our bodies"), the first probable description of death *for* Jesus is that of Stephen in Chapter 7 of the Acts of the Apostles.

This passage incorporates elements that appear consistent in all later martyrologies. In several respects, the description of Stephen's own death harks back to that of Jesus; it is preceded by a lengthy speech that calls for judgment on his adversaries, and the death itself opens heaven to the righteous martyr. In effect, Stephen fulfills the prediction of Jesus before his own death in Luke's previous volume (Lk. 21:12–17): the arrest and trial of his followers, which gives them an opportunity for "testimony" (*martyrion*); the assurance that Jesus himself will give them "a mouth and wisdom" that enables them to refute their opponents; and the promise that their "patient endurance" (the prized and often-reiterated Christian virtue of "*hypomonē*") will "gain their souls (or lives, *psychas*)." Arrested for blasphemy—ironically, through "false witnesses" (*martyras pseudeis*)—Stephen, "with the face of an angel," confronts the Sanhedrin and the High Priest with a powerful recitation of Israelite history and indicts his hearers for the betrayal of the law and the murder of the prophets, leaving them no choice but to execute him by stoning. At the moment before his death, he sees the heavens opened, with Jesus already present in judgment; like Jesus, he forgives his enemies (Acts 7:60; cf. Lk. 23:46).

The importance of Stephen as the first martyr for Christ is emphasized in two sermons by the Cappadocian Father Gregory of Nyssa, who underscores the fact that Stephen's feast-day, December 26, follows the celebration of the birth of Christ on December 25, and describes him in terminology that becomes characteristic in Christian martyr-narratives. Stephen is a *mimētēs*, or an imitator of Christ, and even a "*Christophoros*" (a bearer of Christ, *Homily II*), or an athlete who competes in the stadium and, despite being conquered, actually wins the victor's crown (*stephanos*), in a pun on his name:

> Brethren, let us hasten to the stadium where the great athlete contends against the wicked adversary of human life by stripping himself in the arena by his confession [of faith] [cf. 1 Cor 4.9]. Indeed, as Paul has said [Heb 12.4], Stephen [Stephanos] has become a spectacle to the world, angels and to men. He was the first to have received the crown [*stephanos*] of martyrdom, the first to have paved the way for the chorus of martyrs and the first to have resisted sin to the point of shedding blood. It seems to me that the entire host of transcendent powers, angels, and myriads both assist and accompany them [i.e., the martyrs]. If we hear anything honorable in the heavens from among the principalities, powers, thrones, ruling forces and the entire heavenly assembly, their words provide an

athletic spectacle by contending with an opponent [cf. Col 1.16 & Eph 1.21]. (*Homily I*)[7]

Imitation of Christ through spectacular suffering is the essential qualification of the martyr. This *mimesis* is abundantly clear in a number of martyr narratives, even in those of women. In the *Martyrdom of Perpetua and Felicitas*, for example, the slave Felicitas responds to the servant in prison who taunts her for crying out in her labor pains, replying that in the arena, "Another will be in me who will suffer for me, as I have suffered for him" (15.6). The slave Blandina is described in *The Letter of the Churches of Lyons and Vienne to the Churches of Asia and Phrygia,* which is quoted by Eusebius in his *History of the Church*: "For they looked on her in her conflict, and beheld with their outward eyes, in the form of their sister, him who was crucified for them." Like Stephen, Blandina is praised as a "noble athlete," and "filled with power."

As Alison Goddard Elliott has noted, the protagonist in the martyr-narrative, which she calls "hagiographic epic," competes in an *agon*, that is, a contest that involves both athletic and heroic combat, and is also both physical and verbal.[8] It is thus absolutely necessary in the performance of Christian martyrdom that those "witnessing the witness" must not only hear the testimony, but even more importantly, see the spectacle. The verbal and the physical actions of the martyrdom focus upon the challenge to, and subversion of, the values and norms of the dominant culture with its (illegitimate) authority.[9] As athlete and combatant, moreover, the male martyr uses the socially approved Greco-Roman virtues of bold, open speech (*parrhesia*) and manly courage (*andreia, virtus*), but in a socially inappropriate way: namely, to publicly challenge, rather than to uphold or defend, the social order. To these he adds the humiliation of being treated as a slave, subject to torture and a degrading death that will nonetheless grant him victory. In the *Martyrdom of Polycarp*, for example, as the aged bishop enters the stadium for his trial, a voice from heaven urges him, "Be strong, Polycarp, and show thyself the man!" (IX).[10] When his tormentors finally succeed in killing him (first by fire, then by stabbing him, martyrs generally being extraordinarily hard to kill), Polycarp is praised as a model for the "exercising and preparation" of

---

7. "Two Homilies Concerning Saint Stephen, Protomartyr."

8. Elliott 24. See also Brent D. Shaw, "Body/Power/Identity: Passions of the Martyrs."

9. Streete 31.

10. *Concerning the Martyrdom of Polycarp*.

others who will follow him, seeing that he is a "pre-eminent martyr, one whose martyrdom all desire to imitate, seeing that is after the pattern of the Gospel of Christ" (XVIII–XIX). The mob in Lyons calls all the more strongly for Attalus's death because he is "a person of distinction" who is socially and politically disgraced by confessing his Christianity (*Martyrs of Lyons and Vienne*). Ignatius of Antioch demonstrates martyrdom as an "ethic of imitation"[11] that is also as an exhibition of paradoxical Christian *machismo*: "Let fire and the cross; let the crowds of wild beasts; let tearings, breakings, and dislocations of bones; let cutting off of members; let shatterings of the whole body; and let all the dreadful torments of the devil come upon me; only let me attain to Jesus Christ" (*To the Romans* 5).

Envisioning his desired martyrdom, Ignatius expresses another essential element of Christian martyr narratives: the centrality of the body to the witness. Even when the martyrs do not themselves offer lengthy verbal testimony (as often occurs in the case of female martyrs), their bodies "talk." The public ordeal of the martyrs ironically spotlights their transformation from an identity as defined by "the world," to a new identity that is proclaimed in the spectacle of their dying. Martyrs' bodies are initially seen as distinctly embodied within "the world," that is, within dominant social systems, definitions, and values like marriage, filial obedience, family life, slavery, and citizenship. On the other hand, their bodies are the object of the world's antagonism, and the site of the martyrs' own rejection of embodied "worldliness." In both instances, their bodies are "out of place." Martyrs' worldly bodies are visibly and spectacularly transformed by their annihilation. They may even "disappear," as Ignatius desires in his own martyrdom: "I shall be a true disciple of Jesus Christ, when the world shall not see so much as my body" (*To the Romans* 4). Sanctus's body "externally lost the human shape" because of his torture (*Martyrs of Lyons and Vienne*). The idea of the "resurrection of the body" does not seem to have been applied by martyrologists to a physical, this-worldly body, although some martyrologies, such as the *Martyrdom of Perpetua and Felicitas*, depict the martyrs "out of the flesh," but nevertheless still in some recognizable bodily form, as in the vision of Saturus (*Martyrdom* 11–13). This form is not earthly or worldly, but perhaps was imagined (as Paul envisioned the resurrected body in 1 Cor. 15:35–57), as a spiritual, imperishable body, symbolizing a death that was "swallowed up in victory" (1 Cor. 15:54).

11. Corrigan et al. 224.

Accounts of early Christian women martyrs in particular emphasize the difference between the socially inscribed femaleness of their physical bodies and the "manly" courage (*andreia*) that they "put on" as they do the body of Christ, in anticipation of their imperishable bodies. Their status may vary: martyrs are free, even noble women like Perpetua and Thecla, but also slaves like Felicitas and Blandina. Whether slave or free, however, these women did not have authority over their own bodies. Slave women, the property of their masters, like all slaves, were spoken of as mere "bodies" (*sōmata*). Free women, the guardians of family honor, were not expected to appear or to expose themselves in the public sphere, still less to challenge the authorities dominant in that sphere. Their virtues, typically, were chastity and modesty—virtues carefully guarded by women's not being too "visible." Thus, when women speak or perform a public "witness" (*martyria*), they become "doubly transgressive,"[12] because they are stepping out of approved social roles, and acting in a sphere that is regarded as inappropriate to them. The matron Perpetua (*Martyrdom of Perpetua and Felicitas*), "*honeste nata*" (nobly born) though she is, challenges the authority of both father and governor in refusing to recant her confession of Christianity; and Thecla (*Acts of Paul and Thecla*), the "noble virgin of Iconium," challenges the authority of her mother, her fiancé, and later the Syriarch Alexander by leaving both her household and the socially circumscribed role she was born to play, thereby becoming an "unbride" (*anymphon*)—a social crime so unacceptable that her own mother urges that she be put to death by burning. Perpetua's status in prison is ambiguous: she is a criminal because she is a Christian, but her behavior is that of the free person (*liberaliter instituta*) whom she was raised to be. She asks for and receives better treatment for the prisoners; both her father and her brother address her by the honorific title of *domina* (lady); and she demands that she and her fellow-prisoner, the slave Felicitas, not be degraded by having to wear the clothes of priestesses of Ceres. Christianity makes Perpetua and Felicitas sisters; martyrdom in Christ both levels and ennobles.

But while Perpetua, by her actions, recognizes Felicitas as an equal in Christ, a sister, and a fellow mother and martyr, to her jailers and tormentors, Felicitas is an object of mockery, suffering the pains of an eighth-month delivery while in prison. The slave Blandina, tortured as was the Roman custom for slaves (and an inevitable part of the stories of martyrs), appears to the world as "an insignificant, weak, and despised woman" (*Martyrs of Lyons*

---

12. Streete 31.

and Vienne). The bodies of the women martyrs are, like those of the men, transformed, but first they must be inscribed as specifically female bodies. They exhibit the male virtues of *andreia* and, infrequently, *parrhesia*, and the virtue of endurance (*hypomonē*), but in order to see these virtues we are compelled to witness them as female bodies. Accounts of women martyrs always emphasize—and indeed, often overemphasize—their attributes as women, frequently depicting them naked, in an affront to feminine "modesty," but one that paradoxically turns them into men, for whom nakedness was a sign of virility. As Lisa M. Sullivan notes of Perpetua's "visionary sex change," it is in a sense her "ultimate victory through resistance," appropriating, as a member of a "submissive (female) group . . . the imagery of the dominant (a powerful male body) in order to converse on the dominant's terms."[13] The conversation, however, ends with her death as a woman.

Perhaps the best example of the permeability of the male-female, public-private boundary is offered in the *Martyrdom of Perpetua and Felicitas* which, according to Herbert Musurillo, is "in a sense, the archetype of all later *Acts* of the Christian martyrs."[14] Perpetua describes herself as initially "tormented" with anxiety for her still-nursing son while she is in prison; Felicitas, as mentioned above, suffers the pangs of childbirth, and both are exposed naked in nets in the amphitheater, showing that "one is a tender girl" and the other is a recent mother, her breasts leaking milk. Even the pagan crowd, shocked by this immodest display, demands that they be brought back appropriately clothed. The women are then attacked by a mad heifer as "appropriate to their sex." This encounter leaves Perpetua with a torn tunic and disheveled hair, but she fixes her garment and her loosened hair because of her sense of modesty and appropriate behavior. All of this from a woman who envisioned herself "stripped naked" to fight in gladiatorial combat, becoming a man! As Peter Dronke drily comments, "[The] picture of Perpetua in the arena, covering her legs and tidying her hair after being gored—consorts ill with the dream of the woman who strips naked and is anointed for combat: one who is unafraid to write like that will hardly have gone to her death in a fit of prudery."[15] Yet even her death emphasizes what is deemed appropriately "female": being extraordinarily hard to kill, like other martyrs, she finally has to guide the trembling sword of the young soldier sent to dispatch her to her own throat, in the classic

13. Sullivan 73.

14. Musurillo xxv.

15. Dronke 15.

gesture both of tragic heroines and of pagan female noble deaths.[16] In one of his sermons on the *dies natalis* ("birthday" or Feast Day) of Perpetua and Felicitas, Augustine of Hippo writes that the martyrdom itself made them men (*Sermon* 280 1.1–5).

Thecla, too, as an example of both the valued (male) virtue of *enkrateia* and its Christian version, virginity, appears naked in several episodes of her trials, and indeed in much of her iconography. About to be burned as an example of a woman who refuses to support Iconian society by marrying, she is brought in naked to the stadium (*Acts of Paul and Thecla*). The one whom she follows to Antioch after her ordeal, the apostle Paul, refuses to accept her as a disciple, lest she "act like a coward," using the Greek word, *deilandrēsēs*, which might be interpreted as "failure to act like man, with courage" (*andreia*). But of course she is not a man; she is a woman, who has already shown a good deal of "manliness" in her trials. After rejecting the Syriarch Alexander in Antioch, Thecla is once more brought in naked, to be "exposed" in the arena to the beasts, but after several ordeals, God causes a cloud of fire to cover Thecla's nakedness, thus preserving her modesty at the same time as her chastity is preserved through the agency of a sympathetic local noblewoman, Tryphaena. As if she has been transformed by her ordeals into an active rather than passive participant in them, she boldly leaps into a pool of sea lions in an apocalyptic self-baptism, taking for herself the "seal" that Paul had denied her. Finally, Thecla becomes an apostle herself, albeit "dressed in men's clothing," traveling freely as the male apostle Paul does, preaching and teaching.

The porosity—or erosion, even—of the gender binary in the tales of the martyrs is another aspect of their liminality. The martyrs stand on the borders between the socially acceptable and the socially outcast, humiliation and empowerment, life and death, and the heavenly and the earthly. As Judith Perkins has noted about the *Martyrdom of Perpetua and Felicitas*, "Society's power is not affirmed, but radically reinterpreted."[17] Bodies are also reinterpreted. Women become men, despite their bodily appearance. Slaves, as the case of Blandina shows, become "noble athletes" and win their contests. The body of the aged Polycarp, when set on fire, burns with a sweet fragrance, "like a loaf in the oven" or like frankincense, appearing like refined gold or silver; his remains are treated like "precious stones" by his followers (*Martyrdom of Polycarp*). Ignatius wishes his own body to become "the wheat of God," ground

16. Streete 71.

17. Perkins 105.

by the teeth of the beasts so that it may become "the bread of God," perhaps alluding to becoming Christ's sacrificial body in the Eucharist (*To the Romans* 4). Thecla's naked body is surrounded by fire, and in another version of her story (Pseudo-Basil of Seleucia, *The Life and Miracles of St. Thecla*), although she is a "lowly old woman," she is about to be raped by some scoundrels, when, in response to her prayer for help, her body is safely enclosed in a rock. Thecla's body has thus been "completely translated," perhaps explaining the absence of bodily remains at her shrine.[18] All of this evidence indicates that the martyr's body itself is extraordinary: even in torture it is transformed into a powerful instrument of triumph; and in those cases when the martyr does not verbally testify, as is the case with most of the women martyrs, the martyr's body symbolically "speaks," testifying to the power of God, who is already changing the mortal body into an immortal one, the disempowered to the conqueror. The "crown" of victory in the competition in the arena or in battle is "won" by the besting of earthly opponents. In *The Martyrs of Lyons and Vienne*, despite their terrible tortures, those who confess Christ wear their chains like "beautiful ornaments," appear like "a bride adorned with variegated golden fringes," and are even "perfumed with the fragrance of Christ." Not only do they procure for God a "crown of variegated flowers" signifying his victory; they themselves win "the crown of incorruption."

Yet this victory must be accomplished in death: the victor's crown represents a struggle between the kingdom of God and the kingdoms of this world, and in order to win it, the martyr must no longer be present in the world. In several cases, visions offer this knowledge to martyrs: for example, Perpetua knows, after her first vision, how her life will end. Visions are another indication of the martyr's liminality: standing on the threshold between life and death, the martyr "sees" into the next world, having already symbolically triumphed over "the flesh." Visions are not the reason the martyrs undergo their ordeal, but they seem to show the martyrs and their audiences its outcome: unlike those who must wait for the resurrection of the dead, the righteous will already be in Paradise, as Jesus promised the repentant criminal, who acknowledges him on the cross (Lk. 23:43). During his trial for blasphemy, Stephen's face already appears to the onlookers "like the face of an angel" (Acts 6:15). At the end of his trial, he sees "heaven opened and Jesus standing at the right hand of God," a vision he relates to his interlocutors, which enrages them so much they drag him out of the city and stone him

18. Streete 99; citing Davis 46. Later legend has Thecla being "translated" to Rome, just in time to witness the martyrdom of her former teacher, Paul.

to death as he cries, "Lord Jesus, receive my spirit" (Acts 7:55–59). Polycarp, who has had a vision of his pillow burning, understands that he must die by fire. Although he is burned, he actually does not die that way: he has to be stabbed as well, whereupon a dove emerges with the blood from his body; this perhaps recalls the Holy Spirit descending as a dove on Jesus at his baptism (Mk. 1:10), martyrdom being regarded as a second baptism, or "washing" by blood, like Saturus's death in the *Martyrdom of Perpetua and Felicitas*.[19] In that same martyrdom, both Perpetua and Saturus have visions in their imprisonment. Perpetua's first vision, requested by a brother Christian as a prophetic window into heaven, is exactly that; she climbs a perilous ladder into heaven, where she meets a grey-haired fatherly God and is given sweet cheese to eat, like a small child: it is then she realizes that there is "no more hope in this world." In her last vision, she appears as a male gladiator, defeats her opponent, and is led through the gate of life as a symbol of her victory. Saturus's visions, in the same *Martyrdom*, also open up a window into heaven, where he and Perpetua experience a kind of renewed childhood, as in her first vision, with their fellow martyrs, but are also able to intervene from heaven to settle a quarrel between the bishop Optatus and Asperses the presbyter.

The ability to intercede for others, even if they are dead, is also a feature of the martyrs' liminal existence on the borders between this life and the afterlife, the heavenly and earthly. Not only are Perpetua and Saturus able to reconcile two quarreling clergy from their perch in heaven; as a "confessor," or one imprisoned for her faith, Perpetua is able to ask for and receive a vision on behalf of her fellow Christians and is also able to procure a happy afterlife for her dead brother Dinocrates, whom she sees suffering in her second vision, but in her third vision sees released and playing like a happy child, after her intercessory prayer. In the *Acts of Paul and Thecla*, Thecla is imprisoned in Antioch as a confessor. Her noble supporter Tryphaena has a vision of her dead daughter, Falconilla, beseeching her to ask Thecla to intercede for her to be released "to the place of the just." While the story of the martyrs of Lyons and Vienne, as related by Eusebius, has them refusing the title "martyr," preferring only that of "confessor," they intercede not only for their enemies but for their neighbors: "They begged life, and he [God] gave it to them, and they shared it with their neighbors. Victorious over everything, they departed to God" (*Martyrs of Lyons and Vienne*). These instances reflect not only the special status of confessors as well as martyrs, but also Tertullian's

19. Compare Thecla's decision, "Now is the time to wash!" as she plunges into the pool of carnivorous sea lions prepared for her death (*APTh* 34).

view that Perpetua's vision of heaven proved that only martyrs could enter Paradise: those who die "in Christ" are able to enter the place closed to those "in Adam" (*The Soul* 55.4). Augustine, who notes that the joy of some martyrs is "before, others after, the Resurrection" (*Sermon* 280.1.5), in an apparently anti-Donatist move, nonetheless urges the martyrs to intercede for those still on earth.

Finally, as Elizabeth Castelli remarks, "The discourse of martyrdom is also a discourse of power."[20] Because of their terrifyingly superhuman yet paradoxically triumphant deaths, the martyrs achieve victory and dominion over worldly powers, both social constraints and those of their mortal bodies. The spectacular and graphic accounts of dismemberment and sexual mutilation have an ironic purpose: they indicate that nothing that is done to the bodies of the martyrs can defeat them. Martyrs must die hard deaths; ultimately, however, they do not truly die, but are rather transformed. They conquer their apparent overlords and persecutors with the strength of the weak, which is, ironically, the strength of God: their bodies become the receptacles and transmitters of that strength. Story after story reflects the themes of victory and conquest in battle, in the arena, and in athletic contests. The late first-century book of Revelation, which admits only resistance to empire as true Christianity, glorifies the martyrs as "conquerors" and consistently uses "conquest" as a metaphor for martyrdom: "They [the martyrs] have conquered [the accuser]/ by the blood of the Lamb/ and by the word of their testimony,/ for they did not cling to life/ even in the face of death" (Rev. 12:11). Tertullian's *Apology* denies the triumph of empire: "Therefore we conquer in dying; we go forth victorious at the very time we are subdued." Though horribly tortured, Blandina is "filled with such power" that her torturers grow weary: she and her companions "humbled themselves under the powerful hand [of God] by which they are now highly exalted." Perpetua realizes that her final vision signifies her victory—not over an Egyptian gladiator, but over the devil. In the arena, she cannot die until she guides the sword of her dispatcher to her own throat: "It was as though so great a woman, feared as she was by the unclean spirit, could not be dispatched unless she herself were willing." She and her fellow martyrs have performed "new deeds of heroism." Martyrs are consistently spoken of as gaining the "crown" of victory that symbolizes

20. Castelli 197.

their conquest: Gregory of Nyssa speaks of Stephen as "the great athlete of faith" whose prize was "the crown of immortality" (*Homily I*); and Polycarp and Blandina also win the "crown of immortality." In the end, the martyrs' torture and death is a judgment on those who inflict it: in the *Martyrdom of Perpetua and Felicitas*, Saturus says to his executioners, "You have condemned us, but God will condemn you."

4

Collective Martyrdom and Religious Suicide

THE BRANCH DAVIDIANS AND HEAVEN'S GATE

Catherine Wessinger

THE COMPARATIVE STUDY of new religious movements that become involved in violence illuminates characteristics and dynamics of religious communities whose members believe that in order to achieve salvation they must be martyred or commit religious suicide. Such communities frequently adhere to catastrophic millennial,[1] or apocalyptic, worldviews that devalue earthly existence.

Millennial groups involved in violence may fall into one or more of the following categories: 1) assaulted millennial groups, who are ambushed or confronted by outside agents or agencies; 2) fragile millennial groups, whose members are responding to outside pressures and/or internal stresses that threaten their ultimate concern; and 3) revolutionary millennial movements, who initiate violent actions against forces perceived as oppressive. These categories are not mutually exclusive, and a group may shift from one to another

1. See Wessinger, *How the Millennium*; Wessinger, *Millennialism, Persecution*; Wessinger, "Millennialism in Cross-Cultural Perspective"; and Gallagher, "Catastrophic Millennialism." The other common millennial pattern involving belief that a superhuman agent is overseeing a plan for human progress may be termed "progressive millennialism." Revolutionary progressive millennialism is on the violent end of the progressive millennial spectrum. See Wessinger, *How the Millennium*; Wessinger, *Millennialism, Persecution*; Wessinger, "Interacting Dynamics"; Ashcraft, "Progressive Millennialism."

as members respond to changes in their external and internal environments.[2] This chapter traces the trajectory of a millennial group expecting martyrdom that was assaulted (the Branch Davidians), and the trajectory of a millennial group that resorted to religious suicide due to its fragility (Heaven's Gate). It is possible that in their last moments, the Branch Davidians also became a fragile millennial group.

Both the Branch Davidians and the members of Heaven's Gate lived and died in ways consistent with the logic of their respective worldviews.[3] The Branch Davidians and Heaven's Gate members were committed to their ultimate concern—their most cherished goal[4]—which involved physical transformation and eternal heavenly salvation. They were willing to give up their earthly lives in martyrdom (Branch Davidians) and religious suicide (Heaven's Gate) to achieve their ultimate goal.

The Branch Davidians

History

David Koresh (1959–1993) was one in a particular lineage of prophets who had split off from the Seventh-day Adventist Church, whose members look to Ellen Harmon White (1827–1915) as a prophet who cast "New Light" on the Bible's prophecies about the Last Days. The General Association of the Davidian Seventh-day Adventists (the Davidians), led by Victor Houteff (1885–1955), had settled in the Waco, Texas area in 1935 to live on land they named Mount Carmel. Houteff's printed Bible studies were distributed internationally, primarily to Seventh-day Adventists, and attracted converts to his interpretations of the Bible's prophecies. After Houteff's death, his wife Florence Houteff assumed leadership of the Davidians, sold the original Mount Carmel property, and bought new property nine miles east of Waco, which was also named Mount Carmel. Florence Houteff predicted that God's chastisement of Seventh-day Adventists who rejected the Davidian message would occur on April 22, 1959 during Passover, when the Davidians would be miraculously transported to the Holy Land. About one thousand Davidians gathered at Mount Carmel for the event. After nothing occurred, Florence Houteff disbanded the organization and moved away.

---

2. Wessinger, *How the Millennium*; Wessinger, "Interacting Dynamics."

3. Bromley and Wessinger; Zeller, *Heaven's Gate.*

4. Baird.

Ben Roden (1902–1978) emerged as the next prophet and named his organization the General Association of the Branch Davidian Seventh-day Adventists (or, Branch Davidians). By 1973 he and his wife Lois Roden (1916–1986) had purchased what remained of the Mount Carmel property, where the Branch Davidians lived in cottages. Before his death in 1978 he acknowledged that Lois was the next prophet.

In 1981, a twenty-two-year-old named Vernon Howell, who was born in Houston and was at that time living in the Tyler, Texas area, arrived at Mount Carmel.[5] In 1984 he married Rachel Jones, the fourteen-year-old daughter of long-time Branch Davidians. Lois Roden began to indicate that Howell would be the next prophet after her. The Branch Davidians became convinced that the Spirit of Prophecy had left Lois Roden already, before her death,[6] and now resided with Howell, who legally changed his name to David Koresh in 1990. While in Jerusalem in 1985 with his wife Rachel, who was pregnant with their first child (who would be named Cyrus), Howell claimed to have met with seven angels who traveled through space in a *merkavah*,[7] identified by Koresh as a spaceship that travels by means of refraction of light. He claimed that the seven angels revealed the secrets of the Seven Seals of the book of Revelation to him. He became convinced that he was the new embodiment of Christ for the events of the Last Days, and returned to Texas to teach with authority to his followers.[8]

In 1986, Koresh began to take additional young women as his extralegal wives. In 1989, he taught that all the women in the community were his wives, even if they were already married to other men. All males in the community other than Koresh were instructed to be celibate. Koresh taught that he was to have twenty-four children, who would be the twenty-four elders (Rev. 4:4, 10–11; 5:8, 14) who sit next to the Lord on his throne, where he holds a book sealed with seven seals (Rev. 5:1). The twenty-four elders assist the Lord in judging humanity. Some of the girls with whom Koresh had sexual intercourse were younger than fourteen, which was the legal age at which a girl could be married, with parental consent, in Texas at that time. Texas social

---

5. Haldeman.

6. Pitts 49.

7. In Jewish mysticism, the *merkavah* is associated with the vision in Ezek. 1:4–26.

8. Newport, *Branch Davidians* 180–84; Tabor and Gallagher 58–59, 61–62.

workers investigated Koresh for child abuse in 1992, but closed the case for lack of evidence.[9]

Branch Davidians supported the community by working in various parts of the United States and engaging in business ventures; in 1990 some of the male members began selling guns and ammunition vests at gun shows. They also bought guns for self-defense, in preparation for the assault that Koresh was predicting, based on biblical texts. In 1992, the Branch Davidians dismantled the cottages at Mount Carmel and built a single large residence with a chapel, gymnasium, kitchen, cafeteria, and three towers, with the central tower tall enough to offer a panoramic view of the surrounding landscape.[10]

Hermeneutics

Koresh employed a typological hermeneutic to interpret the King James Version of the Bible, which he learned from his Seventh-day Adventist background and from Lois Roden. Kenneth G. C. Newport describes the "typological method of biblical interpretation" as centering "upon the belief that certain parts of the Old Testament are 'types' or 'foreshadowings' of what was or is yet to come."[11] In Davidian and Branch Davidian theology, passages from various Old and New Testament books are utilized to interpret the symbolism in the book of Revelation in order to unlock its secrets about the imminent Last Days. In this mode of interpretation, the books of the Bible are not read as historical documents influenced by social contexts, nor are the books of the Bible understood as having been impacted by various historical and cultural contingencies which influenced their eventual inclusion in the Bible—both of which are working assumptions for a majority of Bible scholars today.

Christology

Like the Seventh-day Adventists and Davidians before them, the Branch Davidians regarded each of their leaders as a prophet divinely inspired to

9. The jurisdiction of the ATF does not extend to child abuse, so it should not have been used as a justification for the no-knock raid on the community's residence on February 28, 1993 (Tabor and Gallagher 100–03).

10. The way of life of the Branch Davidians is described in Martin; Haldeman; Doyle with Wessinger and Wittmer.

11. Newport, *Branch Davidians* 34.

shed New Light on the Bible's prophecies about the Last Days. Koresh, however, taught that he was more than a prophet; he claimed that he was the Christ for the Last Days. He identified himself with Cyrus (Hebrew, "Koresh"), God's anointed king in Isaiah 45, and the Seventh Angel who holds a "little book" in Revelation 10:1–3, 5–7. Revelation 10:7 states, "But in the days of the voice of the seventh angel, when he shall begin to sound, the mystery of God should be finished, as he hath declared to his servants the prophets." Koresh identified himself with the Lamb in the book of Revelation. The text says that only the Lamb "as it had been slain" (Rev. 5:6) may open the Seven Seals on the book held by the Lord on the throne[12]; Koresh convinced himself and his followers that he could "open" the Seven Seals with his biblical interpretations. The Branch Davidians believed also that Koresh would open the Seals by means of the events of the Last Days.

Koresh taught that he would be assaulted and killed by agents of the United States, identified with the "lamblike beast" or "two-horned beast" in Revelation 13:11–12.[13] Revelation 13:11 reads, "And I beheld another beast coming up out of the earth; and he had two horns like a lamb, and he spake as a dragon." The Branch Davidians understood the lamb-like beast as being a nation—the United States—that claimed to be Christian (affiliated with the Lamb), but which was really of the devil.[14]

Based on the Fifth Seal of Revelation (Rev. 6:9–11), Koresh taught that some of his followers would be martyred, and after a waiting period most of the remainder would be killed. Koresh would be resurrected as the rider on the white horse who would lead an army of the resurrected 200 million martyrs of all the ages in transformed bodies (Rev. 6:2, 19:11, Rev. 9:15–18) to carry out judgment on humanity and set up Christ's Kingdom on Earth, a Davidic Kingdom on a plain created by the miraculous elevation and enlargement of Mount Zion (Zech. 14:4–10), where the righteous would be gathered.[15] The martyrs, including those alive at the time of this resurrection, who had sacrificed their all for God, make up the 200 million members of the "wave sheaf" (Lev. 23:10–14), the first of the "first fruits" in the Lord's

12. Doyle with Wessinger and Wittmer 82.

13. Doyle with Wessinger and Wittmer 92; Newport, *Branch Davidians* 234–35.

14. Doyle with Wessinger and Wittmer 92.

15. Doyle with Wessinger and Wittmer 93, 95.

harvest of souls in the Last Days.[16] In a series of Bible-study lectures held in Manchester, England in 1990, Branch Davidian Steve Schneider taught that if his listeners converted and went to Mount Carmel, they would go through a cleansing by fire—involving death—and then be resurrected as warriors in "an avenging army that would wreak God's vengeance upon the earth."[17]

Koresh did not teach he was the Second Coming of Jesus Christ, who was expected by many other Christian groups and denominations. Rather, he taught that the Christ Spirit, that is, the presence of God on earth, had come many times prior to Yahshua (Jesus), whom the Branch Davidians called "Christ," in different biblical figures such as Melchizedek (Gen. 14:18–20), Elihu (Job 32:2–37), and, according to Branch Davidian survivor Clive Doyle, perhaps as figures in other religions. Koresh was not the return of Yahshua/Jesus; he was the Christ for the Last Days and the creation of the Lord's Kingdom on earth. When he returned after his resurrection, he would not look like David Koresh.[18]

Based on the revelation given to Lois Roden that the Holy Spirit is feminine, Koresh taught that God is both Father and Mother, and that the Son is the Father who has taken on human flesh as a manifestation of God on earth. The Mother aspect is Shekinah (the indwelling presence of God) and Wisdom (*hokhmah*). As the woman clothed with the sun (Rev. 12:1–6), she will play a role in the events of the Last Days.[19] There will be the Marriage of the Lamb in heaven, which members of the wave sheaf will attend,[20] and Christ and his Wife will rule the Kingdom on earth once it is set up. Members of the wave sheaf will live in heaven and travel with Christ to other universes.

Although a violent judgment is part of the events of the Last Days, Christ and the members of the wave sheaf will call persons living on earth to the kingdom in the Holy Land, the first being the 144,000 (Rev. 7:3–8; 14:1, 3–5), who will then call the "great multitude" (Rev. 7:9) from all parts of the world, and even from other religions.[21]

---

16. Doyle with Wessinger and Wittmer 85–86.

17. Newport, *Branch Davidians* 315.

18. Doyle with Wessinger and Wittmer 78–81.

19. Doyle with Wessinger and Wittmer 77, 81.

20. Doyle with Wessinger and Wittmer 88.

21. Doyle with Wessinger and Wittmer 85–86, 89–91, 97.

Beliefs about Apocalyptic Martyrdom

As noted, Koresh taught that the Branch Davidians would be assaulted and martyred by agents of the lamblike beast—that is, the United States. Based on the instruction of Jesus Christ in Luke 22:36 to his disciples to buy a sword for self-defense,[22] Koresh taught that the Branch Davidians should be armed for self-defense against the expected attacks by law enforcement agents. Some of the young men in the community trained in the use of weapons, including Koresh.

Newport has laid out an apocalyptic theology of martyrdom at Mount Carmel going back to Victor Houteff. There was an expectation that at some point the faithful would have to be purified in a baptism by fire. Houteff emphasized the statement of John the Baptist reported in Matthew 3:11: "I indeed baptize you with water unto repentance: but he that cometh after me is mightier than I, whose shoes I am not worthy to bear: he shall baptize you with the Holy Ghost and with fire." Houteff taught that this prophecy did not refer to Jesus Christ but to a later figure, and that baptism by fire would occur by immersion.[23] The name of both properties owned by the Davidians and later the Branch Davidians—Mount Carmel—is evocative of the event when, in response to the prayers of the prophet Elijah, God ignited a fire on Mount Carmel in the Holy Land to consume a sacrificial offering (1 Kings 18:19–39). Lois Roden, Koresh's teacher, gave a Bible study on March 21, 1978, stating that the faithful would undergo a purification and baptism by fire by "full immersion," not just a "sprinkling." She taught that the fire would purify the faithful at "Jerusalem," which was understood by the Branch Davidians as referring to Mount Carmel, as a "gateway" into the Kingdom.[24]

Final Events

On February 28, 1993, the Branch Davidians were assaulted by agents with the Bureau of Alcohol, Tobacco, and Firearms (ATF) when they attempted to carry out a no-knock entry to serve a search warrant for the residence and an arrest warrant for Koresh. ATF agents alleged that Branch Davidians were illegally converting AR-15 semi-automatic rifles to M-16 automatic weapons without filing the requisite paperwork and paying the required fees. Prior to

22. Tabor and Gallagher 65.

23. Newport, *Branch Davidians* 308–11.

24. Newport, *Branch Davidians* 313–14; Wessinger, "Deaths in the Fire" 26–27; Roden.

the raid, visits inside the building by an ATF agent posing as a neighbor had not produced evidence that the Branch Davidians had illegally converted weapons. Through his gun dealer, Koresh had invited ATF agents to come to Mount Carmel openly and inspect his weapons.[25] Before carrying out the raid, ATF agents had sought and received training from Army Special Forces at Fort Hood, Texas. During the raid, the ATF agents received support from three National Guard helicopters, which carried armed ATF personnel.

Arriving in covered cattle trailers, a team of ATF agents stormed the front door where Koresh stood asking that they not shoot, while another team of agents used ladders to climb into second-floor windows into which they threw flash-bang grenades and shot their weapons before entering, and were met with gunfire. More gunfire erupted at the front door. Koresh backed inside, and the steel-encased double front doors were closed. ATF agents and Branch Davidian men exchanged gunfire through the doors, with bullets penetrating the doors in both directions.[26] Koresh's unarmed father-in-law, Perry Jones, received a mortal wound to his abdomen.[27] As soon as the shooting started, Branch Davidian and Harvard-educated attorney Wayne Martin dialed 911 and begged that the shooting be called off for the sake of the women and children in the residence.[28] Five Branch Davidians and four ATF agents were killed as a result of the gunfight. Later that afternoon, Michael Schroeder, a young Branch Davidian who had been working at a car repair shop down the road, was shot and killed by ATF agents as he attempted to walk back to Mount Carmel to rejoin his wife and children. During that night, Branch Davidian parents started sending their children out to the federal agents.

Although Koresh had sustained wounds to his side and wrist, he immediately started giving telephone interviews to media outlets including CNN, explaining his apocalyptic theology of martyrdom. In his discussion on KRLD Radio of Dallas/Fort Worth, Koresh stated, "We're in the Fifth Seal right now."[29] When Koresh spoke to Lieutenant Larry Lynch in the McLennan County Sheriff's Department on the 911 call, he kept explaining

---

25. Wright, "Construction" 76.

26. Hardy with Kimball; Kopel and Blackman; see also Gifford, Gazecki, and McNulty.

27. Doyle with Wessinger and Wittmer 121–25.

28. Reavis 169–76. Martin was married to Sheila Martin and they had seven children.

29. Koresh, KRLD interview.

his theology about the Seven Seals, while Lynch wanted only to deal with practical matters. Koresh replied, "theology really is life and death."[30]

Because four federal agents had been killed, FBI agents took over the site on March 1, 1993, giving the case the designation WACMUR, for "Waco Murder." Koresh's telephone access to the outside world was cut off and a new telephone line was set up to connect him only to FBI negotiators. Koresh promised to come out on March 2 if his audiotaped sermon explaining his apocalyptic theology was played by radio and television outlets. The purpose of the audiotape was to warn members of the public of the impending Last Days, so that they could repent, pray to God for mercy, and thus be spared when Christ returned with "a strong hand" on the Day of the Lord.[31] After the audiotape was played on radio and television, Koresh, while being transported downstairs on a stretcher and in great pain, received a revelation from God dictating that they should remain inside the building.[32] In response, the FBI surrounded the residence with tanks.

From February 28 to March 5, twenty-one children were sent out of the Mount Carmel residence. Between March 2 and March 23, fourteen adults came out as well. Whenever adults exited the building, FBI agents punished the remaining Branch Davidians by turning the electricity off, deriding Koresh in press briefings, using tanks to crush and remove the Branch Davidians' vehicles, directing bright spotlights at the residence throughout the night, and blasting high-decibel, irritating sounds at them. These actions were not conducive to building the Branch Davidians' confidence that they could trust the FBI negotiators[33]; instead, it confirmed the Branch Davidians' belief in Koresh's prophecies, and convinced them that the FBI were indeed the agents of the lamblike beast.

Koresh and Schneider told negotiators that the Branch Davidians would exit the building after Passover week concluded on April 13. On April 14, Koresh sent out a letter for his attorney to give to the FBI agents stating that before coming out, he would write a "little book" on his commentary of the Seven Seals of Revelation. This was theologically significant, because the Seventh Angel in Revelation 10:2 holds "a little book open." Koresh indicated

---

30. Tabor and Gallagher 99; Gallagher, "Theology" 82.

31. Wessinger, "Deaths in the Fire" 31; Koresh, audiotape.

32. FBI, Major Event Log, March 2, 1993.

33. Noesner 94–132; Wright, "Anatomy"; Wright, "Decade after Waco"; Wessinger, "FBI's 'Cult War.' "

that after his Seven Seals manuscript was given to two Bible scholars, Drs. James D. Tabor and J. Phillip Arnold, who had directed a radio discussion of the Bible's prophecies to the Branch Davidians on April 1, he and the Branch Davidians would come out. The FBI Major Event Log shows that on April 14, Koresh also sent out his signed contract to retain his attorney to represent him.[34] On April 16, Koresh reported to negotiators that he had completed his commentary on the First Seal, and the Branch Davidians began requesting supplies needed for their battery-powered word processor. The supplies were finally delivered, along with milk for the remaining children, on the evening of April 18.

During the day on April 18, Koresh got into a shouting match with a negotiator named Henry, after Koresh observed tanks clearing vehicles from around the building in preparation for an FBI assault. Koresh warned Henry that he felt like he was being pushed into a corner, and the FBI agents were preparing to "ruin the safety of me and my children. My life, the lives of my wives, the lives of my friends, *my family*."[35] Not long after Koresh's argument with Henry, surveillance devices, which were monitored by FBI agents, picked up Steve Schneider and Scott Sonobe speaking excitedly about something about to happen, although according to Schneider, "It may be scary!" Schneider joked to Sonobe, "You always wanted to be a charcoal briquette!"[36] Sonobe said, "I told him [Koresh] that there's nothing like a good fire to bring us to the birth." Schneider then gave what he said was his impression of the first man landing on the sun: "Darn our controls are jammed. Here comes Mr. Sun!" Subsequently on this surveillance audiotape, Branch Davidians can be heard speaking about prophecies soon being fulfilled. One woman said, "There's such a thing as fear. I mean, you know you read it, you always think it's *far away*. But it's here."

Later on April 18, Koresh and Schneider made statements directly to FBI negotiators about what could be expected if they were assaulted. Koresh told a negotiator that the Lamb came and tried to reveal the Seals, but "finally God gets pushed in a corner to where God has to fulfill the Seven Seals." Schneider told Henry that if FBI agents started destroying the building, "We're going to be doing something different." When Henry said that he hoped "there will be

34. Wessinger, "FBI's 'Cult War'" 221; FBI, Major Event Log, April 14, 1993.

35. Wessinger, *How the Millennium* 106–12.

36. Clive Doyle explained that before Sonobe converted, he used to say he preferred to be a charcoal briquette in hell than become a Branch Davidian. Wessinger, "Deaths in the Fire" 38.

a time to resurrect, to rebuild," Schneider said, "I think there will be a time to resurrect, but I'm talking about from the dead." Such statements by Branch Davidians to negotiators, as well as statements picked up by surveillance devices, in addition to FBI agents' study of Koresh's theological statements, and interviews with people who knew his theology, gave FBI officials numerous warnings that the Branch Davidians expected to die in a fire if they were assaulted again.[37]

The assault by FBI agents began on April 19, 1993 at 6:00 a.m. Particles of CS, a crowd control agent (also known as tear gas), suspended in a methylene chloride solution, were sprayed into the residence by nozzles mounted on tanks and released by ferret rounds (small plastic rocket-shaped containers that burst upon impact) shot into the building by grenade launchers. Both CS gas and methylene chloride burn skin and mucous membranes. CS converts to cyanide when it comes into contact with water or is burned. CS gas is not intended for use in enclosed spaces.[38]

Tanks drove through and dismantled the building. A couple of Branch Davidian men, directed by Schneider, went outside the front door to signal to FBI agents that they wanted their telephone line to the negotiators, which had been severed by a tank, fixed. A surveillance device picked up Schneider saying they wanted to inform FBI agents about the progress that had been made the night before in typing Koresh's manuscript. When it was apparent that the telephone line would not be repaired, Schneider went upstairs to be with Koresh.[39]

When the assault started, the children and their mothers, including two pregnant women, took shelter in a room with concrete walls, which had formerly been a vault in a previous building on that site. When a fire had consumed that earlier building, the vault had protected its contents.[40] In 1993 the Branch Davidians were using the vault as a storage room and pantry. The door to the vault had been removed when a cooler had been moved inside. At 11:31 a.m., a tank drove through the building and directed CS gas through the vault's open doorway until 11:55 a.m.[41] By 12:07 p.m. the first fire was visible,

---

37. Wessinger, "Deaths in the Fire" 38–39; Wessinger, "FBI's 'Cult War.'"

38. Kopel and Blackman 158–59.

39. Wessinger, "Deaths in the Fire" 40.

40. Doyle with Wessinger and Wittmer 112–13.

41. Hardy with Kimball 275–76, 285. See Wessinger, "FBI's 'Cult War'" 241 on the congressional testimony of a former NYPD negotiator that the New York Police Department would

PHOTO 1 Memorial Image of the 82 Branch Davidians killed during the 1993 siege at Mount Carmel Center east of Waco, Texas. This composite image was created by Matthew D. Wittmer in 2013 using photographs from the former Visitor's Center at Mount Carmel, which was maintained by survivor Clive Doyle from 1998 until 2006, and still photographs taken from videotapes filmed by the Branch Davidians during the siege. Faces are arranged according to the original order of the memorial crape myrtle trees planted on the property for each of the deceased. Rubbings of the memorial name stones are inserted for Branch Davidians for whom no photos were available. Courtesy of Matthew D. Wittmer.

and fire quickly engulfed the entire building. People died from suffocation, smoke inhalation, incineration, and gunshot wounds [See Photo 1].

The complex and contradictory evidence about how the fire started will not be examined here. FBI officials were aware that there was kerosene for lanterns in the building, as well as a large propane tank immediately behind the central tower. FBI officials had approved a decision on April 9, 1993 not to fight a fire if one occurred. A physician specializing in treating burned children was on standby at the Galveston Burn Center on the day of the assault. FBI agents had also contacted the burn unit of the Parkland Memorial Hospital in Dallas ahead of the assault.[42]

---

never use CS gas on a barricaded group that included children, because children have small lung capacity and therefore are less able to tolerate the debilitating effects of CS.

42. Wessinger, "FBI's 'Cult War'" 220, 229.

Graeme Craddock, a survivor of the fire, subsequently testified that during the assault he saw someone in the chapel, on the first level of the residence, pouring fuel. He also testified that moments before the fire started, he heard a shout from the second floor to "light the fire," then a shout that contradicted that order, and then another shout to "light the fire." Immediately after the fire occurred, an FBI spokesman initially stated that he heard similar shouts in audio captured by a surveillance device, but subsequently he retracted that assertion. A retired US Army colonel, who was with FBI agents in Waco listening to surveillance audio on April 19, 1993, stated in 1999 that he and FBI agents heard similar shouts.[43] However, no such audio was produced by the FBI for use in trials or other investigations about the case.

Twenty-two children, from babies to age thirteen, died in the vault. These include two infants who were born during the assault. Fourteen of these children were fathered by Koresh. Seven teenagers and forty-seven adults died in the fire. Eight adults and one teenager escaped the fire, some badly burned. Ruth Riddle jumped out of a second-floor window of the burning building, carrying in her pocket a disk on which was saved the typed manuscript with Koresh's interpretation of the First Seal of Revelation.[44]

Heaven's Gate

History

Like David Koresh, the founders of the group that became known as Heaven's Gate in the late 1990s grew up in Texas, where biblical literalism is common. Bonnie Lu Nettles (1927–1985), married with four children, had a Baptist background, but she was a member of the Houston lodge of the Theosophical Society in America from 1966 to 1973, and was immersed in the New Age movement and familiar with Spiritualism and New Thought. She held séances in her home to contact the dead and claimed to have spirit guides. She also knew how to construct and interpret horoscopes. Marshall Herff Applewhite, Jr. (1931–1997), known as Herff, was the son of a Presbyterian minister, attended seminary briefly, and then became a music professor. He

43. Wessinger, "Branch Davidians (1981–2006)"; Wessinger, "Deaths in the Fire," 43–44; Wessinger, "FBI's 'Cult War'" 235–36; Doyle with Wessinger and Wittmer 169. Rodney L. Rawlings also stated that FBI agents knew the mothers and children were inside the vault because they could be heard "crying, talking and praying" over a surveillance device. See Hancock.

44. See Koresh, "Seven Seals."

lost his job teaching at the University of Alabama in Tuscaloosa after having an affair with a male student, which also led to the breakup of his marriage and loss of contact with his two children. In 1970, he was terminated by the University of St. Thomas in Houston for having an affair with a female student.[45] He began having visions and dreams which made him question his sanity; "In one vision, men dressed in white informed him that he was destined to fulfill a Christ-like role."[46] Nettles was working as a nurse in 1972 and at a low point in her marriage when she met Applewhite. She compared their horoscopes and concluded that they had a spiritual mission which they were destined to carry out together.

Nettles and Applewhite briefly opened a Christian Arts Center in Houston, where they offered classes. Then they opened a center called Know Place, dedicated to the study of metaphysics. During this time, Applewhite studied *The Secret Doctrine* (1888) by Helena P. Blavatsky (1831–1891),[47] the founding theorist of the Theosophical Society. Applewhite and Nettles undoubtedly read other books in the alternative religious milieu during this period, including *Late Great Planet Earth* (1970),[48] the best-selling book by Hal Lindsay (b. 1929), a graduate of the Dallas Theological Seminary, on his Christian Dispensationalist interpretations of current events leading to the imminent Rapture of the faithful, the catastrophic destruction of the world, the Second Coming of Christ, and the resurrection and judgment of all souls.

In January 1973, Nettles and Applewhite left Houston and began driving and camping across the United States. During this time, they concluded that they were the "two witnesses" mentioned in the book of Revelation. In accordance with Revelation 11, they expected their imminent martyrdom and their resurrection after three and a half days, as a demonstration of the transformation which they were offering to others. They began giving talks at New Age bookstores and groups, in which they described their doctrine, which combined their interpretations of passages in the books of the New Testament with themes that rejected the physical/spiritual monism of Theosophy in favor of a dualism of material human life on Earth and material eternal life as extraterrestrials in the Kingdom of Heaven. Nettles and Applewhite taught that they were two extraterrestrials who had taken over human bodies

45. Wessinger, *How the Millennium* 232.

46. Balch and Taylor 210.

47. Balch, "Bo and Peep" 34–38; Wessinger, *How the Millennium* 232.

48. Lindsay with Carlson.

to teach humans how to overcome their humanness and to become genderless extraterrestrials, who would be picked up by a flying saucer and thereby enter The Evolutionary Level Above Human (TELAH, also called the Next Level). Persons willing to detach from human desires and conventional lives, and undertake the spiritual disciplines they offered, would undergo a metamorphosis into immortal extraterrestrial beings.

Applewhite was arrested for car theft in 1974, because he had neglected to return a rental car, and spent six months in jail. He found this experience deeply mortifying, and thereafter "The Two," as they called themselves, were even more careful to avoid law enforcement agents. While Applewhite was in prison he wrote a short statement of their beliefs, which they mailed out to New Age groups. In early 1975, they attracted twenty-four converts from a New Age group in Los Angeles.[49]

Applewhite and Nettles began calling themselves Bo and Peep as they traveled about the western United States giving talks, and called their movement Human Individual Metamorphosis (HIM). In September 1975, they gained over thirty converts after their public lecture in Waldport, Oregon. They attracted about two hundred followers during this period, mostly young seekers in the New Age countercultural milieu. The phenomenon of people leaving their jobs and children and disappearing to follow "Bo and Peep" attracted intense media scrutiny. As a result, The Two went into hiding, and their followers were instructed to travel in groups and pairs, listening for guidance from TELAH. During this time, many people dropped out of the movement.[50]

In 1976, The Two started calling themselves Ti (Nettles) and Do (Applewhite). They instituted the practice of having each disciple choose a new name. An easily pronounced nickname was selected that reflected an aspect of the individual's personality, and then another name was constructed usually consisting of three letters followed by the suffix "ody." "Ody" was said to be a contraction of "Do-Ti," indicating that each follower was a child of The Two.[51]

On April 21, 1976, Ti and Do were speaking at a meeting in Kansas when they were heckled. Ti stood up and announced, "The doors to the Next Level

49. Wessinger, *How the Millennium* 233; Balch, "Bo and Peep" 49–51; Bearak; Balch, "Waiting" 142; Balch and Taylor 212.

50. Wessinger, *How the Millennium* 233–34; Balch, "Waiting" 137–53; Balch and Taylor 213–14.

51. DiAngelo 21–22.

are closed. The harvest is closed." They then traveled and camped in various locations with their followers; during this time, they instituted strict rules for behavior, as well as spiritual disciplines to encourage detachment from human concerns. Their previously amorphous movement became a monastic "class" of students training to overcome their humanness, and thereby transform their human bodies and minds in preparation for entering TELAH. The Two informed their students that the physical demonstration in which they would be assassinated and resurrected had been called off; instead, their "assassination" in the press had fulfilled the prophecy.[52]

Beginning in 1977, the class began the practice of renting a house in which they lived while working at various jobs, although they continued to relocate periodically. Their residence was conceptualized as a "craft," and the students trained in performing tasks with precision and developing "crew mindedness." They told outsiders they were monks. Robert Balch estimates that by the end of 1978, the class had forty-eight students.[53] From time to time, The Two set a date for a flying saucer to pick them up, but it never appeared.[54]

In 1983 Ti had an eye removed due to cancer. However, the cancer spread to her liver, and she died in a Dallas hospital in 1985. Ti's death provoked the crisis of leadership and faith that many new religions face upon the death of a founder.[55] Her death called into question The Two's teaching that after class members had overcome their humanness they would not die, but would instead be picked up by a flying saucer to enter TELAH where they would have genderless, immortal extraterrestrial bodies. Do was distraught at the loss of his spiritual partner, and he expressed doubts in what they had been teaching. He asked a small group of students, "Am I crazy? Should I tell everyone to go home?"[56]

Instead, Do rationalized Ti's death to his students: he explained that her human body could no longer withstand her Next Level energy so it had died; and upon the death of her human vehicle, Ti had returned to the Next Level.[57] Do reinforced his connection with his students by performing a

52. Wessinger, *How the Millennium* 234; Balch, "Waiting" 153–57; Bearak; Heaven's Gate, "'88 Update."

53. Wessinger, *How the Millennium* 237; Balch, "Waiting" 157–59.

54. Bearak; Balch, "Heaven's Gate."

55. See Miller.

56. Bearak.

57. Balch and Taylor 217.

wedding ceremony "in which he gave each student a gold wedding band in an emotional private meeting. Now, just as he was bound to Ti, his students were wedded to him. Students also began sending him 'committal' letters in which they affirmed their devotion." Former students reported to Robert Balch and David Taylor that students' "bonds with Do became intensely personal in ways that once would have been considered thoroughly human."[58] Theologically, Do moved away from teaching a variation of Christian Dispensationalism marked by a physical Rapture of the faithful (the rescue by spaceship), and shifted to a more general, pessimistic, apocalyptic view that the Earth would be destroyed imminently.[59]

Beginning in 1988, the group reached out again to the public with their offer of eternal extraterrestrial life. They mailed out a booklet titled "'88 Update—The UFO Two and their Crew." Calling their group Total Overcomers Anonymous, they produced a twelve-part video series titled "Beyond Human—The Last Call," which was broadcast in 1991 and 1992 via satellite.[60] In 1993, they placed an advertisement in *USA Today* headlined, "'UFO Cult' Resurfaces with Final Offer," warning that the planet Earth, which was a garden in which souls were grown, would soon be "spaded under," because inhabitants were refusing to evolve and the garden had been taken over by weeds. Despite these efforts, the class size dropped to twenty-six students by the end of 1993.

Do began to discuss suicide with his students in 1993 as the means to leave Earth and enter the Next Level. Do expressed admiration for the Branch Davidians for their willingness to "go all the way." Class members purchased weapons, but the guns were eventually locked away "because the students abhorred the idea of not being killed outright."[61]

Some of the male members of the class had been requesting permission from Do to be castrated, so that they might be relieved of sexual impulses. In 1993, one man was castrated, but he suffered painful complications. Even so, in 1994 and 1995, Do and six other men underwent castration as well. Do experienced physical problems caused by the procedure, but former member Rio DiAngelo (Richard Ford, known in the class as Neo or Neoody), who

58. Balch and Taylor 218.

59. Zeller, *Heaven's Gate* 116–17.

60. Transcripts in *Heaven's Gate, How and When.*

61. Balch and Taylor 222.

joined in 1994, reported that the male students who were castrated were happy at being freed from sexual urges.[62]

In 1994, the students held public meetings across the country offering a "last chance" to interested parties. About twenty-five persons joined—some of them former class members—but about half of these left after a few months.[63] "For Do, the poor response confirmed that the harvest was finally over. Other signs that the end was near included wars, earthquakes, volcanic eruptions, and the Waco standoff in 1993."[64] The public lectures were stopped in August 1994.

In September 1994, the group was camping in a warehouse in San Clemente, California. Do explained during a class meeting that when he was Jesus, he permitted himself to be executed and then resurrected to go back to his Father. According to DiAngelo, he said, "leaving the body here is how the Soul of Jesus traveled back to the 'Next Level.'" Do inquired, "What if we had to exit our vehicles by our own choice?" He asked the students if they had a problem with that idea. There was discussion, and Do asked that each student write a private note to him about it. DiAngelo reports:

> As it turned out most people had no problem with that [exiting from their bodies]. They didn't identify with the vehicle anyway and knew they were developing Souls that felt stronger every day. They knew who DO was and knew where they were going. We always had freedom of choice in everything we did. I went along with the idea and possibility of DO being the "Second Coming" just for learning purposes. I knew that leaving the body behind was not for me but wanted to stay until the end.[65]

On that evening Sekody (Seeker) objected, saying, "Are you talking about suicide? If so, look, I've had no problem with everything so far, in fact it has been the most extraordinary time of my life, and you (DO) are obviously

62. Bearak; Zeller, *Heaven's Gate* 187; DiAngelo 64, 83.

63. Balch and Taylor 220.

64. Balch and Taylor 220.

65. DiAngelo 48.

the second coming, but suicide is something that I'm not interested in at all."[66] Sekody packed his bag and left that evening.[67]

Class members researched how they could accomplish their goal, and found a book titled *Final Exit* (1991) by Derek Humphry which included instructions on how to carry out an assisted suicide using phenobarbital. Do and his assistants went to Mexico and purchased phenobarbital.[68]

On September 25–26, 1995, the class posted Do's statement titled "Undercover Jesus Surfaces Before the Departure" on the World Wide Web and to ninety-five UseNet groups. On October 11, 1995, they posted another document written by Do titled, "'95 Statement by an E.T. Presently Incarnate." One person joined the class as a result, but the statements mainly attracted ridicule. Do and the class members decided this meant they were to cease proselytizing and prepare to exit. According to Jwnody (Denise Thurman, 1952–1997):[69]

> [T]he loudest voices were those expressing ridicule, hostility, or both—so quick to judge that which they could not comprehend. This was the signal to us to begin our preparations to return "home." The weeds have taken over the garden and truly disturbed its usefulness beyond repair—it is time for the civilization to be recycled—"spaded under."[70]

Do was in poor health by this time, and he was delegating more responsibilities to secondary leaders such as Jwnody.[71] He spoke of assuming a "professor emeritus" role.[72] Instead of facing another leadership crisis at the death of Do, class members were deciding that they preferred to transition with him to the Next Level. The question remained, however, as to how that would be accomplished.

Do's 1995 UseNet posts reveal that he believed it was likely that they would be attacked by federal agents and killed, as the Branch Davidians had

---

66. DiAngelo 48.

67. Balch and Taylor 222, report that several other students did not like the idea of a self-induced exit. Other students left between 1994 and the exit. Zeller, *Heaven's Gate* 179. Neoody (DiAngelo) stayed until shortly before the exit in 1997. DiAngelo 103–04.

68. DiAngelo 49; Humphry.

69. I thank Benjamin E. Zeller for providing Jwnody's legal name, as well as the names of Lggody and Tllody. Jwnody was in the class for twenty-two years. DiAngelo 77.

70. Jwnody vii.

71. DiAngelo, 77, describes her as an "overseer" of other overseers of different types of tasks.

72. Balch and Taylor 221.

been in 1993. The Heaven's Gate class members were absorbing the theories disseminated by the right-wing, anti-government conspiracy milieu in America. Do thought it was very likely that the class would be assaulted and the members killed by "Luciferian" law enforcement agents. He went so far as to advise anyone who was attracted to his message to purchase weapons, live apart from society, and wait to be attacked: "our total existence is devoted to entering and offering God's World. Our choosing to not 'be submissive'—coupled with 'being armed'—pretty much addresses the 'laying down of our bodies' question."[73]

Neoody and Lggody (John Craig, 1964–1997)[74] designed a monastery-fort made of old tires packed with earth, which the group constructed in New Mexico. However, they found that winter in New Mexico was too cold to live comfortably in such a residence, so they abandoned the monastery-fort and relocated to Phoenix.[75] This was probably when they locked their weapons away and gave up the idea that they would be assaulted.

By the end of 1995, the class was living in a rented house in Rancho Santa Fe, a well-to-do neighborhood of San Diego. They built up their website-design business, named the Higher Source, created an anthology of their materials and put it and other documents on their Heaven's Gate website, and watched for the marker that would be Ti's signal for them to leave Earth for the Next Level. The content of their website attracted the attention of a young couple from Cincinnati. After Do met with them to determine if they were ready, the couple were admitted to the class. The man did not stay but the woman did, and after only six months in the class, she exited with the others.[76]

Hermeneutics

Ti and Do utilized what Zeller terms "extraterrestrial biblical hermeneutics," by which he means that miracles described in the Bible are seen as being physical events involving extraterrestrials. This approach to interpreting religious scriptures and myths is characteristic of the UFO movement.[77]

---

73. Zeller, *Heaven's Gate* 189–94, quotation on 191.

74. Lggody was in the class for twenty-two years. DiAngelo 79.

75. DiAngelo 55–56; Zeller, *Heaven's Gate* 136.

76. DiAngelo 72, 101.

77. Zeller, "Extraterrestrial Biblical Hermeneutics."

The theology of Heaven's Gate was an ET-inspired[78] version of Christianity in which extraterrestrials were seen as being immortal, genderless "angels" in the heavenly kingdom (TELAH), who travel the universe in flying saucers. "Space aliens" (Luciferians) were regarded as being humanoids from other worlds, with greatly advanced technologies, who had rejected TELAH and sought to obstruct the growth of human souls on Earth and keep them from advancing to the Next Level. Their understanding of Luciferians was informed by popular conspiracy theories about a one-world government. Luciferians were regarded as enslaving humanity on Earth through conventional social values that promoted attachments to family, spouses, children, and steady jobs.[79]

In addition to the New Testament, the religious imaginations of Heaven's Gate members were stimulated by television shows such as *Star Trek* and its depiction of a close-knit crew, movies such as *Close Encounters of the Third Kind* (1977) and *Cocoon* (1985) about being taken up into a flying saucer, and the first *Star Wars* trilogy (1977, 1980, 1983), about galactic battles between forces for good and forces for evil.

Christology

Ti and Do taught that they were "walk-ins,"[80] that is, extraterrestrials from TELAH who had taken over the bodies of Nettles and Applewhite to locate their students and teach them how to reach the Next Level. Based on John 15:5–11 ("I am the vine; you are the branches" [Amplified Version]), they taught that the only way to graduate from Earth and enter TELAH was to "graft" onto an Older Member, or Representative, of the Next Level visiting Earth, cultivate dependence on him or her, and depart with him or her to TELAH. They taught that Jesus Christ was just such an Older Member from the Next Level. His crucifixion and resurrection were demonstrations of his ability to regenerate a Next Level body and ascend to TELAH. Jesus departed for the Next Level without his disciples, because they were not ready to enter the Kingdom of Heaven. Two days later in Next Level time, equivalent to two thousand years in Earth time, he returned as Do to locate, train, and depart for the Next Level with his students. On this visit to Earth he was

78. Thomas.

79. Heaven's Gate, "'UFO Group' Resurfaces."

80. Montgomery.

accompanied by his "Father" or Older Member, who was Ti, onto whom he was grafted. Do was the Next Level father of the students in the class, and Ti was their grandfather. They were connected by a "chain of mind" (the "vine") through the Next Level hierarchy tracing back to the Chief of Chiefs, the Creator.[81]

Ti and Do used plant and gardening metaphors derived from the Gospels, such as the parable of the sower who sows seed on good soil and on rocky ground (Matt. 13:18–23; Mark 4:3–9), and the parable of the weeds of the field that will be burned up while the good plants will be harvested (Matt. 13:37–43), to explain the situation of humans on Earth. Ti and Do took literally the passage that reads, "For in the resurrection neither do men marry nor are women given in marriage, but they are like angels in heaven" (Matt. 22:30), as well as Jesus's praise for those who abandoned their families for the sake of the Kingdom of Heaven (Matt. 10:37–39; Matt. 19:29–30; Luke 14:26–27), and the assertion that one's true parents and family are "whoever does the will of God" (Mark 3:35).[82]

Ti and Do taught a dualistic worldview stressing the difference between TELAH and its inhabitants, and the human "plants" in the garden on Earth. Do stressed that the view that matter and spirit are one, found in Theosophy and the New Age movement, was a Luciferian worldview—even, in fact, the Antichrist.[83] Nevertheless, Do and Ti taught the doctrine of reincarnation, as found in Theosophy and Asian religions, including an idea found in Hinduism that reincarnation is no different than changing a suit of clothes (see Bhagavad Gita 2:22).

According to Ti and Do, humans on Earth were merely "mammalian plants" with "spirits" that reincarnate after death. Only those who have received a "deposit" of soul, a seed from the Next Level, have the opportunity to grow their souls for existence in the Next Level as genderless extraterrestrials. Do understood persons with a deposit as being the "elect," indicating the influence of Calvinistic predestinarianism from his seminary days on his thought. Ti and Do taught that only a few mammalian humans receive deposits, thus explaining why such a small number of persons joined their class.[84] They saw a deposit as being received when a human responded

---

81. Wessinger, *How the Millennium* 236; Lvvody; Nrrody; Heaven's Gate, "'88 Update."

82. Wessinger, *How the Millennium* 239.

83. Do, "Aids in Approaching," iv; Heaven's Gate, "'88 Update."

84. Zeller, *Heaven's Gate* 120–22.

positively to information about the Next Level being disseminated by an Older Member or the Representative's students, or when one prayed to be filled with the Next Level Mind.[85] The deposit can ripen fully into a soul only under the direct guidance of an Older Member. In the late twentieth century, that Older Member was Do, who was the second coming of Jesus Christ.

Beliefs about Religious Suicide

By 1995 Do was stressing that not just Ti and Do, but also the students, were beings from the Next Level who had come to Earth as "emissaries" to locate members of the "human-mammalian species" and offer them "liberation" and membership in the Next Level. An unpublished document, dated August 18, 1995, in the Heaven's Gate anthology states:

> They began "touching down" on Earth (evacuating their bodies and the crafts they came in) in the 1940's and subsequently began incarnating in adult human bodies in the 1970's and will evacuate this planet within the next year ('96).[86]

Therefore, like Ti and Do, students in the class were regarded as walk-ins,[87] who had incarnated in their human bodies at the time they heard and responded to the message, which for many of them was the 1970s. According to Zeller, by 1995 their view was:

> [T]hey had come to Earth to complete their final lessons and overcome their humanity, but they did not belong here. While quite different from the earlier teachings of the Two and in fact difficult to harmonize with the movement's long-standing teachings of human individual metamorphosis and human self-development, members' willingness to voice that sort of belief shows how strongly they had come to reject both the world and the bodies they inhabited, their vehicles.[88]

---

85. DiAngelo 26–27.

86. Heaven's Gate, "Heaven's Last Mission."

87. Zeller, *Heaven's Gate* 179–80.

88. Zeller, *Heaven's Gate* 180.

Do told his students to be on the lookout for an indicator that it was time to exit.[89] One of the students sewed sets of identical black shirt and pants for each person to wear for their exit. They bought black Nike sneakers on sale for everyone in the class (the Nike slogan, "Just Do It!" may have seemed appropriate). They designed a shoulder patch that read, "Heaven's Gate Away Team,"[90] and sewed it onto their black shirts. After constructing the Heaven's Gate website containing their materials and anthology, they decided who would be the website's caretakers after they were gone. They put their materials on the website because they believed that anyone who finds them appealing may receive a deposit of a soul, which may be activated the next time an Older Member comes to Earth—in about two thousand years.[91]

The indicator they were waiting for was discovered by Tllody (Michael Carrier, 1949–1997)[92] as he listened to Art Bell's late-night AM radio talk show, *Coast to Coast*, and heard discussions that claimed a space vehicle had been spotted flying behind the approaching Hale-Bopp comet, which would be closest to the Earth on March 22, 1997, a week before Easter on March 30. Even after the flying saucer theory had been debunked by astronomers, Heaven's Gate class members remained convinced that the comet was the marker they had been awaiting. According to DiAngelo, "They were all very excited. Finally they were going home. They were graduating. They knew they were ready and their Souls were strong."[93] The students videotaped exit statements expressing their joy at their imminent transition to the Next Level and their appreciation for their teachers. [See Photo 2][94]

In his final videotaped statements,[95] which Mark and Sarah King, the custodians of the Heaven's Gate website, explain were directed toward the hundreds of former class members,[96] Do spoke of a "message in a bottle" that stressed the apocalyptic urgency of the time. The world would be

---

89. DiAngelo 102.

90. This is a well-known *Star Trek* reference to a small group of crew members who leave the ship to carry out a mission.

91. Wessinger, "Notes"; Goodwin.

92. Tllody was in the class for twenty-one years (DiAngelo 95).

93. DiAngelo 102.

94. DiAngelo 64–100 transcribes a portion of each statement and gives a reminiscence of each student.

95. Do, "Last Chance"; Do, "Planet."

96. Zeller, *Heaven's Gate* 202.

PHOTO 2 The students in the Heaven's Gate class made videotaped exit statements, explaining their rationale for the step they were taking, just before their departure in March 1997. Here (left to right) Jmmody, Ollody, and Dvvody share their happiness at the prospect of departing soon for the Next Level with Do.

imminently spaded under, and this was the last chance to be removed from planet Earth to the Kingdom of Heaven. Do promised that individuals who had received soul deposits but were unwilling to exit at that time would be spared the spading over and would be "in the keeping of the Kingdom Level Above Human, and replanted at another time, and given another chance."[97]

On the Heaven's Gate website, "Our Position against Suicide" defined suicide as turning against the Next Level when it is offered. The group's press release, "HEAVEN'S GATE 'Away Team' Returns to Level above Human in Distant Space," made it clear that the class members conceptualized not only Ti and Do, but also the students, as saviors. They had come to present information about the Kingdom of Heaven to those who recognized it. Ti and Do had offered a "graduation class" on Earth for students who had also come from the Next Level. The press release noted that, for a short period of time, there was the opportunity to enter through Heaven's Gate by calling on Ti and Do with all one's might, which would send out a signal to a spacecraft to come and pick up the soul newly liberated from its vehicle. "Only those

97. Do, "Last Chance."

'chosen' by that Next Kingdom will *know* that this is right for them, and will be given the courage to act."[98]

Final Events

When the time came to exit, the Heaven's Gate members put on their identical clothing and shoes and packed their bags as if going on a trip. The Kings have explained part of their preparations as an expression of their Next Level humor.[99] Each put a $5.00 bill and three quarters in their pockets, as they did whenever they went outside the craft in case they needed transportation back or to make a telephone call on a pay phone. Beginning on March 22 and completing on March 23, 1997, the exit was carried out. Fifteen of the class members, assisted by the others, consumed phenobarbital mixed in pudding or applesauce, drank vodka, and pulled plastic bags over their heads. After the vehicle was dead, surviving members removed the plastic bag and draped each body with a purple shroud, which was Ti's favorite color.[100] Then another group of fifteen class members were assisted in exiting in the same manner. Seven members were assisted in exiting by two women. The last two were found with plastic bags on their heads. Of the thirty-nine, three were in their twenties, two were in their thirties, twenty in their forties, eight in their fifties, four in their sixties, and one woman was seventy-two. Do was sixty-five. An autopsy found that Do had constrictive coronary arteriosclerosis.[101]

Before their exit, the class sent materials to Mark and Sarah King, and to other former members including Chuck Humphrey (Rkkody) and Richard Ford/Rio DiAngelo (Neoody). Rkkody duplicated the materials and donated them to libraries. He tried to exit in May 1997 with Wayne "Nick" Cooke (Jstody, Justin) in a motel room in Encinitas, California, but was revived while Jstody made his exit successfully. In May 1997, James "Jimmy" Edward Pirkey Jr. (Gbbody, Gabby) made his exit in Atlanta.[102] In February 1998, Rkkody finally made his exit while in the Arizona desert.

---

98. Heaven's Gate, "HEAVEN'S GATE.'"

99. Wessinger, "Notes"; Goodwin.

100. Balch and Taylor 224. Purple is a color commonly viewed in the Theosophical and New Age movements as expressing the highest vibration of consciousness.

101. Wessinger, *How the Millennium* 231.

102. Wessinger, *How the Millennium* 231; Simpson.

Conclusions

The Branch Davidians and the members of Heaven's Gate had extreme religious worldviews that devalued earthly existence for the promise of a heavenly one. They both were unconventional Christian groups whose members expected to die near Passover and Easter—one by means of martyrdom, and the other by means of religious suicide—so they could be subsequently resurrected into eternal life. Both groups consisted of faithful persons living in community with a leader to whom they attributed "charisma" (believed access to an unseen source of authority),[103] and for whom they changed their sexual practices and their relationships with spouses and children, indicating that both groups consisted of highly committed members.

The Branch Davidians and the Heaven's Gate class both had a goal of eternal life in the Heavenly Kingdom in new life forms. The Branch Davidians did not want to die, but would be faithful to the best of their ability when assaulted by powerful adversaries. The Heaven's Gate members did want to die to this world, and prepared joyfully for their graduation.

These two groups illuminate different types of trajectories[104] of communities—leading to an assaulted millennial group, and a fragile millennial group—whose members believe that death is the means of salvation within the context of an apocalyptic worldview. Both the Branch Davidians and Heaven's Gate members believed in the imminent, catastrophic destruction of the world, which relativized earthly life in favor of heavenly life.

Catastrophic millennialism promotes a dualistic distinction between earthly life and the next, and between the faithful and others. The Branch Davidians' outlook was less dualistic than that of the Heaven's Gate members, because the Branch Davidians were concerned to extend the possibility of salvation to the rest of humanity up until virtually their very last moments on earth, whereas the Heaven's Gate class turned inward several times to focus on heavenly salvation of members alone.

Many religious believers hold catastrophic millennial ideas without putting themselves in harm's way or taking their own lives. Additional factors had to be involved to prompt the Branch Davidians and the Heaven's Gate members to be willing to die for their ultimate concerns. For the Branch Davidians, it was their experience of being assaulted by federal agents, which

---

103. Wessinger, "Charismatic Leaders."

104. Walliss.

they believed fulfilled David Koresh's prophecies about how the violence of the Last Days would begin with their deaths. For the Heaven's Gate students, it was their belief that the only way to enter the Kingdom of Heaven was with their beloved teacher Do, and the fact that they were all aging. Both the Branch Davidians and Heaven's Gate members held to their ultimate concerns so strongly they were willing to die for them.

It took a particular configuration of interactive[105] events and actors to produce the deaths at Mount Carmel in 1993. Eugene V. Gallagher points out that persons holding a biblically based, apocalyptic worldview interpret events in light of the Bible's prophecies, and they adjust their understanding of the prophecies as the context changes.[106] This is what the Branch Davidians were doing, from the ATF raid, throughout the siege, and then finally during the FBI's tank and CS-gas assault.

The Branch Davidians believed in an apocalyptic theology of martyrdom, but this does not mean that they did not value their lives and the lives of their children. They were armed for self-defense, and used their weapons to defend their community during the ATF assault. FLIR (Forward-Looking Infrared) footage, filmed from an airplane flying over Mount Carmel on April 19, 1993, indicated to an expert that at least two Branch Davidians fired shots in an intense gun battle with agents behind the building—away from television cameras—during the FBI assault.[107] At the beginning of the assault, the children and mothers were placed in the safest room in the building, a former vault. Adult Branch Davidians donned gas masks, and dodged tanks and ferret rounds coming into the building. Five and a half hours into the assault, the children and their mothers were gassed by a tank for nearly twenty-five minutes.

It is possible that after the children and mothers were gassed, the Branch Davidians became a fragile millennial group, in which some of the Branch Davidians lit fires to fulfill the prophecy of a baptism by fire and to preserve their ultimate concern, but this is by no means clear because there were numerous possible causes of the fire.[108] Normal survival instincts prompted eight

105. Wessinger, *How the Millennium*; Hall, with Schuyler and Trinh; Richardson.

106. Gallagher, "Theology."

107. Carlos Ghigliotti had been hired by the House of Representatives to examine the FLIR tapes. See Ghigliotti's preliminary report in Hardy with Kimball, Appendix I, 337–42.

108. See the debate in Newport, "'A Baptism'"; Wright, "Revisiting"; and Wessinger, "Deaths in the Fire." See also Wessinger, "FBI's 'Cult War.'"

adults and a teenager to crawl over rubble or jump out of windows to escape the fire. Others were not able to escape. The deaths of the Branch Davidian children, teenagers, and adults inside the building occurred within an interactive context.

The FBI assault and culminating fire was a "dramatic denouement," defined by David G. Bromley as occurring when

> a movement and some segment of the social order reach a juncture at which one or both conclude that the requisite conditions for maintaining their core identity and collective existence are being subverted and that such circumstances are intolerable.

Bromley further explains that these interactive situations involve "polarization and destabilization":

> Parties on one or both sides thereupon undertake a project of final reckoning under the aegis of a transcendent mandate to reverse their power positions and to restore what they avow to be the appropriate moral order.[109]

FBI officials decided that they could no longer wait to see if more Branch Davidians could be induced to surrender by deescalating the conflict and using normal negotiation procedures.[110] The Branch Davidians were determined to remain committed to whatever God willed for them.

The students in the Heaven's Gate class spent years training to overcome their human attachments to family and loved ones and also to their bodies, while simultaneously cultivating attachments to Do as their Older Member, Ti as their Next Level grandfather, and to their classmates. For several years, they expected to be assaulted and killed like the Branch Davidians. When that did not occur, thirty-eight students, including several who had joined the class recently, proved themselves ready to go with Do into the Next Level existence aboard Ti's spacecraft.

Heaven's Gate can be considered a fragile millennial group, because—from a human, earthly perspective—they committed religious suicide to preserve

---

109. Bromley 11.

110. Wright, "Anatomy"; Wright, "A Decade"; Noesner 94–132.

their ultimate concern from failure. According to former class members Mark and Sarah King, who have listened to, but not made public, the audiotapes of Do's classes, the students were the ones who approached Do with the idea of exiting their human vehicles to relocate to the Next Level. They were all growing older,[111] and according to their theology, the students could enter the Next Level only with Do, their Older Member. Although the Heaven's Gate class acted to preserve their ultimate concern, they did not depart in a dramatic denouement. Instead, they planned and executed a gentle exit from their bodies.

The two Heaven's Gate leaders and their students were affected by interactions with the public in the form of heckling at public lectures and, later, derisive comments on the Internet, at which the group turned inward several times to focus on preparing members to achieve a non-earthly eternal existence. Although the Branch Davidians believed in an apocalyptic theology of martyrdom, they never turned inward. They and Koresh proselytized whenever they could, including to an ATF undercover agent invited into the house, and FBI negotiators during the siege whenever they would listen.

The Heaven's Gate class members prepared themselves to take the enormous step of ending their earthly lives by what Benjamin Zeller terms the "euphemization of violence": "the rhetorical transformation of (self-)violence into a more benign form."[112] Zeller argues that their euphemization of violence was a twenty-five-year process stretching back to Nettles and Applewhite's expectation of a demonstration in which they would be martyred, followed by their metamorphosis into a new life form to be picked up by a flying saucer. Toward the group's end, the human body became considered a mere vehicle for a soul from the Next Level, culminating in the final justification that true death involved the soul only—not an earthly vehicle—and only the Next Level could kill a soul. The religious suicides on March 22–23, 1997, were defined by the Heaven's Gate class as a collective exit for the Kingdom of Heaven.

David Koresh also devalued the earthly body in relation to the anticipated heavenly body. "It's just flesh," he said, pointing to his wounded body in a videotape made during the siege.[113] The violence on April 19, 1993 was euphemized

111. Goodwin; Wessinger, "Notes."

112. Zeller, "Euphemization" 173.

113. Seen in Gifford, Gazecki, and McNulty.

by the Branch Davidians as resulting solely from the actions of the agents of the lamblike beast aimed at martyring the saints, not from refusing to come out, not from pouring fuel inside the building, not from possibly lighting fires, and not from shooting weapons to spare others and oneself the excruciating pain of being burned alive. Anything other than martyrdom was too terrible to contemplate.

5

Martyrdom and its Contestations in the Formative Period of Islam

Asma Afsaruddin

IT IS COMMONLY assumed that the concept of martyrdom, especially military martyrdom, is a particularly well-developed one within the Islamic tradition and must have been so from the very beginning of Islam. The cult of military martyrdom publicly proclaimed and enthusiastically embraced by modern militant groups in Muslim-majority societies in the name of religion conveys the impression that foundational texts in Islam themselves must exhort followers to undertake such acts. If one read only militant literature, with its references to the Qur'an and hadith works, one might be convinced that this were true; however, a deeper, historical survey of early texts easily disabuses us of such notions. As the discussion in this chapter shows, the concept of martyrdom and its purview remained a contested one through most of the formative period of Islam. Early views from the first and second centuries of Islam, in fact, were often dramatically different from those that developed in the later period. A diachronic comparison of such varying perspectives allows us to trace a shifting trajectory of meanings associated with martyrdom that has important consequences for the contemporary period.

This chapter will first of all focus on two critical Qur'anic verses which have been understood to refer to martyrdom, military or otherwise, by influential exegetes across the centuries. It will then proceed to discuss martyrdom as depicted in a number of hadith works compiled between the late second/eighth century and the late fourth/tenth century, and in one treatise on the merits of jihad. These works reveal a lively dialectics on the constructions of piety and religious merit among various groups, and allow us to trace the growth of a cult of military martyrdom by the third/ninth century. The concluding section discusses how this recuperation of contested meanings of martyrdom from the formative period of Islam can serve as an important corrective to deeply entrenched assumptions of the nature of martyrdom in the Islamic milieu.

Martyrdom in the Qur'an

The term *shahīd* used almost exclusively in later literature to refer to a martyr, military or otherwise, does not occur in the Qur'an in this sense. *Shāhid* and its cognate *shahīd* refer in the Qur'an only to a legal or eyewitness, used for both God and humans in appropriate contexts (for example, Qur'an 3:98; 6:19; 41:53). Similarly, *shahada* in its Qur'anic usage signifies "witness/ witnessing" and has nothing to do with martyrdom in the later conventional sense. Qur'anic phrases commonly understood to refer to the military martyr include *man qutila fi sabil allah/alladhina qutilu fi sabil allah* ("those who are slain in the path of God"; cf. Qur'an 2:154; 3:169)[1] and variations thereof. Only in later extra-Qur'anic literature (*sira, tafsir*, and hadith) does *shahid*—and its plural *shuhada'*—acquire the specific meaning of "one who bears witness for the faith," particularly by laying down one's life.[2] Another concept, that of selling or bartering (*yashra/yashrun*) one's self or the life of this world for the hereafter (Qur'an 4:74; cf. 9:111), has been connected to the notion of martyrdom, but the connection itself is not explicit in the Qur'an.

These Qur'anic locutions are therefore ambiguous and do not in themselves clearly refer to military martyrdom. Reflecting this scriptural ambiguity, the rich exegetical literature records a diversity of views among Qur'an commentators on the meaning(s) of these locutions and the interpretation of verses that refer to those who die or are killed in the path of God and those who are identified in the Qur'an as *shahid/shuhada'*. Here we will discuss two such verses—Qur'an 22:58 and 57:19—and their exegeses in order to exhume a broad spectrum of meanings attached to such concepts that, in the ultimate analysis, considerably ameliorate the understanding of martyrdom in

1. See my extensive discussion of these verses in Afsaruddin, *Striving in the Path of God* 102–09.

2. Extraneous, particularly Christian, influence may be suspected in the semantic transformation of these terms. The Syriac word for martyr-witness, *sahda*, is very likely responsible for the Arabic *shahid*'s subsequent acquisition of the secondary meaning of "martyr;" see, for example, Wensinck 91–113; Lewinstein 78–79.

predominantly a military sense, as is endemic in the later juridical literature in particular.

Exegeses of Qur'an 22:58 and Qur'an 57:19

Qur'an 22:58

This verse states,

> Those who emigrated in the path of God and then were slain or died, God will provide handsome provisions for them; indeed God is the best of providers.[3]

In the late third/ninth century the celebrated exegete al-Tabari (d. 310/923) comments that this verse refers to those first-generation Muslims (Companions)[4] who had departed from their native lands and families in order to please God, serve Him, and undertake jihad against His enemies—a clear reference to the Emigrants (*muhajirun*) from Mecca to Medina. Whether they were subsequently killed or died while engaged in such meritorious activities, al-Tabari says, God will confer on them abundant reward in Paradise on the Day of Judgement. Significantly, al-Tabari further remarks that this verse was specifically revealed in regard to certain Companions who differed regarding the status of those who had perished in the path of God. Some were of the opinion that the one who was slain and the one who died were of the same status, while others maintained that the one who was slain had achieved greater merit (*afdal*). Then God caused this verse to come down, continues al-Tabari, in which He informed the Prophet Muhammad that both the one who is slain and the one who dies in the path of God attain the same reward in the hereafter (Al-Tabari 9:182). Al-Tabari notably does not use *shahid* or its derivatives in his explication of this verse.

The sixth/twelfth-century exegete al-Zamakhshari (d. 538/1144) comments that the verse regards all the Emigrants from Mecca to Medina to be equally meritorious, regardless of whether they subsequently were killed during the early battles or survived and died later. God is fully cognizant of their status and confers His reward on them equally (Al-Zamakhshari 4:207).

---

3. Translations of Qur'anic verses are mine, although I have freely consulted existing translations.

4. This term—in Arabic, *al-Sahaba*—refers to the close associates of the Prophet Muhammad from the first generation of Muslims.

The late sixth/twelfth-century commentator Fakhr al-Din al-Razi (d. 606/1210) explains that the phrase "Then they were slain or they died," in Qur'an 22:58 means that God's promise of a handsome provision (*rizq*) encompasses both equally. At the basic linguistic level, he comments, the verse does not indicate either preference or equal status for these two groups, and does not on its surface support those who say that the one slain in jihad and the one who dies in his bed are equal in moral status. This understanding of an equal status finds support in a hadith, however, related by the well-known Companion Anas b. Malik in which the Prophet said, "The one who is slain in the path of God the Exalted (*al-maqtul fi sabil allah ta'ala*) and the one who dies [of natural causes] in the path of God (*al-mutawaffa' fi sabil allah bi-ghayr qatl*) are the equal of one other in regard to the blessings and reward [that they are entitled to]"(Al-Razi 8:244).

A similar range of views is indicated by the Cordoban commentator al-Qurtubi (d. 671/1273) in his exegesis of Qur'an 22:58. He notes that some scholars were of the opinion that the one who is slain in the path of God is better (*afdal*) than the one who dies of natural causes (*mata hatfa anfihi*), but the revelation of this verse affirmed that both were equal in status, and God would accord both a handsome provision in the hereafter. In spite of that, he notes, the religious law as it developed appears to indicate the superior status of the slain (*anna 'l-maqtul afdal*). Some scholars maintained that the one who is slain in the path of God and the one who dies in the path of God are equally martyrs (*shahid*), but the slain individual enjoys a distinctive status on account of "the afflictions he bore for the sake of God" (*ma asabahu fi dhat allah*). But other scholars stated that they were equal, adducing as a proof-text Qur'an 4:100, which states, "Whoever emerges from his home in order to emigrate to God and His apostle, and is then overtaken by death, his reward is already assured with God." Al-Qurtubi cites here the well-known hadith concerning the female Companion Umm Haram, who was thrown from her riding mount and died as a consequence and was not slain (*matat wa-lam tuqtal*). The Prophet is then said to have remarked, addressing her lifeless body, "You are among the first [rank of believers] (*anti min al-awwalin*)" (Ibn Maja, 3:126–27). Other hadiths affirming the equal status of both groups of people are recorded by al-Qurtubi (*Jami'* 12:82–83).

In another significant hadith recorded by al-Qurtubi, the late second/eighth-century scholar Ibn al-Mubarak (reporting from the Companion Fudala b. 'Ubayd [d. ca. 53/672]) relates that two men died at the same place, one on account of having been wounded by a mangonel during a military campaign, and the other of natural causes. Fudala sat down by the corpse of the latter man, and it was said to him: "You abandoned the martyr (*al-shahid*) and did not sit by him?" He replied, "I do not care in which of the two graves I am raised up in." Then he recited Qur'an 22:58 (al-Qurtubi 12:83). Fudala's comment underscores the complete parity in merit between the two men, and his deliberate discounting of military martyrdom as conferring any special status on the believer.

In contrast to such authorities, al-Qurtubi takes note of other scholars who argued that, in fact, the slain individual enjoyed a higher status, according to the hadith in which Muhammad was asked, "Which *jihad* is more meritorious (*afdal*)?" He replied, "[The *jihad* of] one whose blood flows and whose steed is hamstrung." If such an individual is deemed to be "the best of martyrs (*afdal al-shuhada'*)," then, remarks al-Qurtubi, one who does not meet his end in this manner is deemed to be less meritorious (*mafdul*) (al-Qurtubi 12:83).

Al-Qurtubi's commentary indicates the greater reliance on hadith by his time to interpret critical Qur'anic verses with doctrinal implications, even to the point of undermining the explicit meanings of such verses, such as Qur'an 22:58, which makes no prima facie distinction in status between the naturally deceased and the fallen in battle. The cult of military martyrdom, well-entrenched by al-Qurtubi's time, necessitated such a hermeneutic stratagem to circumvent an otherwise transparent stricture in Qur'an 22:58 *against* the very construction of such a cult.

Qur'an 57:19

This verse states,

> And those who believe in God and His messengers are the truthful ones (*al-siddiqun*) and witnesses (*al-shuhada'*) in the presence of their Lord and they have their reward and their light. As for those who disbelieve and give the lie to our verses, they are the denizens of Hell.

The occasion of revelation for this verse is given by the early exegete Muqatil b. Sulayman (d. 150/767) as follows. The previous verse Qur'an 57:18, which states, "Indeed men and women who give alms (*al-musaddiqin wa-'l-musaddiqat*) and thus make a goodly loan (*qardan*) to God will have it doubled for them and for them there is a generous reward," was revealed in reference to Abu Dahdah and his wife, Umm Dahdah, who had given over their orchard "as alms for God and His messenger." On learning about this, Muhammad assured Abu Dahdah of his reward in paradise. At this, the poor lamented that they had no wealth from which they could offer alms or expend on the military jihad. Qur'an 57:19 was subsequently revealed to assure them that those who have affirmed their faith in God and His messengers were indeed among the *siddiqun* (Muqatil b. Sulayman 4:242–43). *Al-shuhada'* in the verse is, however, specifically glossed by Muqatil as "those who were martyred from among them" (*man ustushhida minhum*), presumably from among the *siddiqun*, and who have been promised their reward with God (Muqatil b. Sulayman 4:243). Muqatil's interpretation of *shuhada'* in this verse became quite influential after him, as we shall see.

In the briefest of remarks preserved for us, the Ibadi Qur'an commentator Hud b. Muhakkam (d. ca. 290/903) says that, according to this verse, every believer is a martyr, even if he dies in his bed (*kullu mu'min shahid wa-in mata 'ala firashihi*) (Hud b. Muhakkam 4:297).

The well-known early Shīʿī exegete from the first half of the third/ninth century al-'Ayyashi (d. 320/932) affirms Ibn Muhakkam's expansive understanding of martyrdom. Al-'Ayyashi relates that a certain Minhal al-Qassab had asked the sixth Shīʿī Imām Ja'far al-Sadiq to pray to God on his behalf so that he (sc. Minhal) would be granted martyrdom (*al-shahada*). Ja'far replied, "The believer is indeed a martyr (*inna al-mu'min shahid*)," and then recited Qur'an 57:19 (Al-'Ayyashi 3:157).

The extensive commentary of al-Tabari offers a clear sense of the contested semantics of the term *al-shuhada'* by the late third/ninth century. He commences his exegesis by noting that the verse refers to those who affirmed the unity of God and who believed in the messengers sent by God and their divinely inspired message, thus earning the epithet *al-siddiqun*. As for *al- shuhada', 'inda rabbihim*, al-Tabari indicates the difference of opinion among exegetes concerning this phrase. Some commented that this phrase is separated from the preceding verse concerning those who believe in God and His messengers, and who are thereby called *siddiqun*. A new proposition begins with *al- shuhada'* followed by its own predicate, unconnected to the preceding section. Those who were of this opinion included early authorities such as the Companion Ibn 'Abbas and the Successors (Muslims from the second generation) Masruq b. Ajda' (d. 63/682) and al-Dahhak b. Muzahim (d. ca. 105/723). Masruq categorically stated that the reward and light mentioned in the verse were promised by God specifically to the *shuhada'* (*hiya li-'l-shuhada' khassa*). Similarly, al-Dahhak maintained that the *siddiqun* were only those who believed in God and His messengers; the subsequent part starting with *al-shuhada'* was unconnected to it (*hadhihi mafsula*).

But others were of the opinion that the *shuhada'* were among those who were described as believing in God and His messengers, and that this term is therefore part of the subject of the sentence. The predicate for the whole sentence is therefore to be understood as "for them is their reward and light." Among those who subscribed to this interpretation were a significant number of early authorities, including the Companion 'Abd Allah b. Mas'ud (d. ca. 32/652), who is said to have identified five categories of people who cannot aspire to genuine martyrdom: the man who fights (*yuqatil*) for renown; the man who fights for status; the man who fights for this world; the man who fights for prestige; and the man who fights for booty. If they should expire in battle, none of these men is to be deemed a *shahid*, for only "the man who fights seeking the face of God (*ibthigha' wajh allah*) and the man who dies in his bed is a *shahid*." 'Abd Allah is said to have recited Qur'an 57:19 as a proof-text in this context, thus establishing a clear moral equivalence between the non-combative and combative sincere believer (Al-Ṭabari 11:683).

Al-Tabari next refers to the late first/seventh-century exegete Mujahid b. Jabr (d. 104/722) as an early authority who is said to have remarked, "Every believer is a *shahid*," and had recited this verse as a proof-text. Mujahid is said to have commented further that the *siddiqun* and the *shuhada'* mentioned in this verse referred to those who harbored deep faith in God, and therefore suggested no connection with martyrdom in the case of *shuhada'*. A hadith related by the Companion al-Bara' b. 'Azib states that the Prophet said, "The believers of my community are the *shuhada'*." Al-Bara' is then said to have recited Qur'an 57:19 (Al-Ṭabari 11:683–84). Yet others asserted that the *shuhada'* in this context referred to the prophets who served as witnesses for their communities, as attested to in Qur'an 4:41, which states, "How is it if we brought forth a witness for every community and brought you forth as a witness over these [people]?" (Al-Ṭabari 11:684).

After documenting these early variegated views, al-Ṭabari weighs in and notes that it is more appropriate and accurate to state that the *siddiqun* and the *shuhada'* are two different groups of people described in this verse, and that grammatically, the first part of the verse is not connected to the second. Faith is not the defining attribute of a *shahid*, he comments, unless one means that one bears witness to one's faith and what one holds to be true. Although this argument has some merit, al-Tabari dismisses it as somewhat far-fetched "since that is not its most common meaning." The preferred exegesis of this verse is: "the *shuhada'* who are killed in the path of God or those who perish in His way are in His presence, and for them is reward from God in the next world and their light." In contrast, those who disbelieve and give the lie to

His proofs are the denizens of Hell (Al-Tabari 11:684). Clearly, *shahid* and its plural *shuhada'* came to be widely understood to refer to the military martyr during al-Tabari's time, as he himself attests, and these late meanings were then read back into specific Qur'anic verses that employ these terms.

In his comment on this verse, the well-known fifth/eleventh-century exegete 'Ali b. Ahmad al-Wahidi (d. 468/1076) refers to the exegesis of late first/seventh-century scholar Mujahid b. Jabr, who declared a *siddiq* to be "Everyone who believed in God and His messengers." The two Muqatils—Muqatil b. Hayyan [d. ca. 150/767] and the afore-mentioned Muqatil b. Sulayman—stated that the *siddiqun* are those who "never doubted for one instant the messengers when they informed them [of God's message] nor did they deem them liars." According to another authority, al-Dahhak, the *siddiqun* are the eight people who were the first in their time to embrace Islam: Abu Bakr, 'Ali, Zayd, 'Uthman, Talha, al-Zubayr, Sa'd, and Hamza. The ninth person was 'Umar, whose name was added by God to this list of distinguished persons on account of the sincerity of his intention, according to al-Wahidi. As for "the *shuhada'* in the presence of their Lord," according to Masruq b. Ajda', it refers to the prophets who serve as witnesses for their communities; this was also the opinion of the Qur'an scholars Muqatil b. Hayyan, al-Farra', and al-Zajjaj. But Muqatil b. Sulayman and Ibn Jarir (a reference to al-Tabari here) maintained that it referred to "those who were martyred in the way of God" (*ustushhidu fi sabil allah*) (Al-Wahidi 4:251). Once again, we note that in contrast to an imposing array of early authorities who interpreted *shuhada'* very broadly as sincere believers who witnessed to the truth of God's revelations through His messengers over time, Muqatil and al-Tabari stand out as expounding the minority view in the early period that the term was a specific reference to military martyrs.

Al-Razi in the late sixth/twelfth century begins his exegesis of this verse by pointing out that in contrast to the preceding verse, which compares believers and hypocrites, this verse compares believers and unbelievers. As for the *siddiq* specifically mentioned in this verse, al-Razi considers it to be an epithet applied to one who is exceptionally truthful and sincere, and who evinces these attributes through his or her belief in God and His messengers. Its use in this verse may be understood in two ways. Firstly, it may refer broadly to anyone who believes in God and His messengers. Here, like his predecessors, he references the opinion of Mujahid, who had commented, "Whoever believes in God and His messengers is a *siddiq*." Ibn 'Abbas similarly endorsed this understanding when he glossed "they are the *siddiqun*" as referring to "those who affirm the unity [of God] (*al-muwahhidun*)" (al-Razi 10:462).

Secondly, the term is used to refer to specific people. This was the view of the two Muqatils, who stated,

> The *siddiqun* are those who believed in the messengers when they came to them and did not for an instant deny them, such as the people of Ya Sin, and the believers among the Pharaoh's people. As for our religion, they are the eight who were the first on earth to [embrace] Islam.

And then they proceeded to list the names of the eight Muslims given above, with 'Umar being the ninth (al-Razi 10:462).

With regard to the term *al-shuhada'*, there are two main considerations, continues al-Razi. Firstly, one should note that the term is linked to the first part of the verse, so that one reads it as "those who believe in God and His messengers are the *ṣiddiqun* and the *shuhada'*." Here al-Razi cites Mujahid's statement that every believer is a *siddiq* and a *shahid*. In answer to the possible question as to why every believer should be called a *shahid*, some have replied that that is so "because the believers are witnesses before their Lord for humankind through their actions" in the hereafter. Al-Hasan al-Basri is reported to have said that the reason for considering every believer a *shahid* is that "every believer witnesses to the glory of his Lord." The Mu'tazili scholar al-Asamm (d. 201/816) said that every believer is a *shahid* because everything he does for the sake of God, he does as an act of worship in accordance with the requirements of faith and obedience and in avoidance of unbelief and contumacy. The Successor Abu Muslim (d. 62/684) had remarked that since the *siddiqun* are described as those who are exceptionally truthful and faithful and conjoin faith in God to faith in His messengers, they thereby become witnesses over others (*al-shuhada' 'ala ghayrihim*) (al-Razi 10:462–63).

Secondly, it is possible to regard *al-shuhada'* as disconnected from the previous clause and constituting a new subject, continues al-Razi. From this grammatical perspective, there is still a difference of opinion regarding who is intended by the term. According to the prominent Qur'an scholars al-Farra' (d. 207/822) and al-Zajjaj (d. 311/923), the term refers specifically to the prophets, citing as corroboration Qur'an 4:41. But Muqatil and Muhammad b. Jarir (sc. al-Tabari) were of the opinion that the *shuhada'* were those who were martyred in the path of God. In this context, al-Razi says, one may cite the hadith in which the Prophet asks his Companions, "Whom do you consider to be the *shuhada'* among you?" They said, "the slain (*al-maqtul*)." He said, "then the *shuhada'* among my people would be very few indeed." Muhammad then went on to assert that the slain person is a *shahid*, and the one who dies from a stomach affliction is a *shahid*, as is the one who dies from the plague (al-Razi 10:463). The verse appropriately concludes with a contrasting reference to the unbelievers, notes al-Razi (al-Razi 10:462–63). Al-Razi is therefore unconvinced that *shuhada'* in the verse refers specifically to martyrdom, because the Qur'anic context clearly implies a much broader meaning for it in parallel with the term *siddiqun*.

Al-Qurtubi's discussion of this verse is very similar to that of al-Razi. He discusses whether the *shuhada'* are to be regarded as conjoined to the *siddiqun* in the verse; he cites Mujahid and Zayd b. Aslam (d. 136/753), who affirmed that the two terms were connected and referred in general to the believers (*al-mu'minun*). The well-known Sufi author al-Qushayri (d. 465/1072) is said to have understood the *shuhada'* to be a rung below the *ṣiddiqun* in moral excellence. Al-Qurtubi thinks it is possible to understand Qur'an 57:19 as broadly referring to all those who believed in the messengers through time; *al-shuhada'* may specifically refer to all those who bear witness that God is one (Al-Qurtụbi 17:216–17).

Al-Qurtubi points to two schools of thought regarding the identity of the *shuhada'* in the Qur'an: 1) that they are the messengers who serve as witnesses for their communities as to whether they believed or rejected their message (this was the position of the second/eighth century exegete al-Kalbi [d. 146/763] who drew further on Qur'an 4:41 as a proof-text); or 2) that they are the communities of the messengers who bear witness on the Day of Judgment, either on their behalf regarding their acts of obedience and disobedience (as maintained by Mujahid), or on behalf of their prophets testifying that they had delivered their message to their communities (as also maintained by al-Kalbi). A third position was adopted by Muqatil b. Sulayman, who said that the *shuhada'* referred to those slain in the path of God, as reflected in Ibn 'Abbas's statement that the "martyrs from among the faithful *(shuhada' al-mu'minin)*" are intended here, and *al-shuhada'* is decoupled from *al-siddiqun* in this verse (Al-Qurtubi 17:217). Like al-Razi before him, al-Qurtubi is not convinced by Muqatil b. Sulayman's interpretation of the Qur'anic *shuhada'*, even though it had become an influential one in certain circles by his time.

Martyrdom in the Hadith Literature

The diversity of perspectives encountered in the exegetical literature concerning the identity of the *shuhada'* is mirrored to a considerable extent in the hadith literature as well. A number of early hadith compilations, in particular, preserve a broad range of meanings assigned to the term *shahid*. Thus the *Musannaf* of 'Abd al-Razzaq b. Hammam al-San'ani (d. 211/827) contains a number of early Companion reports (and therefore not attributed to Muhammad) which relate competing definitions of *shahid*. One report attributed to the Companion Abu Hurayra states that the *shahid* is one who, were he to die in his bed, would enter heaven ('Abd al-Razzaq 5:268). The explanatory note that follows states that it refers to someone who dies in his bed and is without sin (*la dhanb lahu*).[5] Another report, related by Masruq b. al-Ajda', declares that there are four types of *shahada* or martyrdom for Muslims: the plague; parturition or delivery of a child; drowning; and a stomach ailment ('Abd al-Razzaq 5:271). Significantly, there is no mention of martyrdom being earned on account of dying on the battlefield in this early report. An expanded version of this report, however, originating with the Companion Abu Hurayra, quotes the Prophet as adding to this list of those who achieve martyrdom, "one who is killed in the way of God (*man qutila fi sabil Allah*)" ('Abd al-Razzaq 5:270–71). It is this expanded version containing the full, five definitions of a *shahid* that is recorded later in the famous hadith compilation known as the *Sahih*[6] of al-Bukhari (d. 256/870; Al-Bukhari 2:420–21).

The *Muwatta'* of Malik b. Anas (d. 179/795) records that the Prophet identified seven kinds of martyrs, in addition to those who died from fighting in God's way. Thus,

> He who dies as a victim of an epidemic is a martyr; he who dies from drowning is a martyr; he who dies from pleurisy is a martyr; he who dies from diarrhoea is a martyr; he who dies by [being burned in] fire is a martyr; he who dies by being struck by a dilapidated wall falling is a martyr; and the woman who dies in childbed is a martyr. (Malik b. Anas 1:366–67)

The *Muwatta'* also records the hadith that all the martyr's sins are forgiven, except for his debt; here the martyr is assumed to be the military martyr (Malik b. Anas 1:365).

5. Cf. Muslim, 3:1204–05 for a variant.

6. The *Sahih* of al- Bukhari is understood by Sunni Muslims to contain only "sound" (*sahih*) reports attributed to the Prophet and is regarded by them as the most important and reliable compilation of hadith. Five other hadith collections by Muslim b. Hajjaj, Abu Da'ud, al-Tirmidhi, Ibn Maja, and al-Nasa'i are also held in great esteem; all these collections are known collectively as "the Six Books (*al-kutub al-sitta*)."

The *Musannaf* of Ibn Abi Shayba (d. 235/849) also records a diversity of early and competing views on what constitutes martyrdom and who qualifies for it. A hadith which is *mursal* (lacking the name of the Companion who would have heard it directly from the Prophet) is narrated by the Successor al-Hasan al-Basri (d. 110/728). In it, Muhammad remarks that the average (pious) person after death is pleased with his or her reward in the hereafter and has no desire to return to this world. But when he becomes aware of the abundance of good things (*al-na'im*) which awaits the martyr (*al-shahid*), then he yearns to go back in order to be slain (Ibn Abi Shayba 4:226). Here the *shahid* is specifically identified as a military martyr, whose moral status in this report is higher than that of a pious non-combatant believer.

But, as in 'Abd al-Razzaq's *Musannaf*, other hadiths and non-prophetic reports recorded by Ibn Abi Shayba challenge such a circumscribed understanding of martyrdom and its purview. Thus the Companion Abu Hurayra, relates,

> I heard the Messenger of God, peace and blessings be upon him, ask, "Who do you regard as *shahid*?" Those present replied, "One who is slain in the path of God (*al-maqtul fi sabil allah*)." The Prophet exclaimed, "Then the martyrs of my community would be few indeed! The one who is slain (*al-qatil*) in the path of God is a martyr; the one who is felled to the ground from his mount in the path of God is a martyr; the one who drowns in the path of God is a martyr; and the one who is stricken by pleurisy in the path of God." (Ibn Abi Shayba 4:227)

In a variant hadith, the Prophet asks a similar question of his Companions regarding those who are to be considered among the martyrs. When they identified as a martyr the one who fights in the path of God and is then slain, Muhammad exclaimed that the martyrs of his community would be too few in number. He consequently proceeded to include among martyrs, beside the one slain in the path of God, the one who dies from a stomach ailment and the woman who dies during pregnancy (Ibn Abi Shayba 4:227). A variant report includes, besides those enumerated above, one who dies from the plague, from being burned or drowned, or from pleurisy (Ibn Abi Shayba 4:227). Other variants are given. A non-prophetic variant report says simply, "The plague is martyrdom; drowning is martyrdom, as is [dying from a] stomach [ailment} and [from] parturition" (Ibn Abi Shayba 4:227).

Two other variants recorded by Ibn Abi Shayba are worthy of note. According to one of them, the Companion ʿAbd Allah b. Masʿud is said to have included the person who drowns in the sea, or falls from the mountains, or is eaten by wild animals among "the martyrs in the presence of God on the Day of Resurrection." The other variant quotes Masruq b. Ajdaʿ as saying, "The plague, the stomach [ailment], parturition, drowning, and whatever afflicts a Muslim constitutes martyrdom (*shahada*) for him" (Ibn Abi Shayba 4:227). In these reports, martyrdom is expansively construed as death resulting from any kind of suffering or pain endured by the faithful during their earthly existence. These reports do not use the phrase *fi sabil allah* ("in the path of God") for non-military afflictions, but the implication is nevertheless clear: earthly suffering of the righteous leading to death earns them martyrdom at least on a par with the military kind. The invocation of these reports also makes clear that the definition of martyrdom and the status of the martyr, both military and non-military, continued to be debated through the first three centuries of Islam.

Hadiths and other kinds of reports which preserve the early expansive meanings of *shahid* and *shahada*, as encountered in the two *Musannafs* and the *Muwatta'* of Malik, are also preserved in early treatises on the merits of *jihad*, such as the *Kitab al-jihad* of the late second/eighth-century scholar-warrior Ibn al-Mubarak (d. 181/797). In a hadith narrated by ʿAtik b. al-Harith as recorded by Ibn al-Mubarak, the Prophet asked some of his Companions what they regarded as martyrdom (*al-shahada*). They replied that martyrdom was being killed in the way of God. The Prophet then responded with the seven categories of martyrs (Ibn al-Mubarak 40).[7] According to another report, when the well-known Companion ʿAbd Allah b. Masʿud heard a martyr being described in his presence solely as one who had died while fighting, he remonstrated that whoever dies from falling off a mountaintop, or from drowning in the sea, or from being attacked by wild animals, will be considered a martyr on the Day of Judgement (Ibn al-Mubarak 40). In another Companion report, ʿUmar b. al-Khattab is said to have remarked, "Indeed there are some people who fight out of a desire for this world, while others fight for glory and renown, and yet others who fight only reactively. But there are those who fight 'desiring/seeking the face of God' (*ibtigha' wajh allah*), and they are the martyrs (*al-shuhada'*)" (Ibn al-Mubarak 19). This last report emphasizes correct and sincere intention (*niyya*)—fighting only for

7. For a more detailed study of Ibn al-Mubarak's treatise, see Afsaruddin, *Striving in the Path of God* 149–57.

the sake of God—in determining genuine military martyrdom, signaling that such determination was exclusively a divine prerogative since humans cannot infer the secrets of the heart.

In comparison with the earlier *Musannafs*, certain reports recorded in the *Sahih* of al-Bukhari clearly assign a more privileged status to military martyrs, with special rewards in the hereafter earmarked for them alone. A hadith on the authority of the Companion Samura b. Jundub states that there is an "abode of martyrs" (*dar al-shuhada'*) which is the best and most excellent of abodes in the hereafter (al-Bukhari 4:409), a report not encountered in earlier collections. Another hadith, narrated by the Companion Anas b. Malik, asserts that only the (military) martyr among the pious will wish to return to earth and be killed repeatedly so as to continue to multiply the abundant posthumous rewards awaiting him (al-Bukhari 4:410). Similarly exalting the status of military martyrs, a hadith on the authority of the Companion Abu Hurayra declares that whoever is wounded in the path of God (and God knows best who is truly wounded in His path) will be resurrected on the Day of Judgment with the color of blood and breath of musk (al-Bukhari 4:412).

Some hadiths warn, however, that the exalted status of the combatant should not lead to the deliberate courting of martyrdom on the part of the faithful by seeking to confront the enemy. As recorded by al-Bukhari, a hadith on the authority of the Companion 'Abd Allah b. Abi Awfa relates that, during a military campaign, the Prophet would customarily wait until the sun had tilted toward the West, and then address his troops thus: "Do not wish to meet the enemy, O People, and ask forgiveness of God. When you meet them, be forbearing (*fa-'sbiru*) and know that paradise lies below the shade of the swords" (al-Bukhari 4:481–82). This report sounds a noteworthy caveat against the deliberate seeking of military martyrdom—that would, after all, be tantamount to suicide, an act explicitly forbidden in the Qur'an (2:195; 4:29).

In the slightly later hadith collection of Abu Da'ud al-Sijistani (d. 275/888) known as the *Sunan*, we encounter an unprecedented report that indicates to us a progressively escalating estimation of the status of the military martyr. Attributed to the Companion 'Ubayd b. Khalid al-Sulami, it states that the Prophet made two men brothers of one another; one of them was slain (it is assumed on the battlefield) while the other died (it is assumed of natural causes) a week or so after the former. Several of the Companions prayed at the latter's grave. When Muhammad asked them what they had uttered, they replied that they had prayed for his forgiveness and that he would be united with his companion. At that the Prophet exclaimed that the prayers, the fasting, and the deeds of the two men in general were not comparable, for "Indeed, [the difference] between them is like that between the sky and the earth!" (Abu Da'ud 2:470–536). Abu Da'ud further records a hadith (from the Companion Abu 'l-Darda') that bestows upon the martyr the right to intercede on behalf of seventy members of his family (Abu Da'ud 2:479). This report is also included by his contemporary Ibn Maja (d. 273/886) in his *Sunan* work (Ibn Maja 3:138–39). The content of such reports, not recorded in earlier compilations, signals to us that by the late third/ninth century, exaggerated exaltation of the status of the military martyr at the expense of the non-military one was being promoted in influential circles.

The *Sunan* of another famed hadith scholar, al-Tirmidhi (d. 279/892), includes a noteworthy report attributed to the second caliph, 'Umar b. al-Khattab, in which he states that he had heard the Prophet enumerate four types of martyrs (*al-shuhada'*): 1) a believing man of strong faith who meets the enemy with resolute and honest intent and is slain (he is the best kind); 2) a believing man of strong faith who on encountering the enemy falters due to a twinge of cowardice and is slain (he is in the second rank); 3) a believing man who mixes good deeds with bad but meets the enemy with honest intent and is slain (he is in the third rank); and 4) a believing man who sins against himself but meets the enemy with resolute intent and is slain (he is in the fourth rank) (Al-Tirmidhi 4:152). Significantly, this report from 'Umar has replaced the five to seven categories of non-combative and combative martyrs (as enumerated in the earlier collections of Malik and al-Bukhari), with only combative ones. The progressively higher moral evaluation of the military martyr over the non-military one is clearly signaled in what is obviously a late report.

In his brief section on the topic of martyrdom (*bab mas'alat al-shahada*), another well-known hadith compiler, al-Nasa'i (d. 303/915), includes a report, not previously encountered by us, which appears to encode early debates concerning which groups of people were entitled to be called martyrs. In this report narrated by the Companion al-'Irbad b. Sariya, one of the pietistic and abstemious *ahl al-suffa*,[8] the Prophet says that military martyrs (*al-shuhada'*) and those who died naturally in their beds (*al-mutawaffawna 'ala furushihim*)

8. This is the name given to a special pietist, impoverished group of early Muslims whose only dwelling was the portico (*suffa*) surrounding the mosque of Medina—hence their name ("the people of the portico"). For Irbad's inclusion among the *ahl al-suffa*, see, for example, Ibn Ḥajar 4:109.

would wrangle in the following manner before God regarding those who had perished from the plague (*yutawaffawna min al-ṭaʿun*):

> The martyrs will say, "Our brothers were slain (*qutilu*) as we were slain," and those who had died in their beds will say, "Our brothers died (*matu*) in their beds as we died." Our Lord will say, "Look at their wounds: if their wounds are similar to the wounds of those who were slain, then they are one of them and with them." And lo! their [a reference to those who had perished from the plague] wounds were similar to their wounds." (Al-Nasaʾi 2:665).

This report is highly significant because it establishes that 1) the issue of whether individuals dying nonviolently in their beds may qualify for martyrdom on a par with warriors was being debated in the earliest period, as the internal reference to the *ahl al-suffa* might suggest, and/or that it remained a contested issue well into al-Nasaʾi's time; and 2) those who perish from non-battlefield afflictions may earn the right to be called martyrs only if proven that their afflictions were as severe as those suffered by the military martyr. It is not surprising that as one of the pietist *ahl al-suffa* suffering from the privations of this world, ʿIrbad propagates this report (or this report is ascribed to him to ensure credibility), which implicitly questions whether the suffering of the battlefield martyr should become the standard against which the sufferings of all others are to be measured before being granted the imprimatur of martyrdom. At the same time, it offers affirmation that those who are subjected to terrible suffering like the victims of plague are indeed to be considered martyrs.

Conclusion

Our discussion in this chapter has allowed us to arrive at the following conclusions regarding the parameters of martyrdom as evidenced in the exegeses of two key Qurʾanic verses discussed above and in the hadith literature.

Detailed analysis of Qurʾan 22:58 and 57:19 and their exegeses reveals that these verses make no distinction in the assignment of merit and posthumous reward between the believer who is slain in the path of God (understood almost exclusively by most of our exegetes to be the military martyr), and the believer who dies of natural causes. Both are equally assured of forgiveness and mercy from God. Consequently, the believer who is slain on the battlefield and the believer who dies peacefully in his or her bed are acknowledged to be morally equivalent, the critical yardstick being the sincerity of their faith and not the manner of their dying.

Qur'an 22:58 asserts, specifically in the case of the Muhajirun (Emigrants), that whoever among them is slain or dies of natural causes will be given handsome provisions (*rizq*) by God in the next world. The verse is understood by our exegetes to point to the greater status of the Muhajirun as a whole over other early Muslims, or of specific Companions from among them; worthy of note is that the Emigrant martyred on the battlefield is not assigned a higher status than the Emigrant who dies naturally. Here the common link between them is their act of emigration in the path of God—an arduous act of faith which, when undertaken for the sincerest intention, is worthy of generous recompense in the next world. Al-Qurtubi in particular draws our attention to the contested definitions of a martyr in the path of God. He acknowledges that despite this verse, some legal scholars in particular went on to assert that the believer who is slain on the battlefield is better than the believer who dies naturally, so that the religious law as articulated by the jurists came to reflect this point of view. But their view, al-Qurtubi points out, clearly contradicts not only this verse, but also Qur'an 4:100, which speaks of the reward due to the Emigrant who dies on the way "to God and His apostle," as well as a number of hadiths which, on the basis of Qur'an 22:58, assert the absolute moral equivalence between the believer who dies a natural death and the believer slain on the battlefield. Those who would argue for the higher status of the slain martyr referred to one hadith in particular in which Muhammad affirms that the jihad of the one who perishes on the battlefield is superior. This entire discussion is highly significant because it underscores the contested definitions of martyrdom through time and the progressively higher moral valuation of the military martyr that occurred in contrast to the earliest period. This trend is clearly encoded in certain purported hadiths which, in spite of countervailing Qur'anic pronouncements, made firm distinctions in status between the combative and non-combative martyr. The growing influence of these legal and exegetical hadiths is signaled in the preferential treatment that came to be accorded to the military martyr over the non-military one.

The contested semantics of the term *al-shuhada'* are even more highlighted in the exegeses of Qur'an 57:19 that we surveyed. Already in the second/eighth century, Muqatil understands this term in this context as a likely reference to those among the *ṣiddiqun* who are martyred from among them (*man ustushhida minhum*). But the term *ṣiddiqun*, according to him, refers to a much broader category of people: namely, all those who publicly attest to the oneness of God and place faith in His messengers—in other words, all believing Muslims. Muqatil's brief exposition reveals to us that there is a considerable blurring of the semantic boundaries between these two terms, given that both groups of people publicly witness to their faith, with the *shuhada'* additionally, in Muqatil's understanding, laying down their lives for it. After Muqatil, however, Hud b. Muhakkam and al-'Ayyashi in the late second/eighth century and early fourth/tenth century, respectively, continued to subscribe to the early position that "every believer is a martyr" (*kull mu'min shahid*), underscoring the basic Qur'anic meaning of *shahid* as a righteous witness, and challenging the annexation of the term *shahid* to the concept of military martyrdom.

Al-Tabari, in the third/ninth century, preserves a broader gamut of exegetical opinions concerning the critical term *al-shuhada'*. A number of Companions, he notes, believed that the *shuhada'* are mentioned separately from the *siddiqun* and therefore the reward and light mentioned in the verse are reserved for them alone. Another group of Companions and Successors maintained that the two groups are mentioned in tandem with one another. On the authority of the Companion Abdullah b. Mas'ud, a *shahid* is declared to be equally one who fights for the sake of God and one who dies a natural death in his bed. The late first/seventh-century exegete Mujahid, as quoted by al-Tabari, subscribed to an even more expansive view of a *shahid*, opining that every believer in God was automatically one; this assertion was supported by a hadith in which the Prophet explicitly makes this equation. The underlying assumption in this equation is that the term *shuhada'* in general is a reference to believing Muslims who attest to their faith through myriad acts of obedience to God. Yet others thought that only the prophets were the true *shuhada'*, because of their role as witnesses for their communities (cf. Qur'an 4:41).

As we have noted, al-Tabari, however, discounts these expansive meanings and opts for what has clearly become the preferable or prevalent view in his time: that the *shuhada* are specifically those who are slain in the way of God, and that they alone are entitled to the reward and light promised in the verse. His method of reasoning that allows him to arrive at this conclusion is rather circuitous. Al-Tabari merely asserts that there is no connection between the first and second clauses of the verse; he does not offer an explanation as to why this should be so. Building on this assertion, he continues by remarking that because there is no connection, the *shuhada'* must be understood to refer to a different category of people entitled to a different kind of reward. Notably, he does not take into consideration here that the verse immediately following talks about the unbelievers who, in contrast to the people described in the preceding verse, will reap hell-fire. If the *shuhada'* were martyrs, specifically military martyrs, the following verse, for effective contrast, might have been expected to refer to those who hesitate to take up arms in self-defense. There is nothing, after all, in the original context of the verse to suggest a military undertaking. In al-Tabari's exegesis, we clearly discern how a higher valuation of the military martyr was either launched or reinforced by him in the context of Qur'an 57:19.

Al-Zamakhshari preserves a similar range of opinions concerning the *siddiqun* and the *shuhada'*. Al-Razi documents both a general and a particular understanding of the *siddiqun*, and once again provides us with a highly relevant discussion of the term *shuhada'*. He presents the key points of view which had crystallized on this matter by his time: that 1) the terms *siddiqun* and *shuhada'* are conjoined in Qur'an 57:19, so that both terms refer expansively to those who believe in God and His messengers and bear witness to it through their actions; or that 2) *al-shuhada'* is severed from the *siddiqun* and refers specifically to the prophets; or that 3) *al-shuhada'* refers to those who are martyred in the path of God, a view held almost exclusively by Muqatil b. Sulayman and al-Tabari in the early period, in contrast to a larger coterie of authorities who subscribed to the other two positions in varying degrees. Al-Razi counteracts this last, highly circumscribed meaning of *shuhada'*, citing the hadith in which the Prophet remarks that in addition to the slain person, one who dies from a stomach ailment or from the plague is also a *shahid*.

Al-Qurtubi describes a similar range of exegetical opinions concerning this verse. With regard to the *shuhada'*, he identifies three schools of thought: 1) that it was a reference to the prophets in their role as witnesses; 2) that it was a reference to the communities who will bear witness on the Day of Judgment to the fact that their prophets had fulfilled their divinely appointed roles in regard to them; and 3) that the *shuhada'* are those slain in the path of God and referred to separately from the *siddiqun*—a view that was uniquely ascribed to Muqatil b. Sulayman, who is the earliest authority on record for this particular interpretation. Al-Qurtubi himself does not express a preference for any of these positions. This discussion reveals that the cult of military martyrdom which emerged later in certain quarters continued to be met with skepticism in pietist and learned circles on the basis of relevant Qur'anic verses, such as Qur'an 57:19, which emphasizes sincerity of faith and purpose as the common link between the pious combatant and the pious non-combatant and disregards the importance of military activity in itself.

With regard to martyrdom, several hadiths and non-prophetic reports specifically challenge those who would understand "being slain in the path of God" as primarily a reference to those who are killed on the battlefield. The early hadith collections in particular—the *Musannafs* of 'Abd al-Razzaq and Ibn Abi Shayba and the *Muwatta'* of Malik b. Anas—offer variegated definitions of those who are slain or die in the path of God; they include those who die from painful afflictions and illnesses as well as those who die on the battlefield. The most expansive definition is contained in the hadith which equates the martyr with the pious believer who dies [peacefully] in his/her bed.

The construction of competing paradigms of moral excellence continues to be evident in the *Sahih* compilation of al-Bukhari and the later *sunan* works of Abu Da'ud, al-Tirmidhi, Ibn Maja, and al-Nasa'i. In reports that are clearly of late provenance, the military martyr sometimes assumes posthumous functions generally denied to other pious Muslims. Both Ibn Maja and Abu Da'ud, for example, record a hadith, not encountered in previous collections, which promises to the military martyr the right to intercede on behalf of seventy members of his family. Another unprecedented report included by Abu Da'ud heralds to us an escalation in the high esteem progressively bestowed on the military martyr. Attributed to the Companion 'Ubayd b. Khalid al-Sulami, it states that the Prophet declared that the difference between the deaths of two men, one of whom was slain (presumably on the battlefield) and the other who died (presumably of natural causes) a week or so after the former, was "like that between the sky and the earth," with the implication that the former was the vastly more morally excellent individual. This report should give us pause when we recall that Qur'an 22:58 asserts the equal moral status of the pious Muslim, in this world and the hereafter, regardless of his or her manner of dying, as was stressed by many of the exegetes in our survey. This purported hadith recorded by Abu Da'ud clearly undermines the Qur'anic equivalence established between these two types of deaths and indicates to us a dramatic transformation in the constructions of piety in Muslim discourses by the late third/ninth century. Certainly, hard-headed realpolitik had a role to play in the reassignment of posthumous rewards away from its Qur'anic recipients and toward the military warrior specifically during times when the faithful needed to be roused to fight against aggressors, actual and potential, as I argue in an earlier study (see Afsaruddin).

Similar narratives of "subversion" are in evidence in the *Sunan* of al-Nasa'i (d. 303/915). The hadith recorded by al-Nasa'i on the authority of al-'Irbad b. Sariya, one of the *ahl al-suffa*, encodes early debates about whether those slain in battle versus those who die in their beds were equally entitled to be called martyrs. Earlier in the late second/eighth century, Ibn al-Mubarak, in his treatise on the merits of jihad, invokes the report from 'Umar b. al-Khattab to remind his readers that genuine martyrdom was attained only through sincere devotion to God (*ibtigha' wajh allah*)—an attribute that defied human judgment.

In summary, martyrdom was undoubtedly an expansive, multivalent concept in Islam's formative period. Peaceful death in one's own bed at the end of a life spent in devotion to God and in the commission of good deeds was clearly the most general definition of martyrdom in the view of many. Death from tragic suffering and painful afflictions also conferred martyrdom. Others would insist that martyrdom's apotheosis was attained only on the battlefield, when the believer waged war against the hostile enemy and expired in its midst. However, active seeking of military martyrdom was generally regarded as reprehensible. This attitude is encoded in the hadith recorded by al-Bukhari in which the Prophet categorically proscribes such activity. Ultimately, most scholars agreed that the moral valence of an individual's actions, particularly those that may qualify for martyrdom, can only be judged by God, who alone can infer true human intention (*niyya*). Such prudence serves as a rebuke to militants in Muslim-majority societies today who noisily arrogate to themselves the right to decide who and how one qualifies for martyrdom, going so far as to glorify self-immolation—in resolute defiance of the moral boundaries set by the foundational texts of Islam.

6

The Death of Mūsā al-Kāẓim (d. 183/799)

KNOWLEDGE AND SUICIDE IN EARLY TWELVER SHĪʿĪSM

Najam Haider

SUICIDE IS PROHIBITED in Islam by the consensus of the larger community. In a seminal article on the subject, Franz Rosenthal summarized juristic and non-juristic attitudes toward suicide through an examination of Qur'anic verses and reports transmitted from and about the Prophet Muhammad.[1] Rosenthal noted an ambiguity that seemed to permit the practice, but he also observed that scholars regularly restricted permissive Qur'anic verses to a specific context or dismissed them through grammatical analysis.[2] Drawing primarily on historical reports of the Prophet, Rosenthal affirmed the categorical prohibition against suicide in the larger Muslim tradition. Muslim jurists were quick to differentiate between suicide and *shahada*, often translated into English as "martyrdom." However, martyrdom fails to adequately convey the proper sense of the Muslim concept of *shahada*. In a 2007 work, Talal Asad surveys some of the term's complicated and nuanced meanings. He notes, for example, that an individual who dies in an unexpected manner or through a

1. Rosenthal 239–59.

2. Rosenthal 239–43. This issue has re-emerged in the early twenty-first century as one particularly prominent legal figure (Yusuf Qaradhawi) argued in 2003 that suicide bombings (which he dubs "martyrdom operations") are not suicide in the literal sense, given the relevant motives and historical circumstances. In 2016, Qaradhawi retracted his argument. See memri.org/tv/sheikh-al-qaradhawi-retracts-fatwa-permitting-palestinian-suicide-bombings-no-need-them-anymore.

natural calamity is considered a *shahīd* ("martyr").[3] This is a far cry from the popular understanding of martyrdom as a bodily sacrifice for a higher purpose. This sense of the term is certainly present in the Muslim sources, but the word "*shahīd*" entails a far larger category of people.

Sunnī and Shīʿī scholars are in complete agreement about the prohibition of suicide, and articulate similar positions on the subject of *shahada*. This agreement may come as a surprise to readers familiar with the centrality of commemorations of the martyrdom of Ḥusayn b. ʿAlī b. Abī Ṭālib (61/680) to Twelver Shīʿī ritual practice. Ḥusayn was the grandson of the Prophet and was revered in the larger Muslim community of the time. Muhammad's love for his grandsons (Ḥasan [d. 49/669–70] and Ḥusayn) is widely attested in the sources, amplified perhaps by the fact that he had no male children who survived to adulthood. Ḥusayn was also the son of ʿAlī b. ʿAbū Ṭālib (the cousin and son-in-law of the Prophet, d. 40/661), whom many considered the rightful successor to Muhammad to the exclusion of the first three caliphs: Abū Bakr (d. 13/634); ʿUmar (d. 23/644); and ʿUthmān.[4] ʿAlī was elected as the fourth caliph following ʿUthmān's murder in 35/656. There is a broad scholarly consensus regarding the seminal importance of ʿAlī's caliphate (35–40/656–61) to the emergence of a distinct Shīʿī identity. Maria Dakake ties the origins of the Shīʿī community to a small group of supporters who took an "all-encompassing oath of spiritual loyalty (*walāya*)" that transcended simple political affiliation.[5] It was far from certain that this bond would transfer from ʿAlī to his sons. The fragility of the bond was reflected in Ḥusayn's inability to garner support for his attempted rebellion against the reigning Umayyad caliph, Yazīd b. Muʿāwiya (rl. 60–64/680–83) in 61/680. The subsequent massacre, which took place in Karbalāʾ (fifty miles northeast of Kūfa) on the tenth of Muḥarram (known as ʿĀshūrāʾ), claimed the lives of Ḥusayn and seventy-two of his companions and family members. The shocking nature of Ḥusayn's killing helped galvanize the growth of a Shīʿī identity that was palpable at the start of the second/eighth century.[6]

The sources suggest that annual commemorations of Ḥusayn's death were first organized by relatives who survived the ordeal, including his son (and

3. See Asad 48–53.

4. For the issues of succession, see Haider, *Shīʿī* 53–66.

5. For the quote, see Dakake 7. For the history of early Shīʿīsm, see Haider, *Shīʿī* 32–35.

6. See Haider, *Origins* for a detailed analysis of this subject. For a general discussion, see Haider, *Shīʿī* 53–99.

the fourth Twelver Imām) ʿAlī Zayn al-ʿĀbidīn (d. 94–95/712–13).[7] These gatherings included public displays of grief and recitations of elegies for the fallen. Shīʿī poets competed to compose elaborate poems that served as the primary means for remembering Ḥusayn (and his companions) through the Umayyad and early ʿAbbāsid periods. By the early second/eighth century, Karbalāʾ (the site of the battle and the graves of the dead) was an important center of pilgrimage for the Shīʿa, and revenge for al-Ḥusayn was a rallying cry for opposition to Umayyad rule. In time, these ritual acts became so central to the articulation of Shīʿī identity that participation alone was sufficient to establish an individual's religious affiliation. There was a fundamental shift in the historical memory of Karbalāʾ in the tenth/sixteenth century under the Safavid dynasty in Iran. This period witnessed the development of new forms of commemoration that included the reenactment of the events of ʿĀshūrāʾ (*taʿziyat khānī*) in accordance with a fixed narrative script (*rawżat khānī*). This period also saw the proliferation of acts of ritual self-mutilation and a further development of poetic forms. The important point to note here is that the centrality of these practices to Twelver Shīʿism did not result from a particular fetishizing of "martyrdom." As discussed above, this concept is equally important to all Muslims regardless of their communal affiliations. The key factor for the Shīʿa, in this instance, was the involvement of Ḥusayn, the third Twelver Shīʿī Imām and the grandson of the Prophet.

A New Question

It would be unproductive to duplicate general discussions about martyrdom in Islam found in other parts of this volume. Instead, this chapter examines a related issue often discussed in Twelver Shīʿī scholarly treatments of Ḥusayn: namely, the degree to which he was aware of his fate prior to his departure from Medina. This controversy raises an interesting dilemma for Shīʿī theologians, who must reconcile two potentially contradictory positions: (1) a maximalist notion of the Imām's knowledge; and (2) a belief that many (if not all) of the Imāms were murdered by their enemies. If both of these premises are true, then is an Imām ultimately complicit in his own death?[8] If he takes no steps to avoid his own murder, then is this suicide?

---

7. For the development of these practices, see Haider, *Shīʿī* 74–80.

8. This controversy was first brought to my attention by Kohlberg's entry on Mūsā al-Kāẓim in the *Encyclopaedia of Islam*.

These are the questions that underlie this chapter, which presents a textual excavation of this singular issue.

Twelver Shīʿī scholars devoted considerable efforts toward confronting these questions beginning in the late fourth/tenth and fifth/eleventh centuries, due (perhaps) to the growth of Muʿtazilī theological influence.[9] The most important of these works were authored by al-Shaykh al-Mufīd (d. 413/1022) and al-Sharīf al-Murtaḍā (d. 433/1044). The subject has continued to garner interest into the modern period, with scholars particularly interested in two historical examples: namely, the murder of ʿAlī and the killing of Ḥusayn. This current chapter differs from these works in two important ways. First, it centers on a case which has received less scholarly attention: the death of the seventh Twelver Imām, Mūsā al-Kāẓim, in Baghdād in 183/799. Second, it examines sources compiled in the late third/ninth and early to mid-fourth/tenth centuries that predate later (more systematic) discussions of the issue.

The three early Shīʿī scholars at the heart of this study are Muḥammad b. al-Ḥasan al-Ṣaffār al-Qummī (d. 290/902–03), Muḥammad b. Yaʿqūb al-Kulaynī (d. 329/940–41) and Ibn Bābawayh (d. 381/991–92). These figures are not necessarily representative of the intellectual landscape of Twelver Shīʿism in the late third/ninth and fourth/tenth century. They were, however, critically important to the articulation of Twelver Shīʿism, and their views offer insight into early debates over the implications of the Imām's (potentially) unbounded knowledge. The discussion that follows in this chapter consciously avoids a grand narrative of change—but it does depict a vibrant scholarly attempt to confront the theological implications of the Twelver Shīʿī community's understanding of the Imām.

This chapter is divided into four sections. The first section details communal divisions over the scope and origin of the Imām's knowledge, which is one of the most important theological debates in the early Twelver Shīʿī community.[10] The second section engages the related questions of whether the Imām is aware of his own death and, if so, whether he is obligated to prevent it. This discussion begins with a brief biography of Mūsā al-Kāẓim before

9. Muʿtazilism is discussed in greater detail below. At this point, it suffices to note that the Muʿtazila were an early (if not the earliest) Muslim theological school. They argued that the foundations of religion could be established on the basis of reason. This led them to advocate for free will, to reject anthropomorphism, and to claim that the Qur'an was a text created in time. For a summary of their views, see Haider, *Shīʿī* 13–17 and Abdulsater, *Shīʿī* chapters 2–3.

10. This debate predates the disappearance of the twelfth Imām, so it would be more apt to refer to this community as the Imāmīs or the Imāmī-Twelvers. In the interests of simplicity (and bearing in mind my audience), I will anachronistically refer to this group as the "Twelver Shīʿa."

examining relevant passages in the works of al-Ṣaffār, al-Kulaynī, and Ibn Bābawayh. The third section details the solutions offered by these scholars. The fourth and final section summarizes subsequent discussions, gesturing to the epistemological shift represented by the writings of al-Mufīd and (especially) al-Murtaḍā.

Knowledge and the Imāmate

In his foundational study of the early history of the Twelver Shīʿa, Hossein Modarressi documents two divisions within the early community over the scope and origin of the Imām's knowledge.[11] One group argued for a maximalist view of the Imām's knowledge. According to this position, God endowed the Imām with a superhuman breadth of knowledge that ranged from esoteric interpretations of Qur'anic passages, to information about the future (e.g., death dates of their followers). A second group maintained a more rationalist understanding of the Imām's knowledge that was limited to areas such as theology and law. This knowledge was acquired through study of books and other special documents which were passed down within the family of the Prophet from father to son. Modarressi traces this divide through a series of crises that culminated with the disappearance (*ghayba*) of the twelfth Imām (Muḥammad b. al-Ḥasan al-Mahdī) in 260/874.

Muḥammad b. al-Ḥasan al-Ṣaffār al-Qummī's (d. 290/902–03) *Baṣā'ir al-darajāt*, one of the earliest extant collections of Shīʿī traditions, was compiled in Qumm during this period of tumult. Al-Ṣaffār's work was intended to support maximalist notions of the Imām's knowledge. According to Andrew Newman, the *Baṣā'ir* was "a repository of traditions devoted primarily to theological issues in which the Imāms are endowed with extraordinary knowledge and abilities."[12] The book is divided into ten sections that cover topics as diverse as the Imāms' familiarity with all human and animal languages,[13] and their abilities to heal the sick or bring the dead back to life.[14] At the same time, al-Ṣaffār counseled the Shīʿa to exercise caution in their dealing with other Muslims and discouraged the general circulation of these ideas. According to Newman, these views were

---

11. Modarressi 17–51.

12. Newman 67.

13. al-Ṣaffār 313–19.

14. al-Ṣaffār 270.

particularly popular among traditionists[15] in Qumm,[16] but the extent to which they were representative of the larger community of Twelver Shīʿa remains unclear.

The considerable influence of the maximalist position in the late third/ninth and early fourth/tenth centuries was also reflected in the work of Abū Jaʿfar Muḥammad b. Yaʿqūb al-Kulaynī (d. 329/940–41). Al-Kulaynī, a devoted traditionist, was born in a small village in the vicinity of Rayy in present-day Iran.[17] He studied in Qumm in the late third/early tenth century before settling in Baghdād, where he spent the rest of his life and died in 329/941. His primary work, entitled *Kitāb al-kāfi*, was a collection of traditions that covered a wide range of topics from law and theology to history. According to Madelung, the book was not greeted with immediate acclaim, and only gained prominence in later periods largely due to its condemnation of anthropomorphism.[18] In time, al-Kulaynī's work was lauded as one of the four most authoritative Twelver Shīʿī collections, and played a critical role in the elaboration of the school's legal rulings.

Al-Kulaynī's voluminous work was meant to convey (his sense of) Twelver Shīʿī orthodoxy in the late third/ninth century, particularly in the area of doctrine and belief. For this reason, it is worth examining the text's understanding of the Imām's knowledge in greater detail. In a section focused on establishing the legitimacy of the Imāmate, al-Kulaynī engages this issue directly. A number of reports suggest a weekly[19] replenishing of the Imām's knowledge, without which it would vanish altogether.[20] The knowledge is restricted to those matters which God makes available to angels and the prophets[21]; such a restriction establishes a clear epistemological divide between God and (even the most privileged of) his creations. In one account, the sixth Twelver Imām, al-Ṣādiq (d. 148/765), reiterates this distinction. He

15. In this discourse, the term "traditionist" refers to scholars who placed primacy on the transmission of "traditions" which are short reports detailing the views of seminal figures. The traditionist approach differs from that of rationalist scholars, which posits human reason as a potential source of religious knowledge

16. Newman 84–86.

17. For a brief sketch of al-Kulaynī's life, see Madelung, "al-Kulaynī (or al-Kulīnī), Abū Dja̲ʿfar Muhammad."

18. Madelung, "al-Kulaynī (or al-Kulīnī), Abū Dja̲ʿfar Muhammad."

19. al-Kulaynī 8:253–54.

20. al-Kulaynī 8:253–55.

21. al-Kulaynī 8:255–56.

adds that, "if an Imām wants to know some matter, then God informs him of it."[22] The assumption here is that the Imām does not have access to all available information at once, but rather seeks it at appropriate moments. The Imām's vast potential knowledge includes information about the past, present, and the future.[23] In many reports, al-Kulaynī cites evidence in support of both predestination and free will without directly addressing this contradiction. Finally, the Imām's access to this repository of knowledge (described as mundane[24]) is acquired at the very moment of the previous Imām's death.[25] The suggestion here is that God bestows this information directly upon the new Imām; he does not acquire it through books or other written documents. Overall, al-Kulaynī describes the Imām as capable of accessing all of the knowledge (including that of the future) that is available to created beings through a weekly process of acquisition.

By the mid- and late fourth/tenth century, the influence of Muʿtazilī theology was increasingly felt in the scholarly discourse of the Twelver Shīʿa, particularly in discussions of the doctrine of the Imāmate.[26] Evidence of this influence is noticeable in the works of a number of scholars, including Ibn Bābawayh (commonly referred to as al-Shaykh al-Ṣadūq). Ibn Bābawayh was born in Khurāsān some time before 311/923 to a rich merchant-scholar family.[27] In 355/966, he settled in Baghdād, where he taught and held a leading position in the community of Twelver Shīʿa until his death (in Rayy) in 381/991. Ibn Bābawayh's most influential work was *Man lā yaḥḍuruhu al-faqīh*, an important legal treatise considered one of the four foundational works of Twelver Shīʿī jurisprudence.[28] Only five of his other ascribed works are extant. Two of these (*ʿUyūn akhbār al-Riḍā'* and *Kitāb al-amālī*) are discussed in greater detail below.

Ibn Bābawayh was generally ambivalent toward theological discourse but he embraced some Muʿtazilī positions, including (most importantly) divine

22. al-Kulaynī 8:258.

23. al-Kulaynī 8:260–62.

24. al-Kulaynī 8:260.

25. al-Kulaynī 8:264–65.

26. This is a complicated and controversial topic that is addressed in great detail by Hussein Abdulsater in his forthcoming book entitled *Shīʿī Doctrine, Muʿtazili Theology*. For a summary of the argument that follows, see Haider, *Shīʿī* 25–27, 41–45.

27. For a very brief biographical sketch of Ibn Bābawayh, see Fyzee, "Ibn Bābawayh (I)."

28. Recall that al-Kulaynī's *Al-Kāfī* was also identified (above) as one of these four books.

justice (*ʿadl*). According to this view, God acts in a manner that aligns with human notions of justice. In other words, humans can discern the motives behind God's actions through rational analysis. This view differs from that of the other main theological school of the time (i.e., the Ashʿarīs), which claimed that God's actions were just by definition. One of the central implications of rational divine justice was an affirmation of free will. This was because a just God would never compel humans to commit sins (as implied by predestination) and then punish them in the afterlife. Final judgment necessitated human volition to make ethical choices, for which he/she was ultimately held accountable. Ibn Bābawayh did not go so far as to accept the Muʿtazilī position on free will; he was only willing to affirm the principle of rational divine justice in a highly restrictive manner, which meant that he accepted the idea in theory, but balked at many of its logical conclusions.[29] Overall, Ibn Bābawayh remained firmly committed to a traditionist perspective that resembled that of al-Kulaynī before him. This included a maximalist notion of the Imām's knowledge, whereby they were familiar with the details of their deaths.

Exploring the Problem of Knowledge of Death

The remainder of this chapter examines the issue of the Imām's potential knowledge of his death as discussed by Twelver Shīʿī theologians from the late third/ninth to the mid-fourth/tenth centuries. The focal point of the analysis is Mūsā al-Kāẓim b. Jaʿfar b. Muḥammad b. ʿAlī b. Ḥusayn b. ʿAlī b. Abī Ṭālib, the seventh Imām of the Twelver Shīʿa. Al-Kāẓim was born near Medina between 127/745 and 129/746–47.[30] His mother (Ḥumayda) was of Berber or Andalusian origins and purchased from a slave dealer by his father Jaʿfar al-Ṣādiq (d. 148/765).[31] Numerous Twelver accounts emphasize Ḥumayda's unique experiences and traits, especially the divine intervention that ensured she was still a virgin at the time of her sale.[32] There are few details regarding

29. For example, the notion of rational divine justice implies that God's threats and promises must be literally true. If the Qurʾan states that a non-believer will be cast into Hell for eternity, then there can be no hope for eventual redemption. Such a harsh view was rejected by many Muslims as too cruel for a merciful God. Other implications of rational divine justice included a rejection of intercession (by the Prophet or others), along with the above mentioned necessity of free will.

30. Ibn Kathīr 13:623; al-Mufīd 288; al-Khaṭīb al-Baghdādī 13:29; Ibn al-Jawzī 9:87. For a summary of his life, see also Kohlberg, "Mūsā al-Kāẓim."

31. al-Iṣbahānī 413.

32. al-Kulaynī 1:476–77.

al-Kāẓim's childhood, most of which are cited by Twelver Shīʿī scholars to establish his right to the Imāmate. In one narrative, he speaks from the cradle and instructs one of his father's followers to change the name he had given his newborn daughter.[33] In another, he is described as a serious child not inclined toward frivolous play.[34] These scattered traditions are meant to highlight al-Kāẓim's superiority relative to his brothers.

Mūsā al-Kāẓim spent most of his life in Medina, with the exception of two periods of imprisonment. The first of these occurred during the reign of al-Mahdī (r. 158–69/775–85), but he was quickly released and allowed to return home.[35] Al-Kāẓim was arrested a second time during al-Rashīd's caliphate (r. 170–93/786–809) and was eventually transported to Baghdād, where he died in 183/799.[36] His body was placed in public display to establish his death before he was interred in a cemetery in north-west Baghdād.[37] The eighth Twelver Imām, Alī al-Riḍā (d. 203/818), was generally acknowledged as his successor, although some Shīʿa denied al-Kāẓim's death and awaited his return as the Mahdī. Such a development was hardly novel, but it was exacerbated in this instance by the high millennial expectations of the period. This group was collectively called the *wāqifiyya* (literally: "those who stop") as a result of their "stopping" with the Imāmate with al-Kāẓim.[38]

The historical sources offer a number of death accounts for al-Kāẓim. Most of the non-Twelver sources dismiss the possibility of poisoning and simply note that he died in prison.[39] In one case, the conditions of his captivity are even described as comfortable.[40] The primary disagreements in these works center on the reasons for his imprisonment, with explanations

33. He had named his child either 'Ā'isha or al-Ḥumayrā' ('Ā'isha's nickname). For this, see al-Kulaynī 1:310 and al-Mufīd 290.

34. al-Kulaynī 1:311; al-Mufīd 290.

35. al-Ṭabarī 4:588; Ibn Kathīr 13:623; al-Khaṭīb al-Baghdādī 13:32; Ibn al-Jawzī 9:87.

36. al-Ya'qūbī 2:360; al-Kulaynī 1:486; al-Ṭabarī 4:647; Ibn Bābawayh, *'Uyūn* 81, 85; al-Mufīd, *Irshād* 288, 298–392; al-Khaṭīb al-Baghdādī 13:33; Ibn al-Jawzī 9:88; Ibn al-Athīr 6:164; Ibn Kathīr 13:624. Al-Mas'ūdī (4: 216) gives a death date of 186/802.

37. al-Ya'qūbī 2:360; al-Iṣbahānī 417; al-Khaṭīb al-Baghdādī 13:33; Ibn Bābawayh *'Uyūn*, 79–82, 85.

38. For an overview of these groups, see al-Nawbakhtī 86–89 and al-Baghdādī 90–92.

39. See, for example, al-Ṭabarī 4:588, 647; al-Khaṭīb al-Baghdādī 23:29–33; 'Alī b. Bilāl 470, 482; Ibn al-Jawzī 9:87–89; and Ibn Khallikān 5:308–10.

40. al-Dhahabī, yr 181–90:417–19.

ranging from his perceived lack of deference to the al-Rashīd, to his (inadvertent) involvement in power struggles within the ʿAbbāsid court.[41] There is a greater diversity on the topic of his death in the Twelver Shīʿī sources, especially with regards to the reasons for his second arrest. All of the authors mentioned below, however, agree that he was fed poisoned dates while in the custody of al-Rashīd's agents in Baghdād. Such unanimity on the cause of death makes al-Kāẓim an ideal case study for this chapter. If he had knowledge of the poison, then why did he eat the tainted fruit?

Al-Ṣaffār

Al-Ṣaffār discusses al-Kāẓim's death in a section that contains twelve traditions regarding the Imāms' foreknowledge of their deaths. These traditions present various Imāms as either explicitly or implicitly cognizant of the time and day of their passing. In one example, Ḥasan and Ḥusayn express their disgust at (an unnamed) Ibn Muljim and predict his role in the killing of their father (ʿAlī). Two reports describe a severely ill Imām quickly recovering his health, while three others present a healthy Imām preparing for his impending death.[42] In a representative example of these accounts, the fifth Twelver Imām, al-Bāqir (d. 114 or 117/732 or 735), notes that, "I have been visited by two (unspecified beings) who informed me that I will not die from this ailment of mine."[43] He later adds, "They told me that I will die on such and such a day." These texts unambiguously assert that the Imām has clear knowledge of his end, as relayed through intermediaries. Al-Ṣaffār presents another account in which he ascribes the deaths of the Imāms to the sinful actions of the larger Twelver Shīʿī community.[44]

In most of these cases, al-Ṣaffār does not directly broach the problem of an Imām's potential complicity in his own death. ʿAlī and Ḥusayn are killed in violent confrontations with their enemies. They certainly are aware of the circumstances, but their actions do not directly contribute to their deaths. Most of the other Imāms mentioned by al-Ṣaffār in this section appear to die of natural causes. The one exception is Mūsā al-Kāẓim, whose murder is ascribed to poisoned dates provided by the ʿAbbāsid official Yaḥyā b. Khālid

41. For the most prominent example of the latter, see al-Iṣbahānī 413–18.

42. al-Ṣaffār 441–43.

43. al-Ṣaffār 441.

44. al-Ṣaffār 441–42.

al-Barmakī (d. 190/805) in two separate reports. In the first, al-Riḍā affirms an Imām's knowledge of his own death, and then explains that al-Kāẓim was aware that the dates were poisoned but was made to "forget it" in order to carry out God's command.[45] The second addresses the potential problem of suicide directly.[46] The questioner asks whether al-Kāẓim's knowing consumption of poison does not constitute complicity in his own death. The Imām responds that, "God placed forgetfulness in his heart so that the divine will was carried out." In other words, God made al-Kāẓim unaware of the poison at the moment of its consumption to shield him from accusations of suicide. Al-Ṣaffār's use of this explanation reflects his unwillingness to compromise on his belief in the maximalist knowledge of the Imām. This "forgetfulness" is a special circumstance that lasts a single fleeting moment. In every other instance, the Imām possesses comprehensive knowledge, with al-Ṣaffar going so far as to argue that an Imām who does not know the details of his own death is not the legitimate Imām.[47]

Al-Kulaynī

In his *Kāfi*, al-Kulaynī addresses the issue of al-Kāẓim's death in two separate sections. The first is biographical and includes a series of small statements that summarize the circumstances surrounding the murder.[48] The first of these (in terms of chronology) centers on al-Kāẓim's betrayal by a member of his family.[49] In this report, the Imām is aware of the impending treachery of his nephew (identified as Muḥammad b. Ismāʿīl b. Jaʿfar al-Ṣādiq), who has been promised a financial award in exchange for false testimony in the ʿAbbāsid court. Al-Kāẓim confronts Muḥammad prior to his departure from Medina, and attempts to dissuade him by offering him both an appeal to common kinship and a considerable sum of money. When questioned about his motives, al-Kāẓim notes that he does not want to sever the bonds of kinship with his nephew, as this would prompt God to shorten his life. Muḥammad rejects these overtures (feigning innocence), travels to Baghdād, and informs

45. al-Ṣaffār 441.

46. al-Ṣaffār 443.

47. al-Ṣaffār 441.

48. al-Kulaynī 1:476.

49. al-Kulaynī 1:485–86.

al-Rashīd that al-Kāẓim has set himself up as a rival caliph in Medina. Al-Rashīd then grants him a hundred thousand *dirhams*, but he is immediately stricken with diphtheria and does not live to receive the money.

As a partial consequence of this testimony, al-Rashīd orders al-Kāẓim's arrest in Medina prior to the Ḥajj on the twentieth of Shawwāl in 179/795–96. He is initially sent to Baṣra, where he is held by an 'Abbāsid official (identified as 'Īsā b. Ja'far b. al-Manṣūr) before being transferred to Baghdad, where he is remanded to the custody of al-Sindī b. Shāhik (d. 204/819) until his death on the sixth of Rajab in 183/799.[50] Al-Kulaynī explicitly identifies the cause of death as poisoning. His account, ascribed to an unnamed but trustworthy Sunnī figure in Baghdād, begins with al-Sindī b. Shāhik summoning eighty prominent men to investigate the conditions of al-Kāẓim's imprisonment.[51] Al-Sindī gestures to the Imām's comfortable quarters and derisively dismisses rumors of mistreatment. He then allows the gathered men to question al-Kāẓim directly. The Imām acknowledges the kind treatment, but then reveals that he has been fed seven poisoned dates that will cause him to turn green the following day and die the day after that. The narrator observes that al-Sindī began to tremble with fear upon hearing this.

The implication of both reports is fairly straightforward: Al-Kāẓim has a clear knowledge of the future. In the first account, he is aware of his nephew's intentions and intervenes in a manner that removes any potential ambiguity from his betrayal. Muḥammad b. Ismā'īl is motivated by avarice and self-interest, as he refuses the Imām's last-ditch effort to help him. Al-Kāẓim's actions suggest a resignation about the outcome of this intervention, but he nevertheless fulfills his familial and Imāmic responsibilities. In the second account, the Imām identifies both the cause of his poisoning (dates) and the progression of the illness that will result in his death. This revelation is particularly shocking to al-Sindī, who has treated al-Kāẓim with kindness to dispel suspicions of foul play. There is no indication here that al-Kāẓim is coerced into eating the dates; rather, al-Kāẓim's revelation is meant to expose the farce of good treatment and convey the true circumstances of his death. Al-Kāẓim makes no documented efforts to avoid the poison or postpone his death.

In a different section of his work, al-Kulaynī directly confronts the question of the Imāms' knowledge of their own deaths. The eight traditions

---

50. For an example of al-Kulaynī's propensity for succinct death narratives, see al-Kulaynī 1:476 and 1:486.

51. al-Kulaynī 1:258–59.

here closely parallel those compiled by al-Ṣaffār and are placed under the unambiguous heading "the Imāms know when they will die and that they die only by their own consent."[52] These reports suggest that the Imāms' deaths were not considered a theologically problematic issue. In most cases, it is assumed that the Imām is aware of his death and acts in accordance with that knowledge. The fourth tradition goes furthest in arguing that the death of an Imām is preordained by God.[53] This idea is further elaborated in other sections of al-Kulaynī's work. In one report, the fifth Twelver Imām, al-Bāqir, responds to a question about the rebellions[54] of the first three Imāms and their subsequent suffering by invoking divine decree (*qadar*).[55] He notes that they were aware of the consequences of their actions, but were not given a choice in the matter. This differs from the fifth and eighth traditions, in which the Imāms are presented a choice whereby they can avoid death.[56] In both cases they choose death, but this is not presented by al-Kulaynī with any sense of alarm. There is no suggestion here that their decision to die is tantamount to suicide.

Al-Kulaynī places the Imāms outside the scope of normal human experience. Their deaths are sometimes decreed with absolute certainly by God. At other times, Imāms are offered choices intimating a degree of agency. In both cases, the apparent complications associated with an Imām's knowledge of his own death are wholly absent.

Ibn Bābawayh

Ibn Bābawayh's discussion of al-Kāẓim's death is considerably more detailed than that of al-Ṣaffār or al-Kulaynī. This is partly a result of his interest in the controversy surrounding the succession of the eighth Twelver Imām, ʿAlī al-Riḍā.[57] The details of this split lie outside the scope of the present study, but the main issue (as mentioned above) concerns whether al-Kāẓim had actually died (the Twelver Shīʿa's view), or whether he remained alive in a

---

52. al-Kulaynī 1:258.

53. al-Kulaynī 1:259.

54. The Arabic term used in the text is *qiyām*.

55. al-Kulaynī 1:261–62.

56. al-Kulaynī 1:260.

57. Such a motivation is clearly evident in Ibn Bābawayh's *Uyūn,* but it also informs his *Amālī,* which is a straightforward collection of Twelver Shīʿī traditions.

state of occultation (the Wāqifī Shīʿa view). Ibn Bābawayh was invested in confirming al-Kāẓim's death and establishing the legitimacy of his successor. This required a careful and systematic narrative that confirmed Imāmic expectations for succession.[58]

Ibn Bābawayh offers four reports that touch on al-Kāẓim's death in a manner that is directly relevant to the present discussion.[59] Two of these accounts overlap (to a certain extent) with parallel traditions preserved by al-Kulaynī. In the first, al-Kāẓim is betrayed by his nephew (in this instance ʿAlī b. Ismāʿīl) in exchange for enough money to cover his debts.[60] Ibn Bābawayh explains al-Kāẓim's knowledge of this betrayal in rational terms. He simply hears of his nephew's intention to leave Medina and surmises his intention; he then offers to pay off the debt himself, but ʿAlī refuses the offer and reiterates his plan to leave the city. The episode ends with al-Kāẓim sending ʿAlī a large sum to cover his travel expenses and asking him not to orphan his (al-Kāẓim's) children. The second common report is al-Kulaynī's death account, wherein outside observers are brought in to attest to his good treatment.[61] Recall the Imām then reveals that he has been poisoned by dates, will turn green the next day, and die the day after that. In isolation, these reports suggest al-Kāẓim's foreknowledge of his own death but—as in the case of al-Kulaynī's text—they do not directly address the potential charge of suicide.

The issue of knowledge also informs two additional accounts mentioned by Ibn Bābawayh. The first reiterates his awareness of the circumstances of his death. The report involves a botched attempt to poison al-Kāẓim that results in the death of an unfortunate dog.[62] At the start of this report, al-Rashīd

58. The next Imām was expected to receive a formal designation from his predecessor (sometimes including a written document). He was then required to carry out the funeral rites of the preceding Imām, including the washing and shrouding of the corpse, and its interment.

59. There is an eighth account (Ibn Bābawayh, *ʿUyūn* 81) related by a number of unnamed Medinans which simply restates the basic facts surrounding al-Kāẓim's death.

60. There is some confusion regarding this betrayal. In al-Kulaynī's account, the ʿAlid informant is specified as Muḥammad b. Ismāʿīl b. Jaʿfar al-Ṣādiq, but Ibn Bābawayh offers two separate reports. In the first, the informant is identified as ʿAlī b. Ismāʿīl b. Jaʿfar al-Ṣādiq, who refuses al-Kāẓim's offer of paying off his debts. In the second, Muḥammad b. Jaʿfar al-Ṣādiq (upheld as the successor to al-Ṣādiq by another Shīʿa group, the Shumayṭiyya) testifies that al-Kāẓim puts himself forward as a rival caliph. Ibn Bābawayh even offers a third name, Yaʿqūb b. Dāwūd (a representative of the Zaydī Shīʿa), as a potential informant. It seems that this was a role ascribed by Twelver Shīʿa scholars to a number of their communal rivals. For these reports, see Ibn Bābawayh, *ʿUyūn* 59–60.

61. Ibn Bābawayh, *ʿUyūn* 79 and *Amālī* 132.

62. Ibn Bābawayh, *ʿUyūn* 82–85.

resolves to murder al-Kāẓim by sending him a plate of dates that includes one he has personally pierced with a needle dipped in poison. He instructs his servant to make sure that the 'Alid consumes all of the fruit by himself. Al-Kāẓim receives the plate and begins to eat the dates using a toothpick. Just then one of al-Rashīd's favorite dogs breaks free of his gold chains and approaches al-Kāẓim, who tosses him the tainted fruit before finishing off the rest. The poor dog dies a horrible painful death. The caliph is both enraged by the death of his pet and frustrated by his inability to harm al-Kāẓim. The Imām's knowledge is self-evident here and there is never a sense that he is in any real danger, despite his imprisonment. He immediately recognizes the poison and effortlessly deflects it, with no fear of the consequences. At other points in Ibn Bābawayh's text, al-Kāẓim even dismisses the concerns of his companions with the confident claim that his death is not imminent.[63]

The narrative now shifts to three days before al-Kāẓim's death, as he casually informs his prison guard (al-Musayyab[64] [d. second/eighth century]) that he is traveling to Medina to designate al-Riḍā as his successor. Al-Musayyab expresses skepticism, but the Imām chastises him for his lack of faith and reveals that he will use the same name of God that allowed the Āṣaf to retrieve Sheba's throne for Solomon.[65] He then recites the name and vanishes. He reappears some time later and refastens his own chains. The implication of this is fairly obvious: al-Kāẓim is capable of escaping prison at any time. The Imām then details the circumstances of his death. He will soon ask al-Musayyab (the narrator) for a drink of water that will cause his stomach to bloat and his skin to turn yellow, then red, and finally green, before culminating in his death. He then provides instructions about his burial and insists that al-Riḍā will appear to perform the funeral rites. After completing this speech, al-Kāẓim asks for the water and dies in the predicted manner. It is unclear whether the water itself is poisoned, or whether he was previously poisoned and the water simply activated the poison. The more likely scenario (the former) suggests that al-Kāẓim knew that the proper moment had finally arrived and took the poison willingly, after making all necessary arrangements.

---

63. See, for example, Ibn Bābawayh, *'Uyūn* 60–61, 62–64, 64–66. The last of these reports is also found in *Amālī* 336–37.

64. Al-Musayyab b. Zuhayr was a confidante of al-Rashid and a jailor of al-Kāẓim. Al-Tustarī (10:78) cites this particular incident as proof of his Shīʿī beliefs.

65. For the Qur'anic story of Solomon (Sulaymān), see Wheeler 266–79. For Āṣaf, see Tottoli, "Āṣaf b. Barakhyā."

But is this embrace of death not a potential theological problem? As noted above, al-Kulaynī exhibits no reservations at all about the fact that the Imām knows of his death and then submits to it (either voluntarily or involuntarily). Ibn Bābawayh, however, addresses this issue in two other reports. The first centers on the figure of al-Faḍl b. Rabīʿ (d. 208/823–24).[66] In this account, the narrator (ʿAbd Allāh al-Qarawī [d. second/eighth century?])[67] recalls standing on the roof of al-Faḍl's house, where he is asked about a spot on the ground of a distant house. ʿAbd Allāh initially believes that it is a piece of cloth, but then realizes that it is the form of a man in prayer. Al-Faḍl reveals the man's identity as al-Kāẓim and relates his extensive daily prayer ritual, which extends throughout the day and the night. After hearing this, the narrator cautions al-Faḍl to refrain from harming the Imām lest this bring misfortune upon him. Al-Faḍl notes that he has received orders to kill al-Kāẓim, but has repeatedly refused to carry them out. Al-Kāẓim is later transferred to the custody of al-Faḍl b. Yaḥyā al-Barmakī (d. 187/803), but al-Faḍl b. Rabīʿ continues to send him food each day. On the fourth day, however, al-Kāẓim's daily rations are provided by his new jailor (i.e., al-Faḍl b. Yaḥyā). Al-Kāẓim then raises his hands to the sky and testifies that he would have been guilty of killing himself had he previously eaten the poisoned food. He then reveals the signs of his poisoning to a doctor who informs the caliph that al-Kāẓim is perfectly aware of the situation.

In a variant report, Ibn Bābawayh offers an alternate perspective on the issue.[68] This report places al-Kāẓim's death in the context of a different court intrigue in which the Imām is (falsely) implicated in an alleged plot against the caliph (the details of which are outside the scope of this chapter). The episode results in the caliph ordering (*yaḥtim ʿalayhī*) al-Sindī b. Shāhik to force al-Kāẓim to eat poisoned dates. There is little ambiguity here, as the Imām is not given a choice at all. Even if the Imām is aware of the poison, he is nevertheless compelled to consume it, thereby absolving him of any potential responsibility for his death.

In these final two reports, Ibn Bābawayh directly engages the potential problem associated with al-Kāẓim's knowledge of his death. The first

66. Ibn Bābawayh, *ʿUyūn* 76–78; and *Amālī* 130–32. The *Amālī* provides the most detailed account, especially with respect to al-Kāẓim's transfer to the custody of al-Faḍl al-Barmakī and his examination by the doctor.

67. In the *Amālī*, the *nisba* is given as al-Farawī with the editor suggesting al-Gharawī as a possible alternative. (Ibn Bābawayh, *Amālī* 130).

68. Ibn Bābawayh, *ʿUyūn* 82–84.

solution (decree) is not wholly satisfying, as it reverts back to the idea of divine decree, but (more importantly) the text acknowledges the dilemma and tries to differentiate complicity in one's own death from an act that is preordained by God. This aligns with Ibn Bābawayh's belief in "pre-estimation," by which God "did not compel an action but created the causal means for its performance."[69] Such a view tries to combine belief in a predetermined outcome with an affirmation of a conditional human agency. The Imām demonstrates a willingness to confront the caliph, but he also possesses knowledge of God's larger plan. His embrace of death may suggest a kind of suicide but it is—in fact—simply an acquiescence to the divine will. The second solution (compulsion) offers more satisfaction and absolves the Imām by removing agency altogether. This might seem like the better solution, but Ibn Bābawayh notably places it outside his section on reliable death reports pertaining to al-Kāẓim. In other words, he gives primacy to the account in which al-Kāẓim's death is an acquiescence to God's will.

Summarizing the Explanations

Four potential solutions to the problem of al-Kāẓim's knowledge of his death are embedded in the works of al-Ṣaffār, al-Kulaynī, and Ibn Bābawayh. The first involves God making the Imām forget this information in the moment prior to those actions that culminate in his death. This is the explanation favored by al-Ṣaffār, whose work is expressly invested in establishing a maximalist view of Imāmic knowledge. The second solution involves a straightforward affirmation of predestination in which the Imām submits to God's decree. Accounts of this variety do not even acknowledge the problem of suicide, as the issue makes little sense given the absolute absence of agency. Al-Kulaynī relies on this type of explanation in a majority of his accounts. Ibn Bābawayh is less categorical but he certainly implies a kind of predetermination within his historical reports. The third solution, by contrast, suggests a kind of agency wherein the Imām is asked to choose between his death and some other outcome. Al-Kulaynī preserves two reports of this type. In the first, God is angered by the Shīʿa and gives al-Kāẓim the choice between protecting himself or his community.[70] He chooses the community and thereby sacrifices his life. In the second, Ḥusayn is offered the choice between victory and reunion with God.

69. Haider, *Shīʿī*, 148.

70. al-Kulaynī 1:260.

He chooses God, which results in his death at Karbalāʾ.[71] The fourth solution contends that the Imām (in this case, al-Kāẓim) was compelled by an agent of the caliph to consume the poison. This view, forwarded by Ibn Bābawayh, defuses the question of complicity altogether.

Looking Forward

The scholars mentioned above were certainly aware of the potential complications resulting from an Imām with prior knowledge of his death. None of them, however, address these complications by explicitly limiting the scope of the Imāms' knowledge. As Modarressi has shown, there were certainly early Twelver Shīʿī scholars who strongly advocated for a rationalist understanding of the Imāmate, which placed limits on knowledge.[72] Beginning in the later fourth/tenth century, the influence of these rationalist ideas were increasingly felt in the work of the community's most prominent scholars who engaged the seeming contradiction between the Imām's knowledge and his death. As mentioned at the beginning of this chapter, such discussions focused, in particular, on the murder of ʿAlī and the events surrounding Ḥusayn's killing in Karbalāʾ.

The two scholars cited most frequently in subsequent discussions of the issue were al-Shaykh al-Mufīd and (most importantly) al-Sharīf al-Murtaḍāʾ. The details of their arguments lie outside the scope of this chapter, but their general conclusions are worthy of mention. Al-Mufīd, who moved to Baghdād as a child (by 347/958), was a leading figure in the Twelver Shīʿī community in the fourth/tenth century. In terms of theology, al-Mufīd held to a number of positions associated with the Muʿtazila (e.g., rational divine justice, free will) but remained a staunch defender of the Twelver doctrine of the Imāmate. In his view, the Imāms possessed special knowledge, as well as the ability to perform miracles. The extent of this knowledge, however, did not necessarily extend to the circumstances of their deaths. As a number of modern scholars have noted, al-Mufīd did not argue that ʿAlī or Ḥusayn were aware of the exact details of their killings. Even if this were the case, he suggested that their actions would not be tantamount to suicide, but rather a mark of honor or an act of grace for the larger community.[73]

---

71. al-Kulaynī 1:260.

72. Modarressi 107–31.

73. Note the connection between this latter reason and al-Kulaynī's explanation that the Imām chooses to die rather than to subject his community to God's wrath for their sinfulness. See Abdulsater, *Climax* 342, footnote 1011 and the primary sources cited therein.

Al-Mufīd's views are reflected in his *Kitāb al-irshād*. This historical work, which includes biographical entries for each of the Imāms, established the basic framework for all future Twelver Shī'ī works in this genre. Al-Mufīd's biography of al-Kāẓim concludes with a single composite imprisonment/death narrative, in which the Imām is caught up in the political intrigues within the 'Abbāsid court.[74] The account includes the betrayal by his nephew (here identified as 'Alī b. Ismā'īl) that precipitates his arrest. After a detailed discussion of court politics, al-Mufīd preserves a death account in which al-Sindī b. Shāhik offers the Imām poisoned food or tainted dates. He falls ill and dies three days later. Prominent figures in Baghdād are then summoned to attest to the fact that his body bears no signs of violence or mistreatment. In accordance with al-Mufīd's view that Imāms (likely) lacked detailed knowledge about their deaths, there is no discussion of the logistics of the poisoning. The text leaves open the possibilities that (1) the Imām was forced to consume the poison, or (2) he was unaware of the poison in the first place. Subsequent Twelver Shī'ī historical works followed closely in the footsteps of al-Mufīd, replicating his death account and similarly eliding the problem of the Imām's knowledge.[75]

Al-Sharīf al-Murtaḍā succeeded al-Mufīd as the leader of the Twelver Shī'ī community in Baghdād.[76] In his theological works, al-Murtaḍā went further than al-Mufīd in espousing views generally associated with the Mu'tazila. The most important of these involved the claim that reason alone (to the exclusion of revelation) could establish the fundamentals of religion and (by extension) validate seminal Twelver Shī'ī beliefs. Given his embrace of rationalist Mu'tazilī discourse, it is not surprising that al-Murtaḍā explicitly rejected the possibility that the Imāms knew the details of their deaths.[77] Whereas al-Mufīd was willing to hedge on the issue, al-Murtaḍā was unequivocal in his view that possession of such knowledge (in combination with his affirmation of free will) would constitute suicide. This was an unthinkable conclusion and was rejected as such.

Al-Murtaḍā's solution to the problem did not permanently settle the matter; rather, the issue of the scope of the Imāms' knowledge remains

74. al-Mufīd 298–302.

75. See, for example, al-Irbilī 3:19–23.

76. For a much-needed biography of al-Murtaḍā, see Abdulsater, *Shī'a Doctrine*, chapter 1 (forthcoming). For a brief summary of al-Murtaḍā's theological positions, see Haider, *Shī'ī Islam* 149–50 and sources cited therein.

77. Abdulsater, *Climax* 307, footnote 902 and primary sources cited therein.

contested into the modern period.[78] In the aftermath of al-Murtaḍā (and al-Mufīd), however, there was a framework for subsequent scholars who composed commentaries on their theological works. The traditions preserved by al-Ṣaffār and al-Kulaynī and the historical reports of Ibn Bābawayh continue to appear in later historical works, but the nature of the discussion is quite different. The central issue is the degree to which Imāms knew the minute details of their deaths, as opposed to more complicated early efforts to reconcile this knowledge (taken as fact) with the reality of their unnatural deaths.

78. For a good (and somewhat controversial) contemporary discussion, see al-Ṣāliḥī al-Najafʾābādī, 433–60 and, in particular, 433–7 and 451–60. I thank Hossein Modarressi for pointing me to this source.

7

Apologia for Suicide

MARTYRDOM IN CONTEMPORARY JIHADIST DISCOURSE

Mohammed M. Hafez

THE LITANY OF suicide attacks perpetrated by militant Islamists against security forces, civilians, and even their coreligionists no longer astonishes their observers. Suicide bombings are reported dispassionately by the news media, and the shocking terror they once evoked in the mass public has gradually faded, as they have become commonplace around the globe. Even in the Muslim world, where the vast majority of these attacks occur, the targeted populations have become resigned to their devastating effect. More perplexing, perhaps, is the seemingly endless supply of "martyrs" who hail from all parts of the world, eagerly willing to kill so many as they kill themselves. This once controversial tactic that defies the instinct of self-preservation—and one that violates so many moral taboos—has become the new normal for militant Islamists.

Violent extremists associated with the Islamic State (ISIS), Boko Haram, and al-Qaeda have standardized the use of human bombs in their repertoire of violence and no longer feel compelled to defend this tactic against their critics.[1] It is hard to recall a time when the act of self-immolation was fiercely debated, requiring extraordinary justification against theological

1. Interestingly, the progenitors of suicide attacks in the Muslim world—Hezbollah and Hamas—have long since abandoned them, although they have not recanted their presumed legitimacy.

objections.[2] After all, suicide in Islam is strictly forbidden; killing oneself is the surest path to eternal damnation. Although the Qur'an cannot be said to be explicitly against suicide, verse 4:29, which reads "Nor kill (or destroy) yourselves" has come to be understood as a prohibition against suicide, as has verse 2:195, which cautions "cast not yourselves by your own hands into destruction" (Rosenthal 243). However, it is in the Prophetic tradition cited in both *sahih* (authentic) canons of Bukhari and Muslim that we find the clearest expression against suicide: "And whoever commits suicide with a piece of iron will be punished with the same piece of iron in the Hell Fire" (al-Bukhari, *Funerals* Chapter 83, and Muslim, *Faith* Chapter 47). Several variations on this theme are found in all compilations of authentic traditions, making the impermissibility of suicide settled doctrine in the Islamic heritage. How, then, did jihadists succeed in turning controversy into convention? By what alchemy were they able to transform that which is forbidden in Islam into a new militant orthodoxy?

Radical Islamists have constructed a permissive ideational structure that apparently anchors suicide attacks in Islamic texts and traditions. This structure rests on three lines of argumentation: the euphemistic labeling of suicide as martyrdom; the elevation of human intentionality above textual forms of authority; and the inference of normative precedent from Islam's formative generation. Jihadists insist that there is a qualitative difference between suicide (*qatl al-nafs* or *intihhar*) and martyrdom (*shahada* or *istishhad*); the former is rejected as religiously impermissible (*haram*), while the latter is venerated in Islam. Contemporary suicide attacks are a form of martyrdom, not suicide. What differentiates suicide from martyrdom is the intention behind the act, in accordance with the authentic Prophetic tradition that "actions are (judged) only according to intentions" (*innama al-a'amalu bil-niyyat*) (Muslim, *Government* Chapter 45). Suicide is designed to kill oneself, while the chief aim of a suicide attack is to kill the enemies of Muslims. Human intentionality is the key to legitimating the act of self-immolation. Lastly, jihadists point out that the companions of the Prophet, upon hearing the rewards of martyrdom, charged the enemy with enthusiasm (*inghimas fil-saf*) in order to hasten their own demise and earn the benefits of martyrdom. Suicide attacks today are a form of *inghimas* that is sanctioned by the normative example of the Prophet's companions.

---

2. For a comprehensive analysis of these earlier debates, see Hatina, Chapter 7; Cook, Chapter 8; and al-Takrouri, Chapter 4.

This chapter explores each of these arguments with a critical eye. It draws attention to the inherent tension between the jihadists' "hyper-textual approach" (Haykel 45) to adducing religious opinions, on the one hand, and on the other, their extra-textual rationalization of a religiously controversial tactic. Suicide bombings today are largely carried out by organizations that refer to themselves as Jihadi Salafists. These organizations have rejected many of the norms and institutions associated with modernity, including democracy and the very construct of the national civil state. They deride interpretive rationalizations that seek to make accommodation with modern values as nothing more than creedal innovation (*bid'ah*) destined to lead their adherents to Hell. Yet, when it comes to suicide bombings, they cast aside their strict constructionist ethos and, instead, choose to interpret away clear and absolute prohibitions against suicide in the inherited tradition in order to justify a modern tactic of utilitarian value. They go beyond the original interpretation (*tafsir*) of jihad verses, reading in them figurative meaning (*ta'wil*) and an inner essence (*ma khalf dahir al-nus*) that permits acts of self-immolation. In doing so, they seek to bolster their religious authenticity at the expense of the Salafist methodology to which they presumably adhere. It is not a surprise, therefore, that this methodological slippage has resulted in other interpretive innovations, such as the permissibility of killing of civilians and coreligionists, which are also clearly prohibited in Islam (Hafez, "The Alchemy of Martyrdom").

Jihadi Salafism and the Suicide Problematic

Contemporary Salafism is a strand of Islamism that idealizes the first generation of Muslims, who lived through the prophetic mission of Muhammad, gave birth to the rightly guided successors (*al-khulafa al-rashidun*), and saw the companions of the Prophet (*sahaba*) spread Islam beyond the Arabian Peninsula. They also venerate subsequent generations of learned scholars who closely followed in the footsteps of the first generation (*tabi'un*). Collectively, they are referred to as *al-Salaf al-Salih* (the righteous ancestors), hence their label as Salafists. Salafism today can be equated with traditionalists who developed their thinking in the eighth and ninth centuries and are known as *ashab al-hadith* (people of Prophetic traditions) or *ahl al-sunna wal jama'a* (adherents of right practice and communal solidarity) (Crone, Chapter 11). They reject heterodoxy and insist on purifying religious practices from the taint of heretical beliefs, speculative philosophy, cultural accretions, and ritualistic innovations.

In practice, Salafist scholars are strict constructionists who prefer narrow interpretations of revealed scripture and Prophetic traditions, and shun reconsideration of historically settled doctrine. This means that when considering an issue of concern to Muslims today, they would first reference the Qur'an and determine what its verses have to say about the matter. They would also reference the authentic traditions of the Prophet and see what he said and did with regards to the issue at hand. A religious ruling (*fatwa*) by a Salafist scholar invariably begins with citations of a plethora of verses from the Qur'an and Prophetic traditions. To the extent that the Salafist scholar calls on other authorities to make a case for a particular position, he relies on the sayings and deeds of the Prophet's companions, as well as the rulings of tradition-minded scholars who insisted on textual forms of authority and were hostile to speculative theology, philosophical rationalism, and allegorical interpretations (*t'awil*). If verses in the Qur'an are deemed clear (*ayat muhkamat*) and their commands absolute (*ahkam qat'iyyah*), and if Prophetic traditions clearly support their meaning, then the matter is virtually closed for discussion. The explicit and unequivocal scriptures (*muhkamat*) must be treated as eternal and ineligible for reinterpretation, as they are the foundations (*umm al-kitab*) upon which scholars build their jurisprudence and clarify verses that may carry multiple meanings (*ayat mutashabihat;* Bazmool 12–13). Thus, when it comes to settled doctrine, contemporary Salafists encourage their followers to adhere closely to the revealed text, and downplay the role of human interpretive capacity and extra-textual rationality in their methodology (*manhaj*).

Jihadi Salafists, in contradistinction to quietist Salafists who emphasize obedience to Muslim rulers and prefer preaching to militancy, have actively sought to legitimate suicide attacks. As a result, they have encountered a barrage of criticism from traditionalists, who point out that these operations involve that which God has forbidden: namely, suicide. Notable Salafist scholars and grand muftis, such as Sheikh Naser al-Din al-Albani, Sheikh Ibn al-'Uthaimin, Sheikh Abdel Aziz bin Baz, and Sheikh Abdel Aziz 'Al al-Sheikh, rejected suicide attacks because of their presumed violation of the plain Islamic prohibition against suicide. (It must be said that some of these scholars equivocated in their opposition, largely due to the popular support suicide bombers received in the context of the Arab-Israeli and Chechen conflicts.)[3] They also objected

3. Al-Albani, for instance, ruled that this tactic could only be ordered by an Islamic commander waging a jihad under the banner of an Islamic state, not an individual act or one by a zealous group. Al-'Uthaimin conditioned the permissibility of suicide attacks upon bringing great advantages to Muslims. If they bring harm, as they appear to do, then they cannot be

to the indiscriminate nature of suicide bombings, their prevalence outside of clearly demarcated arenas of legitimate jihad, and their authorization in the absence of a clearly established Islamic leader presiding over a state. Even some radical ideologues have raised questions about the seemingly limitless use of this tactic, and its controversial targeting of civilians and coreligionists (al-Maqdisi, and al-Tartusi). Others approve its use under clearly defined conditions, which would practically make its deployment a rare occurrence.[4]

The principle argument of critics is a rather simple one: Islam is unequivocally against suicide. The preponderance of evidence from the Qur'an and the tradition supports this view, they argue, making the matter closed for discussion. In addition to the aforementioned verses and hadith, we may add the following to the list:

> Qur'an 2:258: "My Lord is the one who gives life and causes death."
> Qur'an 3:145: "And it is not [possible] for one to die except by permission of Allah at a decree determined."
> Qur'an 6:151: "And do not kill the soul which Allah hath forbidden [to be killed] except by [legal] right."
> Hadith: The Prophet said of a man who hastened his own death by leaning on his sword after he was severely wounded in battle, "indeed, he is amongst the people of the (Hell) Fire." (al-Bukhari, *The Book of Jihad* Chapter 77)
> Hadith: "None amongst you should make a request for death, and do not call for it before it comes, for when any one of you dies, he ceases (to do good) deeds and the life of a believer is not prolonged but for goodness." (Muslim, *Remembrance of Allah* Chapter 4)

Based on these verses and Prophetic traditions, classical Islamic scholars converged in the opinion that suicide is a grave sin, even though they disagreed as to whether it makes one an unbeliever (Rosenthal 42).

---

used. Sheikh 'Al al-Sheikh simply did not deem them viable per Islamic jurisprudence. See al-Takrouri 105–06, 173–74, and 178–79, respectively.

4. Sheikh Salman al-'Ouda, a renowned Saudi Salafist scholar, laid down five conditions that must be met before authorizing a martyrdom operation: 1) the goal must be to raise God's law on earth; 2) the operation should have high probability that it would harm the enemy; 3) the target must be unbelievers who had declared war on Muslims; 4) the operation must be inside a Muslim land that is under attack or occupation (i.e. defensive jihad); and 5) the proposed martyr must seek the permission of both parents. See al-Takrouri 166–67.

Opposition from tradition-minded scholars poses a challenge to Jihadi Salafists who, on the one hand, wish to uphold their image of authentic bearers of Islamic legitimacy, and, on the other, recognize the operational and strategic advantages of human bombs. Consequently, proponents of suicide bombings had to find a way to anchor their military preferences in classical Islamic sources and traditions. In this regard, they benefited immensely from early scholarly support for "martyrdom operations" in the context of the Arab-Israeli conflict.[5] A number of radical Islamists, including Salafists, have stepped forward to assert that suicide bombings are indeed religiously sanctioned. They did so by abandoning their strict constructionist reading of revealed texts and traditions. They turned, instead, to *ta'wil* (figurative interpretations) to frame martyrdom verses and traditions, as well as examples from Islam's formative period, as permissive of suicide operations.

Martyrdom, Not Suicide: The Euphemistic Labeling of Self-Immolation

Jihadists reject the labeling of operations that involve self-destruction as suicide attacks (*'amaliyat intihariyah*). Rather, they insist that these should be characterized as martyrdom operations (*'amaliyat istishhadiyah*), Jihadi operations (*'amaliyat jihadia*), or sacrifice operations (*'amaliyat fida'iyah*) (Muhammad 203–04). Moreover, their perpetrators should be called martyrs in this world, and it is up to the Lord to determine whether they are indeed martyrs (*shuhada'*, singl. *shahid*), based on the sincerity of their intentions and legitimacy of their cause (al-'Ayiri; al-Takrouri).

Jihadists begin their case by insisting that the Qur'an recognizes and venerates the category of the martyr in verses 2:154, 2:207, 3:169, 4:69, 4:74, 4:95–96, and 9:20–22 (Farghal; al-'Amili). The two most-cited verses, however, are the following:

> Qur'an 9:111: "Allah hath purchased of the believers their persons and their goods; for theirs (in return) is the garden (of Paradise): they fight in His cause, and slay and are slain: a promise binding on Him in truth."
>
> Qur'an 61:10–12: "O you who have believed, shall I guide you to a transaction that will save you from a painful punishment? [It is that]

---

5. For the many religious rulings from various Sunni authorities permitting suicide attacks against Israel, see al-Takrouri 119–72.

> you believe in Allah and His Messenger and strive in the cause of Allah with your wealth and your lives. That is best for you, if you should know. He will forgive for you your sins and admit you to gardens beneath which rivers flow and pleasant dwellings in gardens of perpetual residence. That is the great attainment."

Moreover, God commands Muslims to fight the unbelievers with whatever means are at their disposal, including their lives:

> Qur'an 9:41: "Go forth, whether light or heavy, and strive with your wealth and your lives in the cause of Allah. That is better for you, if you only knew."

They go on to point out that Prophetic traditions are equally replete with references to martyrdom:

> Hadith: "Nobody who dies and has something good for him with Allah will (ever like to) return to this world even though he were offered the whole world and all that is in it (as an inducement), except the martyr who desires to return and be killed in the world for the (great) merit of martyrdom that he has seen." (Muslim, *Government* Chapter 29)
>
> Hadith: Upon affirming that the Prophet declared, "Surely, the gates of Paradise are under the shadows of the swords," a man bid his friends farewell, broke the sheath of his sword and advanced towards the enemy and fought them until he was slain. (Muslim, *Government* Chapter 41).

In the first tradition, martyrdom can be desired, even if not self-induced. In latter traditions, however, the act of breaking the sheath of the sword implies certainty of death, because the fighter presumes that he will not return to sheath his weapon.

Based on these verses and Prophetic traditions, proponents of suicide operations aver that Islam presents Muslims with two paradigms: suicide and martyrdom. One is clearly prohibited, but the latter is sanctioned and venerated (al-'Ayiri 5). Suicide is associated with a lack of patience (*sabr*), or failing God's trial, as per verses 2:155–56: "And We will surely test you with something of fear and hunger and a loss of wealth and lives and fruits, but give good tidings to the patient, who, when disaster strikes them, say, 'Indeed we belong to Allah, and indeed to Him we will return.' " Martyrdom, on the other hand, is about faithful righteousness, or heeding God's command to exchange one's life for the hereafter (*ishtara al-akhira bi dunya*).

Suicide is sinful, earning one a place in Hell; martyrdom is noble sacrifice rewarded generously in the hereafter (al-'Ayiri 5). Classic Islamic scholars debated whether it is permissible to pray for those who committed suicide, but there were no debates as to the status of martyrs, because according to the Qur'an (verse 4:49), they are "in the company of those whom God has favored," a category that includes the prophets, the saints, and the righteous. Suicidal persons seek to escape their personal misery, whereas martyrs seek heroic death in order to redeem their nation and bring benefit to Muslims. Martyrdom is inherently about personal strength (whereas suicide betrays feebleness); optimism (whereas suicide is rooted in pessimism); and the will to victory (whereas suicide is the ultimate expression of defeatism) (al-Qardawi 34).

A critic may point out that the euphemistic labeling of suicide attacks as martyrdom operations leaves unaddressed the issue of God's prerogative over terminating life, as per the aforementioned verse 3:145. Fighting in the path of God and seeking martyrdom in the Islamic tradition invariably involved waging battle, taking extraordinary risks, and dying at the hands of the adversary, which, theoretically speaking, leaves inviolate God's domain over life and death (Ayoub 164–65). As one Salafist detractor of these attacks points out, Qur'an verse 3:140, which declares, "We alternate among the people so that Allah may make evident those who believe and [may] take to Himself from among you martyrs," is textual proof that, ultimately, it is God's prerogative to select who becomes a martyr and who is spared (Suhaymee). It is said that the Muslim commander Khalid Ibn al-Walid, whose appellation "The Sword of God" honors his prolific conquests, was deeply saddened on his deathbed that he did not die as a martyr. Suicide attacks, therefore, cross the boundary that divides probabilistic outcomes, which leave one's ultimate fate up to God's will, and deterministic ones in which the outcome is preordained by someone other than God.

Human Intentionality is the Sine Qua Non of Martyrdom

The key to understanding the distinction between suicide and martyrdom is the intention of the actor. There is a qualitative difference between the intention of a person committing suicide to kill oneself, and one using his or her body to deliver explosives to kill enemies in a jihad. In the first instance, the primary objective is to put an end to one's life, and the only target is the self. In a martyrdom operation, the primary objective is to dispatch one's adversaries—but for that objective, the actor would not contemplate harming himself. Moreover, whereas suicide is intended for its own sake and in violation of Islam's commandment against self-destruction, martyrdom is never intended for its own sake, but rather, for the purpose of elevating God's word on earth and in the general interest of the Muslim nation (al-Falistini).

Proponents of suicide attacks point to the Prophetic tradition in which Muhammad narrates a pre-Islamic story of the boy (*al-ghulam*) and the impious king. The boy becomes a believer after encountering a monk, and others become believers after encountering the boy who, due to his faith in God, is able to cure blindness and leprosy. The wicked king orders his men to kill the young man unless he recants his faith, but the boy refuses to do so, and all attempts to kill him fail, due to divine intervention. Finally the boy, in an act of martyrdom, offers the king the method by which to kill him. He tells the king to gather the people around, tie him to a tree, take an arrow out of the boy's quiver, and shoot it at him while declaring "In the name of Allah, the Lord of the boy." The death of the young man confirms his divine inspiration and leads others to declare their faith in God, further enraging the king. He orders his men to dig a pit of fire and force those who refuse to renounce their faith to jump to their fiery deaths. All accepted their fate, but a woman with a child hesitated to jump until her child spoke: "O mother, endure (this ordeal) for it is the Truth" (Muslim, *Piety and Softening of Hearts* Chapter 17).

This narrative is presented as a proof-text that embracing death with the intention of elevating God's creed on earth is legitimate martyrdom, not suicide. The boy facilitated his own death to make manifest God's existence, not to end his personal misery. The "Companions of the Pit" (*ashab al-ukhdud*) choose death over recantation, and the Qur'an (verse 85:11) notes of them, "Indeed, those who have believed and done righteous deeds will have gardens beneath which rivers flow. That is the great attainment." In other words, in the eyes of God, they are worthy of paradise, not suicides deserving damnation. Similarly, suicide bombers sacrifice their bodies not for the sake of death, but in order to advance the causes of Muslims. Their martyrdom should be viewed in similar light and presumed to have the proper intention.

However, others suggest that proper intention alone is insufficient to deem self-immolation legitimate martyrdom. The act must also be linked to collective benefits (*maslaha al-'amma*) for Muslims.[6] Abu Qatada al-Falistini, a radical Salafist ideologue, anchors the legitimacy of martyrdom operations in the notion of Muslim interests. The death of a suicidal person benefits no one, but the death of a martyr brings all Muslims great advantages. Martyrdom operations dispatch many enemies in a single blow, and do so with only few Muslim fighters. They strike terror in the hearts of the enemy, making manifest the firm determination of the faithful (*salabat al-muslimeen fi din*) and their desire for the eternal afterlife over this fleeting world. Such dedication and sacrifice demoralizes the enemy and deters them from further attacks on Muslims. A martyr's death, moreover, might serve as inspiration for others to fight, or shame bystanders (*al-qa'idun*) into action (al-Falistini).

The notion of human intentionality in assessing conduct seems well anchored in the aforementioned Prophetic tradition, "actions are (judged) only according to intentions." However, for strict constructionists at least two issues arise. The first relates to the Islamic rejection of the consequentialist principle of "the ends justify the means." It is a generally accepted jurisprudential principle that if the means are forbidden, the ends they seek to affect cannot justify them. The second issue relates to how to balance the inherently subjective assessment of the presumed benefits (*masalih*) of suicide attacks against the absolute and clear imperative to refrain from the evils (*mafasid*) of suicide, especially when other means of combat exist.

Jihadists insist that in their present condition of defensive warfare and military feebleness, "necessity renders prohibited things permissible" (*al-dharourat tubih al-mahdhourat*). This jurisprudential principle (*qa'ida fiqhiyah*) is derived from the Qur'an verse 2:173, which gives Muslims permission to eat that which is prohibited if forced by necessity. The necessity of fighting effectively to save Muslims from subjugation renders suicidal operations permissible.

Moreover, they argue that when one encounters two evils (in this case individual suicide or defeat at the hands of the enemy), one chooses the lesser evil as per the jurisprudential principle that "the greater evil is repelled by the lesser evil" (*daf'a a'adham al-dararayn bihtimal akhaffihima*).[7] They point

---

6. Other than some Maliki jurists, classical scholars generally required that these acts must inflict harm on the enemy. The intention of martyrdom alone is insufficient to justify self-sacrifice. See al-Takrouri 79.

7. Qur'anic verse 2:217 is referenced to support this principle. "They ask you about the sacred month––about fighting therein. Say, 'Fighting therein is great [sin], but averting [people] from the way of Allah and disbelief in Him and [preventing access to] al-Masjid al-Haram and the expulsion of its people therefrom are greater [evil] in the sight of Allah."

to the historic precedent of killing Muslim human shields (*qatl al-turse*) as proof that suicide operations are permissible, as long as they bear benefit to Muslims. Based on this precedent, Hanbali scholar Ibn Taymiyyah (1236–1328) ruled that it is permissible for Muslims to kill their co-religionists if they are used as human shields against invaders (Haykal 1329). In this case, while killing fellow Muslims is a grave sin, the greater evil is to permit enemies of Islam to achieve victory. The latter harms the collective interests of Muslims, while the lesser evil is the private harm incurred to those who are fatally wounded as a result of attacks on the human shields (al-Azdi). In accordance with this ruling, if it is permissible for Muslims under certain circumstances to inflict harm on other Muslims to benefit the entirety of the Muslim nation, then surely it is permissible for Muslims to inflict self-harm to benefit their community. Killing human shields involves two evils: the death of an innocent Muslim (tragedy) at the hand of a believing Muslim (sin). Yet, the two evils are permitted to avoid a third and greater evil, which is defeat at the hands of unbelievers. Suicide operations, on the other hand, involve only one evil—suicide (sin)—to avoid the greater evil of defeat at the hands of unbelievers. Given the hierarchy of lesser and greater evils, if the rule permitting the two evils associated with the killing of Muslim human shields is valid, then it is logical that the ruling concerning the permissibility of suicide attacks is also valid since the latter involves one less sin than the former.[8]

Charging the Enemy: Normative Precedents from the Companions

It is vitally important for Jihadi Salafists to find normative precedents from the first three generations of Muslims to solidify their claim that self-induced martyrdom is legitimate in the contemporary era. In their view, examples from the Prophet's companions are acceptable proof (*dalil*) that their deeper construal (*ta'wil*) of martyrdom verses is not mere speculative interpretation (*ta'wil biduna dalil*). Here they point to the precedent of charging the ranks of the enemy (*inghimas fi al-saf*) as proof that the pious ancestors permitted self-sacrifice. During Islam's formative period, the Prophet's companions, upon learning the benefits of martyrdom, charged the enemy and plunged

8. See the fatwa by Sheikh Hamoud bin 'Aqla al-Shu'aybi in al-Takrouri 156–61.

into battle knowing that the odds of survival were infinitesimal—indeed, many hoped that they would die as martyrs.[9]

This paradigm of charging the enemy was considered as martyrdom seeking, not suicide. None other than the venerable Ibn Taymiyyah deemed *inghimas* as a legitimate act of warfare (Ibn Taymiyyah). The example of al-Bara bin Malik al-Ansari is often cited as proof that the companions approved of *inghimas*. During the apostasy wars following the death of the Prophet, Muslims loyal to Abu Bakr as-Siddiq waged battle with the tribe of Banu Hanifah, led by Musaylimah bin Habib ("The Liar"). As the latter began to suffer defeats in the Battle of Yamama, his men retreated to a garden with high walls. After fortifying its gates, Musaylimah's men attacked the army of Khaled Ibn al-Walid with arrows from their secure position. One of the fighters was al-Bara bin Malik, who asked his men to lift him above the wall so he could enter the garden and open its gates, knowing that he will likely die as a martyr. When his men refused, he insisted that they do so. After leaping over the wall, he fought off many of Musaylimah's men and managed to open the gates. Interestingly, despite sustaining severe wounds, he survived and eventually recovered. His desire for martyrdom, however, did not abate. He eventually achieved his wish during the conquest of Tustar in Persia.[10]

Critics of this argument point out that *inghimas* still leaves the door open for survival and one's ultimate fate to God alone; suicide operations infringe on God's prerogative of selecting martyrs at the time of his choosing, as in the case of Bara bin Malik who survived the apostasy wars and died in the conquest of Persia. Moreover, there are strict conditions that constrain this behavior, making it an exception to the rule, not the new norm in jihadi operations. Ibn Taymiyyah and other scholars have concluded that *inghimas* is permitted in actual battle, when Muslim fighters are outnumbered in the field, and when there is a clear collective benefit for the Muslims (Hatina 48–49). In other words, they should be carried out when there appears to be no other options for waging battle against the opposing side. This is not the case in the early twenty-first century, where suicide attacks are nearly daily events. Moreover, many suicide attacks target civilians and Muslims deemed unbelievers (i.e. Shīʿa) by jihadists, and these operations take place not on

---

9. For many examples of *inghimas* in early Islamic history, see al-ʿAyiri.

10. It is noteworthy that Al-Qaeda in Iraq named its suicide brigade the Bara bin Malik Brigade.

the battlefield, but in cities, markets, religious processions, and even mosques (Hafez, "Takfir and Violence").

Conclusion

The rate of suicide bombings carried out by so-called jihadists around the world is mind-boggling. Many of these militants adhere to the Salafist strand of Islamism, which is known for its strict constructionist reading of the Islamic tradition, elevating scripture and Prophetic traditions above reason, and chiding those who would seek to reinterpret settled doctrine. Their approach to Islamic jurisprudence is known for its outright antipathy to creedal innovation (*bid'ah*), which they associate with heterodoxy and modernist interpretations of Islam. Given the strict constructionist orientation of the Jihadi Salafist movement, how could their ideologues justify suicide attacks that require self-immolation, which involves a grave sin?

This chapter notes that Jihadi Salafists have reverted to a hyper-interpretive (*ta'wil*) methodology that contravenes their strict constructionist orientation to textual authority. When it serves their objectives, they do not hesitate to set aside clear verses (*muhkamat*) and traditions concerning suicide which have bequeathed absolute rulings (*ahkam qatiyya*) against self-immolation throughout the Islamic heritage. Instead, they have anchored their apologia for suicide in jihad verses, traditions, and historical precedents that are subject to multiple interpretations (*mutashabihat*), and in which the desire for martyrdom through extraordinary risk is equivalent to suicide. While they appear to draw their opinions from textual sources and normative traditions, in this respect they ignore the inclination of tradition-minded scholars and jurists to reconcile apparent tensions within Qur'anic verses and prophetic traditions by privileging *muhkamat* verses over ambiguous ones, establishing the conditions that permit exceptions to general rules, and relying on the jurisprudence of abrogation (*naskh*), where later revelations supersede earlier ones when they appear to be in conflict. In short, it is no mere exaggeration to say that the Jihadi Salafists opportunistically shift between jurisprudence methodologies to justify their strategic and tactical inclinations in their wars against a host of enemies. Perhaps it is they whom the Qur'an was referencing in verse 3:7:

> It is He who has sent down to you, [O Muhammad], the Book; in it are verses [that are] precise (*muhkamat*)––they are the foundation of

the Book - and others unspecific (*mutashabihat*). As for those in whose hearts is deviation [from truth], they will follow that of it which is unspecific, seeking discord and seeking an interpretation (*ta'wilih*) [suitable to them]. And no one knows its [true] interpretation (*ta'wiluhu*) except Allah. But those firm in knowledge say, "We believe in it. All [of it] is from our Lord." And no one will be reminded except those of understanding.

8

Hindu Ascetic Death

Mary Storm

> The one who tries to escape from the trials of life by committing suicide will suffer even more in the next life.
>
> —Yajur Veda

THE ANCIENT ADMONITION from the *Yajur Veda* (ca.1200–1000 BCE) quoted above is in keeping with modern Hindu attitudes toward suicide, which is usually interpreted as a violation of the ideal of *ahiṃsā,* or non-violence. Modern Hinduism usually interprets suicide as the violence of self-murder and the willful waste of a precious human birth.

Historically, however, Indian religions have expressed conflicting attitudes toward self-immolation. Indian religions have usually condemned suicide as a violent emotional act that has a negative karmic impact on future lives. Suicide has been rejected as an act of hubris, as only the divine can measure out our allotted lifespan. Conversely, at times, self-sacrifice to the gods, or as an act of ascetic discipline, has been condoned as the most precious of oblations.

This English translation from Vedic Sanskrit of the Yajur Veda uses the word "suicide," which despite its Latin-sounding origins, was not used by ancient Romans. "Suicide" is an artificial term first appearing in English in 1651, formed from the Latin *sui,* "of oneself" and *occidere,* "to kill." Romans would have translated *suicidium* as "death of a pig," and instead, Romans employed euphemisms such as *mors voluntaria,* or "voluntary death," or *liber mori,* or "free death." *Mors voluntaria* reflects a complex cultural attitude toward self-killing in classical Western antiquity. During the early days of the Roman Republic, Romans accepted self-killing as the dignified end to a life that had reached crisis. Gradually however, suicide was condemned, especially when it was committed not by patricians, but by slaves, which thus deprived Roman citizens of their property (Colt 151).

India also has a long and complex relationship with the idea of voluntary death. At times, suicide was condemned, and at other moments, especially during the miseries of war, famine, disease, religious persecution, or other forms of social or biological upheaval, suicide was honored. Sanskrit has various terms to describe suicide that reflect these diverse attitudes and approved methods of self-oblation. Some terms carry opprobrium, such as *ātmahatyā* (self-murder). Some terms imply approval such as or *ātmayāga* (self-sacrifice) or *ātmaparityāga* (total self-sacrifice), *tanutyāga* ("body-abandonment" with the implication of bravery), and *dehatyāga* ("body-abandonment" with the implication of a spiritual abandonment of the corporeal mass). Some of these terms reflect specifically approved methods of voluntary death, such as: *prāyopraveśa* (embracing starvation), *jalpraveśa* (entering water), or *agnipraveśa* (entering fire).

One contested issue for a Western understanding of these concepts is the nature of the self that reputedly is killed. It has been posited, not without opposition, that the concept of "self" is the product of the Reformation and the development of the notion of independent religious agency, and then further development under the Enlightenment and the secular identity ideologies of the modern age. In the premodern past, people may have understood their individual identities as something quite different from the contemporary constructions of self, and probably something quite different from the present sociopolitical notions of identity. In contemporary global culture, we believe that individuals enjoy self-determination and unique rights. The Western "self" is usually portrayed as an aware and unified being, connected to consciousness and acting with individual agency.

But we may ask, in contrast, what did the "self" and self-sacrifice mean in Indian antiquity? Historically, Indian religions defined the self, in the sense of ego-awareness, as the major factor in our destructive ensnarement in *māyā,* or delusion. Most Indian religions posit that to understand ego was to be free from its grasp and to achieve the liberation of *mokṣa* (spiritual release and realization). What then, did it mean to self-sacrifice, considering that the notion of "self" was so different from the contemporary globalized construction? It may be a challenge for our contemporary selves to understand the motivations for *mors voluntaria* in societies so removed by time and philosophical history.

Indian religions have always emphasized that realization, or *mokṣa,* is predicated on a self-knowledge which leads to escape from the bonds of a dichotomous perception of self. The Indian *śramaṇa*, or striver, is expected to determine the differences between *ātman*, or the universal self, and the discrete empirical self of "I," and to integrate these differences. Most Indian schools of thought have been concerned with cultivating the right behavior, or dharma, in the physical or empirical world, which will then lead to metaphysical realization and liberation (*mokṣa*) from that same empirical world. The fear or denial of our own empirical death and of individual extinction is the ultimate challenge for spiritual and psychological wholeness.

With Émile Durkheim's nineteenth-century study of suicide, Western scholars began to consider suicide outside the realms of timeless religious strictures and morality, and to locate it instead within specific social-scientific contexts. Durkheim considered suicide from the standpoint of societies with sufficient individuation and insufficient individuation. In societies where caste, sub-caste, religious orthodoxy or heterodoxy, feudal status, or family identification are stronger than notions of individual agency, the altruistic or "obligatory altruistic suicide" is more common (Durkheim 222–25). If such altruistic suicide is the overarching type of voluntary death in India, two subtypes should be considered: "optional" altruistic suicide, in which social factors make self-inflicted death praiseworthy, thus encouraging it without requiring it; and "acute" altruistic suicide (of which "mystical" suicide is the ideal), in which the victim kills himself/herself for the pure joy of sacrifice and self-renunciation. The altruistic suicide of the optional, acute, and mystical varieties is the major expression under discussion here.

Condemnation of Self-Destruction in Early Texts

Suicide is disruptive to the fabric of society. It is therefore closely controlled and often condemned in religious or social law. Suicide is often freighted with moral opprobrium and is usually a statement of aggression toward the self, but it also addresses the failures of society. As Arthur Miller puts it in *After the Fall*, suicide is meant to have an impact beyond the victim-self: "A suicide kills two people, Maggie, that's what it's for!" (104). Its permitted use is usually controlled through ideals of bravery, heroism, and religious devotion. Suicides performed under these circumstances carry the message that these are outlier acts, but nevertheless permitted expressions of individual heroism, freely performed, with no criticism of the larger social structure.

Early texts, such as the *Iśavasya Upaniṣad* (3), denounced the individual who took his own life: "Those who take their lives reach after death the sunless regions, covered by impenetrable darkness." The *Śatapatha Brāhmaṇa* (10.2.6.7) prohibited suicide, stating: "And therefore one should not die, desirous of heaven, before one's [allotted] lifespan [is complete]."

The *Manu Smṛti* (ca. 300 BCE–200 CE) condemned suicide and denied funeral libations to the suicide (5.89), but simultaneously permitted suicide for the expiation of sin. For example, a man who seduces his guru's wife could expiate his sin by embracing a heated metal image of a woman. A man accused of killing a *brāhman* could expiate his sin through death in battle or by entering fire (Muller 184).

The statesman and legal philosopher Kauṭilya (350–283 BCE) condemned self-destruction. Kauṭilya states that those who take their own lives due to love, jealousy, anger, or other sinful impulses could not be cremated; rather, their bodies were to be left at the crossroads, to be scavenged by wild animals. Anyone who performed the funeral rites for such a person should himself be deprived of funeral rites. Any *brāhman* performing such funerals would be denied the rights of performing sacrifices or obtaining donations for one year (IV, 7).

Sanctioned Forms of Voluntary Death

There is no central textual authority or supreme leader within Hinduism; this gives Hinduism great flexibility in its reactions to social change. There were many Hindu strictures forbidding suicide, but there were also many dispensations allowing suicide, depending on the extenuating circumstances.

It was argued at various times in India's long religious history that the most intimate and generous of oblations is the free offering of the body through self-chosen death. The following are exemptions to the sin of suicide: a retainer could ensure his king's victory by a pre-battle self-sacrifice to a war goddess; a warrior in battle could seek death in prodigal acts of heroism; and a loyal subject of the king could make a self-offering to a deity to insure the stability of the royal lineage (Storm, "Hero Stones," 63–64).

A person who died while protecting the young, the elderly, a woman's honor, a *brāhman*, or a cow, would not be condemned as a suicide. A widower, overcome by the death of his wife, could choose voluntary death. A widow could be released from her inauspicious state by seeking death as a *sati.* Rather than become victims of war, women and children could self-immolate in the act of *jauhar.*[1] An elder, unable to conform to the rules of

1. *Jauhar* was a sanctioned form of a mass suicide performed by Rajput women, their children, and their retainers. Upon recognizing an imminent defeat in battle, with the inevitable rape, pillage, and slavery which would follow, women would self-immolate in a great fire.

Hindu orthopraxy, could seek death by drowning, starving, or a pilgrimage exhausting unto death. A criminal could seek expiation of sin by self-sacrifice in honor of a deity. A holy man could force a king to change a discriminatory law, or policy, by threatening or performing religious self-sacrifice. A *sadhu* could gain merit and spiritual power and obtain *mokṣa* by performing certain types of arduous *ātmayāga*.

The Self-Sacrifice of the Ascetic

The voluntary death of the *sannyāsin* was the most commonly sanctioned form of *ātmayāga*. In contrast to the usual criticisms of suicide, the *Kanṭhaśruti Upaniṣad* (ca.100–30 BCE) stated: "The *sannyāsin*, who has acquired full insight, may enter upon the great journey, or choose death by voluntary starvation, by drowning, by fire, or by a hero's fate." The *sannyāsin* or *sādhu* (female: *sannyāsinī* or *sādhvī*) is a Hindu ascetic who has vowed to achieve spiritual liberation by breaking the bonds of ego. This path is usually followed after the traditional three stages of life have been completed as student (*brahmacārin*), householder (*gṛhastha*), and retired forest dweller (*vānaprastha*). In unusual situations, the *saṃnyāsa* life might also be pursued after completion of the first *brahmacārya* phase of life.

As a renunciant, the *sannāysin* has no engagement with material concerns and is ritually detached from worldly obligations. His or her austere ascetic discipline is believed to erode the ties to secular life. This ascetic process helps the renunciant to move beyond the passionate and emotionally destructive entanglements of daily life—and thus the ascetic's actions fall outside the laws of secular life.

Ideally, the *sādhu's* life is contemplative and nonviolent. The *sādhu's* self-chosen death is often deemed acceptable because the self-aware death does not engender karmically destructive passion. The *sādhu* is already ritually dead to himself or herself, to society, and to Indian law (Olivelle, *Ashrama*, 88–91). As part of the initiation to the life of renunciation, a symbolic funeral is held for the *sādhu*-to-be, thus removing the ascetic from the rules of the secular social contract. These funeral rituals, called *ātma śrāddha* (self-funerals), are then followed by the *yajña vīraja* (sacrifice of the passions). These processes

---

Jauhars could number in the thousands of victims. In 1294 at Jaisalmer, twenty-four thousand women performed *agnipraveśa*, rather than be dishonored by Sultan Alla-ud-din. In the *jauhar* at Chittorgarh in 1533, thirteen thousand women and children entered the fires rather than submit to Bahadur Shah's troops.

of *ātma śrāddha* and *yajña vīraja* allow the ascetic to choose death without harming his karmic status.

The poet and Vedic sage Atri states in the Jābāla Upaniṣad (ca. 100 CE):

> This is the procedure for becoming a recluse. (For one who is weary of the world but not yet fit to become a recluse the following are prescribed), he may choose a hero's death (by following the path of the warrior in the battlefield), he may fast unto death, throw himself into water or enter fire (burn himself to death) or perform the last journey (walk unto death). Then the wandering ascetic who (puts on) orange robes, who is shaven, who has non-possession, purity, non-enmity, lives on alms, obtains the state of Brahman. If he is diseased he can renounce by mind and speech. This is not to be done by one who is healthy. Such a renouncer becomes the knower of Brahman, so said the venerable Yajñavalkya. (Olivelle, *Ascetics* 220)

When considering voluntary death in the Hindu ascetic traditions, self-sacrifice should be considered in the context of this history. For an Indian ascetic who has striven for a passionless observation of existence, achieved self-integration with *ātman*, and overcome the fear of death, *ātmayāga* must be understood as a very different act than emotional and physical violence and the karmically ensnaring act of suicide. It is thus essential to distinguish between suicide *(ātmahatyā)* and self-sacrifice *(ātmayāgya).*

Methods of Self-Sacrifice

Ascetic voluntary death could be performed in many ways: by drowning, burning, starvation, dismemberment, falling from trees, exhausting pilgrimage, or decapitation. All forms of self-destruction carry some form of symbolism.

The *Kūrma Purāṇa* states that suicide anywhere in the Ganga will not be a sin and that salvation will be obtained. Voluntary drowning *(jalprevśa)* was usually performed at one of the confluences of holy rivers, such as the intersection of the Yamuna and the Ganga at Allahabad. This intersection of holy waterways, called Prayāga, was considered such an especially sacred place that it would assure redemption of sin. We are told in the *Uttara Kanda* of the Rāmāyaṇa that Rāmā renounced his life by entering the Sarayu River, watched by hundreds of people along the banks, who then in their grief followed him by drowning. The seventh-century Ikṣvakū king Rāmā, like the legendary

Rāmā, was said to have died by voluntary drowning along the Sarayu River, accompanied by his closest retainers, as his courtiers watched from the banks of the river (Sircar 212). King Dhruva of the Rāṣṭrakūṭa Dynasty (r. 780–793 CE) probably died by drowning at Prāyaga (Thakur 99). The Candella King Dhaṅgadeva, having lived to be over one hundred years old, took his life at Prayāga in the eleventh century (Thakur 101, ftn.2). King Vallāsena of the Sena Dynasty (r. 1168–1178) also probably died at Prayāga (Thakur 98).

Voluntary death could also be performed by immolation in fire *(agnipraveśa)*. Unlike the negative Western symbolism surrounding fire as the punishing environment of hell, Indian symbolism saw a death by fire as an auspicious, renewing, and cleansing method of obtaining salvation. *Agnipraveśa* was preferred for *satis* and performers of *jauhar*. The *agnipraveśa* ritual also carried the antiquity and sanctity of the Vedic fire sacrifice, lending it historic authority and sanctity. King Kumarāgupta (ca. 554) of the Gupta Dynasty voluntarily died by entering a slow-burning fire of cow dung cakes. King Jayapāla of Kabul and Lahore is also said to have committed *agnipraveśa* in the year 1001.

Self-controlled starvation *(prayopaveśa)* was an accepted form of self-sacrifice. Jain ascetics, especially, favored slow voluntary death by starvation (*sallekhanā*), which could be accomplished thoughtfully, with full insight. Historically, many Jains ended their lives in this manner and some continue to do so, with mixed social acceptance. Although Jains especially favored death by fasting, Hindu ascetics also embraced this method of voluntary death. *Sadhus* up to the present day have used the threat of *prayopaveśa* as methods of social and political manipulation and persuasion. During India's struggle for independence, Mahatma Gandhi's hunger strikes repeatedly forced political changes. Historically, this has been a powerful tool of religious manipulation upon Indian secular institutions: the threat that, unless a policy change was enacted, a respected holy man would die, shifted the karmic consequence from the *sadhu* to the ruler.

We know from texts such as the *Kālikā Purāṇa* and also from epigraphical evidence that dismemberment was highly valued and special temples were established with priests trained to help those who wished to perform death by dismemberment. Each part of the body held special symbolic value, and was no doubt reminiscent of the original dismemberment of the primordial man, Puruṣa. The *Ṛg Veda* X.90 describes the original sacrifice, the dismemberment of Puruṣa, from whom all creation was structured and ordered into moon and sun, castes and duties, animals and plants. By participating in this form of voluntary death the devotee was participating on a microcosmic level with the macrocosmic act of creation.

Falling from trees *(akṣayavaṭa)* was a favored method of religious self-offering. Trees carry the symbol of sanctified authority; religious figures are often associated with trees. The Buddha, who was born under an ashoka tree, experienced his first transcendent meditation under a jambu tree (rose apple), found enlightenment under a *ficus religiosa* (pipal or bodhi tree), and died under two sal trees. Asko Parpola posits that pre-Vedic human sacrifice may be associated with the deity of the pipal tree. Parpola cites the evidence of an Indus Valley civilization steatite seal, which is incised with the depiction of a devotee offering a head to a deity standing in a pipal tree (227–36). Trees often symbolize authority, as teachers, judges and kings would sit under a tree to teach, adjudicate or rule. The banyan tree is associated with Yama, the Lord of Death, and is often planted near cremation grounds. It is also associated with immortality, as its aerial root system allows the tree to keep renewing itself over large areas and over many centuries. The "undying" banyan tree *(akṣaya vaṭa vṛksham)* at the confluence of the Ganga and Yamuna, at Allahabad (Prayāga), is especially revered as a personification of Śiva, and it was from this very large and famous tree that numerous people chose to die (Garg 342), assured that their deaths would earn them liberation. King Gāṅgeya and his one hundred wives jumped from this tree at Prayāga in 1073 (Thakur 97).

An exhausting pilgrimage leading to death was another honorable form of self-destruction. Elders, or people unable to conform to Hindu orthopraxy, or those with incurable illnesses, could honorably end their lives by walking a pilgrimage unto death. This form of voluntary death is mentioned in the *Mahābhārata*, in the *Mahāprasthanika Parva*, as the method by which Draupadī and the Pāṇḍāvas ended their lives. As they traveled across India and then into the Himalayas, Draupadī died first, followed by the others, one by one. Only Yudiṣṭhara survived to reach Mt. Sumeru. We are told that eventually, they were all united in heaven.

The most symbolically complex form of sacrifice was self-decapitation. In most cultures, the head is the location of identity. Therefore, decapitation not only assures a quick death; it also symbolically destroys the ego. The head represents rational life, rule, and control. Because of this symbolism, decapitation denotes a loss of power, position, and prestige. In self-sacrifice rituals, the oblate seeks a merger with the divine; decapitation is therefore a specifically self-effacing act, which relieves the offerer of the burden of ego and allows union with the divine in specifically symbolic ways not connected to other forms of self-destruction. The head has power as the locus of the soul and the seat of the self. *Ātmayāga* by self-decapitation was the offering of the unique and intimate self. Therefore, self-decapitation represented submission to the deity and the rejection of self before the greater reality of the divine; it graphically displayed the void of self and the realization of nonattachment to self. On a more pragmatic level, a decapitation represented the loss of power, and the transfer of that power to the divine recipient of the sacrifice (Storm, *Head and Heart*, 147–48).

Many societies have multi-headed mythological beasts, but India, in particular, makes much of multiple-headed deities and the symbolism each head offers. Many stories explore decapitation. Recall that the very founding of the world starts with the dismemberment of the Puruṣa. Each part of Puruṣa's body became an element of the cosmos, but it is from his head that brāhmans and their speech emerged, to renew the world through the precise enunciation and repetition of sacrificial ritual. Many stories revolve around multiple heads as in the story of the three-headed Brahmā. These stories question who we are and which caste, which personality, which virtues, or which vices represent our true selves.

In addition, the head is laden with sexual symbolism. Many ancient Indians believed, as did the Greeks, Romans, Jewish Kabbalists, and medieval Christian alchemists, that semen was stored in the head. Sexual vitality was proportionate to the length and the luxuriance of hair. Hair piled high symbolized the rich store of semen that the Hindu ascetic controlled through his austerities. Cutting the hair of a Hindu ascetic would result, as it did with Samson in the Bible, in a loss of virility and control. The touching of another's head and hair carried a message of sexual intimacy, and the hair and head often are associated with the sex organs. Therefore, in Indian myth, as in the myths of other cultures, a decapitation can represent a symbolic castration and the return to an ideal childlike or desexualized state, as the devotee approaches the divine.

One illustration of a heroic head-offering is that of the Chauhan chieftain, Hammīr of Ranthambhore. After defeat by the armies of Sultan Alā-ud-din Khalji in the 14th century, Hammīr of Ranthambhore took his own life by self-decapitation before a Śiva lingam image. With this offering, Hammīr became a paradigm for the resolve of a true hero: a person who could commit to oblation and turn defeat into self-abnegation, not to an enemy, but to a god (H. Shastri 35–40). Numerous paintings exist commemorating Hammīr's head-offering.

It may be noted that many of these deaths were performed by *kṣatriya* caste members—that is, rulers or warriors. That may be because we have better evidence for the deaths of historically significant people, but it may also be because some medieval writers condemned voluntary death of brāhmaṇs. Gradually, however we know that many ordinary people, and not just those from the princely caste, sought heroic death by self-sacrifice. These deaths are memorialized in numerous literary references, as well as in hero stones, shrines, and the formal iconographic programs in the great South Indian temples.

Religious Precepts

Religion posits that it is possible for man and god to communicate, and this communion is usually performed through the rituals of sacrifice. Sacrifice *(yajna)* is founded on the assumption that men and gods need and feed each other in a relationship of reciprocity. In Indian sacrifice, men and gods interact in a constant contractual process of maintenance and renewal. As such, sacrifice forms the heart of social communion and structures the relationship between god and mortal, and sanctity and violence.

Sacrifice must address not only the willingness of the offerer, but also the appetite of the gods for violence. Even if death is voluntary, self-sacrifice sanctions human destruction and the bloody appetite of the gods. Self-sacrifice, no matter how ardently embraced, was therefore an indicator of an inherently violent sacred. Human life is marked by both the understanding and acceptance of the immediate actuality of life, and the intangible enigma of death. Self-chosen death was metamorphosed in ancient India to control the balance of creation and destruction that lies at the heart of this dichotomy. Self-sacrifice addresses the inevitability of death, as the inexorable and unfathomable counterpart to life. It may be argued that, by controlling the time of death through self-destruction, the offerer perceives himself or herself to be in a contractual reciprocity with God, the administrator of death. The question arises, however, as to whether this is hubris, as only the divine can measure out our lifespan—or, is this the ultimate act of self-abnegation?

The answers to these questions varied over time, traditions, and audiences. Early Vedic religion, which emphasized complex and costly sacrificial rites and rituals controlled by the brāhman elite, had appealed to the priestly and ruling classes. Its elitism and concern with control, manipulation, and consolidation of power did not pertain to those members of the population outside of the upper echelons of society. However, Indian religious life gradually developed forms of spiritual expression that included other members of society: non-brāhmans, low caste, out caste, indigenous, and women.

Over the centuries, reactions to Vedic religion emerged. During the Reform or Śramanic period (800–200 BCE), some heterodox practitioners, such as Ajivikas, Buddhists, and Jains, broke away from basic Vedic structures, especially the control of the caste system and the necessity of the brāhmans to be intermediaries with the gods. Within Hinduism, during the Purāṇic period (ca. the year 200–tenth century and onwards), non-elite forms of practice developed in the charismatic worship of bhakti, which eschewed the power of the brāhmans and encouraged intense personal devotion to the gods without the intercession of priests. The Purāṇic literature is vast and covers many topics, but it is primarily focused on the personal narratives of the gods and goddesses, and the various paths of devotion that might lead to an intimate connection to the divine. Tantra developed an even more rebellious approach to religion, intentionally rejecting the hierarchies, taboos, and orthodoxies of Vedic practice and embracing socially transgressive beliefs and practices. Eventually, many Brāhmanical, Purāṇic, and Tantric systems merged and influenced each other.

Regional, non-Sanskritized worship continued to accommodate those culturally and geographically liminal members of the population. Gradually, all of these non-Vedic forms of devotion evolved into more formalized types of bhakti and tantra, and were then finally subsumed into Sanskritized practice.

This process of assimilation included deities. As North Indian Sanskritic culture moved into areas with already established non-Vedic deity cults, such as South India, Vedic rituals and brāhmanical deities had to accommodate or merge with indigenous traditions. Local deities were aligned or merged with their Sanskritic counterparts. Often these conflated deities retained their non-Vedic penchant for blood sacrifice *(bali),* which was then retained or reinforced with the development of bhakti and tantra.

Although some regional non-Vedic deities retained their anonymity, such as the Tamil hero-warrior-god Ayyanar, many local deities integrated with the deities of the "Great Tradition." For example, the Tamil war goddess Koṟṟavai merged her identity with the North Indian goddess Durgā; sculptures reflected this, with images incorporating symbolism of both goddesses. In South Indian temple sculptures, Durgā is indicated with her *vāhana* (mount), the lion, and Koṟṟavai is indicated by her *vāhana,* the stag, and often one goddess will be merged and depicted with both *vāhanas.* Other local gods found their place in Sanskritic Hinduism through marriage, such as the marriage of the Tamil goddess Minakshi to the Sanskritic deity Śiva. In this process of assimilation, non-Vedic rituals and devotional ideology did not wholly disappear, but rather were adapted, and found expression in the more accommodating rituals of bhakti and tantra.

In the early centuries CE, innovations in South Indian Hindu bhakti devotionalism were evidenced in the rise of the twelve Vaiṣṇava Āḻvārs and the sixty-three Śaiva Nāyaṉmārs. These groups of saints were of immense importance in the development of South Indian piety. The saints came from many different occupations and castes; their hymns and deeds became paradigms of devotional surrender. Some of these saints were of proven historicity, but others appear to have been purely mythic. Their extravagant devotion must have had great impact on society. They served as archetypes of grace, piety, and self-abnegation.

Saints and Self-Abnegation

Numerous stories attest to these bhakti saints' self-giving love of God. They called themselves "Slaves of the Lord," with the implication being that they belonged, body and soul, to the divine. Their self-sacrifices were presented as the ideal expression of piety.[2] Nāyaṉmār bhakti stories, such as the tale of Ciṟuttoṇṭar who sacrificed and fed his child to the god Śiva, make it clear that the gods were entitled to ask the most fearsome sacrifices of their devotees, even human sacrifice. Besides the story of Ciṟuttoṇṭar, other stories related various forms of self-mutilations and self-sacrifices, such as those of Kaṇṇappa, who gave his eyes to Śiva (Shulman 20–30); Arival-Taya Nāyaṉmār, who was about to decapitate himself with a sickle before Śiva intervened (Shulman 156–57); Kanampullar, who pulled out his own hair to use as temple lamp wicks (Shulman 158); and King Pugal Cholar, who killed himself in remorse for the death of a Śaiva devotee, (Shulman 160–61).

During the early centuries CE, at the same time that bhakti encouraged radical forms of dedication to the gods, the Tantric practices of the Kāpālika, Kālamukha, and Pāśupata cults developed socially transgressive expressions of that devotion. There is ample evidence from contemporary literary sources, such as the *Tevāram* cycle of poems and the *Mattavilāsa,* that the Tantric sects flourished in ancient South India. Certain sites such as Kanchipuram, Mayilapur, Kodumbalur, and areas of Thanjavur are mentioned in literature as having been associated with Tantric sects dedicated to either the

2. A number of the Nāyaṉmār saints, including a Pallava commander-in-chief of the army, Ciṟuttōṇṭar (active ca. 642), possibly two Pallava monarchs, Siṁhavarman (ca. 550–575), and Rājasiṁha (ca. 700–728), and four of the Āḻvār saints, came from the Pallava region.

goddess in her angry or *ugra* aspects, or to the terrible form of Śiva Bhairava (Minakshi 180–81). Tiruvarur is referred to as the location of the goddess who demanded animal and human sacrifice. It is alleged that the Vedāntic philosopher Śaṅkaracārya (ca. 788–838) visited Tiruvarur during the Pallava period and subdued the goddess by closing her mouth and throwing her image down a well (Archaeological Survey of India 68). However, sculptural evidence from the later Cōḷa period indicates that the ideal of self-sacrifice in the form of self-decapitation continued or was re-instituted at the shrine after Śaṅkaracārya's visit. Other sites, such as Mahabalipuram and Tiruchirappali, indicate by ample sculptural evidence that self-sacrifice took place in honor of the goddess during the Pallava period; therefore, if Śaṅkaracārya did have success with the eradication of extreme forms of Tantric goddess worship, his reforms were short-lived.

Clear examples of self-offering can be seen in the sculptural programs at the Pallava site of Mahabalipuram (seventh and eighth centuries). These images attest to the practice of self-sacrifice in honor of the goddess. In the small Draupadi Ratha, in the Varāha Cave, and on the north wall of the Shore Temple we see ascetics kneeling and cutting off their own heads in oblation to the composite form of Durgā/Koṟṟavai.

Historical Motivations for Self-Chosen Death

In the early twenty-first century world, globalized identity politics drive shifts in the notion of self as it is posited within larger social structures (Kinnsall). We constantly ask to be located within a social frame of "identity" that connects us to political, cultural, sexual, religious, and linguistic debates, and of course these frames have shifted over time. In the same way, attitudes about self-sacrifice shifted in Indian history, depending on numerous factors, including especially the changing perception of the self and the relative power of individual agency. Indian religious attitudes toward self-chosen death often reflected changes in religious, social, or even biological situations: heterodox religious developments such as tantra or even bhakti could legitimate voluntary death. So too, persecution, war, famine, and epidemics created stressful environments that legitimated zealotry. The old adage "there are no atheists in the foxhole" reminds us that in high-stress situations, it is common to make extravagant promises for safety, security, health, or life.

Over the centuries, Indian religion deviated from the early strictures against suicide, opening up to the possibility of its permitted performance. With the development of the charismatic structures of bhakti and the transgressive practices of tantra, complete sacrificial surrender to the divine became an ideal form of devotion. However, it was often a "perfect storm" of conditions that would allow the oblate to conceive of voluntary death as an acceptable act. Developments in religion, which gave permission for extreme acts of devotion, coupled with the stress of warfare, the paranoia induced by persecution, and the physical exhaustion brought about by famine or disease, combined to make voluntary death a reasonable, or even honorable, option for a life in crisis.

Once an ascetic was permitted self-sacrifice as a karmically neutral act, what were the occasions that would inspire this extreme form of oblation? There were several situations in which Indian society condoned, or even approved of, self-sacrifice. Common reasons for self-sacrifice were petitions for victory in battle, stability of the monarchy, expiation of sin, or release from disease or infirmity. Self-sacrifice could also be performed to address an injustice, forestall a calamity, or force political change. Some forms of self-sacrifice even seem quite mundane, such as insurance of construction safety. These acts could be considered "altruistic suicides," as they were performed to protect society, to maintain social stability, or to address an ethical dilemma.

Devotees could make a vow, or *vrata,* to petition the gods; by performing self-sacrifice the oblate could seal the contract, and the deity could be persuaded to act on the oblate's behalf. The most common recipients of self-sacrifice were usually *ugra*, or violent forms of tantric gods or goddesses, such as Śiva Bhairava, Viṣṇu Narasiṃha, Durgā, Kālī, Koṟṟavai, or Camuṇḍa. The practitioners of self-sacrifice to these deities were usually acting within a tantric tradition, which endorsed fervent heterodoxy.

Human instinct for self-preservation prevents casual implementation of self-sacrifice. Even the most pious devotee was unlikely to perform voluntary death unless there was a supportive culture and a triggering event or atmosphere of crisis. War, famine, epidemics, and persecutions were often initiating events, but self-sacrifice still must have been supported by the community.

Due to its human-divine contractual nature, sacrifice offers the potential for psychological control over the chaos of life, and medieval India was often a chaotic place, demanding structure and reprieve from the miseries of life. After the mid-seventh century, Muslim invasions threatened Hindu culture. As Muslim armies sought conquest, both political and religious structures were under siege.

Certain periods of Indian history were not only beset by conquering armies, state failures, persecutions, and forced conversions, but also suffered from the resultant famines and diseases that inevitably follow war. Elsewhere, the seventh to fifteenth centuries experienced relentless biological disasters. The world's first plague pandemic, the Plague of Justinian, raged from 541 to 775 (Norris 4). It was followed by outbreaks such as the Plague of Emmaus of 639, and other outbreaks in the seventh and eighth centuries. In India, plague caused such devastation that, by the eleventh century, the *Bhāgavata Purāṇa* was giving instructions for its prevention (Nathan 42).

The fourteenth century was perhaps the worst period of global misery; it saw the expansion of unsustainable population growth, followed by weather-related crop failures, and then the global devastation of the "Black Death"—that is, the bubonic plague, which is estimated to have killed at least a third, if not half, of the world's population in the fourteenth century.[3] This pandemic, named for the black gangrenous pustules it formed in the lymph nodes of the neck, underarms, and groin, is thought to have originated somewhere in the steppes of Central Asia. The bubonic plague bacterium (*Yersina pestis*) is found in fleas that infest black rats, which traveled with the disease across the globe via trade ships and the camps of the marauding Mongol armies. The effects of these disasters are well understood in European history, but are less so in South Asia. However, firsthand observations from visitors, such as Ibn Battuta, who visited India in 1345 during the time of the Black Death, referred to its relentless fatalities: "When I reached Madura [Madurai, Tamil Nadu], I found that an epidemic was raging there and that the people afflicted with it died in no time. Whoever caught infection died on the morrow, or the day after, and if not on the third day, then on the fourth. Whenever I went out I saw people but diseased or dead" (Hussain 104–05, 230).

Pandemics historically have engendered radical response. Thucydides wrote about the extreme behavior of the usually rational Athenians in the face of sudden lethal contagion in the epidemic of 427 BCE. Eyewitnesses as diverse as Giovanni Boccaccio and Pope Clement VI reported on the religiously hysterical behavior engendered by epidemics in medieval Europe. The masochistic flagellants were an expression of the frenzied response to the ravages of the fourteenth-century European eruptions of the plague. Flagellants believed that the Black Death was the result of God's wrath levied upon the sinful; by emulating the Passion of Christ, they hoped to atone for their sins by scourging themselves with spiked whips for thirty-three days (because Jesus lived for thirty-three years). This kind of massive social upheaval often resulted in the leveling of hierarchies and the questioning of accepted ideas,

3. The estimates of deaths are controversial, with most recent estimates increasing the numbers previously estimated (Alchon 21).

and thus engendered new approaches to the status quo in religion, morality, and devotion. We might deduce, from the reports we have from the Western response to pestilence, that similar responses happened in South Asia. For example, like the Christian flagellants, anti-*purāṇic* tantric adepts also indulged in extreme forms of self-harming devotion.

Ascetic Sects Associated with Self-Sacrifice

Yamunācārya, the eleventh-century teacher of Rāmunāja, identified anti-*purāṇic* tantric adepts as Maheśvaras, or worshippers of Śiva Bhairava as the supreme lord. Yamunācārya identified these Maheśvara sects as Śaivas, Paśupatas, Kāpālikas, and Kālamukhas (Banerjea 450–52). Maheśvaras, such as the Kāpālikas ("Skull Bearers"), often performed a like-for-like self-sacrifice if they had accidentally killed a brāhman *(brahmahatyā),* or if they had not killed a brāhman, but wished to gain great powers. These ascetics took a "Great Vow"—the Mahāvrata—which emulated the story of Śiva Bhairava, the form of the god as sinner and destroyer (Lorenzen 87). In one of the many variations of the Bhairava story, Śiva had cut off one of the lord Brahmā's original five heads. The offending head had insulted the goddess Sarasvatī, the daughter of Brahmā, by spewing crude and incestuous comments; Śiva was so disgusted by Brahmā's incestuous behavior that he had decapitated the insulting head. This act left Śiva as a proponent of the social moral code against incest, but also marked him as committing a patricide and a brāhmanicide, the worst possible violations of the Vedic code. Śiva was condemned by the other gods and was forced to wander as an ascetic with Brahmā's skull attached to his palm, until he could redeem himself by immersion in the holy river Ganga at Kashi (Varanasi).

Self-sacrifices by Kāpālika Mahāvratins commemorated Bhairava's impious decapitation of Brahmā. The Kāpālika ascetic was required to withdraw from society, wander in an ascetic pilgrimage for twelve years, carry a human skull (*kāpāla*) and a skull-topped staff (*khatavanga*), and dust himself in cremation ash. When the Kāpālika reached the Ganga he could be cleansed of sin by the sacred river and his final oblation of eight parts of the body: hair, skin, blood, flesh, sinews, fat, bone, and marrow (Lorenzen 76). This could easily culminate in accidental death, or the final conscious choice of self-decapitation. This brought the devotee into the arena of divine emulation where the oblate was playing many roles: devotee, divinity, renegade, sinner, and victim. Because of their extreme lifestyle, the Mahāvratins were both the most reviled of criminals and the holiest of ascetics; above all, they were considered powerful. The power of the Mahāvrata resulting in death was supreme. The Skanda Purāṇa VI.22.76 states: "he who dies in Kashi [Varanasi] does not incur the sin of suicide, but secures his desired object."

Those Who Chose Death

The earliest indications of socially sanctioned forms of self-sacrifice are mentioned in South Indian and Deccani texts, so it should not be surprising that self-sacrifice was performed in South India from the seventh to the sixteenth centuries in the Pallava, Pāṇḍya, Cōḷa, Cāḷukya, Reḍḍi, Kākatīya, and Vijayanagara areas.

Ancient Indian monarchies fought seemingly endless wars for empire. This required the support of their goddesses, violent deities who did not give their favors without exacting a high price. Early Tamil literary sources, such as the epic poem called the *Cilappatikāram* (fifth century), describe self-sacrificing rituals performed in honor of the war goddess Koṟṟavai. To ensure victory in battle, select warriors would offer their heads to Koṟṟavai in a pre-battle sacrifice. The *Cilappatikāram* describes a rite in which a virgin was dressed as the goddess. The girl was placed on a stag (the vehicle or *vāhana* of Koṟṟavai). A dance was performed in her honor and then the rite culminated with a warrior self-decapitating. His blood was offered to the girl, who represented the goddess (Adigal 76–85). In another scene, the *Cilappatikāram* describes warriors: "[O]ffering their fierce heads to the sacrificing priest, they cried, 'The king will return victorious!' and their dark hairy heads fell upon the altar" (Adigal 20).

Tamil poetry often refers to the devotee as being in a *veṟi*, or frenzy; he is said to be mad, demonic, enslaved, or idiotic (Nammalvar 117). This state of being "outside of one self" builds a vision of suicide as an act done, not to oneself, but to an abstracted and disconnected self, thereby lessening the instinct for self-preservation. We might imagine this scene: a nighttime gathering, music, chanting, the press of bodies, and the persuasion of arena culture, with warriors going to a temple and calling up the goddess Koṟṟavai to give victory to their king and his army, and then offering themselves as the first fruits of battle. This would have been perceived as a supremely noble and valorous act, the ultimate form of social altruism (Storm, *Head and Heart* 95–96, 143–44).

Military offerings were not the only forms of self-sacrifice rituals. During the medieval period special temples were established for the offering of body parts. These temples were sometimes constructed under royal patronage. In

1377, King Anavema Reḍḍī had the Viraśaiva Mallikārjuna temple constructed in Srisailam for the explicit purpose of religious self-mutilation and self-sacrifice (Rao 103–38). [See Figure 8.1]

There was a specially constructed hall for self-decapitation, the Vīraśiro Maṇḍapa ("Hall of the Heroes' Heads"). The inscription there states:

> How wonderful it is that here in this *maṇḍapa* hosts of Ekāṇgavīras [protector-heroes], who proudly make a votive offering of their eyes, hands, heads, and tongues, by cutting them off, attain instantaneously a brilliant body of blessed limbs. The next moment, endowed with three eyes, ten arms, five faces and five tongues, they shine as if they were *aṣṭamūrti* [eight-bodied Śivas].

FIG. 8.1 Devotee offering his head to the Goddess, Lower Rock Fort, 8th C. Paṇḍya Period, Tiruchirappalli, Tamil Nadu [author].

A thirteenth-century group of twenty sculptures (sixteen male figures and four female), from the Nalgonda area in Andhra Pradesh, indicate that both men and women were willing to make complete self-sacrifice. [See Figure 8.2]

These images probably represent Viraśaiva ascetics. Viraśaivas, also called Liṅgayats, were members of a populist South Indian sect that was militantly anti-brāhmanical (Zybendos 525). The twelfth-century social reformer, philosopher, and poet Basava founded the group and rejected the power and stratification of the caste system. He also opposed social or gender discrimination and took the unusual step of writing in the local language of Telegu, rather than exclusively writing in Sanskrit. The Viraśaiva bhaktas rejected many of the strictures of the caste system and worshipped Śiva with great fervor. The *Basava Purāṇa of Palkuriki Somnatha* expresses a strong proclivity for violent devotion. Self-mutilation and self-decapitation are endorsed alongside

FIG. 8.2 Female devotee self-decapitating, Nalgonda, 14th c. Reḍḍi Period, Andhra Pradesh [author].

intolerance and violence toward upper caste nonbelievers or non-Śaivas (Rao and Roghair 12).

Symbolism of Suicide

Many cultures explore self-sacrifice stories as the trope for the enforcement of social rules and taboos. Ensconced in the safely symbolic remove of myth, we can explore the violations of the social order that would be too contentious to discuss directly (Obeyesekere). Greek myths are full of the tales of social wrongs "righted" by suicide: Jocasta, both the mother and wife of Oedipus, killed herself upon discovering her incestuous relationship; and Phaedra fell in love with her stepson Hippolytus, but then killed herself when her passion was made public.

Indian myths also explore the ideas of social taboos in the stories of suicide. The goddess Satī self-immolated when her husband, Śiva, was not invited to a great sacrifice arranged by her father, Dakṣa. Enraged and humiliated at the disrespect shown to her husband, Satī spontaneously burst into flames and died. Śiva then in rage destroyed the sacrifice and turned Dakṣa into a goat, the typical animal of sacrifice. The message is that upon marriage, loyalties must shift from father to husband. Śiva in his grief would not release the body of Satī, but instead carried it to every part of India, and each place where a part of her body fell became a sacred site associated with her worship. Like the story of Purusa, the dismemberment of the goddess gave structure and hierarchy to Hindu rituals and gave sanctity to place.

Deities Who Received Sacrifice

As Indian religion moved from sacrifice to devotion, orthodox Hindu practitioners viewed violence and blood sacrifice with increasing suspicion. However, some powerful gods and goddesses still demanded blood offerings. Hindu reformers, such as the eighth-century Śankārācārya, questioned the morally ambiguous place of blood sacrifice. The devotee performed a violent act that was destructive to his or her karma, and the deity receiving sacrifice was placed in a position of inferior moral standing. This placed the deity and worshipper in a complex relationship, where worship took place in a chaotic nexus of violence and sacrality, where agency shifted from the whims of the divine to the decision of the worshipper making the offering.

The recipients of self-sacrifice tended to be violent deities. They were often the outliers of the Hindu pantheon and were singled out as liminal, transgressive, and "non-vegetarian." They were described as operating outside the bounds of orthodoxy (*adharma*). Their properties are referred to as angry and "hot;" they needed the cooling offering of blood. Despite this, *ugra* deities were powerful, and if their demands were met, their very *adharmic* nature made them both dangerous and powerful.

Goddesses were particularly desirous of blood sacrifice. Goddess worship in India probably had non-Vedic or even pre-Vedic roots. Judging by the numerous female images discovered in the Indus Valley sites (ca. 3000–1750 BCE), it is indeed possible that the goddess was a supreme deity in early Indian society. There are few goddesses mentioned in the Vedas, and those that are tend to be personifications of rituals or auspicious attributes, rather than full-fledged deities with a distinctive narrative. However, in the post-Vedic period, as Indian religion moved away from the elite rituals of the Vedas and toward personal and charismatic worship with the development of bhakti, goddesses became institutionalized, their stories were developed and embellished, and they took on dangerous roles as patrons of war, disease, childbirth, old age, and death.

The goddesses were often described as operating on the edges of society, both ritually and geographically. Durgā, the preeminent form of the Mahādevī, or Great Goddess, was often referred to by her liminal sobriquets, such as Vindyavāsinī, the goddess of the Vindya Mountains, which for many centuries marked the southern edge of Sanskritic culture (Kinsley 99). South Indian goddesses, such as the war goddess Koṛṛavai, were only barely removed from their local context. To be acceptable to the more sedate patterns of the "Great Tradition," local goddesses had to be Sanskritized by association to North Indian goddesses such as Durgā, who themselves were still liminal at the time of their incorporation into South Indian religious practice.

Other blood-drinking goddesses, such as Kālī, Cāmuṇḍā, Caṇḍī, Chinnamastā, Jyestha, and Śitalā, were liminal, untamed, and associated with danger, disease, decay, destruction, and death. The goddesses were not easy to love. They were both nurturers and destroyers; they were the acknowledgement that decay and death are parts of existence, and that mothers can be dark and demanding as well as nurturing and giving. Kālī, in particular, took on the conflicting roles of mother and destroyer and the recipient of sacrifice. In the Agni and Garuḍa Purāṇas, Kālī is mentioned as black, gaunt, and fanged, wearing a garland of corpses, riding a ghost, and residing in the cremation ground. The approximately tenth- to twelfth-century Kālikā Purāṇa describes the goddess as black, terrible, ogre-ish, beautiful, and charming. References in the Kālikā Purāṇa (71–73) note the goddess's need for human sacrifice and the detailed rituals for achieving the sacrifice.

Male deities also received blood sacrifice. Śiva Bhairava was marked out as the god of the cremation pyre, the outcast, and the sinner. His images portray him as fanged, decorated with serpents, carrying a trident with skull impaled, wearing a necklace of severed heads, smeared with cremation ash, accompanied by a scavenging dog and various ghouls and ghosts. Like the violent forms of the goddess, Śiva Bhairava gained his power by his *adharmic* behavior. He was the antithesis of the ideal Brāhmanical Hindu, having gained his power through heterodox sin and redemption rather than orthopractic adherence to rules and taboos. The sacrificial practices of ascetic devotees of Bhairava asserted both control and violence, like the god himself.

Conclusion

Sacrifice is at the core of many religions; it is a contract of communication between the human and the divine. In crossing the threshold of death, the Indian bhakta (devotee) made a commitment to the transcendent possibility of merger with the sacred.

The biological imperative for self-preservation, coupled with a shift toward secular culture, render the idea of religious self-sacrifice inconceivable for most people in our contemporary globalized society. We cling to our unique identities and our delusions of individual agency. An annihilation of self or merger with the gods is now, if at all, a mystical symbol and not a physical process. Sacrifice is now used primarily as an allegory, rather than a bloody reality.

Can we understand this "other" world of the bloody reality? Even if the ancient Indian method of self-sacrifice seems extravagant, we can understand the need to find a greater meaning for our individual struggles and our desires to be of service to society. Our fears have not changed so much from antiquity, but we have lost the language of ritual. We are still held in the jaws of death and are gripped by the terror of annihilation. Sacrifice rituals were attempts to control the chaos of uncertainty (Heesterman 24), and we continue to live in uncertain times.

9

Sati

David Brick

WITHOUT A DOUBT, one of the most widely known forms of ritual suicide in world religions is the traditional Hindu practice of widow self-immolation, or more precisely, the practice of a Hindu widow committing suicide by ritually ascending the funeral pyre of her deceased husband. A number of terms both in English and in Indian languages have been used to denote this practice, which has been discussed in an array of sources, including newspaper articles, colonial administrative reports, missionary accounts, and scholarly publications, not to mention the body of premodern religious texts that are the major focus of this essay. Although English sources often refer to the practice simply as "widow-burning," they perhaps more frequently use the term "sati" to denote it—a convention that I will here adopt both for the sake of convenience, and because it has become rather standard usage in scholarly works. Given its currency in modern English, one might reasonably regard the term "sati" (which is often given the alternative spelling "suttee" in older sources) as effectively an English loanword rather than a properly foreign word. In any case, its derivation from the Sanskrit *satī* during the British colonial period is clear. Importantly, however, the shift from the Sanskrit *satī* to the English "sati" involves more than simply the loss of italics and a diacritical mark; it involves a significant semantic shift too, for the word *satī* in Sanskrit sources never refers to the practice of widow self-immolation, but rather denotes a good, virtuous woman. The explanation for the semantic shift from woman to practice in the process of English borrowing is undoubtedly that certain Hindus came to regard a good, virtuous woman—a *satī*—as one who, among other things, ascended her husband's funeral pyre. Thus, what was at first a term associated with a self-immolating widow became in English the standard term for widow self-immolation itself. Contrary to English usage, however, Sanskrit sources use several different—typically euphemistic—terms to denote the Hindu practice of widow self-immolation, specifically: *sahagamana* ("going with"), *anugamana* ("going after"), *sahamaraṇa* ("dying with"), *anumaraṇa* ("dying after"), and *anvārohaṇa* ("ascending after").

Before proceeding directly to discussing the history of sati, it is necessary to point out that a number of other cultures historically have observed strikingly similar practices, which we may collectively describe as ritualized forms of widow suicide or "following into death" (in German, *Totenfolge*). Such practices are attested, for instance, in premodern Japan and China, in an array of colonial and precolonial African societies, and among the medieval Rus people and at least a few native tribes of North America.[1] Hence, from a certain perspective, one might say that sati is hardly a uniquely Indian cultural practice and might sympathize with those who resent the Western fascination with it as part of the Orientalist legacy, committed to showing the inherent backwardness of traditional Indian society. Nevertheless, there are at least three salient features of sati that seem to set it decidedly apart from most other forms of widow suicide and, therefore, make it arguably an object worthy of special scholarly attention. The first of these is that while most cultures that have had institutionalized forms of widow suicide or following into death abandoned the practice altogether by the early twentieth century at the latest, sati is a notable exception. Indeed, as Joerg Fisch (345) notes in his masterful study of widow suicide as a global phenomenon, "India is the only region in the world in which following into death can be proved to exist even today."[2] The second rather distinctive feature of sati—and one that is likely related to the first—is its historical spread beyond royal circles to larger segments of Indian society. For while widow suicide in most societies seems to have been effectively restricted to select members of the ruling class, sati in India eventually came to be an established custom among Hindu widows of virtually every social stratum, although members of the higher castes do seem to have engaged in the practice more frequently.[3] The final unique feature of sati is that it is much

1. For an extensive discussion of ritualized widow suicide outside of India, see Fisch 23–209.

2. For scholarly discussions of the most recent known act of sati, that performed by the Rajput widow Roop Kanwar on Sept. 4, 1987, see Narasimhan 1–10; Oldenburg 101–30; and Nandy 131–59.

3. See Fisch 258–59; and Mani 22.

better documented, and thus better known, than any other form of widow suicide (Fisch 9).

Earliest Sources

Turning now to the history of sati, there is no evidence of the practice whatsoever from the earliest period of Indian history—namely, the period of the Indus Valley Civilization (ca. 2600–1600 BCE), from which no deciphered written records survive. Furthermore, even in the following period, the so-called Vedic period (c. 1200–500 BCE), during which the various religious texts that make up the Vedas were composed, one finds no clear evidence of sati. Past scholars have sometimes cited the following verse of the *Ṛgveda* (10.18.7), the earliest surviving South Asian text, as an oblique reference to sati:

> Let these women, who are not widows, but rather have good husbands, enter together with fresh butter as ointment! Without tears or afflictions and possessed of fine jewels, let the wives ascend the womb first!

However, the precise meaning of this verse, including particularly the identity of the "womb" (*yoni*) that the wives are supposed to ascend, is decidedly unclear. Although it does seem to refer to a funerary rite of some type, the verse explicitly speaks of women who are "not widows" (*avidhavāḥ*). It therefore provides an extremely shaky basis upon which to hypothesize the custom of sati in the early Vedic period, especially when one considers the complete absence of references to the practice in the subsequent Vedic literature, which significantly includes rather detailed and explicit descriptions of late Vedic funeral ceremonies.

Perhaps the earliest surviving references to sati come not from India itself, but rather from several Western Greek sources, specifically from the *Geographica* of Strabo and the *Bibliotheca historica* of Diodorus Siculus, both authors belonging to the first-century BCE, who apparently rely upon earlier historians connected with Alexander the Great for their descriptions of sati.[4] Hence, Greek sources indicate that the practice of sati was current in at least Northwestern India as early as the fourth century BCE. Moreover, the specific

4. For a detailed discussion of Greek and Latin sources on sati, see Garzilli.

content of these sources suggests that it was practiced largely or perhaps even exclusively by members of the ruling class, specifically by the widows of kings.[5]

Probably the earliest references to sati in Indian literature come from the *Mahābhārata*, the longer of the two great Sanskrit epics. In keeping with its narrative focus on kingly culture and warfare, the *Mahābhārata* contains numerous literary descriptions of how royal women conduct themselves after the deaths of their husbands. In fact, the eleventh book of the epic, the *Strī Parvan* or "Book of Women," centers fundamentally around such descriptions. Tellingly, however, the *Strī Parvan* makes no mention whatsoever of sati, and occurrences of sati throughout the entire epic are rare and restricted almost exclusively to the widows of kings and princes.[6] This suggests that sati was a rather exceptional practice in North India, during the period in which the epics as we have them took shape (ca. 300 BCE–300 CE). It furthermore confirms the general impression gathered from early Greek sources that it was observed mainly, or perhaps exclusively, by members of royal families.

To give just one concrete example of sati from the *Mahābhārata* that is fairly representative of its treatment throughout the epic, we can examine the story of the death of Pāṇḍu, the father of the epic's five chief protagonists, the Pāṇḍava brothers. Prior to his death, Pāṇḍu has renounced his role as king of the city of Hastināpura and taken up a life of ascetic celibacy, because a Brahmin sage has fatefully cursed him to an immediate death should he ever again have sexual intercourse. Despite his sworn celibacy, however, Pāṇḍu's two young wives, Kuntī and Mādrī, accompany him to the forest. Then, on a beautiful day in spring—the season most associated with sexual love in India as in the West—Pāṇḍu takes a stroll through the forest accompanied only by his younger wife Mādrī (MBh 1.116.2–5); becomes deeply smitten by her beauty (6–7); forces himself upon her despite her attempts to resist him and, thereby, save his life (8–10); and dies at once (11–12). Kuntī then hears Mādrī's piteous lament (13); comes quickly with their five young sons to investigate (14); learns what has happened and grieves her husband's passing (15–21); and thereafter decides to perform sati as his eldest lawful wife (23–24). Mādrī,

---

5. If Garzilli (221) is correct in her suggestion that the Kathaioi mentioned in Strabo should be identified with Brahmins of the Kāṭhaka Vedic school, this would constitute an important exception to the above statement.

6. References to sati in the *Mahābhārata* include: 4.22.5–25, where the kinsmen of Kīcaka, king Virāṭa's brother-in-law, unsuccessfully try to burn Draupadī on Kīcaka's pyre (here the wicked character of the perpetrators would seem to account for the element of overt coercion); 12.144.1–12, where a grief-stricken dove performs sati; 16.8.18, where several wives of king Vasudeva resolve to perform sati; and 16.8.71, where several wives of Kṛṣṇa perform sati.

however, asks Kuntī's permission to perform sati in her stead for two basic reasons (25–30). Firstly, Pāṇḍu has died out of a sexual desire for her and only by following him in death can she carry out in the hereafter her wifely duty of fulfilling her husband's desire. Secondly, she claims that she is incapable of treating Kuntī's sons as lovingly as her own should she have to act as their mother. Mādrī's arguments immediately persuade Kuntī, who lives on as the Pāṇḍavas' sole surviving mother throughout the epic, while Mādrī ritually ascends her husband's funeral pyre (31). As readers can see, this narrative reveals two crucial features of sati as it is presented in Hindu religious texts of the ancient and medieval periods. The first of these is that it is a strictly voluntary undertaking; it is not presented as a mandatory practice, nor does physical coercion constitute a motivating factor in its lawful execution. The second feature of sati is its special goal, which is the unbroken continuation in the next life of a wife's faithful and devoted service to her husband—the very reason for her existence according to many classical Hindu texts.

Another early description of sati comes from a work that belongs to an entirely different South Asian literary tradition, the so-called Sangam literature, written exclusively in South India in the old Tamil language, the precursor of modern Tamil and Malayalam. The specific work referred to is the *Puṟanāṉūṟu*, a collection of four hundred short poems on kingship that has been dated to the second or third century (Hart and Heifetz xvi). In particular, poems 246 and 247 of the *Puṟanāṉūṟu* deal with sati. The former is ascribed to Peruṅkōpeṇṭu, the wife of a recently deceased Tamil king, who conveys her ardent desire to ascend her husband's pyre despite the plans to the contrary of her male guardians. The essential reason given in the poem for her decision to perform sati is a profound aversion to the ascetic hardships of South Indian widowhood, which include the consumption of only bland food and sleeping on the bare ground.[7] The latter poem is ascribed to a male witness to Peruṅkōpeṇṭu's sati, who expresses his wonder at her undertaking. Together these poems confirm the exceptional nature of sati, its voluntary character (at least in the literary imagination), and its restriction to the ruling classes in early South Asia. Their rather realistic tone—in contrast, for instance, to the Sanskrit epics—also supports the impression that sati was an actual cultural practice at the time, rather than a mere literary trope. And the general provenance of the *Puṟanāṉūṟu* shows that even fairly early on, sati was practiced in both South India and North India.

---

7. For more on widow-asceticism in early India, see Hart, and Brick, "Widow-Ascetic."

Following these early literary references to sati, there also begin to appear around the sixth century an increasingly large number of inscriptions that record specific instances of sati, as well as uninscribed stones that clearly memorialize acts of sati.[8] These objects and inscriptions attest both to the actual practice of sati throughout much of the Indian subcontinent, and to its gradual spread to new segments of society beyond high-caste ruling families. For instance, a Kannada inscription dated to the year 1057 records, in laudatory language, how the daughter of a provincial governor of explicitly low-caste origin performed sati, despite her parents' objections.[9] Unfortunately, not enough research has been done to map the spread of sati geographically and socially with any real precision on the basis of inscriptional sources. One can note with some confidence, however, on the basis of both inscriptional and literary evidence that it spread historically from royal circles to the rest of Hindu society,[10] and that this spread began in the second half of the first millennium, and gained special momentum in the first half of the second millennium. The precise reasons for the spread of sati during this period are unclear, but plausibly include the perceived threat of Islamicate power, the important role of hypergamy in classical Indian society, and Brahmanical rivalry with the ruling warrior class (Fisch 251–54; Brick, "Widow-Ascetic," 277–81).

Whatever the underlying causes of sati's spread, we have not yet touched upon arguably the most important set of premodern sources on the practice—sources that allow us to track changing attitudes toward sati with unequaled clarity and reveal a major pan-Indian debate on its very validity. These sources are the numerous works belonging to the tradition of Hindu law known as Dharmaśāstra, which is the branch of classical Brahmanical scholarship most directly concerned with delineating the bounds of right conduct. It is these texts to which we now turn.

Sati Under Hindu Law

The scholastic and literary tradition known as Dharmaśāstra, often referred to in English as "Hindu law," is, as its name suggests, the *śāstra* or branch of Brahmanical scholarship that takes as its subject dharma, a term denoting

8. On these, see Kane vol. 2, 629; and Fisch 226–28.

9. See *Epigraphia Indica* vol. 6, 213–19.

10. Fisch (12–15, 248–54) refers to this as a shift from institutionalized following into death to individual following into death—the latter form being particularly characteristic of sati throughout much of its history.

in this context the rules of right conduct governing virtually all aspects of Brahmanical Hindu life. As such, Dharmaśāstra prescribes sets of specific normative rules—"laws" in a certain sense of the term—for a massive and varied array of topics, including personal etiquette, the settlement of legal disputes, expiatory rites, world-renunciation, and gifting. This prodigious legal tradition spans over two millennia of Indian history, from roughly the third century BCE to the eighteenth century CE; and during this time, important Dharmaśāstra works were composed in virtually all areas of the subcontinent. Thus, taken in its entirety, Dharmaśāstra literature is incredibly vast—surprisingly so to nonspecialists. Broadly speaking, however, it can be divided into two periods, a basic understanding of which is essential, if one wishes to understand the history of Hindu religious views on sati. During the first period, which extends from approximately the third century BCE to the seventh century CE, authors working within the Dharmaśāstra tradition composed works called "Smṛtis," which typically present themselves as divine revelations, and eventually took on the status of sacred scriptures second in authority only to the Vedas. In the second period, which covers more or less the eighth to eighteenth centuries and which scholars loosely refer to as "medieval," Dharmaśāstric authors composed primarily exegetical works—i.e., commentaries and digests—that strive to create a clear, comprehensive, and systematic account of the rules of right conduct prescribed in the earlier Smṛtis. From a historical perspective, the fundamental value of the Dharmaśāstra tradition is that it provides a uniquely long and thorough record of Indian beliefs and customs—if admittedly perhaps only the beliefs and customs of a powerful, pan-Indian class of Brahmins.[11]

Turning specifically to the treatment of sati within Dharmaśāstra, the first thing to note is that like the earlier Vedic literature, the earliest works on Hindu law[12] contain no mention whatsoever of the practice—a striking omission given the breadth of Brahmanical customs that these texts treat in significant detail. In fact, of all the extant Smṛtis of the Dharmaśāstra tradition, only the two most recent (relatively speaking), namely, the *Viṣṇu Smṛti* (25.14)[13] and the *Parāśara Smṛti* (4.29–31), make any mention of sati.

11. For a detailed defense of this thesis, see Lariviere.

12. For a brief and authoritative account of the relative and absolute dates of the early Dharmaśāstra works, see Olivelle, "Dharmaśāstra." For the dates of the later digests and commentaries, see Kane, vol. 1.

13. This work is also sometimes referred to as either the *Viṣṇu Dharmasūtra* or the *Vaiṣṇava Dharmaśāstra*.

Specifically, both works present the practice as a meritorious alternative to ascetic celibacy for Brahmanical widows. Moreover, the *Parāśara Smṛti,* at least, clearly regards sati as the superior of these two alternatives, for while it cites simply "heaven" (*svarga*) as the reward of ascetic celibacy, it elaborates upon the otherworldly rewards of sati in far greater detail. In particular, it explains that a woman who performs sati not only dwells in heaven for as many years as there are hairs on a human body, but also leads her husband there, even if his sins would ordinarily have made residence in heaven impossible—a telling violation of classical Hindu laws of karma that attracts the attention of several commentators, as will be discussed below.

In any case, aside from the above references to sati found in the extant Smṛtis of Viṣṇu and Parāśara, an examination of the later commentarial literature reveals a number of passages advocating sati ascribed to authors of Smṛtis that are now lost. Such authors include Aṅgiras, Uśanas, Paiṭhīnasi, Vyāsa, Hārīta, and Bṛhaspati.[14] Taken together with the previous citations from Viṣṇu (25.14) and Parāśara (4.29–31), these passages constitute the entirety of Dharmaśāstric injunctions regarding sati. However, a complete account of Hindu scriptures on the practice must also include several passages from the Purāṇas and Sanskrit epics.[15]

Considering the complete absence of any mention of sati in both Vedic literature and the earliest works of the Dharmaśāstra tradition, it seems reasonable to conclude that this practice first gained enough popularity within Brahmanical culture to warrant mention at approximately the time when Viṣṇu, Parāśara, Aṅgiras, and the other writers of Smṛtis mentioned earlier composed their works on Hindu law. Consequently, in order to establish the period during which sati first became a recognized custom within orthodox Brahmanical culture, it is necessary to establish the provenances of these works. Unfortunately, however, the available evidence does not allow us to do this within very narrow limits. Perhaps the best that can be said is that they were composed somewhere in India probably during the second half

14. See Medhātithi 1.157; *Mitākṣarā* 1.86; Aparārka 1.87; Mādhava 4.30–31; *Madanapārijāta* 196–200; *Smṛticandrikā* (*Vyavahārakāṇḍa*) 596; *Śuddhimayūkha* 68–69; and *Nirṇayasindhu* 438–39.

15. For instance, Aparārka (1.87, specifically p. 111), the *Kṛtyakalpataru* (*Vyavahārakāṇḍa* 634), and the *Nirṇayasindhu* (438) all cite an identical passage that they ascribe to the *Brahma Purāṇa* and the *Nirṇayasindhu* (438–40) also cites passages ascribed to the *Skanda, Vāyu, Bṛhannārada,* and *Brahmavaivarta Purāṇas*. For references to sati in the *Mahābhārata*, see note 6.

of the first millennium.[16] In any case, it is clear from citations found in later commentaries that by the twelfth century, these works and the practice of sati were widely known to orthodox Brahmins throughout India.[17]

Importantly, however, not all Smṛti passages that mention sati endorse the practice, for beginning with the commentator Vijñāneśvara (c. 1076–1127), authors working within the Dharmaśāstra tradition cite a number of authoritative scriptures that explicitly prohibit Brahmin widows from performing sati.[18] For example, one such oft-cited Smṛti reads:

> Due to Vedic injunction, a Brahmin woman should not follow her husband in death, but for the other social classes, tradition holds this to be the supreme law of women.

Although all medieval exegetes who cite this passage and others like it manage to greatly reduce their proscriptive scope, to a neutral reader their purpose is clearly to issue a general prohibition against sati in the case of Brahmin widows. Hence, they inform us that while their authors, who were undoubtedly Brahmins, had no specific objection to non-Brahmin widows performing sati, they strongly objected to this practice among widows of their own social class. This, in turn, may be taken to confirm that sati was well-established among certain other social groups at the time these scriptures were composed, but still relatively new and, therefore, controversial among orthodox Brahmins.

With this in mind, it should come as no surprise that Medhātithi (ca. 825–1000 CE), the author of probably the earliest extant commentary to discuss the issue, staunchly opposes the practice. Specifically, Medhātithi (in *Mānava Dharmaśāstra* 5.155) puts forth two different arguments against sati. First, he

16. Olivelle ("Date and Provenance") puts forth a convincing argument for the provenance of the *Viṣṇu Smṛti* in particular, which settles the date of the text within somewhat narrow limits as 600–800 CE. This may be used to approximate the dates of the less well-established Dharmaśāstras in question.

17. The following Dharmaśāstric works/authors all discuss sati at some length: Medhātithi 5.155 (c. 825–1000, Kashmir); the *Mitākṣarā* 1.86 (c. 1076–1127, Karnataka); Aparārka 1.87 (c. 1125, Goa); the *Vyavahārakāṇḍa* of the *Kṛtyakalpataru* 632–36 (c. 1110–50, Kannauj); the *Vyavahārakāṇḍa* of the *Smṛticandrikā* 596–97 (c. 1150–1225, South India); Mādhava 4.30–31 (c. 1330–60, Vijayanagara); the *Madanapārijāta* 196–201 (c. 1350–1400, U. P.); the *Śuddhitattva* (c. 1510–80, Bengal); the *Śuddhimayūkha* 68–71 (c. 1610–50, eastern U. P.); the *Nirṇayasindhu* 438–40 (1612, Benares); and the *Dharmasindhu* 384–86 (1790–91, Maharashtra).

18. See Aparārka 1.87, *Mitākṣarā* 1.86, *Madanapārijāta* 197, *Śuddhimayūkha* 69, and *Nirṇayasindhu* 438.

argues that those Smṛtis that evidently prescribe it are in direct contradiction with those statements in the Veda that prohibit suicide.[19] And since it is an accepted exegetical principle of Hindu law that the Vedas are of greater authority than the Smṛtis, one can safely construe the various Smṛti statements that appear to advocate sati as, in reality, conveying a different meaning. Medhātithi's second argument against sati is considerably more technical and deals with an obscure Vedic ritual—the *śyena* or "falcon" sacrifice—whose explicit purpose is to kill a man's enemies. According to the traditional interpretation, this rite is unlawful, because there is a general prohibition against violence. The Vedic text laying down the *śyena* sacrifice (*Ṣaḍviṃśa Brāhmaṇa* 3.8.1) simply conveys that if a person wants to kill his enemies, this sacrifice is one means of accomplishing his goal. It does not, however, enjoin the killing of one's enemies, so there is no specific scriptural injunction that would override the general prohibition against violence. Using the analogy of this sacrifice, Medhātithi argues that the Smṛtis do not actually enjoin sati, because they explicitly mention its result: namely, heaven. They only state that if a widow wants to be reborn in heaven, sati is one possible means. In other words, according to Medhātithi, the various Smṛtis on sati are simple statements, rather than legal injunctions or recommendations. Thus, as in the case of the *śyena* sacrifice, the general prohibition against violence still applies. It is on the basis on these two arguments that the earliest commentarial work within the Dharmaśāstra tradition to address the topic of sati takes a position that is completely opposed to the practice.

However, beginning with the *Mitākṣarā* (ca. 1076–1127), Vijñāneśvara's highly influential commentary on the *Yājñavalkya Smṛti*, this position starts to weaken in several distinct ways. To begin with, Vijñāneśvara attempts to reconcile those Smṛtis that generally enjoin sati with those that apparently prohibit the practice in the case of Brahmin widows. And, importantly, he does this in a way that allows Brahmin women to perform sati with little restriction. In particular, Vijñāneśvara (1.86) argues that those Smṛtis that apparently prohibit Brahmin women from performing sati really only prohibit them from performing it on different funeral pyres than those of their husbands. And, in support of this interpretation, he cites a previously unknown scriptural passage that appears to express precisely this idea. Via this argument, Vijñāneśvara effectively does away with any objections aimed specifically at the right of Brahmin widows to perform sati.

19. Of these, the standard passage that is cited is *Śatapatha Brāhmaṇa* 10.2.6.7.

Furthermore, it is noteworthy that Vijñāneśvara's line of argumentation on this point appears to have exerted considerable influence on a large number of later exegetes. For instance, both Aparārka (1.87) and Madanapāla (197–98) clearly adopt Vijñāneśvara's exact thinking on this point.[20] Beyond this, some later commentators even go so far as to do away with Vijñāneśvara's restriction that Brahmin widows ascend the same funeral pyre as their husbands. For example, the *Nirṇayasindhu* (439), an influential digest composed in Benares in 1612, introduces a novel interpretation of those scriptures that issue prohibitions against Brahmin women performing sati: instead of referring to separate funeral pyres, they could refer to cases where a woman's husband either was an outcaste or had died in the process of repenting for some grievous sin. If accepted, such an interpretation would virtually eliminate any special restrictions placed on Brahmin widows. Furthermore, the *Nirṇayasindhu* proceeds to explain that in any case, a woman can avoid the sin of ascending a separate funeral pyre by immolating herself together with either the bones of her dead husband or a wooden replacement for him. Again, such a position—even more so than Vijñāneśvara's—effectively eliminates any special restrictions placed on Brahmin widows. From the presence of such statements and the complete absence of contrary ones, it is evident that starting with Vijñāneśvara, commentators within the Dharmaśāstra tradition differ markedly from the authors of some earlier Smṛtis in that they feel no particular reservations about Brahmin widows performing sati.

To return specifically to the *Mitākṣarā*, after severely limiting the prohibitive scope of those Smṛtis that seemingly proscribe sati for Brahmin widows, Vijñāneśvara then attempts to demonstrate that the practice is dissimilar to the *śyena* sacrifice and, therefore, completely lawful. In other words, at this point Vijñāneśvara responds to Medhātithi's earlier discussion of sati, with which he was clearly familiar, and specifically tries to refute one of Medhātithi's two basic arguments against the practice. To this end, he postulates two possible lines of reasoning that might explain why the *śyena* sacrifice is unlawful to perform, and then attempts to show that neither line of reasoning works in the case of sati. Vijñāneśvara's argument here is particularly ingenious.[21] It is highly technical and involves a number of ideas specific to classical Brahmanical hermeneutics,[22] but the significant point of

---

20. For a detailed discussion of this, see Brick, "Dharmaśāstric Debate" 208–10.

21. Interested readers should consult Brick, "Dharmaśāstric Debate" 210–12 for a detailed explanation.

22. For a detailed discussion, see Brick, "Dharmaśāstric Debate" 210–12.

difference between sati and the *śyena* sacrifice that Vijñāneśvara latches onto can be easily summarized: the problem with the *śyena* sacrifice is its result, which is the death of one's enemies, whereas the result of sati—i.e., heaven—is clearly unproblematic. Importantly, this part of Vijñāneśvara's exegesis on sati appears to have been highly successful, for no subsequent work of Dharmaśāstra attempts to use analogy with the *śyena* sacrifice as grounds for rejecting the practice or, indeed, makes any mention of the possibility even to refute it.

Despite his strong refutation of the *śyena* analogy, however, Vijñāneśvara appears not to have wholly approved of sati, for he cites two arguments against the practice that he regards as unobjectionable. The first of these arguments against sati is essentially the same as Medhātithi's earlier argument that Vedic statements prohibiting suicide effectively negate Smṛti statements that enjoin widows to immolate themselves on their husbands' funeral pyres. The second unobjectionable argument against sati that is mentioned by Vijñāneśvara is markedly more peculiar, at least from a Western religious perspective. It begins by noting that, although certain Smṛtis do enjoin sati as a means of attaining heaven, heaven itself is an inferior goal to *mokṣa*—that is, liberation from the cycle of rebirth altogether—which is the highest soteriological goal in classical Indian religions. From this the conclusion is drawn that since the alternative practice of ascetic celibacy can help a woman to attain *mokṣa*, this alternative is undoubtedly superior. Vijñāneśvara's judgment of these two arguments as unobjectionable shows that while he does not appear to share Medhātithi's strong opposition to sati, he does have considerable reservations about the practice.

It is noteworthy that none of the commentators or digest-writers in the centuries following the *Mitākṣarā* takes up the position that Vedic statements prohibiting suicide negate those Smṛtis that apparently enjoin sati. And this—it should be noted—is the only argument accepted by Vijñāneśvara that would actually prohibit sati, rather than merely demote it to the lesser of two alternatives. Moreover, Aparārka (1.87), who likely wrote only a few decades after Vijñāneśvara, explicitly refutes this line of argumentation by proposing what is technically called a *viṣayavyavasthā*, that is to say, a resolution of apparently contradictory scriptures by ascribing to them different spheres of applicability. According to his analysis, those Vedic statements that proscribe suicide or otherwise stand opposed to ending one's life prematurely are only of a general nature, whereas those Smṛti statements that prescribe sati are of a specific nature. Therefore, since it is a standard principle of Brahmanical hermeneutics that a specific rule overrides a general one, the

Smṛtis that enjoin sati are of sufficient authority in this case to overrule Vedic texts. In other words, Aparārka concludes that those Vedic passages that prohibit suicide apply everywhere except for the specific case of sati, where the less general rules of the various Smṛtis apply. Significantly, a number of later authors accept the very same position on this issue as Aparārka and none attempts to refute it.[23]

In addition, both Aparārka (1.87) and the *Kṛtyakalpataru* (*Vyavahārakāṇḍa* 634) approvingly cite a line ascribed to the *Brahma Purāṇa*, according to which a woman who performs sati is not guilty of suicide due to some unspecified statement of the *Ṛgveda*. And, unsurprisingly, these commentators both identify the statement referred to as *Ṛgveda* 10.18.7, which has been cited above. As has already been mentioned, it is extremely unlikely that this rather cryptic verse has anything originally to do with sati. Despite this, however, the *Brahma Purāṇa*, Aparārka, and the *Kṛtyakalpataru* all apparently regard it as in some way sanctioning the practice. The underlying reason for this highly dubious interpretation is undoubtedly their desire to find Vedic support for sati. Beyond this, there is also the distinct possibility that within the context of the Dharmaśāstric debate on sati, *Ṛgveda* 10.18.7 underwent certain changes to make it appear more germane to the practice. Of these, the most important is the possible change of the word *agre* ("first") in the verse to *agne* ("O fire") or *agneḥ* ("of fire").[24] The result is that rather than speaking of wives ascending the "womb first," the verse speaks of wives ascending the "womb of fire" or "womb, O fire!"

In this regard, it is also significant that both the *Nirṇayasindhu* and the *Dharmasindhu* attest to the recitation of *Ṛgveda* 10.18.7 as a part of the performance of the sati rite. In particular, the earlier of the two works, the *Nirṇayasindhu* (438), describes its recitation as a practice peculiar to Bengal, while the *Dharmasindhu* (385; a work from Maharashtra, not Bengal) cites it as part of the standard ritual. Hence, these texts suggest that the verse may have been a rather late addition to the sati rite in much of India. Whether or not this was the case, their testimony further indicates that certain elements within the Brahmanical community were not content to refute, through strictly exegetical arguments, the objection to sati on the grounds that it contradicts the Veda. Instead, by including *Ṛgveda* 10.18.7 as a liturgical

23. See, for example, Mādhava's commentary on *Parāśara Smṛti* 4.30 (cited in Brick, "Dharmaśāstric Debate" 214n.).

24. See Hall; Kane vol. 2, 634; and Rocher.

formula, they appear also to have constructed the sati rite itself in such a way that it conveys an aura of Vedic authority. And if this is in fact so, we have here a further Brahmanical argument in favor of sati, albeit of an oblique and unconventional sort.

To return one last time to the *Mitākṣarā*, although the argument against sati on the grounds that it contradicts the Veda quickly falls out of favor after Vijñāneśvara, the other argument accepted by him—namely, that sati is an inferior option to ascetic celibacy, because it yields the inferior result of heaven—has at least one later supporter: Devaṇa Bhaṭṭa, who probably wrote his *Smṛticandrikā* in South India between 1150 and 1225.[25] After this author, however, even support for this weakened position against sati seems to cease. Furthermore, two rather late digests, the *Nirṇayasindhu* (438) and *Dharmasindhu* (384), cite a previously unquoted Smṛti passage that lists liberation from the cycle of rebirth as an explicit reward of sati. In light of the earlier commentarial debate, this passage appears tailor-made as a refutation of the last remaining objection to the practice. That is, the content of this Smṛti and its absence as a cited scripture in the preceding commentaries combine to strongly suggest that it is a relatively recent creation of the Dharmaśāstra tradition—a creation whose purpose was to refute claims regarding the inferiority of sati vis-à-vis ascetic celibacy.

Nevertheless, despite the eventual disappearance of all objections to sati within the Hindu legal tradition, it is important to note that the practice never becomes an obligatory act. Instead, authors consistently regard it as optional, although given the especially lavish praise it often receives, for many it was probably not just optional, but in fact supererogatory. The first commentator to explicitly mention the optional character of sati appears to be Aparārka (1.87); and it is Madanapāla (198–99), in the fourteenth century, who argues this point in greatest detail. Nonetheless, it can confidently be stated that all other Dharmaśāstra works, whether exegetical or scriptural in nature, either explicitly or implicitly accept this position as well.

Furthermore, even beyond this, several commentarial works specify that if the widow loses her resolve to perform sati, her husband's younger brother or another male relative should intervene and lift her up from the funeral pyre.[26] Moreover, rather unusually, none of these texts cites any scriptural

---

25. See *Smṛticandrikā* (*Vyavahārakāṇḍa*) 596–97.

26. See Aparārka 1.87; *Nirṇayasindhu* 438; and *Dharmasindhu* 385. It is perhaps worth noting that when these texts instruct a widow's brother-in-law to lift her up from her husband's funeral pyre, it is almost certainly intended as a literal act, rather than an oblique reference to leviratic

evidence in support of this rule. Hence, it seems a distinct possibility that here these classical Hindu jurists may, for once, be implicitly acknowledging the harrowing nature of the sati rite and allowing a role for general compassion in what it is otherwise treated as a matter of dry scriptural analysis. At the very least, it shows that these authors believed strongly in the voluntary nature of sati.

Finally, many authors in the Dharmaśāstra tradition explicitly stipulate that sati is prohibited for women who are either pregnant or have young children. For example, Vijñāneśvara (1.86) summarizes the injunctions regarding sati as the "universal law for all women right down to Cāṇḍalas [untouchables], provided that they are not pregnant and do not have young children." Perhaps somewhat surprisingly, the earliest commentators to make this stipulation, including Vijñāneśvara, cite no scriptural passages in support of their position.[27] From this, we might infer that the justification lies not in specific scriptural prohibitions, but rather in the basic ethical principle that sati may harm only the widow herself and no one else, including her born and unborn children. In other words, the prohibition against pregnant women and women with small children performing sati is essentially an application of the general prohibition against violence. It is noteworthy, however, that two later exegetical works, the *Parāśara-Mādhava* (4.31) and *Nirṇayasindhu* (439), both cite several verses that provide an explicit scriptural basis for this prohibition.

To summarize then, one can loosely arrange Hindu legal writings on sati into three historical periods. In the first of these, which roughly corresponds to the second half of the first millennium, Smṛti texts that prescribe sati begin to appear. However, during approximately this same period, other Brahmanical authors also compose a number of Smṛtis that proscribe this practice specifically in the case of Brahmin widows. Moreover, Medhātithi—our earliest commentator to address the issue—strongly opposes the practice for all women. Taken together, this textual evidence suggests that sati was still quite controversial at this time. In the following period, opposition to this custom starts to weaken, as none of the later commentators fully endorses Medhātithi's position on sati. Indeed, after Vijñāneśvara, in perhaps the early twelfth century the strongest position taken against sati appears to be that it

marriage, which, by the medieval period, the Hindu legal tradition had come to uniformly reject. On leviratic marriage under Hindu law, see Kane vol. 2, 599–607.

27. These are the *Mitākṣarā* (1.86), *Kṛtyakalpataru* (*Vyavahārakāṇḍa* 635), and *Madanapārijāta* (196).

is an inferior option to ascetic celibacy, since its result is only heaven rather than liberation from the cycle of rebirth altogether. Finally, in the third period, several commentators refute even this attenuated objection to sati, for they cite a previously unquoted Smṛti passage that specifically lists liberation as a result of the rite's performance. They thereby claim that sati is at least as beneficial an option for widows as celibacy and perhaps even more so, given the special praise it sometimes receives. These authors, however, consistently stop short of making it an obligatory act. Hence, the commentarial literature of the Dharmaśāstra tradition attests to a gradual shift from strict prohibition to complete endorsement in its attitude toward sati.

Lastly, before turning briefly to the history of sati during the colonial and postcolonial periods, it is worth remarking on the special purpose of the practice according to classical Brahmanical thought. This purpose is reflected in a number of oft-cited Smṛti passages, such as the following[28]:

> A woman who follows her husband in death shall dwell in heaven for thirty-five million years or as many years as there are hairs on a human body. And just as a snake-catcher forcefully lifts up a snake out of its hole, so does this woman lift up her husband from hell and then rejoices together with him.

As this passage indicates, sati is held to possess two special powers. Firstly, it ensures the continuation in the hereafter of the marital union and the close personal bond between husband and wife and, secondly, it brings about a rebirth in heaven for a widow's husband, even if his past actions would ordinarily have resulted in a less desirable rebirth.

Hence, the vision of the hereafter and the soteriology underlying sati differ markedly from the standard classical Hindu view on these matters, for according to this view, one's future rebirths depend solely upon one's own past actions, not the actions of any others, including one's wife. As such, a person's journey through various rebirths can be regarded as highly individualistic in that his or her social position and personal relationships in one life do not generally carry over to subsequent ones. In its special otherworldly effects, therefore, sati reflects a notable departure from classical Hindu soteriology. And this is quite unlikely to be a coincidence, for Joerg Fisch

28. *Parāśara Smṛti* 4.30–31 (discussed briefly above). See also Aparārka 1.87 (specifically p. 110), and *Madanapārijāta* 199–201.

(10–11) has persuasively argued that a major precondition for the practice of following into death to develop and endure in a given society is a belief that the social order of this life extends into the next life as well. And yet, as he readily acknowledges and as is generally well-known, classical Indian religions, including Hinduism, espouse a markedly different soteriology from this, one based fundamentally upon laws of karma. Thus, the preservation of sati within Hinduism seems to require it to be exceptional from a soteriological point of view. And, indeed, in its special telos, sati appears to contain a combination of older and newer soteriological elements. The practice reflects an older soteriology, in that a woman who performs it and her husband continue on as a married couple in the hereafter. Yet it also reflects a newer soteriology based on karma, in that the union of husband and wife in the next life is not simply assumed. Instead, it is only through the extraordinary and highly meritorious act of sati that this, as well as an especially long stay in heaven, becomes possible. Fisch (463) aptly characterizes this development as the "moralization" of sati.

Moreover, several commentators within the Dharmaśāstra tradition make special note of the unusual otherworldly effects of sati and take pains to explain how these effects do not, in fact, violate the accepted laws of karma. Aparārka (1.87), for example, argues that by performing sati, a woman does not actually lead her sinful husband to heaven; he gets there purely through his own past good deeds. His wife's act of self-immolation simply removes for a time the sin that blocks him from experiencing such a happy rebirth. And, according to an influential strand of classical Brahmanical thought, to remove an obstacle is not the same thing as to produce an effect.[29] Hence, because sati does not technically cause a husband's heavenly rebirth, it does not violate the accepted laws of karma. The *Madanapārijāta* (199–202), by contrast, in an especially long exposition offers two alternative explanations as to why certain Smṛtis present sati as salvific for both the widow and her husband. Firstly (200), it argues that one might interpret the relevant Smṛtis as instances of a recognized type of scriptural statement called *arthavāda*, which are statements intended merely to inspire the carrying out of scriptural injunctions and not to be taken at face value.[30] If interpreted as such, a particular scripture can effectively be disregarded according to standard Dharmaśāstric exegesis. Secondly, in a rather convoluted passage, the *Madanapārijāta* argues that sati

29. On this notion in Advaita Vedānta philosophy, see Potter 32–33.

30. On *arthavāda*, see Kane, vol. 5 1238–44.

has no impact on a husband's sins that are far from bearing fruit; temporarily suspends the effects of his sins that are currently bearing fruit, but does not destroy them; and completely destroys his sins that are about to bear fruit in a manner analogous to a ritual penance (200–01). And interestingly, the *Madanapārijāta* defends its position that sati can expiate some of a husband's sins by arguing that as in other rituals, a husband and wife jointly perform sati and, thus, jointly enjoy its rewards (201–02).

Later Developments

With the founding of the Delhi Sultanate in 1206, Islamicate political power became established in the heartland of North India. And, as is well-known, Muslim rulers came to reign over most of the Indian subcontinent during the course of the following centuries. Given that, like Christianity, Islam essentially rejects all forms of following into death, it is unsurprising that Muslim rulers in South Asia tended to discourage the practice of sati, sometimes restricting it and at other times apparently prohibiting it, at least in certain regions (Fisch 345–52). Furthermore, early European colonies in India, such as that at Goa, generally treated the practice in a similar fashion (Fisch 362–63). Nevertheless, despite the disapproval of many local rulers, a reasonably large number of Hindus clearly continued to actively observe the custom of sati from the thirteenth to the early nineteenth century. Indeed, it was only in 1829, under the rule of the British East India Company, that sati was finally abolished as a practice throughout most of India, the sole exceptions to this abolition being the various semi-autonomous princely states, where the practice was not fully banned until 1862.

Well before 1829, however, British colonial administrators widely expressed strong abhorrence for the practice of sati and criticized it on the basis of both Christian and Western secular ethics, although they often expressed their criticisms in the language of moral universals. Yet, at the same time, these administrators were extremely reluctant to impose what they viewed as foreign personal laws upon their subjects, especially when these laws were held to be in conflict with explicitly religious beliefs. Therefore, in the eighteenth and early nineteenth centuries, British colonialists felt simultaneously a strong impulse to ban sati on moral grounds, and an extreme reluctance to do so on the grounds that this would constitute an intolerable interference in Hindu religious practice and incite rebellion. In order to resolve this conflict, attempts were made to ascertain the extent to which Hinduism actually sanctioned sati. And, consequently, in keeping with the prevalent European assumption at the time that religion ultimately resides in holy texts, the British colonial authorities closely engaged with Hindu scriptures on sati and the traditional interpretations thereof. To this end, Hindu pundits connected with the colonial courts were consulted and, prior to abolition, a number of old restrictions on sati prescribed in earlier Dharmaśāstra works were reapplied. These restrictions include that a woman performing sati could not be pregnant; that she could not have young children unless she made explicit provisions for their care; and that if she were of Brahmin caste, she could only perform sati on the same funeral pyre as her husband.

In addition to British opposition to sati, Hindu opponents of the practice became politically mobilized in the process leading to abolition. By all accounts the most important of these Indian opponents of sati is Rammohun Roy, a prominent intellectual and the leading Hindu reformer of the early nineteenth century. Roy argued against sati in a number of polemical pamphlets written in both Bengali and English.[31] Although his arguments in these pamphlets occasionally appeal to universalistic morals, they are more often of a traditional exegetical character, intended presumably to sway orthodox Hindu defenders of sati. Particularly interesting in this regard is that Roy effectively revives the *Mitākṣarā*'s old argument against sati on the grounds that it leads merely to heaven, rather than the higher soteriological goal of liberation. Indeed, despite the fact that this argument really only reduces sati to the lesser of two alternatives, it is central to Roy's case against the practice. Roy, however, strengthens the *Mitākṣarā*'s argument considerably by stressing the debased character of striving merely for the sensual enjoyments of heaven, rather than unity with the supreme godhead, so that it effectively becomes a rather harsh condemnation of sati.[32]

Following its legal prohibition, the practice of sati undoubtedly became far less common throughout South Asia to the point that occurrences of it eventually became extremely rare. Nevertheless, the practice did not disappear entirely, as the widely publicized sati of Roop Kanwar in 1987 clearly shows.[33] And, in this regard, sati is a rather unique form of following into death, as Fisch (345) astutely points out. The reasons for the persistence of sati—at least when compared to other forms of following into death—are

31. English versions of these are reprinted in Ghose 121–92.

32. On the colonial debate on sati, see Fisch 364–446; and especially Mani.

33. For a discussion of instances of sati after its legal prohibition, see Fisch 1–3, 446–57. On the sati of Roop Kanwar specifically, see note 2.

not entirely clear, but two plausible reasons present themselves. Firstly, certain Hindu texts and ideologies developed in explicit support of the practice. Thus, sati had—and for some Hindus still has—the status of a sacred religious institution. Secondly, although it was in all likelihood originally restricted to Indian rulers and their close associates, Hindu widows of virtually every social class eventually came to practice it, albeit in a minority of cases as an extraordinary act of wifely devotion. Thus, the disappearance of Hindu monarchs did not necessarily spell the end of sati, as one might otherwise have expected.

10

Dying Heroically

JAINISM AND THE RITUAL FAST TO DEATH

Anne Vallely

LEGEND HAS IT that the conquests of Emperor Chandragupta Maurya were known throughout the ancient world while he was still an adolescent. Capitalizing on the power vacuum that followed Alexander the Great's retreat from India, he vanquished the remaining satrapies in the west, freeing India of Hellenistic rule, before unleashing his might on the Nanda empire in the east (Mookerji 21). Then, in swift order, he subjugated all the kingdoms from Bangladesh to Afghanistan, establishing India's first and largest empire. From his palace near present-day Patna, he surveyed the lands around him, and as far as his eye could see, he had conquered them all. But according to Jain sources, he knew that the greatest and fiercest of battles still awaited him; he still needed to summon the courage to enter the terrain of his own desires, subdue his body, and slay his ego. Finally, at the height of his power, he voluntarily abdicated his throne in favor of his son, Bindusāra, so that he could pursue a life of renunciation. He became an itinerant mendicant under the leadership of the great Acharya Bhadrabāhu, the last acharya (mendicant leader) of an undivided Jain sangha. The emperor-cum-monk soon became Acharya Bhadrabāhu's chief disciple, traveling with him to the south of India, and attending to him during the acharya's fast to death on the top of a hill in the town of Sravanabelgolā (Mookerji 40). Twelve years later, on the same hill that now bears his name (Chandragiri), Chandragupta entered his final battle. He embraced the vow of sallekhanā, and embarked on a ritual fast to death. With courage and equanimity, he subdued his fiercest of enemies—namely, the cycle of birth, death, and rebirth—attaining the greatest of spiritual heights.

Chandragupta's renunciation to pursue a life of ascetic nonviolence is not depicted in the Jain tradition as an abrupt about-face, or some kind of a road-to-Damascus conversion experience. Instead, it is understood as an elaboration, interiorization, and deepening of the resolve that had already served him throughout his life as emperor (Titze and Bruhn 52; Settar 3). To be sure, as a Jain renouncer, his life and death were informed by strict nonviolence. Death through sallekhanā is the pinnacle of nonviolence because it presupposes the total eradication of the passions which are the root cause of violence. But sallekhanā is first and foremost understood by Jains as a heroic death—as the culmination of a courageous, detached, nonviolent life. Indeed, an appreciation of the centrality of heroism within the Jain tradition is fundamental to a proper situating of the practice of sallekhanā. In its absence, the practice loses its rationale, significance, and prestige. Chandragupta's death, like the hundreds of others who undertook the fast to death on Chandragiri Hill, is marked by a memorial stone that is "equivalent to the hero stones erected all over the subcontinent in honor of those who died a gallant death in battle" (Dundas, *Religion and Violence*, 43). Sallekhanā was a befitting end for a (former) emperor, as it was for a monk.

Clearly, the heroism of sallekhanā has ancient roots. Phyllis Granoff, in her essay, "Fasting or Fighting: Dying the Noble Death in Some Indian Religious Texts," argues that Jainism's ancient glorification of the renouncer's death parallels the depictions of battles in the great India epic, the *Mahābhārata*. Although in Jainism the ultimate battle is an interior one, waged within oneself, she writes that its texts are filled with descriptions of the death of renouncers in terms of battles and the courage of the warrior (4).

The equation of sallekhanā with heroism is a straightforward one in the Jain imagination, and continues to govern the way in which the religious death is understood and practiced by Jains in the contemporary period. Sallekhanā is a culmination of Jainism's rigorous ethic of nonviolence, which censures harm to all living beings, including the smallest and simplest, and disavows anything that interferes with the jiva's (soul)'s realization. Ultimately, in its fullest expression, it leads to complete self-abnegation—that is, a total disregard for all worldly needs, including that of social standing and physical comfort. The pursuit of nonviolence is an extraordinarily exacting path that few have the courage to fully embark upon. For this reason, it is conceptualized as the highest and most noble expression of heroism. It reaches its pinnacle in the ritual fast to death, where the path of nonviolence and heroism become concretized and homologized. Importantly, heroism frames not just those exceptional practices of bodily mortification, but all aspects of the tradition. Indeed, a "proper" (i.e., emic) understanding of the Jain path would be to see it as an extraordinary, heroic undertaking of self-restraint in a cosmos characterized by self-indulgence and violence. This is where we begin.

The Heroism of Nonviolence

> [S]uch heroes are free from passion, they destroy anger and fear, they don't kill creatures.
>
> *Sūtrakrtānga Sūtra,* 1:2:1

The Jain tradition is widely recognized for its emphasis on not harming living beings, so much so that the declaration "ahiṇsā parmo dharm" (nonviolence is the supreme path) has become the defining epithet of the tradition, and one that plays a role of near-creedal authority. The emphasis on nonviolence has been a fundamental component of the Jain tradition since its historical emergence[1] in the sixth century BCE, with the ascetic teacher Mahāvīra (also known by his childhood name, Vardhamāna). Mahāvīra's teachings, preserved in the tradition's most ancient scripture, the *Acāranga Sutra,*[2] provide a powerful rationale for nonviolence as the one and only means to escape the cycle of birth and death. The teachings also reveal a profound degree of sensitivity to the sufferings of embodied existence, and express a striking solidarity with all life. The *Acāranga Sūtra* states:

> The Arhats and Bhagavats of the past, present, and future, all say thus, speak thus, declare thus, explain thus: all breathing, existing, living, sentient creatures should not be slain, nor treated with violence, nor abused, nor tormented, nor driven away. (Jacobi, *Acāranga Sūtra* 1:4:1)[3]

---

1. Jains argue that the teachings of the Jinā are eternal, transmitted through prophetic teachers who appear during specific eras during the great cycles of time. Mahāvīra is merely the twenty-fourth and final teacher within the current time cycle. He is important to Jains because, chronologically, he is the most recent, and to scholars because his historicity has been established.

2. The *Acāranga Sutra* is the oldest text of the Svetāmabara canon.

3. A contemporary Jain translation of this passage from the *Acāranga Sutra* reads: "As sorrow or pain is not desirable to you, so it is to all which breathe, exist, live or have any essence of life.

A contemporary Jain translation of this passage reads:

> As sorrow or pain is not desirable to you, so it is to all which breathe, exist, live or have any essence of life. To you and all, it is undesirable, and painful, and repugnant. That which you consider worth destroying is (like) yourself. That which you consider worth disciplining is (like) yourself. That which you consider worth subjugating is (like) your self. That which you consider worth killing is (like) yourself. The result of actions by you has to be borne by you, so do not destroy anything." (Bothra iv)

The Jain emphasis on ahiṇsā—including its specific rejection of Vedic animal sacrifices and its advocacy of vegetarianism—was widely shared by the world renouncing or shramana groups of ancient India, including Buddhist groups (Jaini 33). What distinguished the teachings of Mahāvīra from the others was, therefore, not the value they placed on ahiṇsā, but rather the remarkable degree and breadth of its application. For followers of the *Jinā*, the concrete and meticulous application of ahiṇsā governed all aspects of the religious life. The unyielding ascetic practices by which Jain mendicants became renowned are outcomes of this impetus to avoid harm in thought, word, and deed to the panoply of living beings that abound, both visible and invisible, on earth. The members of early mendicant community that formed around Mahāvīra's charismatic leadership, both nuns and monks, were called nigaṇṭhas ("unattached") (Jaini 27). They led austere lives centered on purifying their souls of the "knots" (gaṇthas) of karma through such ascetic practices as vegetarianism, extensive fasting, and celibacy. Many ended their lives through the voluntary and passionless death of sallekhanā, considered to be the highest expression of nonviolence because, by eradicating the passions, it eliminated the source of violence. The path that Mahāvīra prescribed was a rigorous one, aimed at purifying the *jiva* (eternal, immaterial essence; soul) of all its deleterious karma, which would thereby pave the way for its eventual liberation in a state of mokṣa (release).

Observers of the Jain tradition have been understandably quick to celebrate the tradition's emphasis on ahiṇsā, but in so doing they have often

---

To you and all, it is undesirable, and painful, and repugnant. That which you consider worth destroying is (like) yourself. That which you consider worth disciplining is (like) yourself. That which you consider worth subjugating is (like) yourself. That which you consider worth killing is (like) yourself. The result of actions by you has to be borne by you, so do not destroy anything" (Bothra iv).

downplayed its robust language of battles, heroes, and conquerors as merely allegorical (Tobias 11). This may stem from the common tendency to equate nonviolence with pacifism, which Jainism does not espouse. Jains, of course, do make a sharp moral distinction between an action that results in violence (hiṇsā) and one that endeavors to avoid it (ahiṇsā). Harming another living being results in an inflow of negative karma, which threatens to sabotage the spiritual path. But Jains do not treat the ethic of nonviolence and that of martial valor as stemming from contrastive value systems. Instead, as with the example of the emperor who became a monk, self-discipline, exactitude, and fearlessness are seen by Jains as values common to both. Paul Dundas makes this argument when he describes Jainism as "a way of heroism" (vīryamārga) and claims,

> World renunciation of the sort followed by the Jains, Buddhists and other groups was an institution which entailed not so much the abandonment of social ties for a career of mendicant quietism as an entry into a heroic way of life which derived a great deal of its ethos . . . from an affinity with the early Indo-Aryan warrior brotherhoods . . . [and which effectively entailed a] reconfiguration of warrior codes of bravery and physical control in the ascetic search for spiritual power and mastery. (*Religion and Violence*, 42–43)

The heroism of the renouncer path has always been central to the tradition's self-understanding, and finds unambiguous expression in the words the community uses to describe itself. The very self-appellation "Jain" derives from the Sanskrit "Jina" meaning "conqueror." Jains are followers of those dispassionate "conquerors" who prevailed over the most powerful and ferocious of all enemies—namely, egotism and the passions of the self—and then taught the path of freedom to others. The most recent of the Jinās was "Mahāvīra," an epithet that means "Great Hero." He lived approximately 2600 years ago in northeast India, in the area of present-day Bihar. Born into a ruling kṣatriya (ruling-warrior caste) family, as a young man he chose to abandon his life of power and luxury to pursue a path of world renunciation—considered by all to be an act of unsurpassed courage. Importantly, Mahāvīra ended his life through the ritual fast of sallekhanā, as do all Jinas.

Mahāvīra's birth into, and subsequent renunciation of, a ruling kṣatriya family followed the same life trajectory of every previous and future Jinā-to-be. The mytho-historical affiliation of the Jinās with royalty remains a central theme in Jain narratives, as well as in devotional practices. Within the

Svetāmbara tradition of Jainism, for example, images of Jinās, adorned with crowns and regal garb, are the main focus of worship. And the Jain community, which is now squarely within the vaishya/ baniya caste, traces its origins to the ruling-warrior (kṣatriya) castes of ancient India from which both the Jinās and their early followers descended. It is significant that Jains never disowned their kṣatriyas roots, nor do they comprehend their tradition in terms of a supersession of the earlier, worldly and thus flawed path. On the contrary, Jains remain supremely proud of their kṣatriya origins, and the connection with a tradition of nobility, bravery, and discipline that it provides them. It is as if the difficulty of the renouncer path, and the courage needed to pursue it, made its association with the kṣatriyas inescapable.

The arduousness of the renouncer path is universally recognized, and only those who possess the requisite mettle are permitted initiation. Those who embark on the path must forsake all worldly comforts and attachments: they do not have a home; status; personal belongings; nor familial support. To avoid attachments, they wander in small groups from place to place throughout the year,[4] and are dependent upon the generosity of householders for alms. The heroic nature of the path is taken as a given, and revealed in the most common salutation by which householders refer to them: "mahāraja" (lit. "great king," a title that is also used for nuns[5]).

The renouncer path is one that is singularly dedicated to freeing the soul of karma, allowing it to manifest its own inherent powers. Because the soul is understood to be physically ensnared in karmic matter, practices of body mortification (tapas), most quintessentially fasting, are employed to purge karma and inhibit its return. Jain scriptures describe such practices of body mortification "in the same way as one consciously picks up a weapon to fight an enemy" (Dundas, *Religion and Violence* 51). If asceticism is a kind of warfare, renouncers are its courageous combatants. As the Acāranga Sūtra remarks of the renouncer: "On the decay of the body (he does not despond, but deserves) his appellation, 'the leader of the battle'" (Jacobi, Book 1, 1:6). The ultimate battle on which they have their eyes set is that of sallekhanā

4. They walk for eight months of the year, staying no more than a few days at each location. During the four-month-long rainy season (caturmaas), they remain in one location, because travel during that period would result in unnecessary violence to the plants, water, and insects that are in abundance.

5. Nuns (sadhvis) no less than monks (munis) are referred to as "mahāraja." For example, Jainism's only female ācāraya—Ācāraya Sadhvi Chandandji—is affectionately called "Tai Mahāraj." "Tai" feminizes the epithet, because it is a term that denotes "elder brother's wife."

(ritual fast to death). It is a battle every bit as heroic and unforgiving as the legendary Mahābhārata, but fought in a state of absolute nonviolence.

The Labyrinth and its Escape

From a Jain point of view, the world is a stampede of craving, grasping, desire-ridden lunges, impelled by ignorance, hurtling headlong into death and rebirth. All living beings of the cosmos are caught up in this circus of longing, utterly terrified of death and unaware that escape is possible. It is not just kings and noblemen, and those lives of obvious consequence, who yearn for immortality, but all life seeks preservation. Even simple gnats, slugs, and parasites guard their lives jealously, and seek to fend off death at all costs. The rush to life and retreat from death constitutes the warp and woof of all samsaric existence. Against this backdrop, the Jain message of restraint is extraordinary. It proclaims another way of being, one that is extremely rare among living beings. Jainism understands itself to be a discipline for the realization of that which is pure, blissful, and eternal in oneself, an element Jains call *jiva,* or "life force." It is common to all living beings, irrespective of embodied form, size, species, or intelligence. Through the inspiring legends of its heroes, which include both renouncers and householders (referred to as "illustrious beings"),[6] as well as through its ethical teachings and its powerful purifying mantras, Jainism seeks to spark an awareness in the individual of its own eternal non-corporeal nature and to lay out a path for its realization. Given that the odds are so spectacularly stacked against the message (of escape) being received, those beings who do hear it are already considered privileged. Jain cosmography is complicated, but a basic understanding of it is important for our discussion of death, because it reveals the privilege of human birth and the urgency of the renunciatory path—an urgency that does not diminish, but is rather heightened, as one nears death.

The Jain tradition asserts that the cosmos is an uncreated phenomenon. This is significant. "Creation" implies some kind of purpose, and some form of inherent meaningfulness in its design. Jains reject such a formulation, and insist that no omnipotent being was as its source, nor is in charge of its functioning. The cosmos's myriad spheres, continents, mountains, and

---

6. The Jain time cycle is divided into two half-rotations: an ascending time cycle (utsarpiṇī), and a descending time cycle (avasarpiṇī), which we are presently in. During each half cycle, sixty-three illustrious beings (trīṣaṣṭiśalākāpuruṣa) appear, serving to inspire others to follow the path of the Jinā.

oceans, as well as its great time cycles, are without beginning or end. They operate according to natural laws, not the whims of a deity or deities. The cosmos contains three distinctive realms: an upper realm (home to the gods); a middle realm (home to humans, animals and plants); and a lower realm (home to hell beings). Its shape resembles three equilateral triangles stacked on top of each other (with the middle one inverted). It is commonly depicted as a cosmic person (purush) standing upright with his arms on his hips, and his legs slightly apart. Human beings are only found in the middle realm, called the Madhyaloka, and then only in small sections of it. The Madhyaloka contains eight continents, three of which support human life, and of these, only one of which, Jambūdvīpa (the "rose apple" continent), permits liberation. If this wasn't dire enough, only a small, territorial section of Jambūdvīpa supports liberation. The continent is divided into seven "fields" (kṣetra)[7]—self-contained lands separated from each other by immense mountain ranges. Of these, enlightenment is only possible in three: namely, Bharat Kṣetra, in the southern part of the continent; Mahavideha Kṣetra, in the middle region; and Airavat Kṣetra, in the north. What makes these three areas distinctive is that they give rise to experiences of both pleasure and suffering—and suffering is a key ingredient in spiritual awakening. It is precisely because suffering is absent in the other four kṣetras of Jambūdvīpa that these areas are not suitable environments for enlightenment. Like the heavenly realms above, such pleasure abodes (bhogbhumi) allow humans to live lives of ease and pleasure but, in the absence of the catalyst of suffering, they deprive them of the impetus to seek truth. The soul (jiva), intoxicated with pleasures, slumbers in ignorance. Correspondingly, those in the hell realms in the lower region of the cosmos are so singularly engulfed in their suffering that they too cannot gain enough purchase on their lives to pursue enlightenment. Only Bharat Kṣetra, Mahavideha Kṣetra, and Airavat Kṣetra have the right mixture of pleasure and pain to act as a catalyst for dharma ("religion"). Called "karma lands" (karmabhumi), life here involves struggle, and struggle brings insight. For this reason, Jinās take birth in these areas alone to preach the path of release, but only during those time periods favorable to the dissemination of their message. There is always a Jinā present on Mahavideha Kṣetra because it is not subject to time cycles, and remains in a favorable state. By contrast, Bharat Kṣetra and Airavat Kṣetra, the southern and northern parts of the continent, respectively, are subject to the influences of the time cycles, and

7. The seven kshetre are Bharat Kshetra, Mahavideh Kshetra, Airavat Kshetra, Ramyak, Hairanyvat Kshetra, Haimava Kshetra, and Hari Kshetra.

undergo periods that are more and less suitable for release. Only during the favorable phases of the declining and ascending time cycles do Jinās appear.

The details of Jain cosmology can be overwhelming. Everything is given in superlatives: measurements are immense, distances are unfathomable, and numbers are beyond ordinary comprehension. For example, we learn from the celebrated *Tattvārtha Sūtra*[8] that the continent of Bharata is 526 6/19ths yojanas wide, and that the inhabitants of Mahāvideh can live up to one pūrvakoti, which is 8,400,000 (to the power of 2) X 10 (to the power of 7) time units (Umāsvāti 83). Outside of the few specialists for whom systematizing the workings of the cosmos is a form of sādhanā (spiritual exercise), for most Jains, the impact of this knowledge is surely a deep sense of wonder--or perhaps dread. Mircea Eliade, writing on Hinduism, suggests that such cosmological elaborations function to induce a desire for mokṣa (27). At a minimum, such knowledge communicates to Jains the enormous privilege of human birth. To be born human in a part of the cosmos that is favorable to spiritual release, and during a time when the teachings of the Jinā are accessible, is unimaginably fortunate.[9]

The fact that all of this cosmological knowledge can be grasped at all is extraordinary. Most living beings of the three realms live in total ignorance of the workings of the cosmos. Knowing the correct path and having the ability to act on it is an immense privilege that is deliberately forsaken only by fools. It follows that to squander such an opportunity would be nothing short of tragic. Such is the central message of the Jain renouncer, who unwearyingly admonishes householders to capitalize on human birth by remaining vigilant at all times, arresting the inflow of new karma (a process called saṃvara) and shedding old, accumulated karmas (a process called nirjarā). Saṃvara and nirjarā are understood to be real, physical processes that cannot be accomplished on the basis of the mind or intentionality alone. Nirjarā, in particular, involves a literal scouring of karma from the soul, of which fasting is the most effective method. Together saṃvara and nirjarā inform all practices

8. The Tattvārtha Sūtra is the only ancient scripture that all Jain "sects" (sampraydays) accept as authoritative. A modern (1970) text, *Saman Suttam*, has gained similar acceptance.

9. It must be acknowledged that things *could* be more favorable. To be born human in the third or fourth time cycle, in the presence of a living Jinā, would be most preferable, as would birth on Mahavideh Kshetre in the presence of a living Jinā, which would effectively ensure liberation. But Bhagwan Simandhar Swami, one of the twenty Jinas currently alive in Mahavideh Kshetra, made a commitment ("runa nu bandhan") to help living beings of Bharat Kshetra to reach him on Mahavideh Kshetra. One can do so by acquiring knowledge of the true self through Akram Vignan, a devotional practice that entails spiritual surrender to Simandhar Swami.

of bodily discipline and serve as the rationale behind Jainism's mandatory vows. Incumbent upon all Jains (both mendicants and householders) are the five cardinal vows: Ahiṇsā, i.e., non-injury; Satya, i.e., truthfulness; Asteya, i.e., non-stealing; Brahmacarya, chastity/celibacy; and Aparigraha, i.e., non-attachment. For mendicants, these five vows, called "Mahāvratas" or Great Vows, are absolute and uncompromising. For lay Jains, they are "partial," fulfilled to the greatest extent possible within a householding life. Because they are not absolute, lay Jains observe additional supplementary vows, namely three guṇavratas (or "reinforcing vows") and four śikṣāvratas ("vows of discipline"). Householders who fully observe the twelve vows approximate mendicants in their discipline and resolve, and have progressed enough spiritually to take the vow of sallekhanā, or the voluntary termination of life by fasting. Sometimes considered a thirteenth (and non-obligatory) vow, sallekhanā concludes a life of discipline. As the Tattvārtha Sūtra proclaims, "One who has observed all the vows to shed the karmas, takes the vow of sallekhanā at the end of his life" (7: 22). In sum, the conscious death is an aspiration of all Jains, and one that is enshrined within the final lines of their daily prayer[10]:

> Cessation of sorrow,
> Cessation of karmas
> Death while in meditation,
> The attainment of enlightenment.
> (*Jaini* 226)

Sallekhanā and Scriptural Solidarity

> When the bonds fall off, then he [the sage] has accomplished his life.
>
> *Acāranga Sūtra*, Book 1, 7:8

The sacred scriptures of Jainism[11] are unanimous in treating the practice of sallekhanā as the ideal end to a human life. Although Svetāmbara and

10. The "universal prayer" concludes the observance of sāmāyik, a daily contemplative practice centered on soul awareness and worldly detachment.

11. Although Svetembara and Digamabara sects of Jains do not accept each other's scriptures as authoritative, the scriptural canon of both sects (sampradayas) hail the practice of sallekhanā as the ideal end of a human life.

Digamabara Jains differ over a great many important issues (e.g., the nature of the Jinā, correct mendicant practice, the spiritual potential of women), and despite their rejection of each others' scriptures as incomplete or inauthentic, both treat sallekhanā as the most noble end to a human life. The scriptural unanimity on sallekhanā is significant, repudiating claims of the practice's peripherality to the tradition.[12]

Both Svetāmbara and Digambara scriptures consider sallekhanā as the consummate end of a human life, provided the life in question has been lived in the pursuit of soul realization (atma darśan). In other words, all concur that sallekhanā should never mark a rupture with what came before, but instead should be its natural conclusion. Indeed, it is agreed that sallekhanā would be impossible to achieve in the absence of a life dedicated to renunciation. Sallekhanā is a hard-won achievement, the crown on a noble life. In the words of the Âcârya Samantabhadra, "To be able to control one's conduct at the moment of death is the *fruit* of renunciation" (Book 6, 2, 123).

The *Acāranaga Sūtra* is the earliest known record of the Jain tradition, and belongs to the Svetāmbara canon. It is believed to contain the teachings of Jinā Mahāvira, spoken over 2600 years ago.[13] The ideal of a voluntary, non-violent death appears in several passages. Mahāvīra declares:

> If this thought occurs to a monk: "I am sick and not able, at this time, to regularly mortify the flesh," that monk should regularly reduce his food; regularly reducing his food, and diminishing his sins, "he should take proper care of his body, being immovable like a beam; exerting himself he dissolves his body." (I, 7, 6)

and again,

> This is the truth: speaking truth, free from passion, crossing (the samsâra), abating irresoluteness, knowing all truth and not being known, leaving this frail body, overcoming all sorts of pains and

12. In 2015, the High Court of Rajasthan banned the practice of sallekhanā on the grounds that it is a form of suicide and that it is a "non-essential" component of Jainism.

13. Digambara Jains do not recognize the authenticity of the *Ācāranga Sūtra;* they claim the early teachings of Mahāvira were lost.

> troubles through trust in this (religion), he accomplishes this fearful (religious death). Even thus he will in due time put an end to existence. This has been adopted by many who were free from delusion; it is good, wholesome, proper, beatifying, meritorious. Thus I say. (Book I, Lecture 7, Lesson 6)

The Seventh Lesson of the Seventh Lecture in the Acāranaga Sūtra is entitled "Liberation." For those courageous few who are "intent on such an uncommon death," it provides meticulous instructions, and reads like a how-to manual for mendicants. Fascinating in its detail, I quote it in its entirety:

> Knowing the twofold (obstacles, i.e. bodily and mental), the wise ones, having thoroughly learned the law, perceiving in due order (that the time for their death has come), get rid of karman. Subduing the passions and living on little food, he should endure (hardships). If a mendicant falls sick, let him again take food.
>
> He should not long for life, nor wish for death he should yearn after neither, life or death. He who is indifferent and wishes for the destruction of karman, should continue his contemplation. Becoming unattached internally and externally, he should strive after absolute purity.
>
> Whatever means one knows for calming one's own life, that a wise man should learn (i.e. practice) in order to gain time (for continuing penance). In a village or in a forest,
>
> examining the ground and recognizing it as free from living beings, the sage should spread the straw.
>
> Without food he should lie down and bear the pains which attack him. He should not for too long time give way to worldly feelings which overcome him.
>
> When crawling animals or such as live on high or below, feed on his flesh and blood, he should neither kill them nor rub (the wound). Though these animals destroy the body, he should not stir from his position.
>
> After the âsravas have ceased, he should bear (pains) as if he rejoiced in them.
>
> When the bonds fall off, then he has accomplished his life.

(We shall now describe) a more exalted (method) for a well-controlled and instructed monk.

This other law has been proclaimed by Gñâtriputra:

He should give up all motions except his own in the thrice-threefold way.

He should not lie on sprouts of grass, but inspecting the bare ground he should lie on it.

Without any comfort and food, he should there bear pain.

When the sage becomes weak in his limbs, he should strive after calmness.

For he is blameless, who is well fixed and immovable (in his intention to die).

He should move to and fro (on his ground), contract and stretch (his limbs) for the benefit of the whole body; or (he should remain quiet as if he were) lifeless.

He should walk about, when tired of (lying), or stand with passive limbs; when tired of standing, he should sit down.

Intent on such an uncommon death, he should regulate the motions of his organs.

Having attained a place swarming with insects, he should search for a clean spot.

He should not remain there whence sin would rise.

He should raise himself above (sinfulness), and bear all pains.

And this is a still more difficult method, when one lives according to it: not to stir from one's place, while checking all motions of the body.

This is the highest law, exalted above the preceding method:

Having examined a spot of bare ground he should remain there; stay O Brâhmana!

Having attained a place free from living beings, he should there fix himself.

He should thoroughly mortify his flesh, thinking: There are no obstacles in my body.

Knowing as long as he lives the dangers and troubles, the wise and restrained (ascetic) should bear them as being instrumental to the dissolution of the body.

He should not be attached to the transitory pleasures, nor to the greater ones; he should not nourish desire and greed, looking only for eternal praise.

He should be enlightened with eternal objects, and not trust in the delusive power of the gods; a Brâhmana should know of this and cast off all inferiority.

Not devoted to any of the external objects he reaches the end of his life; thinking that

patience is the highest good, he (should choose) one of (the described three) good methods of entering Nirvâna. Thus I say. (2–25)

The *Acāranga Sūtra* addresses "the monk" or "the sage" as its main audience, reflecting the strong mendicant bias of early Jainism. Although Mahāvīra established a "fourfold community" of monks, nuns, male householders, and female householders (caturvidyāsangha), he did not do this in recognition of diverse spiritual paths. Instead, in so doing, he ensured that all members of society would be united in support of the renouncer ideal: renouncers made progress by devoting their lives to soul purification; and householders did so by supporting renouncers. While this dynamic remains an important feature of the tradition, with time the lay path gained a greater legitimacy of its own. Other avenues for spiritual merit, such as devotional practices, temple work, and philanthropy, became recognized as legitimate. Nevertheless, renunciation remains the axle upon which the tradition revolves, and householders orient their lives to the same lofty goal of mokṣa as renouncers, albeit less singularly. They engage in practices of tapas (restraint, detachment, and purification), constrained only partially by this-worldly demands of family and social life. One's householder status, therefore, need not be an impediment to the spiritual life, and should not interfere with the observance of the vows. At the end of one's life, when physical decline threatens to impair the observance and integrity of the vows, sallekhanā is understood to safeguard them. As Ācārya Amritchandra writes in his *Puruṣārthasiddhyupāya*, "sallekhanā enables a householder to carry with him his wealth of piety"[14]

The "story of Ānanda," found in the *Upāsakadaśāh Sūtra*,[15] encapsulates the householder ideal, and the central role of sallekhanā within it. Ānand, who had

14. The *Puruṣārthasiddhyupāya* is a text written by Digambara Ācārya Amritchandra during the tenth century. It is primarily concerned with householder dharma.

15. *Upāsakadaśāh,* translated as "Ten Chapters on Lay Attenders," is said to have been promulgated by Māhavīra himself, and composed by Gaṇadhara Sudharmāswāami, as per the Śvetámbara tradition.

the great privilege of living at the time of the last Jinā, was an exemplary householder. He had great wealth, honestly earned, was exceptionally generous, and was beloved by all. One day, after hearing, for his first time, a sermon by the Jinā Mahāvīra, he decided on the spot to adopt the twelve vows and thereby become "a true disciple of renunciation," called śramaṇopāsaka. From that point on, his life was marked by progressively rigorous ascetic practices that eventually culminated in his decision to undertake the ritual fast to death. He reflected:

> Truly, though these ascetic exercises, I have become reduced to a skeleton. While there is still within me the vigor and energy of faith, therefore, I should, after sunrise tomorrow, devote myself to a determined sallekhanā that ends in death, renouncing all food and drink and patiently awaiting my end. (*Upāsakadaśāh Sūtra*)

As a result of his fasting, he attained clairvoyant knowledge and, at the moment of his soul's release, was reborn in a celestial abode. Scriptural accounts, such as Ānanda's, while not prescriptive, serve as powerful ideals for Jain householders. For instance, the life and death of Mr. Amarchand-ji Nahar, as described by James Laidlaw[16] in his article "A Life Worth Leaving: Fasting to Death as Telos of a Jain Religious Life," bears a striking resemblance to that of Ānanda's. Amarchand-ji undertook sallekhanā in the 1980s. He had been a successful businessman, and a highly respected member of his Jaipur Jain community when, in middle age, he embraced the strict regime of a renouncer while remaining a householder. For the final many years of his life, like Ānand, he lived in a tiny, windowless room. He slept on a thin mattress on the floor, ate from a single wooden bowl, and fasted on alternate days. Laidlaw writes, "Even on days when he did eat, Amarchand-ji always carefully weighed and measured his daily allowance of grains and water and, progressively, as the years went by, simplified and reduced his diet" (180). He ended his life through the fast to death and, like Ānand, his moment of death was extraordinary. It was reported that when he died "there was rain of saffron and inside there was a sound of cracking and a wound appeared in his head" (181)—perhaps, as with Ānand, indicative of rebirth in a celestial abode.

The body for "a real Jain" like Amarchand-ji (as he was called) is not an end in itself, but rather serves the higher purpose of dharma. Only when it can no longer serve its essential purpose, that of spiritual purification, is

16. See also Laidlaw's discussion of Jain religious fasting in *Riches and Renunciation: Religion, Economy, and Society Among the Jains*.

sallekhanā embraced. For Amarchand-ji, no less than for Ānand, death was a performance, a momentous accomplishment, rather than a passive acceptance of annihilation. As Laidlaw writes,

> The iconography of Jain religious suicide might suggest passivity, since the dying samadhi-maran sits patiently in meditation . . . but in another sense the Jain religious suicide is active rather than passive, because death will nevertheless be the result entirely of his or her own deliberation, decision, effort and action. (183)

Jainism, in common with the vast majority of religious traditions the world over, insists that the dying process can be a time of powerful insight. As the jiva (soul) becomes dislodged from its material encasement (body), it is less bound by its constraints.

For householders such as Ānanda—no less than for renouncers—sallekhanā was an end that was both desirable and attainable. It was surely with such householders in mind that the second-century Ācārya Umāsvami wrote: "The householder courts voluntary death at the end of his life"[17] (cited above). A text from the same time period as Tattvārthsūtra is the *Ratna Karanda Śrāvakāchāra*,[18] composed by the Digambara Ācārya Samantabhadra swami. As the title indicates, it is similarly concerned with the religious conduct of householders (shravaka). Chapter Six discusses sallekhanā in terms of a practice available to pious householders. Again here, it is worth quoting at length:

> The most excellent of men describe the giving up of the body on the arrival of unavoidable calamity, distress, senescence and disease, with a view of increase of spiritual merit, as sallekhanā. To be able to control one's conduct at the moment of death is the fruit (culmination) of asceticism; all systems are at one as to this; therefore, one should apply oneself to attain sallekhanā death to the extent of one's power. Giving up love, hatred, attachment and possession, with a pure mind, one should obtain, with sweet speech, forgiveness from one's kinsmen and attendants, and

17. The *Tattvārthsūtra* is the only traditional scripture recognized by both Śvetāmabar and Digambara as authoritative.

18. Also called the "householder's dharma."

> should also forgive them oneself. Renouncing duplicity and reflecting on the sins committed in any of the three ways[19], one should take all the great vows of asceticism for the rest of one's days. Banishing grief, fear, anguish, attachment, wickedness and hatred and bringing into manifestation energy and enthusiasm, one should extinguish the fire of passions with the nectar of the Word of God [i.e., Scripture]. Giving up solid food by degrees, one should take to milk and whey, then giving them up, to hot or spiced water. [Subsequently] giving up hot water also, and observing fasting with full determination, he should give up his body, trying in every possible way to keep in mind the five-fold obeisance mantra.[20] Entertaining a desire to live, wishing for [speedy] death, displaying fear, desiring to see or to be remembered to friends, looking forward to future sense- enjoyment [in the life to come]—these have been described as the transgressions of sallekhanā by the Jinendra. He who has qualified the nectar of dharma [such an observer of the sallekhanā vow] becomes freed from all kinds of pain and drinks from the endless, unsurpassed and exalted "ocean" of blissfulness of mokṣa. That which is free from birth, old age, disease, death, grief, pain and fear [which is] eternal, blissful [and of the nature of] pure delight is called nirvana. [Those who perform sallekhanā] dwell unexcelled for all eternity, in the joy of final beatitude, endowed with [infinite] wisdom, faith, energy renunciation, bliss, satisfaction and purity. (122–32)

Although there have been historical ebbs and flows in the observance of the vow of sallekhanā, the practice and its idealization have always been a defining feature of the Jain tradition. Beginning in the post-Gupta period, however, one finds texts that evince a greater sensitivity to distancing it from suicide. In the sixth century, for instance, Ācārya Pujyapāda offered a commentary on the Tattvārthsūtra passage[21] cited above, with the express aim of establishing

19. The three ways by which a sin can be committed are: by an act of mind, speech, or body (krita); by inciting others to commit such an act (karita); or by approving the commission of such an act by others (anumodana).

20. Namo Arhantanam (I bow to Arhants)
Namo Siddhanam (I bow to Siddhas)
Namo Aiyaryanam (I bow to Acharyas)
Namo Uvajjhayanam (I bow to Upadhyas)
Namo Loe sarva sahunam (I bow to all Sādhus)

21. "The householder courts voluntary death at the end of his life" (*Tattvārthsūtra* 7:22).

the nonviolent character of sallekhanā, and differentiating it from suicide. He begins by describing the intention behind the practice: "To make the body and the passions thin is sallekhanā," and then elaborates on its nonviolent, non-destructive essence, stating:

> It is argued that it is suicide, since there is voluntary severance of life etc. No, it is not suicide, as there is no passion. Injury consists in the destruction of life actuated by passion. Without attachment etc. there is no passion in this undertaking. A person, who kills himself by means of poison, weapons, etc., swayed by attachment, aversion or infatuation, commits suicide. But he who practices holy death is free from desire, anger and delusion. Hence it is not suicide. "It has been taught by Lord Jina that the absence of attachment and the other passions is non-injury and that the rise of feelings of attachment and the other passions is injury." For instance, a merchant collects commodities for sale and stores them. He does not welcome the destruction of his storehouse. The destruction of the storehouse is against his wishes. And, when some danger threatens the storehouse, he tries to safeguard it. But if he cannot avert the danger, he tries to save the commodities at least from ruin. Similarly, a householder is engaged in acquiring the commodity of vows and supplementary vows. And he does not desire the ruin of the receptacle of these virtues, namely the body. But when serious danger threatens the body, he tries to avert it in a righteous manner without violating his vows. In case it is not possible to avert danger to the body, he tries to safeguard his vows at least. How can such a procedure be called suicide? (Jain 205)

In the tenth century, Ācārya Amritchandra, in his *Puruṣārthasiddhyupāya*, uses nearly identical language in his characterization of sallekhanā, and similarly aims to differentiate it from suicide:

> When death is imminent, the vow of sallekhana is observed by progressively slenderizing the body and the passions. Since the person observing sallekhana is devoid of all passions like attachment, it is not suicide.[22]

22. The *Puruṣārthasiddhyupāya* is a text written by Digambara Acharya Amritchandra during the tenth century. It is primarily concerned with householder dharma.

Differentiating sallekhanā from suicide was likely always an important task for the minority Jain tradition. The community's support for voluntary death made Jains conspicuous, and distinguished them from the majority population. If not well understood, it could have provoked misunderstanding and condemnation.[23] But the task of distinguishing sallekhanā from suicide became a legal matter first during the British Raj, when colonial jurisprudence deemed suicide and its abetment illegal and punishable by law. The colonial government, however, seems to have accepted the Jain distinction between a death motivated by self-actualization and a death motivated by self-destruction, if the lack of legal action against the former is any indication. In recent years, this has all changed.

Spiritual Heroics

Śrimati Bai was ninety-two years old in the summer of 2015 when she asked her family for permission to take the vrat (vow) of sallekhanā. The request was not unanticipated, as her entire life had been governed by religious observance, including daily temple visits, devpuja, meeting with mendicants, performing the meditative practice of samayik and, especially, the observance of extensive fasting. Although she never formally adopted the twelve vows or six obligatory actions[24] of an ideal householder, her life was governed by them. At the age of fifty-five, after she and her husband took the vow of celibacy in the presence of their guru, she steadily but without fanfare made progress along the pratimas—the series of progressively more rigid stages of renunciation that lead the householder to the point of complete renunciation. Most importantly, however, Shrimati had informed her family many times of her intention to take the vrat of sallekhanā, so that she could "abandon her body" (kayostarg) consciously as death approached. Sallekhanā cannot be undertaken without the consent of family and guru, so this she obtained. Lying on a sheet directly on the hard floor, she embarked upon her final fast. A great many in her community came to receive her darshan during her final days. And after just one week without food, she consciously and

23. This is true even in a nation where the practice of *samadhi maran* (death in meditation), is not infrequently undertaken by Hindu renouncers. In the Jain community, sallekhanā plays a more central ideological and defining role for the community, and this may be why it seems to need to be continuing defended.

24. Equanimity; praise of the Jinās; obeisance to the Jinās, teachers, and scriptures; confession; resolution to avoid sinful activities; and "abandonment of the body" (standing or sitting in a meditative posture). See Dundas, *Jains* 173.

dispassionately left her body. Shrimati Bai's sallekhanā was auspicious and heroic, like that of so may others throughout Jainism's long history—with one important exception: it was illegal.

On August 10, 2015, in a much-publicized ruling by the High Court of Rajasthan, sallekhanā was equated with suicide, and designated as a criminal offense, punishable by law. No announcement of Shrimati Bai's auspicious death appeared in the local paper, and the family disavowed its association with sallekhanā. For the first time ever in 155 years of Indian Penal Code jurisprudence, the practice of voluntary death was decreed illegal. But the matter had been brewing for years. As early as the 1970s, human rights activists began to raise concerns about sallekhanā's potential for abuse (particularly elder abuse) and agitated to have the practice criminalized as suicide. In the climate of growing misapprehension, the late Justice T. K. Tukol (former judge of the High Court in Mysore and chancellor of Bangalore University) wrote a declarative text with the unambiguous title, "Sallekhanā is Not Suicide." In it, he surveyed the historical evidence of the practice and its rationale, concluding on the basis of his research and legal work that "the vow of sallekhanā as propounded in the Jaina scriptures is not suicide" (preface).

The specific catalyst for the 2015 ruling came from Nikhil Soni, an advocate in Jaipur when, on May 9, 2006, he submitted a writ petition before the High Court of Judicature for Rajasthan. Soni described santhara (a word often used interchangeably with sallekhanā)[25] as a "social evil," and stated, "It is submitted that a voluntary fast unto death is an act of self-destruction, which amounts to 'suicide'" (Soni v. Union). In the August 2015 ruling, the Rajasthan High Court sided with the plaintiff, declaring: "Santhara or fast unto death is not an essential tenet of Jainism," and that it would henceforth be treated as "suicide" and "accordingly made punishable under the pertinent sections—Section 309 (attempt to commit suicide) and Section 306 (abetment of suicide)—of the Indian Penal Code."

The Jain community's response was swift, decisive, and (seemingly) univocal. Large-scale demonstrations were organized throughout India (Rajasthan, Gujarat, Madhya Pradhesh, Uttar Pradesh, and Maharashtra). In Jaipur thousands marched in silence, many of the men with their heads shaved in protest, to the Rajasthan High Court, where the judgment had been made. Expressions of solidarity came from the Jain community throughout the world. Within just two weeks, on August 31, the Supreme Court of India

25. The writ employs "santhara" interchangeably with sallekhanā. Technically "santhara" refers to the straw mat upon which one lies when in the final stages of the fast.

(Delhi) stayed the Rajasthan High Court judgement, restoring the Jain practice. As of 2017, it exists in a legal limbo, and a Supreme Court judgement may yet be years away.[26]

At least six petitions challenging the High Court of Rajasthan's ruling have been filed from members of the Jain community, with one coming from the United States. Jaipat Singh, a lawyer living in New Jersey and former president of Siddhāchalam Mission, traveled to India to file his petition. In it he objects to the Rajasthan High Court's ruling. He writes,

> The distinction between the two [sallekhanā and suicide] . . . is as basic and sharp in Jainism as is between night and day. One concerns the manner of passionless death in samadhi meditation at the end of natural life in specified circumstances, and the other concerns intentionally and unnaturally terminating life overcome by passion. (Preamble, Singh v. Union)

Several fasts to death have been undertaken since the Supreme Court stayed the High Court ruling. To show support for the otherworldly heroics which they make manifest, and in defiance of a judgment deemed odious, they have been publicly and widely celebrated within the Jain community.

That the Jain community's efforts to differentiate sallekhanā from suicide have become more, rather than less, contentious in the postcolonial period is revealing. Modern nations secure their status as "modern" in large measure by delineating and compartmentalizing the "religious" from the "non-religious." "Modernity" is a rhetorical concept that implies functionally differentiated social spheres of religion, science, education, politics, economics, and so on—each ostensibly distinguishable from the other (cf. Luhmann). But the sphere of "religion" is more than just one among many, because the religion/nonreligion divide underpins all the others.

Demarcating religious or "transcendent-centric" dispositions from the non-religious or anthropocentric/humanistic ones is one of the most daunting challenges of modern democracies, and often proves impossible. For example, Nikhil Soni (petitioner in the case before the Supreme Court), describes the religious practice of sallekhanā as "abhorrent to modern thinking" and describes his own position, which champions "the right to life of an individual," as reflective of "modern thought and thinking." Ironically, in support

26. The matter may have become moot with the Indian Parliament's recent Mental Healthcare Bill of 2016, which decriminalizes suicide.

of his position, he draws upon the Section 309 of the Indian Penal Code which criminalizes suicide[27]—a statute that bears the mark, in a very straightforward way, of India's Judeo-Christian colonial past.

Shekhar Hattangadi's documentary film *Santhara* explores the current legal dispute over the Jain ritual fast to death as a confrontation between two divergent "religious" worldviews. In an article in *The Hindu,* he writes,

> The basic contradiction between a statute founded largely on a Christian-inspired bioethic and the essentially Eastern variant of the idea of spiritual advancement through abstinence and renunciation rears its head whenever an ancient religious practice like Santhara collides with contemporary law. The conflict becomes particularly glaring in a faith-based society like ours whose polity has embraced norms of governance and administration that are transplants from an alien soil.

Modern humanist ideals and norms of governance place an absolute premium on individual freedom and agency, and treat human flourishing as an end in itself. By contrast, faith-based ideologies, in the main, identify a value beyond that of personal liberty, and do not treat human flourishing as an end in itself, but rather as a means to a higher end. These worldviews cannot be readily harmonized; one must be subservient to, and subsumed within, the other. For example, in the writ petition of Nikhil Soni, the "religious" must be subservient to the more all-encompassing "secular." He writes, "All persons are entitled to freedom of conscience and the right freely to profess, practice and propagate religion. A practice, however, ancient it may be to a particular religion, *cannot be allowed to violate the right to life of an individual*" [italics added].

The preservation of life—understood within secular ideology to be the preservation of the biological processes of the body and the brain—is an indubitable, axiomatic good. As such, sallekhanā appears as the most flagrant violation of this good. The voluntary elimination of the body and brain can only be seen in this view as "self destruction," and therefore as an unequivocal "social evil," as Soni describes it. For Jains, however, life is not reducible to body and brain; the latter are but vehicles for the jiva, and sallekhanā is not self-destruction, but rather, self-actualization.

---

27. Section 309 of the IPC reads, "Attempt to commit suicide: Whoever attempts to commit suicide and does any act towards the commission of such offence, shall be punished with simple imprisonment for a term which may extend to one year or with fine, or with both."

That the same practice elicits such conflicting views is nicely brought out in the opening pages of Dalrymple's celebrated book *Nine Lives: In Search of the Sacred in Modern India,* wherein he confronts a Jain nun undertaking a fast to death. "No, no: sallekhana is not suicide," insists the nun who endeavors to disabuse Dalrymple of his misunderstandings. He challenges her, countering with the bare facts: "But you are still trying to end your life." Her response reveals the incompatibility of their visions: "Really—it can be so beautiful: the ultimate rejection of all desires, the sacrificing of everything." She adds, smiling, "You have to understand: we feel excited at a new life, full of possibilities."

To conclude, sallekhanā is at the center of a legal controversy because it crystallizes, so starkly, the different assumptions, ideals, and heroics of modernity. Bioethicist and Jain scholar Whitney Braun, in an interview on the legal controversy surrounding sallekhanā, encapsulates the deep incompatibility of worldviews when she says: "The crux of it is how do you hold onto your old gods, if you will, in an era dominated by science and technology?" The "old gods" of which Braun speaks are those "transcendent-centric" ideals—non-utilitarian, non-rational, metaphysical, teleological, non-material aspirations upon which human life is meaningfully grounded, and for which human life is lived, but upon which contemporary "modern" society often stumbles.

Secular heroics are unabashedly anthropocentric, centered on the advancement of human potential and the preservation, integrity and dignity of human life. Human well-being is an end in itself, and is the telos toward which all social life is oriented. In Jainism, by contrast, the purpose of human life is the pursuit of dharma; mokṣa is the telos toward which all life is oriented, and heroics revolve around those extraordinary testimonies to the transcendent dimension of human life.

11

The Tropics of Heroic Death

MARTYRDOM AND THE SIKH TRADITION

Louis E. Fenech

The sky-resounding kettledrum is struck!
Aim is taken, wounds inflicted. The warrior
enters the battlefield. Now is the time to fight!
The person is recognized as hero who fights on behalf of the
  oppressed (dīn).
Though cut limb from limb, they do not abandon the field of battle.

Kabir, Rāg mārū 2:1–2, *Adi Granth*

THE EPIGRAPH ABOVE, found within the sacred utterances of the Hindu *sant* Kabir (ca. fifteenth century) that are included within the principal Sikh scripture, the *Adi Granth* (hereinafter AG), today conveys the Sikh understanding of the sacrifice of the martyr without naming it as martyrdom, the most common Punjabi term for which today is *śahīdī* or *śahādat* from the Perso-Arabic *shahīd*, "witness." The battle metaphors noted here are reminiscent of the popular representation of seventeenth- to eighteenth-century Sikh history, in which Sikhs fought against a series of murderous foes whose sole goal was the extermination of Sikhism (and, by extension, all that was righteous). Sikh Gurus and heroes, tradition notes, fought these villains and their nefarious schemes, often nonviolently, but with weapons when all other means had failed, and died in the process for no purpose other than to ensure the victory of righteousness and truth and the right of Sikhs and all people to live freely and in good conscience. These were struggles that became a part of a Sikh's *sevā,* or the selfless service to humanity, service that is essential to securing salvation, according to the Sikh Gurus. As an early nineteenth-century Sikh martyrologist suggests, *sevā hari gur thīṁ qurbān*: "To become a sacrifice for the sake of the Guru is the true service of God" (Garja Singh 54).

Within popular Sikh tradition, such service begins with the founder, Guru Nanak (1469–1539). In this reading, Nanak's age is an era of intolerance and brutality in which regular people are exploited to uphold a system that grinds them down. Well aware of the danger of speaking out in the face of such cruelty, Guru Nanak nevertheless does, severely responding to a draconian regime that could easily kill him:

> The dark age is the knife,
> the king the butcher;
> righteousness has grown wings and flown off.
> Nowhere is visible the moon of truth
> in this dark night of falsehood. (*AG* 145)

Courage and defiance in the face of injustice become the two qualities often extracted from Nanak's hymns to portray him as a fearless defender of truth and social justice. And with such virtues placed foremost, the tradition of martyrdom interprets Guru Nanak's hymns as directed toward a singular goal—namely, the defense of truth regardless of the consequences: "O Nanak, falsehood must be destroyed. In the end truth will prevail" (AG 953). This commitment is Nanak's "game of love," a sport, tradition claims, regularly played by his successors, all nine of whom embodied Nanak's qualities in their confrontation with the state's injustice. Some quarrels ended amicably, with emperors accepting the counsel of the Gurus; but others terminated less so, as the Gurus demonstrated the requisite courage required to stand for the truth that the emperors were violating, and offered their lives in its service. Both Guru Arjan (d. 1606) and Guru Tegh Bahadar (d. 1675) were executed on the command of the tarnished Mughal emperors Jahangir (d. 1627) and Aurangzeb (d. 1707), becoming martyrs and providing shining examples to the whole world of steadfastness in the face of oppression.

It was partially in response to the martyrdom of his father, Tegh Bahadar, that the tenth Guru, Gobind Singh (1666–1708), inaugurated the Khalsa, a martially inclined order of Sikhs, admission into which required the Sikh to symbolically offer the head as a sacrifice to truth and justice. This symbolic offering transformed the individual Sikh into a *sant-sipāhī,* or "soldier-saint," attired in battle gear comprising the so-called five Ks: *kes* (sanctified hair that must never be cut); *kaṅghā* (comb); *kaṛā* (bangle); *kirpān* (dagger); and *kacchahirā/kacch* (undershorts). Such a commitment, tradition notes, made it inevitable that Khalsa Sikhs would pursue sovereignty, ushering in a rule of humility in which Khalsa Sikhs fought for all that was just, with no concern for themselves. The result of this devotion was the formation of the Sikh kingdom under Maharaja Ranjit Singh (1780–1839), which flourished from 1799 to 1849.

In such popular Sikh histories, Khalsa Sikh martyrs embody the doctrines of the Gurus, living lives and dying deaths fearlessly by following the supreme examples of the Sikh Gurus, and thus also following the will of God perfectly. By such action Sikh martyrs are believed liberated from *samsāra*, the illusory world with its cycle of birth, death, and rebirth prior to their sacrifice, having mastered already that most tenacious of foes, *haumai* (I-me), the self-centeredness that entices the selfish and corrupt in Sikh soteriology. From a Sikh perspective, *haumai* is the force against which all of us are pitted, and that all Sikhs must first defeat in order to achieve martyrdom while also combating tyranny and oppression; these last two are deemed disruptions of the divine order or *hukam* and are portrayed as the social manifestation of *haumai*. As Guru Nanak proclaims, *mani jītai jaggu jītu* (*Japu* 28, AG 6), "conquering the self conquers the world." It is only at this point of conquering that one can offer the gift of martyrdom, and it is only at this point that one can fully love and be victorious in the game of love, which begins by benevolently offering the head (AG 1412) in love for the Truth that is God. Guru Gobind Singh seconds this in his Dasam Granth, another significant sacred Sikh text: *jin premu kīo tin hī prabhū pāio*, "that very person dyed in love is the one who obtains the Lord" (*Tva-prasādi Savaiye* 9:29, Dasam Granth [hereafter DG] 14). Through martyrdom, therefore, Sikh martyrs are portrayed, ipso facto, as true lovers of the divine liberated from the mundane world while yet alive.

What makes our introductory epigraph by Kabir such an intriguing addition to Sikh martyrology is its implicit admission that martyrs are created not only through their sacrifice, but also through the work of the martyrologist, who recognizes the sacrifice as such and conveys it to an audience, generally for the purpose of edification. The criteria of such recognition, however, have altered as Sikhs and the Sikh tradition have evolved over the centuries. Indeed, in early nineteenth-century Sikh accounts, these criteria became more intricately linked to Sikh sovereignty, while in the 1980s and 1990s, these principles became more associated with Sikh self-determination in a globalized world. In the latter context, certain desperate liberties were taken with aspects of earlier Sikh tradition underscored as sacrosanct: those articles of the Sikh faith for which eighteenth-century Sikhs died, for example, were cast off, albeit reluctantly, in order to help secure this self-determination. This was the case with Sukhjinder "Sukha" Singh and Harijinder "Jinda" Singh, two young Sikh men who cut their hair (otherwise a form of apostasy) in order to get close to General A. S. Vaidya, the chief architect of Operation Bluestar in 1984 (of which more later), and assassinate him.

The meaning of the utterances of the Gurus are also reinterpreted. Both the above-noted Kabir's *Rāg mārū* 2:1–2 and Guru Nanak's *Japu* 28, for example, were not intended initially to refer to the heroic Sikh martyr or *śahīd* who dies on the battlefield. These hymns were instead addressed to yogis, replete as they are with the terminology of yoga, underscoring *haṭha* yoga concepts that were animating the thoughts of both the Sikh Gurus and sants like Kabir, who had to contend with the popularity of yogis in their lifetimes. Just such a transformation may be recognized in the beautiful poetry of Bhai Gurdas Bhalla (d. 1637), easily the most important Sikh intellectual of the seventeenth century apart from the Sikh Gurus. Note, for example, a line from his *vār* 30, *pauṛī* 14, my translation of which follows:

> *Laṛi maraṇā tai sati hoṇu gurmukhi panth pūraṇ partāpai* (Vir Singh 1997: 477–78)
>
> The glorious path of unqualified perfection that those oriented towards the Guru (*gurmukh*, lit., 'Guru-facing') tread is dying in battle and manifesting truth [while so doing].

The most easily adapted words in this line are *satī hoṇu*, meaning "to become truthful" or "becoming true" which was, in the time of Bhai Gurdas, indicative of controlling the senses in the logic of yoga, in the battle against self-centeredness and pride—a battle all yogis had to overcome to achieve *sahaj* or equipoise. A recent translation, however, perfectly provides the point I make above; Rahuldeep Singh Gill's fresh interpretation suggests far more than simply calming the senses and defeating the ever-active self: "to die in battle and to be a martyr [*satī*] is the way of the perfect Gurmukh's path" (Gill 245). Such a retrojection of martyrological concepts and interpretations is quite commonplace in contemporary general accounts of Sikh martyrdom. This draws a clear line from the Gurus to later and contemporary Sikh martyrs—thus transforming historians into the very martyrologists they are examining. Such uncritical backward projections obliquely suggest that the ideology of the Gurus has remained static (something against which the Fourth Sikh Guru, Guru Ram Das (1534–1581), tacitly warns in AG 442), and thus beckon us to begin our analysis of the Sikh martyr tradition in a period of Sikh history that is much later than that of the Sikh Gurus (namely, 1469–1708). As I have implied and will argue in this chapter, the idea of martyrdom may appear sporadically in the early period of Sikh history, but it does not begin to take hold of the Sikh imagination until the eighteenth century, sparingly at first, after which, in the nineteenth and then throughout the twentieth centuries, it is intimately refined in response to contemporary contingencies.

These facts notwithstanding, it is correct to claim that martyrdom is a living tradition within Sikhism. There can be no doubt that martyrological narratives have inspired Sikhs to perform deeds of rare and daring courage as well as acts of extraordinary piety, benevolence, and love, and have thus played an important role in framing much of the militancy and oppression that occurred between the 1970s and 1990s. These narratives may therefore be firmly placed within the mythology of Sikhism, particularly that of Khalsa Sikhism, the normative variety of the tradition whose members are enjoined to follow a code of conduct known as the *rahit*, enshrined today within the *Sikh Rahit Maryādā*, the normative Khalsa Sikh code of conduct completed in 1950. This is not mythology in the sense of something inherently untrue that estranges one group from another; rather, it is the mythology conveying those narratives that Sikhs tell themselves about themselves and about their community, stories that give Sikh life meaning and purpose, that provide archetypes or blueprints of the comportment that Sikhs are enjoined to adopt in certain circumstances. Hence these are supplementary to the *rahit*, which prescribes, among other things, how to live the good Sikh life (McLeod, *Who is a Sikh?*). These aggregate Sikh cultural and symbolic capital, in stories that Sikhs know intimately well, but regularly gather together to hear again and again. To be sure, martyrdom is but one component in this construction of Sikhness, but it is now a supremely important one, with its foremost models regularly remembered in the Sikh congregational prayer, the *ardās* (petition). As such, Sikh martyrology and Sikh martyrs merit the utmost respect.

The Specter of 1984

In order to trace the evolution of the Sikh concept of martyrdom, therefore, I will turn our attention first to the events over the last fifty years in northern India, which were germane to the idea's more robust entrenchment within the Sikh imaginary. From the late 1970s until the year 2000, the Sikh Panth (community), especially in India, went through a series of tumultuous events that have left an indelible mark upon it. These were set in motion by even earlier political actions. These events included the partition of the British Indian state of the Punjab, the Sikh homeland, between Pakistan and India in August 1947, and the bloody riots which followed in the wake of its division;

the failure of the new Indian government to establish a Punjab state within the truncated Sikh homeland that was circumscribed by the mother tongue of its residents (Punjabi); a criterion that was used to create new Indian states after Independence (for example, West Bengal was delimited along the areas the people of whom spoke Bengali); the distribution to nearby states of the Punjab's much-needed river water; and the inability to uncouple Sikhs from Hindus and Buddhists in Article 25 of the Indian Constitution, which identified Sikhs as Hindu, a classification that the majority of Sikhs found offensive, among many others.

Such disappointments, exacerbated by the poor showing of Sikh politicians in the Punjab state elections of the early 1970s, persuaded Sikh leaders from the predominant Sikh political party, the Akali Dal, to gather in the city of Anandpur to organize a Sikh response to the government. The result was the Anandpur Sahib Resolution of 1973 which offered the government of India a way to rectify Sikh and Punjabi grievances. For the most part the government ignored these requests for rectification, which helps to explain the fierce resistance mounted by the Akali Dal to the Emergency of 1975–77, during which Prime Minister Indira Gandhi became dictator in all but name.

Although events in 1978, a year after the Emergency was ended, saw the rise of the charismatic leader Jarnail Singh Bhindranwale and growing Sikh militancy in the Punjab, the situation reached a boiling point when Sikhs en masse were terribly mistreated by Indian authorities and police in Delhi during the Asian Games of 1982. This resulted in a loud call for Sikhs to secede from the Indian union and to take the Punjab with them. To this end, many frustrated young male Sikhs took to militancy and violence, a choice that ultimately led to growing hostilities between them and the Indian government and the former's fortification of the Golden Temple complex (the most sacred of Sikh sites) in the city of Amritsar. In June 1984, the Indian army attempted to flush these Sikh militants out of the complex, launching Operation Bluestar, in which over six hundred Sikh worshippers were killed and substantial sections of the Golden Temple campus damaged or destroyed, including the library, which housed hundreds of unique, handwritten manuscripts dating back to the time of the Sikh Gurus. In response, Mrs. Gandhi was assassinated by her Sikh bodyguards almost five months later, an act which engendered widespread rioting in Delhi in early November 1984, during which hundreds of Sikhs were singled out and butchered in the streets, as the police and politicians simply looked on. For the next eight years, the situation in the Punjab remained exceedingly tense, featuring excesses by both the Punjab police and Sikh militants. The Sikh diaspora also loudly chimed in at this time. Traumatized by the destruction of their holiest shrine, Sikhs abroad funneled large amounts of cash back to India in order to help Sikhs finally secure self-determination, all the while gathering political allies throughout those countries with a substantial Sikh diaspora. The goal was to pressure the Indian government to meet certain Sikh demands and to build a narrative of the India-wide persecution of the Sikhs. Prime Minister V. P. Singh's public apology for Operation Bluestar at the Golden Temple in 1989 helped slightly ease tensions between Sikhs and the Indian government and the situation has incrementally improved ever since—as manifested, for example, in the elevation of the Sikh politician Manmohan Singh to the prime ministership in the national elections of 2004, a position he held until 2014. During this time there was only the occasional flare-up, sparked in large part by the fact that the well-known perpetrators of the anti-Sikh pogroms of 1984 have yet to be brought to justice. Despite the diminishing militancy today, however, 1984, as it has come to be known by the Sikhs, was a seminal moment in the construction of the Sikh identity.

It was during this period that Sikh martyrological narratives began to appear in both India and abroad in far greater numbers with far greater resonance, a trend that reflected the rapid growth of the Sikh diaspora across the United Kingdom, Canada, and the United States. It was also at this time, not surprisingly, that the field of Sikh studies began to discover its voice in the Western academy and to attract the attention of scholars of South Asia. Of course, the serious study of the Sikhs by non-Sikhs has a long history, stretching back to the mid-eighteenth century, when the British East India Company attempted to better understand the Sikhs and their tradition in the context of the Company's increasing global presence and expansionist policies. The British government inherited this interest after 1858 when the company's monopoly in India was terminated, an interest which ultimately resulted in the 1909 publication of M. A. Macauliffe's six-volume tome *The Sikh Religion: Its Gurus, Sacred Writings and Authors*, editions of which are still published today and widely read. Although severely marred by Macauliffe's Orientalist bias, this series nevertheless captures the type of traditional historical narrative (with martyrology prominently featured) that late nineteenth-century Sikh intellectuals, influenced by the ideals of the European Enlightenment, lovingly crafted over the forty years prior to 1909 (Macauliffe 1909). But it was under the stewardship of a small number of scholars in the 1960s, such as J. S. Grewal, Ganda Singh, W. H. McLeod, and Harbans Singh, that Sikhism as a field of study began to attract more serious critical attention outside of India. By the mid-1980s, their efforts had succeeded in a new diasporic environment, as a number of universities in Canada and the United States began to toy with the idea of establishing chairs of Sikh studies.

It was during the period of defiance in the late 1980s that I first took serious notice of the Sikh tradition of martyrdom. I discovered that martyrdom was not merely constructed as an aspect of the Sikh tradition overall, sitting equally with, for example, other features of the tradition such as those expressed by Guru Nanak in his famous series of compositions known as *Siddh Goṣṭi: gurmukhi nāmu dānu isnānu* "That Person Who Faces Towards the Eternal Guru Cultivates the Divine Name, Charity, and Purity (AG 942)," underscoring the Sikh emphasis upon the cognitive, the communal, and the personal, in the words of Pashaura Singh (234). Rather, martyrdom was cast as the central feature that combined the best elements of these and of Sikhism overall and drew them to their ultimate, ethical conclusion and, as such, was the component toward which many Sikhs collapsed their entire tradition. As one young Punjabi scholar tellingly noted in 1990: "One can say that Sikh history is the history of martyrs" (Kang 187). Listening to Sikh homilies, viewing Sikh art, and reading Sikh material from this period certainly supports this notion.

Although I was living vicariously through the many events, my interest in the Sikh tradition of martyrdom was sparked predominantly by an appeal in the Sikh newspaper the *Akālī* (September 2, 1920) by Sardul Singh Caveeshar, at the beginning of the Sikh Gurdwara Reform Movement. This action (1920–1925) saw a widespread move by Punjab-based Sikhs to purge their temples (known as *gurdwāre,* singular: *gurdwārā*) of British-backed custodians who were generally understood to be corrupt and marginally Sikh: "Wanted: 100 martyrs to defend Sikh gurdwaras."

Although the appeal was from several decades ago, reading it proved to be my epiphany. I could understand how this petition could generate an enthusiasm and determination which saw thousands of Sikhs daily offer their lives, suffer harsh beatings by British and Indian police alike, and court long periods of incarceration to secure Sikh sacred space and to offer to Indians as a whole their first major victory in the subcontinent's long battle for independence from the British. The Sikh-centered events through which I was living in the 1980s and 1990s seemed eerily reminiscent of these. Once again it appeared as if Sikhs were confronted by a near-intractable foe who acted with impunity and from whom they believed they were attempting to reclaim their sacred territory—a territory consecrated in large part not only by the footsteps of the Sikh Gurus but also through the copious Sikh blood that had been spilled upon it in the defense of righteousness.

The task of understanding the Sikh tradition of martyrdom ultimately led me to critically question some of the most dearly held assumptions of the Sikhs (Fenech). I began (and completed) my project under the direction of W. H. McLeod, whose own work on the life of Guru Nanak was swept up into Sikh ethno-nationalist discourse as early as the late 1960s. At this time (the 1990s), a fellow student of McLeod's, Pashaura Singh at the University of Toronto, came under fire for his dissertation on the Sikh scripture. As word of our projects spread not only did we find encouragement and support from many Sikh corners, but we also faced vitriol against our supervisor (and against us, his students) from certain Sikh groups interested in defending the scripture and the tradition of martyrdom from any kind of so-called academic onslaught. This led a small number of Sikhs in Canada, the United States, and the United Kingdom to organize a number of conferences and to write articles about the topics and their centrality within the teachings of the Sikh Gurus. Many of these were not written by trained scholars of the tradition, I should add, but rather by Sikh professionals, which is indicative of the threat that regular, non-academic Sikhs felt at the time from both critical academics and the Indian government.

These aspersions were of course situated within, and no doubt stimulated by, the volatile ethno-nationalist context described above, in which many Sikhs within India felt threatened and oppressed by the Indian state. Since the standard history of the Sikh people plays such a crucial role in the construction of Sikh personhood, any attempts at the time to critically assess that history, especially when such activity brought the glorious, normative historical narratives of the Sikhs martyrs into question, was taken as a direct attack on individual Sikhs, on the collective Sikh community, and indeed, on their perceived value (or not) as citizens of India. Consequently, critical scholars of the Sikh tradition, especially those who were now ensconced as newly established chairs of Sikh studies programs in North America, were often labeled as agents of the Indian government, with their work portrayed as simply one more attempt to eradicate the genuine heritage of the Sikh Panth (an erasure tacitly equated to the Indian army's assault on the Golden Temple in 1984, which destroyed the Sikh Reference Library). Critical scholarship was interpreted as one more bid to destabilize and ultimately destroy the Sikh community. This was when it struck me that the very work of understanding Sikh martyrdom was imbricated with a traditional Sikh martyrological discourse, which exercised its own kind of tyranny on Sikh identity. "*Panth khatre vich*" went the common Punjabi rallying cry: "The Sikh Panth is in danger!"—and it was in danger in part because of us, or so it was claimed.

The Gurdwara Reform Movement

Up to this point in this chapter, the focus has been on historicizing the very study of martyrdom within Sikhism today, situating it within the trauma initiated by the storming of the Golden Temple and the subsequent Sikh pogroms of 1984. These events are artistically captured in the magisterial painting by the Singh Twins titled, after George Orwell, "Nineteen Eighty Four," the name of which indicates the seminal nature of this event in the contemporary Sikh imaginary and the dark and degenerate nature accorded to the Indian government. Although it has been in the background since the early nineteenth century, the presence of martyrdom within Sikhism and its renegotiation within the Sikh tradition emerges anew whenever the Sikh community is constructed as threatened. This should elicit little surprise, as at its very heart, martyrdom is a discourse not only of difference and identity, but also of resistance, a point which clearly emerges throughout its appropriation in the many Sikh struggles of the nineteenth and twentieth centuries, and within the oft-told narratives of the Sikh past in which martyrological themes are retrojected. This is not to suggest that Sikh writers are being disingenuous and falsely assigning ideas to their Gurus which do not accord with early Sikh tradition; it is obvious that righteousness and truth are interpreted differently within different contexts. Certainly within the ideology that may be extracted from the hymns of the Gurus known as *gurmat*, truth and righteousness are some of the most oft-mentioned virtues. It is but a small step to incorporate these virtues into a martyrological discourse in which martyrs are willing to have their bodies broken for their commitment to both this truth and their duty to restore or maintain righteousness.

It is best to start this historical discussion in the relatively recent Sikh past and to work our way backward, to the time of the Sikh Gurus. I begin with an event already referred to: the Gurdwara Reform Movement. Much has been written on this event, which was initially sparked by the attempts of the British government in India in 1913 to remove a boundary wall to a Sikh gurdwara in Delhi, known as Gurdwara Rakabganj. The British government was laying the groundwork for the new capital city of New Delhi. Although World War I intervened, the issue was picked up again in 1920, and led to the appeal by Caveeshar noted earlier. Put simply, Sikh gurdwaras became the focal point of resistance to the British government among Sikhs during the

Indian independence movement, prompted in large part by the government's failures to appeal to the Sikhs (Fox 1985). As intimated earlier, this event helped to further entrench the credible rhetorical strategy that Sikh authors would use throughout twentieth-century Sikh struggles in order to secure aims which were deemed both in the interest of all Sikhs worldwide, and loftily espoused in the hymns of Sikh Gurus. For example, Guru Nanak said, "Truth is the highest of all; yet higher still is truthful living" (AG 62)—surely one of the most significant ethical statements in the Sikh religious canon.

The Gurdwara Reform Movement may nevertheless seem like an odd place to commence such a discussion, especially given that popular Sikh tradition traces conceptualizations of martyrdom to the very times of the Sikh Gurus—indeed to Guru Nanak himself, whose hymns are often inserted into Sikh martyrologies to demonstrate that all Sikh martyrs meet their untimely ends while keeping the words of the Gurus foremost in their minds. In many ways the leaders of the Gurdwara reform movement were all functioning under an idea of selfless Sikh sacrifice that they believed was entirely situated within the period of the Sikh Gurus (1469–1708).

I single out the Gurdwara reform movement because, during this collective undertaking—indeed, this seminal moment in the construction of contemporary Sikhness—martyrdom was hailed as the most significant aspect of the Sikh tradition, through both the powerful writings of these Sikh leaders, and their commanding oratory, delivered as Sikhs were galvanizing to fight for their sacred space. All Sikhs were strongly encouraged to emulate the behavior of past Sikh martyrs at this point: "If you cannot sacrifice like Bhai Mani Singh . . . then why not simply declare that the Golden Temple no longer belongs to the Sikhs!" (Fenech, *Martyrdom* 226).

Such taunts were indeed effective, and were often embedded into what I call the Sikh rhetoric of martyrdom. But the authors of these texts did not restrict their activities to the written or spoken word, powerful as these were. The process of activating the tradition of martyrdom through its performance put Sikh martyrology on display for the entire world to witness (as in the example of the thousands of Khalsa Sikhs who courted beatings, arrest, lengthy stints in jail, and in some cases, death [Teja Singh 1922]). This action became a dramatic performance that ultimately led these leaders, and the Sikhs generally, to cement a particular interpretation of Sikhism and Sikh history that was advocated and reified in large part by the Sikh intelligentsia of the late nineteenth century. This intelligentsia was composed of a more "radical" group within the larger Singh Sabha movement that began in 1873, the Tat Khalsa or true Khalsa, which aimed to reform Sikhism in order to bring it into line with more contemporary global sensibilities in regard to religion. The Tat Khalsa's ideologies were promulgated by the later Sikh organizations earlier mentioned such as the Akalis, the "followers of *akāl* (God)" pledged to liberate the gurdwaras from the hands of their corrupt managers. Indeed, the *morche* (battle lines) of the Gurdwara Reform Movement became "models of what they believe, and models for believing it . . . plastic dramas [in which] men attain their faith as they portray it" (Geertz 113–14). Put crudely, the Tat Khalsa adapted the rules of "the game of love," while the Akalis and the Shiromani Gurdwara Parbandhak Committee (SGPC) played that game successfully, suffering beatings and risking death as they sought to liberate the gurdwaras from British-backed custodians. These latter actions, witnessed on a daily basis between 1920 and 1925 further enhanced the credibility of this strategy of reading current struggles through a martyrological lens, and ultimately ensured the dominance of a particular interpretation of the Sikh tradition in which martyrdom prominently figures, a tradition attained through its portrayal. Sikh publications, which widely circulated during the Gurdwara reform movement (and were often read aloud to illiterate Sikhs), seconded this understanding of Sikhism. In the process, these newspapers also explained the basic political program of not only the Akalis and SGPC, but also that of the Indian National Congress, which advocated the nonviolent resistance of M. K. Gandhi and vowed noncooperation with the British government, in part through the wide scale adoption of homespun cloth known as *swadeśī*. Nearly the entirety of the Gandhian-Nehruvian strategy to secure freedom from British rule was explained through the rhetoric of martyrdom: *swarāj* (self rule); *satyāgrah* (passive resistance); and *namilvartaṇ* (non-cooperation); and all of the political tactics utilized by Indian freedom fighters, the origins of which were traced back to the sacrifices of both the Sikh Gurus and eighteenth-century Sikh martyrs, and couched in a martyrological rhetoric with which all Sikhs in the 1920s were thoroughly familiar (Fenech 255–75). The implication in such an exegesis was also directed toward a foreseeable future in which Sikhs would once again liberate India from an oppressive regime. Sikh tradition often claimed that, in the eighteenth century, Khalsa Sikhs kept the Mughals at bay—and so it seemed only logical to prognosticate that in the twentieth century, the Khalsa Sikhs would once again rid India of the new Mughals, the white Mughals (*pace* William Dalrymple)—that is, the British. Implied in such claims was the understanding that a new rule would be established in India, displacing that of the British. This perception was predicated upon Guru Arjan's understanding of *halemī rāj*, the "rule of humility" (AG 74), in which all people lived peacefully.

The regular use of the rhetoric of martyrdom in the struggle to liberate the gurdwaras allows us to observe clearly the progression from the Tat Khalsa to the Gurdwara reform movement. The Tat Khalsa conveyed their particularly potent understanding of the Sikh tradition through this rhetoric; as their interpretation displaced numerous other ways of being Sikh, the language in which they couched that interpretation, and persuaded Sikhs that theirs was the genuine way to understand Sikhism, became seen as central to the Sikh tradition. In the process, this understanding helped transform Sikhism into a religion predominantly composed of heroic martyrs. Of course, Tat Khalsa Sikh authors were tapping into a tradition of martyrdom that was already apparent within Sikh history well before the end of the Sikh kingdom in 1849, and which was relatively well known. However, they elaborated it through their writings consistently, to a point that was hitherto unknown, and did so in such a way as to affect the way Sikhs behaved and thought—especially what they thought about themselves, their community, and the tradition handed down to them by their ancestors. Once again they appropriated discourses of martyrdom in order to influence a foreseeable future. This influence was indeed felt by the time of the Gurdwara reform movement some thirty years later, as activists had been weaned on the stories of Sikh martyrs since childhood; in many ways, these traditions and tales became the models for their own sacrifices, and the frames through which they interpreted their own historical moment. This would be the first chance Sikhs had to bring their traditions (back) to life, as it were, transforming the powerful myth of the Khalsa martyr into the Sikh ritual of martyrdom, and collapsing time as rituals symbolically do, thus allowing the past, heroic Sikh Panth to merge with the contemporary community warrior, and in the process reconstructing Sikh society in much the way that the re-membering of well-known mythology does. Indeed, today's Sikh Ardas (the Sikh prayer) mentions eighteenth-century martyrs in the same breath as those of the Gurdwara reform movement, thus equalizing their sacrifices.

This tactic proved to be quite successful, ultimately forcing the British government in 1925 to acquiesce to the demands of the SGPC, which included granting it the right to manage all Sikh gurdwaras within British Punjab, and a mandate to form a clear legislative statement defining who was a Sikh—a definition which was made official that same year. Explicit in this definition was the outline of normative Sikh identity, that is, Khalsa identity; implicit was the Tat Khalsa interpretation of the heroic Sikh past, the trajectory by which that specific Khalsa Sikh identity was formed (McLeod 82–121). In the process of enshrining their understanding of Sikhism within the Sikh imaginary, leaders of the Akali movement entrenched the norms of identity within the rhetoric of martyrdom and the heroic Khalsa myth to the point that it is entirely normative in the early twenty-first century.

As noted, the myth that animated the Akali rhetoric of martyrdom was constructed and utilized first by the Tat Khalsa. Between 1879 and 1909, Sikh writers associated with the Tat Khalsa, especially such pioneers as Ditt Singh, Gurmukh Singh, and Vir Singh, created a Sikh narrative which relied on traditional Sikh sources—but traditional sources refracted through a lens polished by the forces of the European Enlightenment and British modernity. This was a Sikhism that easily came to terms with the modernity ushered in by the British—which, indeed, led the British to proclaim a type of kinship with the Sikhs—and transformed Sikhism from a provincial religious tradition to one of the great religions of the world.

This rhetoric was the most effective strategy Tat Khalsa writers employed to mobilize Sikhs in large numbers to act against what they considered to be the greatest of all dangers: namely, a Sikh tradition that was understood as Hindu, a threat which they described in terms that emerged from classic British Orientalism, a Sikh sapling overwhelmed by a Hindu jungle. The Tat Khalsa was not elaborating a Sikh tradition that was new. As already discussed, there were strong precedents for their interpretation, and many sources and examples on which they could draw in its construction. But there were also both other Sikh groups and Hindu groups who contested the narrow interpretation of the Tat Khalsa, and whose own understandings of a more generous Sikhism also had strong historical precedent underscored in part by the current, more plural state of the Sikh tradition, and by the image of Guru Nanak as a quietistic, spiritually inclined teacher and reformer of Hindu tradition. These other groups were nevertheless unable to establish a rhetorical strategy to parry Tat Khalsa claims, nor were they able to adopt this same rhetoric of martyrdom to deflect those claims—despite the fact that it was eminently possible, given that many Sikhs of the past were believed to have been martyred in order to save Hindus.

The Tat Khalsa's Ditt Singh was the first writer to make consistent use of this rhetoric in his newspaper articles and popular martyrologies (Ashok 1977). His message was straightforward: how is it, Ditt Singh asked, that Sikhs in the past chose death, rather than abandon the sacred symbols of the Sikh tradition, while Sikhs today arrogantly cast these off? Bhai Taru Singh, he reminds us, was horribly tortured and died for refusing to cut his sacred *kes*:

> But the young Sikhs of nowadays are too proud of their good looks and sit in the upper storeys of their houses cutting their own heads with scissors. Within the heart there is no shame whatsoever. This is the enemy of the Sikh way of life (*sikhī*). (Ashok 210)

Slightly later in the 1890s, Vir Singh would pen similar sentiments in his wildly popular novels, in particular, *Sundarī* (1898) and *Bijai Siṅgh* (1899), in which ordinary Sikh men and women become heroes and heroines, abandoning their conventional lives to fight for the survival of the Sikh Panth against the forces of tyranny. It was, Tat Khalsa narratives made clear, the very initiatory elixir of the Khalsa that made possible Sikh sacrifice and martyrdom and, by extension, the very freedom of India. Vir Singh's novels so closely captured this Khalsa narrative of the past that they actually inspired many Sikhs to join the Gurdwara reform movement.

Literary Foundations for Sikh Martyrdom

Before the annexation of the Punjab in 1849, and indeed well into the twentieth century, before the Singh Sabha/Tat Khalsa achieved its prominence, stories of Sikh heroism and martyrdom were predominantly the subject of traditional Sikh intellectuals, who passed on these traditions orally. Many of these stories were in turn at least partially derived from the written work of Santokh Singh, especially his voluminous *Gur-pratāp Sūraj Granth* of 1843 (popularly known as *Sūraj Prakāś*). Although *Sūraj Prakāś* contains many Sikh martyr stories, Sikh martyrs and their intimate relationship to the sovereignty of the Sikh Panth, and thus the future of the Khalsa, were even more strongly championed by Ratan Singh Bhangu's *Srī Gur-panth Prakāś*. This work was authored at the behest of the British sometime after 1813, and brought the issue of martyrdom from the periphery of the Sikh tradition to the center. Bhangu's work, the supreme exemplar of the Sikh *gur-bilās* genre, is a testament to Sikh bravery, daring, and martyrdom in a time of great distress, and is the work which comes closest to the spirit of the Khalsa Sikhism embraced and refined by later Tat Khalsa intellectuals (Dhillon 2004). Although both make use of narratives of martyrdom, Bhangu, unlike the Tat Khalsa, is not primarily concerned with the question of a unique Khalsa Sikh identity struggling to stay afloat in an overwhelmingly choppy Hindu ocean. Certainly Bhangu's understanding of the Sikh tradition is quite similar to that we discover in other *gur-bilās* texts which predate Bhangu, but Bhangu elevates the martyrological component to a point not matched by any previous Sikh writer, portraying martyrdom as the very essence of the ideology of the Sikh Gurus.

Perhaps Bhangu's fascination with the heroism and bravery of Sikh martyrs stems from the fact that he was the grandson of the great heroic martyr Mehtab Singh. Such an emphasis was therefore in his own interest and that of his family, while simultaneously allied with his own deep, personal devotion to the Tenth Guru and the Khalsa he founded. What makes Bhangu stand out even further from all other earlier Sikh writers of the *gur-bilās* genre is that he is the first to engage in what J. S. Grewal has insightfully called the "metaphysics of martyrdom" (Grewal 263), that is, the miraculous ability to have the future altered through the individual sacrifices of Khalsa Sikhs. The later Tat Khalsa also projected their interpretation of Sikh martyrdom to carve out a potential future for all Sikhs. While these writers aimed to place agency into the hands of the Sikhs themselves, as they individually and collectively fought against the temptation to engage in "Hindu" practices, Bhangu, rather, allocates agency to the Divine, who alters the present as a response to the extraordinary sacrifices of the Sikhs, sacrifices that demonstrate the truth in the Tenth Guru's gift to the Khalsa of sovereignty. For Bhangu, therefore, the Mughal execution of the great martyr Gurus, and the martyrdom of the four sons of Guru Gobind Singh, inevitably resulted in the destruction of that once-great empire, and suggested a new dawn of righteous Khalsa Sikh rule. Implied here is Bhangu's claim that all Sikh martyrs, Shahid Mehtab Singh included (and by extension his family, to which Bhangu belonged), also participated in this downfall, and would contribute to its replacement. Indeed, in later episodes of *Srī Gur-panth Prakāś* it is made apparent that the Mughals themselves rule in the late eighteenth century as a result of the munificence of the Khalsa.

This suggests that, for Ratan Singh Bhangu, sovereignty and martyrdom became inextricably linked. As Grewal has suggested, the ability to sacrifice one's life for a righteous cause, without any concern for personal gain, activates the ideas of sovereignty and humility that were earlier articulated by all of the Sikh Gurus, enhancing the power of the Sikhs on earth and thus ensuring the righteous rule of the Khalsa (Grewal 265). "*Rāj karega khālsā,*" goes the popular Sikh battle cry: "the Khalsa Shall rule!" Indeed, the Khalsa is particularly fit to rule because of the altruistic benevolence behind the martyrdoms of Khalsa Sikhs, warriors of righteousness who place concern for others above their own desires and needs. Such a heroic, triumphalist interpretation of the Sikh past was intriguingly aligned with the values the British, as ideally reflected in their own Victorian, "muscular" Christianity (the defense of the oppressed, for example). This similarity may have influenced the Tat Khalsa's adoption of Bhangu's privileged place for martyrdom within the Khalsa Sikh tradition (Jakobsh 58–69). Tat Khalsa writers retold the narratives of Sikh history in a style that of course differs from, but is nevertheless reminiscent of, Bhangu's own, a style that appeals to a "modern" Sikh individual shaped in part by the forces unleashed by the British presence in India. This privileged place may be seen throughout *Srī Gur-panth Prakāś*, but is best expressed at the end, while Bhangu is telling his reader of the benefits one accrues from reading his narrative of the Khalsa's ascendance. Here in a short passage—which may have been added by Vir Singh in the first printed edition of the text—we read that,

> The enlightened mind who listens to [the contents of *Sri Gur-panth Prakāś*] will be unable to turn away from battle. At the time this warrior expels his final breath that fighter will meet with the martyrs, merging with the martyrs in the same way that a drop of water combines with the ocean. (Dhillon 436)

The drop in the ocean, of course, is a commonly employed metaphor to describe the annihilation of the self that is believed to be the hallmark of the enlightened state in both Sufi and mystical Hindu traditions. The suggestion here is stark: merging with martyrs is akin to annihilation within the divine, thus tacitly equating martyrs with the highest of beings—the divine itself. Thereby the divinity is allocated to the Khalsa in a way similar to that of the Sikh doctrine of Guru Panth, wherein the presence of the eternal Guru manifests in any gathering of five Sikhs, and thus, by extension, the assembled Khalsa.

The word Bhangu uses exclusively for the Sikh martyr is *śahīd*, which, as earlier mentioned, is the term that Sikhs have thoroughly embraced today to the exclusion of all others. The Punjabi term is derived from Persian and Arabic, and as in these languages, it can mean not only "martyr," but also "witness." But the definition of *śahīd* as solely that of the martyr who witnesses to the truth, and in the process sacrifices life for a righteous cause, is not something that was unique in Bhangu's time. Certainly we find this meaning favored in other Sikh works, most prominently that of Sewa Singh Kaushish, whose *Śahīd-bilās*, the martyrology of the famous Bhai Mani Singh who was executed in 1741, predates Bhangu's by more than a decade. This work appears to offer the first sustained use of this category to describe the specifically Sikh martyr. But this fact notwithstanding, by the time Sewa Singh is preparing his text in the late eighteenth century and into the nineteenth, the word "*śahīd*" conveys any number of supernatural beings that inhabited the enchanted landscapes of the Punjab. Bhangu's own "metaphysics of martyrdom" makes clear that Sikh martyrs have supernatural power. To offer just one example, the curse uttered by Bhai Taru Singh, that the ruler who ordered Taru Singh's scalping will suffer a painful ordeal, comes true (Dhillon 277–83).

The term "*śahīd*" could, moreover, be applied to people who died in any number of ways, including murder during a robbery, or being eaten by a tiger (Fenech 164). It is perhaps for these reasons that the term appears so rarely in early Sikh literature, and when it does, it is the rarest occasion to see it defined solely as meaning "martyr." This meaning does appear in the lengthiest chapter of the Dasam Granth, the *Pakhyān Charitr*, but in order to ensure that the term is not open to misunderstanding, the word "*śahīd*" is qualified with the adjective "*pāk*" or "pure," which indicates that many apparently "less pure" understandings of the term were present during the author's time (DG 948). It is only by the late nineteenth century that the term, at least in Sikh circles, comes to indicate solely the person who dies in the defense of righteousness. This was due in large part to the appropriation of the term and its regular use by the Tat Khalsa in their rhetoric of martyrdom. The transformation to the singular meaning is indicated by the fact that it is at this time that we begin to see the title "*zindāśahīd,*" or "living martyr" to describe those Sikhs, like Bhai Takht Singh of Ferozepur, who struggle against near insurmountable odds to accomplish good but continue to live. The addition of *zindā* or "living" to *śahīd* to describe such people indicates that the privileged meaning of *śahīd* alone is that of the martyr who suffers persecution and dies as a result.

Another reason for the lack of use of *śahīd* in early Sikh sources was its sole association with Islam in the earliest Sikh writings, including its rare appearance in both the *Adi Granth* and within the odes of Bhai Gurdas. These authors understand the *śahīd* as a specifically Muslim martyr. There was a bias against Islam in eighteenth-century Sikh literature that was prompted by the fact that Sikh authors portrayed the antagonists of the Khalsa predominantly as Muslim, whether they were Mughal, Afghan, or Irani. For this reason it seems highly unlikely that these authors would use the term *śahīd,* identified as it was with Islam, to describe the Sikh martyr in the eighteenth century.

But although the term *śahīd* very rarely emerges in eighteenth-century Sikh literature in its sole meaning as the martyr, the concept of martyrdom is not rare at all, appearing frequently and often designated in this century's Sikh literature with terms that previously indicated humility such as "*sīs deṇā,*" "offering the head," a phrase we find for example in the *bāṇī* (sacred utterances) of Guru Nanak. Among others we also note "renouncing the body" ("*deh tiāgāṇā*") or "renouncing breath" ("*prāṇ tiāgaṇā*") in the service of righteous causes, and "sacrifice" ("*qurbān*"), all of which are still used in stories of Sikh martyrs. The eighteenth century is often understood as the most heroic of Sikh periods, in which the Sikh Khalsa, facing overwhelming odds and persecution, managed nevertheless to sporadically rule parts of Mughal Punjab, culminating in the 1760s with the occupation of the most important town in the *subā*, Lahore and then, in 1783, Delhi, which was the Mughal seat of power. By the final decade of the eighteenth century, the entire Mughal province was in Sikh hands. From the vantage point of authors like Kaushish and Bhangu, who lived through this period and were aware of the great strides that Sikh warriors had made, it may well have appeared as if the Sikh ability to sacrifice allowed the Khalsa to achieve these impressive ends.

But this of course speaks to the latter eighteenth century when, although clearly in the ascendant as we have noted, Sikh doctrines of martyrdom had yet to overtake the Sikh imagination as they will in the nineteenth, as evinced by the work of Sewa Singh and Bhangu in particular, followed afterwards by that of the Tat Khalsa. Prior to the eighteenth century there is very little to suggest that Sikhs were thoroughly intrigued by the concept, but this should not suggest that it was altogether absent in this earlier period.

The fascination originates early in the eighteenth century. In regard to Guru Tegh Bahadar's execution, for example, there can be no doubt that he was understood as a martyr by the start of the eighteenth century, as underscored in the *Bachitar Nāṭak* ("The Wonderful Drama"), in the *Dasam Granth* and attributed to Guru Tegh Bahadar's son, Guru Gobind Singh, which forms the basis of all later retellings of the Ninth Master's death in the *gur-bilās* literature. One can therefore understand the author of the *Bachitar Nāṭak* as the first successful Sikh martyrologist, who transformed the death of one Sikh into martyrdom. In this account Guru Tegh Bahadar, while his head is being severed from his body, maintains his resolve to protect the rights of all those who are oppressed, dying *dharam heti*, "for the sake of righteousness" (DG 54). The fact that this passage is so often repeated in the eighteenth century suggests that it animated the thoughts of Sikh writers, who perhaps were attempting to prepare Sikhs to confront a rather tumultuous political environment, during which Mughal power was devolving. In this turbulent period, stories of martyrdom may have inspired Sikhs to bear their tribulations and to resist the powers, much like so many other regional powers in India at the time were resisting and carving out their own territories and sovereignties. Clearly the message of Guru Tegh Bahadar is that of resistance and sacrifice.

While the first effective martyrologist is the author of the *Bachitar Nāṭak,* the first literary voice to promote the theme is arguably that of Bhai Gurdas, who speaks to us in poetry. Writing in metaphors, Bhai Gurdas devotes an inordinate amount of space to the symbols and tropes of suffering, Islamic martyrology, and ultimate redemption through such in his poetry (Gill 56–66). A study of Gurdas's manuscripts has also suggested that it may well have been the execution of Guru Arjan that prompted Bhai Gurdas to compose the *vār* which appears first in the earliest manuscripts of thirty-four odes. This *vār* deals with the death of Guru Arjan, the response to that event, and the glorious Sikh future that will be secured as a result of Arjan's death.

For Bhai Gurdas, the loss of the Sikh Guru who was also his cousin would have affected him dramatically, regardless of the circumstances of Guru Arjan's death. Let me be clear that nowhere in his poetry does he explicitly make the connection to martyrdom in the same way that the author of the *Bachitar Nāṭak* does with Guru Tegh Bahadar's death. One can surmise that as a close companion to the Guru, Bhai Gurdas would have offered some leadership to the young community with a concern to their future With an eye to the future, the last thing he would have wanted to do is further enrage the temperamental emperor who had executed the Guru by accusing him of such and having the repercussions of this visited upon the young Sikh Panth. As Gill forcefully has claimed, the future of the Sikh community, and the idea that the Sikhs, although small in number, could accomplish a great deal, were paramount ideas found throughout the writings of Bhai Gurdas writings (Gill 3). Martyrdom as a concept may be easily aligned with such concerns for the future.

But whether Bhai Gurdas understood Guru Arjan's execution as martyrdom is not the focus here; rather, the primary concern is whether Bhai Gurdas effectively transformed Guru Arjan's death into martyrdom for the seventeenth-century Sikh Panth. The answer, as far as I can tell, is no, given that there is no mention of Guru Arjan's execution—nor indeed of his execution as martyrdom—in Sikh literature until more than 150 years after the event. Were martyrdom a significant component of seventeenth-century Sikh tradition, there is no doubt that Guru Arjan's execution would have occupied far more space in Sikh literature than it does (which is none). Even Sikhism's first martyrologist, presumably Guru Gobind Singh as the author of the *Bachitar Nāṭak*, as well as the later authors of the earliest *gurbilās* literature in which martyrological themes of suffering and sacrifice are present, fail to mention it as such. Although Guru Arjan's execution is implied in the narrative portions of the Chaupa Singh *rahit-nāmā* dated to the 1740s it is not until 1769, with the completion of Kesar Singh Chhibbar's *Bañsāvalīnāmā* that we hear of the death of Guru Arjan as an execution: *ek mās śram pāi tin prāṇ tiāge*, writes Chhibbar, "after a month's worth of hardship [Guru Arjan] relinquished his life (*prāṇ tiāge*)" (Padam 82). Although one may only conjecture that martyrdom is what Chhibbar has in mind, it is not until Bhangu's text that the connection to martyrdom is firmly established (Fenech 20–31).

Perhaps a reason for Bhai Gurdas' lack of success in translating Guru Arjan's execution into martyrdom is that his poetry was simply not well known enough. Although Gill challenges a number of the predominant interpretive narratives regarding Bhai Gurdas, he does not go so far as to suggest that Bhai Gurdas was anything other than popular among Sikhs in the seventeenth century, despite the lack of evidence, intimating this popularity through his claim that Sikhs had become accustomed to the idea that Bhai Gurdas' work was extracanonical (Gill 12, n.7). The first time we hear Bhai Gurdas quoted as authoritative is in the *rahit* text attributed to Chaupa Singh Chhibbar, the non-narrative portion of which has been roughly dated to 1700, and this occurs only once. It will not be until the mid- to late eighteenth century that Bhai Gurdas will be mentioned again in Sikh literature. Sarup Das Bhalla's *Mahimā Prakāś* (1776) alludes to five of his poems in an authoritative manner (Bhalla 464); this is coupled with the appearance of the *Sikhān dī Bhagat Mālā*, an exegesis of the eleventh ode of Bhai Gurdas (Bedi 31). It does not appear to be a coincidence that, at the same time that Gurdas's poetry becomes understood as an important contribution to the Sikh scriptural inheritance, there is mention of the execution of Guru Arjan in Sikh literature.

This late eighteenth-century period marks a seminal moment in which Sikh power is on the rise with the displacement of Mughal power in Lahore and then Delhi, a time which very soon afterwards sees the appearance of Guru Arjan's execution narrative in Kesar Singh Chhibbar's *Bañsāvalīnāmā*. Martyrdom as a concept begins to exert a firm hold on the Sikh imagination at this time—a time in which this mid- to late-eighteenth-century seed will sprout and be watered first by Sewa Singh in 1802, then by Bhangu in the second decade of the nineteenth century, and finally by the Tat Khalsa in the latter part of this century. It is at this point that the idea of martyrdom is retrojected into the times of the Sikh Gurus to form the perfect interpretive circle that the martyr tradition in Sikhism today suggests.

12

The Meanings of Sacrifice

THE LTTE, SUICIDE, AND THE LIMITS OF THE "RELIGION QUESTION"

Benjamin Schonthal

MANY INQUIRIES INTO religion and suicide are driven by questions of motivation and justification: what sorts of religious ideas or rituals appear to justify suicide?[1] How are these ideas or rituals used to motivate others to commit acts of self-harm? At the heart of these questions lies a taxonomic impulse, a desire to distinguish between religious and non-religious suicide, between voluntary deaths motivated and justified by religious rationales and those undertaken for other reasons.

This line of questioning has played an important role in scholarship on the Liberation Tigers of Tamil Eelam, or LTTE, a militant group that for thirty years battled Sri Lanka's army to create a separate Tamil state in the island's north. The LTTE was well known for its use of suicide attacks and the group even maintained its own special squad of suicide bombers called Black Tigers.[2] In addition, LTTE soldiers regularly undertook military campaigns in which soldiers faced almost-certain death. Observing these tactics, many outside observers viewed the LTTE as a prototypical suicide-rationalizing organization, a singularly compelling example of a

1. Parts of this chapter draw upon, while also revising and expanding, sections of Schonthal, "Translating."

2. For example, an LTTE Black Tiger suicide bomber assassinated Rajiv Gandhi in 1991.

group that succeeded in persuading its soldiers to commit acts of voluntary death.[3]

It was not just the LTTE's use of suicide attacks that prompted scholars to ask questions about the links between religion and suicide in the group; equally important was the LTTE's extensive use of propaganda and ceremonial to eulogize the soldiers who died in battle. In a context of deprivation (of water, petrol, cement, and other primary goods), the LTTE spent enormous resources on building statues, monuments, and graveyards. It mandated that all persons living in LTTE-controlled areas observe regular ceremonies and memorials to pay homage to the group's war dead. These commemorative edifices and practices, scholars argued, played a central role in insuring motivation among the LTTE's fighters and in gaining support from Tamil populations in Sri Lanka and abroad.

Since the 1990s, scholars have asked questions about the links between voluntary death, commemoration practices, and religion among members of the LTTE and its supporters: what role did religion play, if any, in the group's practices? One line of scholarship concluded that religion was, in fact, the active ingredient: LTTE commemorations, these scholars argued, were infused with religious imagery and ideas, which in turn worked to motivate and justify acts of self-sacrifice for the organization. Although LTTE cadres came from diverse religious backgrounds (mainly Christian and Hindu), analysts nonetheless characterized LTTE soldiers' fierce commitment to the organization as a kind of shared religious zeal that was generated and sustained by the group's memorial ceremonies. These ceremonies functioned, in this view, as a type of religious ritual that fused together martial discipline with Christian and Hindu symbols, such that soldiers' deaths came to be interpreted by cadres and their families as acts of Christian martyrdom or Hindu asceticism.[4]

A second line of scholarship took the opposite position, disavowing any tight links between religion and LTTE memorialization practices. Although LTTE commemorations used phrases and symbols traceable to Christianity or Hinduism, the argument went, they were not, in themselves, religious. To view LTTE commemorations as religious was, in this view, to misunderstand the nature of LTTE ceremonial, by confusing (religious) symbols with

3. Analysts disagree as to how much was encouragement and how much was compulsion. For a good example of scholarship which portrays the LTTE in this way, see Pape.

4. For sophisticated arguments of this type see Roberts, "Saivite Symbols," "Tamil Tiger 'Martyrs,'" and "Pragmatic Action."

(religious) substance, or by mistaking deep commitments to an organization for some kind of Hindu or Christian piety.[5] Moreover, it was to contradict the claims of the LTTE itself, which regularly declared its commitments to being a "secular" (Tamil: *matacārparra*) organization, pursuing the creation of a "secular, socialist" state.

In this chapter, I want to reevaluate this debate—and others like it—by reconsidering the question that stands at the center of it: the question of whether LTTE memorialization does or does not root itself in religion. I argue that while framing inquiry in these terms may help illuminate some important features of LTTE commemoration practices, it also leads scholars away from asking other important questions. I show how, when it comes to the LTTE, "the religion question" has misled scholars, by urging them to seek interpretive singularity in symbols, rhetoric, and events that may in fact be conspicuously and deliberately multivocal, and by inclining them to see consistency in practices that have changed substantially over time. Looking at LTTE commemoration practices outside the context of the religion question allows one to see that, rather than religious or non-religious, LTTE memorialization practices were purposefully ambivalent, calibrated to communicate both religious and non-religious meanings. Moreover, it allows one to recognize how the nature of that ambivalence, itself, has changed since the 1990s.

To demonstrate this, I look closely at one small but important instance of LTTE commemoration: a single section of a single speech from a 1997 "Heroes Day" ceremony, the most important annual memorialization event organized by the LTTE. (The year 1997 was also notable as a particularly bloody period in the conflict between the LTTE and the Sri Lankan army.) Through a detailed translation and explication of the language used in this speech, and a brief analysis of the transformations of this speech over time, I not only cast light on how and why asking the religion question offers limited analysis, I also propose an alternative approach to the study of religion and suicide. This approach eschews the question of whether religion does or does not justify and motivate actors, and instead urges scholars to pursue a more flexible and patient examination of the potential functions of ambivalence and ambiguity in the discourses and practices of groups that praise acts of self-sacrifice.

5. For sophisticated arguments of this type, see Schalk, "Present Concepts of Secularism," and "Beyond Hindu Festivals."

LTTE Memorialization

From its rise to power in the early 1980s to its military defeat in May 2009, the LTTE undertook a sophisticated and costly regime of memorialization for its war dead. This regime included large funerals, military cemeteries, roadside statues, posters, memorial songs, videos, speeches, and regular celebrations. According to the LTTE itself, these memorial practices were intended to transform fighters' deaths from tragic events into inspiring ones. Rather than signs of loss, the group insisted, soldiers' bodies became "seeds" (Tamil: *vittu*) out of which would grow a future Tamil homeland (Hellmann-Rajanayagam 124). Through symbolism and rhetoric, even suicide bombing was presented less as an act of "self-destruction" (Tamil: *tar̲kolai*) than an act of "self-giving" (Tamil: *tar̲koṭai*) (Chandrakanthan 164).

To this end, by the mid-2000s, the LTTE erected dozens of concrete and stone monuments around the island's northern and eastern regions (areas over which the LTTE had influence). Even in army-occupied towns, such as Jaffna, LTTE propagandists would frequently work at night, using the darkness of the early morning hours to mount posters and stencil graffiti on exposed walls surrounding busy streets. In many areas, the LTTE maintained lavish military cemeteries, complete with lush, irrigated gardens and rows of generator-powered lights, which remained illuminated at night to ensure that soldiers' graves were always visible (see Figure 12.1). These activities were not simply ad hoc; rather, the LTTE maintained a special bureaucratic department to oversee these projects staffed by soldiers who had been injured on the battlefield. The department was called the Office of "Great Heroes (*māvīrar*)."

The Office of Great Heroes administered nine memorial "festivals" (*viḻā*) each year. The largest and most important of these was called "Heroes Day (*māvīrar nāḷ*)." Celebrated on November 27, Heroes Day has been observed by LTTE supporters both in Sri Lanka and around the world.[6] In Sri Lanka, before 2009, the event was observed at LTTE military cemeteries called *māvīrar tuyilum illam*, or "the home of sleeping Great Heroes." Outside of the island, members of the Sri Lankan Tamil diaspora organized (and continue to organize) Heroes Day events at community centers and convention halls in Toronto, Geneva, London, Melbourne, and many other cities.

6. Since the end of the war in 2009, the Sri Lankan government has banned the celebration of Heroes Day and other LTTE ceremonies on the island.

FIG. 12.1 Kopai māvīrar tuyilum illam, one location of Heroes Day ceremonies. Photographed by author Sept. 2005.

While performances differ from site to site, the basic format of Heroes Day has tended to center around displaying images of deceased LTTE soldiers and paying tribute to them through speeches, songs, and the lighting of lamps.[7]

A central feature of Heroes Day gatherings was the broadcasting of an official speech given by the leader of LTTE. Prior to his death in 2009, the speech was given by Velupillai Prabhakaran, the man who founded and served as "head" (*talaivar*) of the LTTE from the early 1980s. Prabhakaran normally gave the speech from the LTTE's headquarters in Kilinocci, a town 330 kilometers north of Colombo, which was, until 2009, controlled by the LTTE. From Kilinocci, the speech was relayed live to ceremonies all over the island by the LTTE's pirate radio station, "The Voice of the Tigers." At Heroes Day events overseas, the speech was transmitted (as audio recordings, and as Tamil transcripts along with English translations) via the Internet.

---

7. Field notes, informal interviews, Jaffna, September 2005. For interpretations of the events, see Roberts, "Saivite Symbols" along with Schalk, "Revival," and "Beyond Hindu Festivals."

A Heroes Day Speech

For those interested in the links between religion, memorialization, and suicide, Heroes Day speeches are tantalizing texts. The transcripts of these speeches contain sweeping visions of the LTTE's aspirations and rationales, as well as extended paeans of praise for dead LTTE cadres. In these speeches, one finds a series of religiously resonant phrases and images, which scholars have identified as taken from Hindu and Christian texts.

As mentioned above, scholars have been quick to latch onto these phrases and images either to affirm or debunk their religiousness. However, one may also approach these phrases in another way: one may view them as sites of purposeful ambivalence, which permit and even encourage multiple types of translation and interpretation. To demonstrate this I engage in my own act of multivalent "simultaneous" translation, one designed to illustrate this ambivalence for a non-Tamil-speaking reader.

In Figure 12.2, I have taken the official Tamil transcript of Prabhakaran's Heroes Day speech from 1997 (obtained from a pro-LTTE website, which has since been shut down) and prepared two English translations: in Translation 1, I translate the Tamil transcript and place maximal stress to the religious connotations of Tamil words used in the speech. That is, I try to make the Hindu-centric meanings of Tamil terms legible to an English reader by deliberately rendering them using English terms that, as much as possible, suggest the category of religion.[8] In Translation 2, I translate the same Tamil words but place minimal stress on the words' religious connotations, choosing English terms that do not conspicuously implicate the category of religion. Translation 3 is an unaltered reproduction of the LTTE's official English translation of the speech, taken from the same website, and arranged spatially to correspond with my own translations.[9]

These three translations of the Heroes Day speech are juxtaposed in columns in order to cast light on two rhetorical features. First, this arrangement foregrounds the striking presence of dozens of religiously ambivalent terms: these are words that, on the one hand, have a lexical value in the

---

8. This is not to say that the chosen English terms have exclusively religious connotations (if such terms even exist), only that they are terms that are regularly used by English speakers and writers to describe religious actions, experiences, and concepts.

9. I have no knowledge of how official LTTE translations were prepared, or whether Prabhakaran himself vetted them.

Translation 1 (my religion-maximal rendering of Tamil speech)	*Translation 2 (my religion-minimal rendering)*	*Translation 3 (Published LTTE Translation)*
My beloved and esteemed people of Tamil Eelam,	My beloved and esteemed people of Tamil Eelam,	My beloved people of Tamil Eelam,
[1] Today is Heroes' Day. It is a **sacred** day for us to remember and honor our beloved **martyrs**, who **sacrificed** their precious lives for the freedom of our nation, and who continue to fill all our hearts. These **martyrs**, who committed themselves to the one great ideal of freedom for [our] people, lived for that ideal, struggled unwaveringly to achieve that ideal, and **sacrificed** their very life in a war for that ideal, they are magnificent human beings.	[1] Today is Heroes' Day. It is a **special day** for us to remember and honor those beloved **patriots**, who **committed** their precious lives for the freedom of our nation, and who continue to fill all our hearts. These **great heroes**, who committed themselves to the one great ideal of freedom for [our] people, lived for that ideal, struggled unwaveringly to achieve that ideal, and **dedicated** their very life in a war for that ideal, they are magnificent human beings.	[1] Today is Heroes' Day, a **sacred** day in which we honour and remember our beloved **martyrs** who have **sacrificed** their lives for the cause of freedom of our nation. Our **martyrs** were **extra-ordinary human beings**. They chose the noble cause of liberating our people. Having lived and struggled for such a cause they finally **sacrificed** their precious lives for that higher ideal.
[2] I honor these **martyrs** as **sacred individuals**. They, who are pulled by a common feeling of **devotion** to the freedom of their mother country, fully **renounce** the solitary **bonds of their worldly desires** and **material attachments**. They gave up **the worldly pleasures** of their individual life and are embracing the lofty values of a public life. They dare to **sacrifice** their very-own lives for that common ideal. I regard this as act of **holy asceticism**! We should **worship** these **martyrs** who shine as **exemplars of this sacred asceticism**, as nothing other than **sacred individuals**.	[2] I honor these **great heroes** as **flawless individuals**. They, who are pulled by a common sense of **commitment** to the freedom of their mother country, completely **give up** their own solitary **interests and close relations**. They gave up **creature comforts** of their individual life and are embracing the lofty values of a public life. They dare to **dedicate** their very-own lives for that common ideal. I regard this as an act of **flawless commitment**! We should **honor** these **great heroes** who shine as **exemplars of this flawless commitment**, as nothing other than our **flawless individuals**.	[2] I **venerate** our heroes since they **renounced their personal desires and transcended their egoic existence** for a common cause of higher virtue. Such a **noble act of renunciation** deserves our veneration.
[3] Our liberation organization awards great prestige and respect to its **martyrs** because they are supreme **martyrs** who selflessly destroy even themselves in the service of freedom, without expecting any benefit for themselves. We **worship** our **martyrs** as national heroes, as historic leaders in the war for our beloved freedom. We observe these **memorial ceremonies** for them, so that they should remain firmly in our hearts, where their memories do not fade with time. We honor them, raising memorials for them. Sowing the seed-bodies of the **martyrs** with **rituals** to **worship** the hero, planting memorial stones, **worshipping** their graves **as sacred symbols**, and **worshipping** their final sleeping homes are as **sacred sites of pilgrimage**, [all these practices] have become beloved customs for our people.	[3] Our liberation organization awards great prestige and respect to its **great heroes** because they are supremely **dedicated** persons, who selflessly destroy even themselves in the service of freedom, without expecting any benefit for themselves. We **acclaim** our **great heroes** as national heroes, as historic leaders in the war for our beloved freedom. We hold these **memorial festivals** for them, so that they should remain firmly in our hearts, where their memories do not fade with time. We honor them, raising monuments for them. Sowing the seed-bodies of the **great heroes** with **observances** to **honor** the hero, planting memorial stones, **honoring** their graves as **symbols of purity** and **honoring** their final sleeping homes are as **places of purity**, [all these practices] have become beloved customs for our people.	[3] Our liberation movement pays highest respect and reverence to our **martyrs** for their **supreme sacrifice**. We honour our **martyrs** as national heroes, as creators of the history of our national struggle. We **commemorate our heroes** and erect them **memorials** so that their memories should remain forever in our hearts. It has become a popular norm to bury our **martyrs** with honour, erect stone monuments for them and **venerate** these war cemeteries as **holy places of tranquility**. The practice of **venerating heroic martyrdom** has become an established tradition in our society.

FIG. 12.2 Three different translations of 1997 LTTE Heroes Day Speech.

context of Hindu religious practice[10] and, on the other hand, have important semantic value outside of those contexts, connoting qualities such as selfless heroism, military valor, or patriotism.[11] Second, this vertical arrangement illuminates how the LTTE translated these ambivalent Tamil terms in its own English translations.

Comparing these versions, one sees the markedly different ways in which Tamil listeners/readers and/or English listeners/readers may have understood the Heroes Day speech. Tamil Translations 1 and 2 suggest quite different narratives depending on whether one understands soldiers to have "sacrificed" or "committed" themselves to the LTTE cause (in the case of the Tamil word *īkamceytu*), or to have "sacrificed" or "dedicated" themselves (in the case of the Tamil word *arppaṇittu*). By choosing to render the Tamil terms as "sacrifice," Translation 1 selectively amplifies the religious valence of a word that has connotations extending in the direction of both Hindu ritual devotion and non-religious loyalty to a cause. As a consequence, Translation 1 valorizes soldiers' deaths in battle as acts of self-offering, offering oneself to the "ideal of freedom for [our] people" as one would offer an oblation to the divine.

Contrasting images of death and commemoration may not be plainly evident when comparing the translations of single words. (After all, "sacrifice" in English shares much of the Tamil terms' ambivalence.) However, different understandings of soldiers' deaths, and of the potential religious significance of them, form when one takes into account the broader imagery of an entire paragraph. Consider, for example, the possible connotations of paragraph 3. The passage gives a significantly different picture depending upon whether the person chooses to interpret Heroes Day as a "memorial ceremony" (*niṉaivu viḻā*), consisting of worship (*vaḻipaṭuvatum*), rituals (*caṭangku*), and pilgrimage sites (*puṉita talangkaḷ*), (Translation 1) or as a "memorial festival" consisting of honor, observances, and places of purity (Translation 2). In the first case, deceased soldiers' graves are cast as holy places, similar to Shaivite pilgrimage places (*s/talam*), and are to be treated in a manner usually reserved for sacred Hindu sites. In the second case, soldiers' graves are treated as monuments, places for solemn reflection, but not specifically objects of ritual action.

---

10. By terms used in "Hindu religious practice," I mean terms that have specialized in meanings in the context of temple (*kōvil*)-based deity devotion or are associated with certain, authorized (*śruti* and *smṛti*) Sanskrit or Tamil texts (*sūtras, śāstras, purāṇas,* and *āgamas*).

11. There are some Christian connotations as well, but, for the sake of focus, I will only look at Hindu connotations.

The degree of religious significance that analysts attributed to LTTE Heroes Day speeches frequently hinges on how they interpret key terms that Prabhakaran used to describe soldiers. Scholars frequently place great emphasis on the etymologies of these words and their potential links to terms contained in important Sanskrit or Tamil religious texts. However, even terms that can be traced to ancient religious texts acquire ambivalent connotations in modern Tamil usage. This is seen particularly in one word which many scholars (and, in some cases, the LTTE) have translated as "martyr." The Tamil word is *tiyāki*.[12] Many observers argue that *tiyāki*, as used by the LTTE, was a specifically Hindu term with linguistic roots (as Sanskrit *tyāgin*) that can be traced to Patañjali's *Yoga Sūtras*, the *Bhagavadgītā*, and other Sanskrit texts. Although *tiyāki* has these etymological moorings, the modern Tamil term *tiyāki* is used quite differently. In the *Bhagavadgītā*, for example, *tyāgin* refers to one who acts without consideration for the results, goals, or "fruits" of that action.[13] However, in the above Heroes Day speech, *tiyāki* refers to a rather different actor: not someone who renounced the goals of action, but someone who renounced his or her life for a political goal. In each case, one acts selflessly, but, in its usage by Prabhakaran, *tiyāki* describes a focused, goal-oriented, goal-motivated actor, not someone who has abandoned worldly aspirations. This use of *tiyāki* in the 1997 Heroes Day speech shows affinities with the writings of Dravidian nationalists in India, who used the term in the 1960s to describe, for example, activists who died while protesting legislation that would make Hindi the state's official language (*moḻi tiyāki*; Ramaswamy 229). *Tiyāki*, like so many terms in LTTE speeches, suggests both a religious agent (a *deva-bhaktin*, or divine devotee) and a political agent (a *deśa-bhaktin*, or patriot), depending on which linguistic genealogy one invokes.

The LTTE's own English translation of the Tamil speech, Translation 3, renders the Tamil terms in ways that tack between preserving and muffling the words' religious valences. This oscillation can be seen, in particular, by tracking how the LTTE translated the Tamil word *puṉita*, a term that contemporary

12. The LTTE were not the only Sri Lankan Tamil organization who use the term *tiyāki*. In September 2005, I observed a poster near the center of Jaffna advertising an event hosted by a formerly militant Tamil nationalist group, the EPRLF (Eelam Peoples Revolutionary Liberation Front). The flier mentioned an EPRLF memorial day on the June 19, 2005 called "*Tiyāki's* Day" (*tiyākikaḷ tiṉam*) that commemorated the killing of an EPRLF leader, K. Patmanāpa, on June 19, 1990.

13. See *Bhagavadgītā* 12(11), where Krishna tells Arjuna to abandon the fruits of all action, *sarvakarmaphalatyāgam*.

Tamil writers often use to translate the English words "holy" or "sacred,"[14] and a word that Translation 2 renders as "flawless."[15] In the above Tamil speech, *punita* is used as an adjective to describe Heroes Day (*puṉita nāḷ*), the dead soldiers (*puṉitārkaḷ*), soldiers' acts of dedication (*punita turavaram*), and graves (*puṉita ciṉṉangkaḷ, puṉita talangkaḷ*). In the English translation, the LTTE rendered *puṉita,* as I have in Translation 1, as "sacred" or "holy," when it refers to Heroes Day (a "sacred day") or soldiers' graves ("holy places"). In other cases, such as the second paragraph of Translation 3, LTTE translators ignored the word completely—here omitting the phrase which I translated as "sacred individuals" in Translation 1. In yet other places, the LTTE translated the word using an English term that does not implicate the category of religion in obvious ways, such as in paragraph two of Translation 3, where the LTTE rendered *puṉita* as "noble." The LTTE translation of *puṉita* echoes the religious ambivalence of the Tamil text by alternating between English terms that are marked and unmarked for religion.

The LTTE's translation (Translation 3) also makes particular semantic interventions to silence sect-specific Hindu theological ideas. In paragraph 2, the LTTE's English translation leaves a large section of text untranslated, substituting the shortened phrase "renounced their personal desires and transcended their egoic existence" for a longer section of Tamil text that describes (in the religion-maximal sense in Translation 1) how martyrs are to be venerated as ascetics (*tuṟavaṟam*) who piously renounced (*turantuviṭukiṟārkaḷ*) the tethers of worldly desire (*pācavuṟavukaḷaiyum*) and the bondage of sensual pleasures (*cukapōkangkaḷai paṟṟukkaḷaiyum*). The terms are strung together in the Tamil original with phrases that refer clearly to a fundamental theological idea in *Shaiva Siddhanta* religious philosophy: namely, the idea that followers of Shiva should strive to eliminate mundane concerns (Tamil: *pācam*, Skt: *pāśa*) in order to prepare their souls (Tamil: *pacu*, Skt: *paśu*) for spiritual union with Shiva (Tamil and Skt: *pati*). In other words, according to the part of the speech that the LTTE translators omitted, LTTE soldiers are compared to a particular kind of Shaivite ascetic (*tuṟavaṟam*). Yet the LTTE's English translation silences these specifically Shaivite connotations, choosing a phrase that suggests more generic (less theologically specific) Hindu ideals of selfless action.

---

14. *Punita* is also used for the modern Tamil transformation of Christian concepts Good Friday and Holy Ghost (*puṉita veḷḷi, puṉitāvi*).

15. *Punita* derives from the Sanskrit past participle *punīta,* meaning purified.

Religious Ambivalence in 1997 and After

By juxtaposing the translations above, one can see that depending on which section of the text one reads, with which interpretive tendencies, in which language, LTTE commemoration can be regarded as a project that eulogizes dead soldiers in Hindu terms, or as a project that honors soldiers as exemplary (but not holy), persons, or as a project that combines elements of both. In this light, LTTE memorializing practices appear to resist (or confound) the very question that scholars so frequently ask of them. In this instance, the language of LTTE commemoration is not readily identifiable as religious or non-religious; it appears as both. Moreover, this religious ambivalence seems to be carefully crafted by the authors and translators of the Heroes' Day text.

This observation—that the Heroes Day speech appears to have been purposefully ambivalent in the way it plays with religious and non-religious meanings—provokes an important question. Why would the LTTE construct its rhetoric of remembrance in such deeply ambivalent ways? One answer is that the LTTE used religiously ambivalent language in the Tamil-language versions of its Heroes Day Speeches in order to render commemorations persuasive and compelling to a diverse audience, consisting of many types of listeners and readers with different relationships to Hinduism. These audiences included Tamil-speakers and non-Tamil-speakers, persons inside and outside of Sri Lanka, Hindus and Christians, sympathizers and critics, foreign governments, journalists, and even academics. The Hindu valences of the speech may have proved uniquely comforting to Tamil Hindus who had lost family members or friends in the fighting, because these valences served to solemnize soldiers' deaths through meaningful and familiar—and therefore consoling—idioms of holiness and asceticism.[16] However, those very Hindu themes, if rendered more baldly, could alienate other audiences whose support the LTTE actively courted, both inside and outside of Sri Lanka. These included secularist Marxists, who were well represented in the LTTE's high command (Schalk, "Present Concepts"; Balasingham), Tamil Christians (particularly Catholics), who constituted a significant portion of the LTTE's cadres (Hellman-Rayanayagam 117), and non-elite-caste (non-*Vellalar*) Tamil

16. For further reflection on this as it pertains to the symbolism of LTTE graves, see Natali 287–301.

Hindus, for whom certain types of Hinduism had been associated with caste discrimination and social exclusion.[17]

In 1997, the LTTE's English-language translation of the Heroes Day Speech (Translation 3) seemed to reflect similar considerations of audience. It conveys to non-Tamil-speaking or reading audiences inside and outside of Sri Lanka a vision of commemoration streaked with generically religious hues, but without a specific Hindu theology. However, the following year, this began to change. Beginning in 1998, the LTTE altered the content and format of its English-language translations. Instead of publishing complete translations of the Tamil Heroes Day speeches, the LTTE released only partial translations, leaving out the most religiously ambivalent section of the speech, the introductory dedication (which I translated above). Moreover, beginning in 1998, these English translations were distributed not in the form of transcripts, but in the form of press releases, as official statements from the office of the "Tamil National Leader, Hon. V. Pirapaharan" (Liberation Tigers of Tamil Eelam (English). The new content and format of the LTTE's translation seemed to sanitize the English version of most of its religiously ambivalent terms, and to further highlight the political overtones of the speech (the LTTE's specific grievances and rationales for war) over and against the eulogizing of soldiers.

The LTTE's move to reconfigure its English-language propaganda after 1997 likely reflected an attempt to cultivate a more clearly "secular" international image on account of growing public concern with incidents of "religious" terrorism. (In 1997, the LTTE was placed on the United States register of global terrorist groups (Hoffman)). This concern became particularly acute after September 11, 2001, and the subsequent moves by foreign governments and international organizations to combat religious "extremism" and terrorist violence (Kleinfeld). The LTTE's 2001 Heroes Day speech, for example, made the case explicitly, even in the Tamil transcript, which underscores at one point:

> We [The LTTE] are a national liberation organization. We are fighting for the sake of our freedom against racist cruelty, against foreign military occupation, against state terrorist violence. Our struggle has a definite, legitimate political objective. Our struggle is based on the right to self-determination, a principle endorsed by the United Nations'

17. A large proportion of the LTTE came from the karaiyar fishing caste. On Hinduism and caste discrimination in northern Sri Lanka, see Pfaffenberger, *Caste,* and "The Political."

> Charter. We are not terrorists. We are also not lunatics who engage in reckless acts of violence impelled by the fury of racism or religious fanaticism (*matavāta*). We are fighting and giving our lives for the love of a lofty cause, human freedom. We are ones who yearn for freedom; we are *freedom fighters*. (Liberation Tigers of Tamil Eelam [Tamil])

Beginning in 2001, then, the LTTE began to limit the religious ambivalence of its Tamil Heroes Day transcripts as well. Post-2001 speeches describe soldiers using the Tamil phrases "eminent persons" (*uṉṉatamāṉavarkaḷ*) or "great human beings" (*makattāṉa maṉita piṟavikaḷ*), rather than "sacred (*puṉita*) individuals." In many cases, the speeches emphasize soldiers' mortal nature by adding an extra adjective to their descriptions, *māṉava*, meaning "human." While post-2001 Tamil transcripts still describe Heroes Day as a holy day (*puṉita nāḷ*), they now explicitly refer to the objects of reverence as heroic men and women, not Hindu ascetics. Instead of enjoining audiences to worship (*pūcittal*) deceased soldiers, these speeches enjoin audiences to bow their heads (*cirantāḻttutal*), commit [the soldiers] to memory (*niṉaivukūrtal*), or pay homage (*kauraviceytal*).

Considering the hazards associated with linking the group with religion, especially after 2001, why did the LTTE not eliminate all religiously ambivalent terms from its Tamil and English speeches altogether? One explanation lies in the fact that such terms provide a convincing and concise language for articulating monopolistic claims on loyalty, morality, and legitimacy—a ready-made vocabulary of what Paul Tillich called "ultimate concern" (1). In this sense, Heroes Day speeches might be compared to speeches given by other institutions that assert authority and demand allegiance over their members: for example, a eulogy at Arlington National Cemetery, or a State of the Union address from a US president. Some scholars would argue even further, insisting that the very grammar of national sovereignty (a goal to which the LTTE aspired) necessarily draws from religion either because nationalism is, in fact, a form of religion (Renan 153; Smith 159), or because the conceptual structure of politics derives originally from theology (Schmitt 36; Schmitt 23). Interpreted in this way, the LTTE's Heroes Day speeches could not help but employ religious ideas or language, because those ideas and that language were incipient in (or cognate with) the political goals that they were pursuing.

Yet for the LTTE, religiously ambivalent language not only had instrumental value for expressing nationalism, it also had aesthetic value in Tamil literary culture. In classical and modern Tamil, punning, or as it is termed (from Sanskrit) *śleṣa*, has been considered a mark of beautiful, well-adorned (*alangkariya)* literature. Classical Tamil poets and commentators celebrated authors' abilities to write in two registers simultaneously, to compose songs, prose, and poetry that communicated multiple meanings to readers and audiences depending upon how they chose to gloss the terms and parse the sentences. This was especially valued in Tamil bhakti writing, which often communicates two narratives at once: a mundane narrative involving temporal events and actors; and a theological narrative describing the attributes of the divine (Rao). In modern Tamil writing and speaking, this tradition continues, with punning being employed widely as a rhetorical device in movies, literature, and political oratory.

Conclusion

By asking the question of whether LTTE memorializing is or is not religious, scholars have both gained and lost. They have gained a deeper appreciation for the history behind the symbolism and rhetoric that have defined LTTE propaganda. However, they have lost attentiveness to the quality and function of ambiguity itself in LTTE memorializing. When it comes to the 1997 Heroes Day Speech, asking "the religion question" too quickly preempts an examination of how and why the group decided to communicate in both religious and non-religious registers. It forecloses an appreciation of the religiously ambivalent quality of LTTE rhetoric and it short-circuits an analysis of how and why—as well as when—the LTTE may have chosen that rhetoric. These decisions may reflect considerations of audience, politics, or aesthetics—or even combinations of all three.

Yet, this examination of LTTE practices also suggests a broader point about how scholars analyze the links between religion, commemoration, and suicide. Commemoration practices (along with the aural and visual media that constitute them) are rarely designed for a single audience and a single purpose. The practices that scholars analyze are almost never "intercepted" on their way from in-group producers to uniform collections of in-group audiences. LTTE speeches, like other media, are scripted with multiple imagined audiences in mind: among others, Tamil-speakers in Kilinocci and Toronto; Sinhalese communities in Colombo and London; officials in Washington and Geneva; academics and journalists; and supporters and critics. The artifact that scholars interpret may be singular (for example, a particular speech), but the broader economy of reception in which it circulates is almost always plural.

This is not to assert that scholars should avoid interpreting commemoration practices such as those of the LTTE altogether. These practices are undeniably important and ripe for scholarly examination. Instead, this chapter has suggested an alternative approach for analyzing these practices, one that remains aware of and attentive to the role of rhetorical and symbolic ambivalence in those practices, and the ways in which that ambivalence might change over time. Interpretation need not be an act of disambiguation; sometimes one can learn more by exploring the texture of multivalence, rather than by focusing on whether a given text is or is not religious.

13

To Extract the Essence from this Essenceless Body

SELF-SACRIFICE AND SELF-IMMOLATION IN INDIAN BUDDHISM

Reiko Ohnuma

WHEN CONSIDERING INDIAN Buddhist attitudes toward elective death, it is essential to distinguish among several different forms. Ordinary suicide, or the act of voluntarily and intentionally taking one's own life, is largely condemned in Indian Buddhist literature as a manifestation of both desire (P. *taṇhā*)[1] and delusion (P. *moha*)—desire because the "desire for non-existence" (P. *vibhava-taṇhā*) is one of the three types of desire that characterize an unawakened person, and delusion because the person who commits suicide is profoundly mistaken if he or she believes that suicide will solve his or her problems. In fact, in a universe characterized by karma and rebirth, suicide will only result in the person being reborn into another existence in which he or she will have to suffer the negative karmic fruition of the act of suicide itself, given that killing oneself is an inherently immoral act, because it violates the most important Buddhist moral precept, which is to abstain from taking life.[2] We can see the negative judgment cast upon ordinary suicide in

1. Throughout this chapter, foreign terms are cited sometimes in Pali and sometimes in Sanskrit. When not clear from the context, Pali is indicated by P. and Sanskrit is indicated by S.

2. To abstain from the destruction of life (P. *pāṇātipāta*) is the first of the five moral precepts incumbent upon both monastics and laity, as well as the first of the ten wholesome ways of acting (P. *kusala-kamma*). It thus constitutes the most important element of moral behavior (P. *sīla*) in Buddhism.

a famous story from the Pali Canon (of the Theravāda school) in which the Buddha teaches his monks the meditative practice known as "cultivation of the foul" (P. *asubha-bhāvanā*), which involves contemplating rotting corpses in the cremation ground in order to foster detachment with regard to one's own body. The monks, however, soon become so disgusted with their bodies that they begin killing themselves and each other en masse—clearly not what the Buddha intended. He quickly puts a stop to the situation (replacing "cultivation of the foul" with a focus upon the breath) and makes abetment to suicide an offense entailing expulsion from the Sangha—the most serious category of monastic offense.[3] Although there are some examples in early Buddhist literature of monks who commit suicide and are not condemned for doing so, these examples are small in number, ambiguous in nature, and characterized by multiple constraints: (1) the monks in question are suffering from a painful disease and have exhausted all other options for relief; (2) they become liberated arhats (that is, they achieve the ultimate goal of nirvana) at the very moment of taking their lives and are thus incapable of acting out of either desire or delusion, nor will they be subject to rebirth; and (3) although the Buddha exonerates these monks of any wrongdoing, their acts are not explicitly condoned.[4] Buddhism thus agrees with other major religious traditions in largely condemning the act of suicide.

Self-mortification or asceticism to the point of death—such as we find in the highly respected Jain practice of sallekhanā, or the ritual vow to fast unto death—is likewise not condoned by the Indian Buddhist tradition; indeed, it was explicitly rejected by the Buddha, because it violates the fundamental idea of his path as a Middle Way between the two extremes of sensual indulgence, on the one hand, and ascetic self-mortification, on the other. Although the Buddha himself does voluntarily "renounce the life-principle" (P. *āyusaṅkhāraṃ ossaji*) three months before he dies (or attains *parinibbāna*), this act is fairly abstract in nature and seems quite distinct from the practice of mortifying the physical body to the point of death.[5] Likewise, martyrdom, which I define as voluntarily accepting death in response to religious persecution, does not appear to be a very relevant category for Indian Buddhism, and it is difficult to come up with representative examples.

---

3. For a translation of this story, see Horner, *Disciplines* i, 116–23.

4. These cases, and the issues surrounding suicide in general, are discussed in Wiltshire, Keown, and Lamotte.

5. See Walshe 247.

There are, however, two forms of elective death that are both textually represented and highly celebrated in Buddhist literature from India—as long as they are carried out by the appropriate actors, with the proper motivations, and under the correct conditions. These are self-sacrifice, which I define as compassionately sacrificing one's life for the welfare of others, and self-immolation, which I define as killing oneself as a sacrificial offering in a ritual act of devotion. The bulk of this chapter will be devoted to the former, supplemented by a brief discussion of the latter.[6] We will see that both are depicted as extraordinary acts, appropriately undertaken only by the most highly idealized beings. Rather than unproblematic valorization, however, these acts are greeted with discomfort and ambivalence.

Self-Sacrifice, or the Gift of the Body

Buddhist authors in India composed, recited, and passed down an enormous collection of stories of several different types, including many stories relating the previous lives of the Buddha and describing the innumerable deeds of virtue and compassion he performed during his eons-long career as a bodhisattva (a being traveling on the path that ultimately leads to buddhahood). These so-called *jātakas,* or past-life stories of the Buddha, which are voluminous in extent (the Theravāda collection, for example, contains 547 stories), were adapted from pre-Buddhist Indian folklore, borrowed from other Indic religious traditions such as Hinduism, or composed anew by the Buddhists themselves. They found expression through oral traditions and written literature, simple prose and elaborate verse, pictorial art and ritual performance. Persisting in popularity throughout the entire history of Buddhism in India, they also spread far and wide to other parts of the Buddhist world, and continue to play a prominent role in many forms of contemporary Buddhism.

Although these *jātakas* are extraordinarily diverse in subject matter and depict the bodhisattva in countless different ways, it is striking to note what a significant number of them involve astonishing and gruesome acts of bodily self-sacrifice, sometimes (but not always) leading to death. Indeed, the propensity of the bodhisattva to sacrifice life and limb on behalf of others, in one rebirth after another, is a persistent theme in the Indian Buddhist tradition. Indian Buddhist literature is replete with stories in which the Buddha, during his previous lives as a human being or animal, willingly sacrifices his own

6. See Ohnuma (on which this chapter is based) for a much more thorough discussion.

head, eyes, flesh, blood, skin, or entire body on behalf of somebody in need. In his previous birth as King Śibi, for example, the bodhisattva gouges out his eyes and gives them to a blind man, so that the blind man can see.[7] In his birth as Prince Mahāsattva, he allows his body to be devoured by a starving tigress in order to keep her from devouring her own cubs.[8] In his birth as a virtuous hare, he immolates himself in a fire in order to feed a wandering supplicant.[9] And the list goes on and on. Although only some of these stories result in the bodhisattva's death, I place all of them under the general category of "self-sacrifice," because in all of them, the bodhisattva is always willing to die, with his death being prevented, in many cases, only by magical and supernatural means, or because the being for whom he is sacrificing his life puts a stop to the process before death occurs. Such stories dramatically illustrate the great selflessness, compassion, and altruism cultivated by the Buddha during his long career as a bodhisattva.

What type of elective death is this, and why is it celebrated rather than condemned? The act of self-sacrifice is variously referred to in Sanskrit as *ātma-parityāga* ("self-sacrifice" or "renunciation of the self"), *śarīra-parityāga* ("renunciation of the body"), *adhyātma-dāna* ("internal gift"), and *kāya-dāna* or *deha-dāna* ("gift of the body")—which suggests that it is simultaneously a sacrifice, a renunciation, and a gift. The category of the gift is perhaps most relevant, for in terms of the bodhisattva's cultivation of the various moral "perfections" needed for buddhahood,[10] such acts are almost always classified as preeminent examples of the "perfection of generosity" (*dāna-pāramitā*): so generous was the bodhisattva, these stories suggest, that he gave away not only material goods, but even his own body and life. Even outside of the *jātakas*, in fact, Buddhist scholastic treatises contain long discussions of the virtue of generosity (*dāna*), with the gift of one's body or life in an act of self-sacrifice consistently idealized as one of the highest forms of the gift. Because such acts

---

7. For example, in *Jātakaṭṭhavaṇṇanā* 499; *Cariyāpiṭaka* 1.8; *Jātakamālā* 2; *Avadānaśataka* 34; and *Mahajjātakamālā* 44.

8. Chapter 18 of the *Suvarṇabhāsottama Sūtra*. The story involving the starving tigress occurs in multiple versions, but the protagonist is variously named; see, for example, *Jātakamālā* 1; and *Avadānakalpalatā* 95. The same story also appears as one of several episodes in *Divyāvadāna* 32; and *Avadānakalpalatā* 51.

9. For example, in *Jātakaṭṭhavaṇṇanā* 316; *Cariyāpiṭaka* 1.10; and *Jātakamālā* 6. In *Avadānakalpalatā* 37 and 104, the hare sacrifices himself for a human ascetic companion rather than a wandering supplicant.

10. The standard list (in Sanskrit) includes six such "perfections" (*pāramitā*): generosity (*dāna*), morality (*śīla*), forbearance (*kṣānti*), zeal (*vīrya*), meditation (*dhyāna*), and wisdom (*prajñā*).

are motivated by pure generosity and compassion (rather than desire or delusion), they result in enormous karmic merit for the bodhisattva and further advance him along the path to buddhahood. Moreover, because such acts so often result in saving the lives of other beings, as well as setting a powerful moral example (whose widespread effects are generally depicted), the fact that the bodhisattva may be violating the moral precept against the taking of life seems to be mitigated or drop out of view. In general, then, these acts of self-sacrifice are praised, lauded, and celebrated in Buddhist sources as a testament to the ideal character of the bodhisattva or buddha-to-be. Nor is the act of self-sacrifice unique to the historical Buddha alone, for some texts maintain that all bodhisattvas must make five gifts throughout the course of their careers—those of wealth, children, wife, body parts, and life[11]—and in the Mahāyāna tradition, many manuals on the bodhisattva path routinely treat self-sacrifice as an essential element of the bodhisattva career.[12]

Nevertheless, the willful taking of one's own life—even if on behalf of others—always, no doubt, raises troubling questions about the relationship between self and other, between the individual and the community, between self-interest and genuine altruism—and the bodhisattva's gift of his body is no exception. Buddhist sources from India grappled with the extreme nature of such an act, and their discussions are often characterized by anxiety and ambivalence.

Self-Sacrifice and the Discourse of Self and Other

How can we distinguish between self-sacrifice, motivated by compassion and altruism, and suicide, motivated by desire and delusion? How can we be sure that the bodhisattva is offering up his life purely out of a concern for the welfare of others, and not in order to gain something for himself? The praiseworthy nature of the bodhisattva's self-sacrifice depends wholly, of course, upon the purity of intention that lies behind it—particularly because Buddhist moral theory is characterized by an ethics of intention. But, intention is purely mental and invisible to the outside observer, so how do we know for sure? Buddhist sources routinely depict the bodhisattva

11. This statement is made, for example, in the commentary to the *Cariyāpiṭaka*; see Horner, *Minor Anthologies* Pt. 2, 14, n. 1.

12. In Śāntideva's *Śikṣāsamuccaya,* for example, the bodhisattva's gift of his body is one of the central, structuring elements of the bodhisattva path as a whole (as shown in Mrozik, *Morality and the Body*, and *Virtuous Bodies;* and Mahoney).

making explicit statements about his intentions, and these statements are formalistic in nature, conventional across a wide range of stories, and immediately recognizable as a group. Let us look at a few representative examples:

> [By means of this gift,] there is nothing I wish to obtain in this world. Rather, having benefited all beings, I strive to obtain unsurpassed, perfect, full awakening. (*Avadānakalpalatā* 55 [Vaidya ii, 337, v. 52])
>
> If I sacrifice my body, it is not in order to win riches, nor for sensual pleasures, nor for the love of my wife, children, or relations. What I covet is awakening, so that I can procure the welfare of all beings. (*Kalpanāmaṇḍitikā* 64 [Huber 337–38])
>
> The merit that I obtain from giving my head to you is not for the sake of [acquiring rebirth as] Māra, Brahmā, Śakra, or a cakravartin,[13] nor because I desire the pleasures and enjoyments of the three worlds. Rather, I do this [only] because I wish to attain unsurpassed, perfect, full awakening, and to rescue all beings and establish them in nirvana. (*Sūtra of the Wise and the Fool* 22 [Schmidt 144–45])
>
> This is not an attempt to win for myself a happy destiny, or the royal majesty of a cakravartin, or heaven with its singularly excellent joys, or even the bliss of liberation. But by whatever merit I gain [from this] . . . may I become the savior of the world . . .. (*Jātakamālā* 30 [Vaidya 212])
>
> I make this sacrifice not for the sake of kingship, not for the sake of wealth, not to become Śakra, not to acquire the territories of kings and cakravartins, and how much less for anything else! Rather, when I have awakened to unsurpassed, perfect, full awakening, may I tame those who are untamed, ferry across those who have not crossed, liberate those who are not liberated, comfort those who are despondent, and bring to complete nirvana those who have not attained complete nirvana. (*Divyāvadāna* 32 [Cowell and Neil 478])

---

13. Māra, Brahmā, and Śakra are traditional Indian deities, but Buddhism considers them to be particular stations of rebirth (inhabited successively by one being after another). A cakravartin is an emperor who rules over the entire world; again, Buddhism understands cakravartin-hood to be a particular station of rebirth.

Examining these passages, it is clear that all such statements are concerned with the denial of unacceptable motives for the gift and the affirmation of acceptable motives for the gift. The unacceptable motives denied by the bodhisattva include three basic types of inappropriate desire: the desire for a high karmic station (such as kingship, cakravartinhood, Śakrahood, Mārahood, or Brahmāhood); the desire for the rewards of such high stations (such as kingdoms, wealth, glory, sensual pleasures, sons, or family); and the desire for individual tranquility, final emancipation, or final bliss. Unacceptable motives for the gift thus include all worldly and heavenly goals, all karmic goals, and even the goal of individual liberation, if it does not include a consideration of the welfare of others. The acceptable motives affirmed by the bodhisattva are overwhelmingly limited to two: the desire to attain omniscience or awakening or buddhahood, and the desire to help beings, to rescue beings, to work for the welfare of the world, and so forth. Particularly clever in this regard is the bodhisattva's statement (in *Jātakamālā* 1) that he gives the gift only *parārthasiddheḥ*—a phrase which, as Speyer has pointed out, can be interpreted as either "in order to benefit others" or "to attain the highest goal [of buddhahood]," thus suggesting both acceptable motives within the same phrase (Speyer 6, n.1).

The bodhisattva's self-sacrifice is thus characterized by an intriguing mixture of self-interest and other-interest. On the one hand, it is not a completely disinterested and pure gift, because the bodhisattva acts partially out of self-interest and gives his gift with the desire to attain something for himself—namely, the ultimate goal of buddhahood. On the other hand, "attaining buddhahood" appears to be the one "self-interested" motivation that does not compromise the altruistic purity of the gift, since buddhahood—though pertaining to oneself—is desired for the sake of all beings. This is why the *Bodhisattvabhūmi* is able to describe the "pure gift," without contradiction, as one given "with no expectation of reward" but made "seeing supreme awakening [alone] as a benefit" (Dutt 94). The gift made "with no expectation of reward" is made possible only by aiming for the ultimate reward—the attainment of perfect buddhahood. It is only at the level of this purest motivation of all that self-interest (*svārtha*) and other-interest (*parārtha*) finally merge together, for the bodhisattva (as the *Mahāyānasūtrālaṃkāra* puts it) "cannot be happy unless others are happy," and "his own happiness is inseparable [from the happiness of others]" (Lévi Ch. 17 v. 53). In what Stephen Jenkins has described as a "productive paradox," self-interest and other-interest are here mutually intertwined, for nothing is more beneficial to one's own self-interest than to act solely for the interests of others, and conversely, one cannot be effective in furthering the interests of others without paying due attention to the development of oneself.[14] Or, as Śāntideva states in the *Bodhicaryāvatāra,* "All those who suffer in the world do so because of their desire for their own happiness. All those happy in the world are so because of their desire for the happiness of others" (*Bodhicaryāvatāra* Ch. 8 v. 129 [Crosby and Skilton 99]). In this way, Buddhist thought seeks to make a space for the possibility of a purely altruistic act and to rationalize the idea of self-sacrifice for others.

The delicate confluence between self-interest and other-interest that alone justifies the act of self-sacrifice can easily go awry, however, and soon begin to suggest the wrong kind of "self-interest." In fact, this problem seems to become increasingly worse, as the gift itself becomes increasingly altruistic: the more one insists on the other-directed nature of one's generosity, the more one draws attention to one's concern with oneself. The act of self-sacrifice is perhaps particularly prone to this problem, for while giving up one's body and life for the sake of another would seem on the surface to be the ultimate denial of self, it is, at the same time, an ultimate act of self-will—an aggressive assertion of the self's right to dispose of itself as it pleases (others be damned). Perhaps this is why another standard feature of these *jātakas* is for the bodhisattva's "selfless" gift to encounter serious opposition and resistance from those around him—from his officials and ministers, when he is a king, or from his family, friends, and dependents. In *Jātakamālā* 8, for example, when King Maitrībala insists on feeding his own flesh and blood to five hungry demons, his ministers protest:

> O Lord . . . you bear the burden of kingship solely for the benefit of your people, [but] your determination to give away your flesh runs contrary to your own intentions! So let it go! . . . What kind of dharma is this by which the Lord would make the whole world fall into misfortune for the sake of these five demons alone? (Vaidya, *Jātakamālā* 48)

Likewise, in the *Maṇicūḍāvadāna,* when King Maṇicūḍa slices up his own body to feed yet another hungry demon, he is met by the spirited response of his wife, the queen:

> Alas, alas, Lord, you who are supremely virtuous and greatly compassionate, Hero in Generosity, Protector of the World! Where have you

14. See Jenkins, for a thorough discussion of this notion.

> gone, abandoning me without a protector, extremely depressed and wandering in the wilderness? . . . O Lord, I am blameless, yet you have abandoned me. Alas, Illustrious One, I am ruined, miserable, and depressed . . . O Sinless One, you even promised Bhavabhuti, my father, that you would never abandon his daughter. Did you make such a promise in vain? (Handurukande 40–41)

It is in the arguments of these opposers, perhaps, that we see which "self" the bodhisattva really wishes to give away: the self entangled within and defined by its obligations and duties to others, the self that must engage in reciprocity. Whereas the bodhisattva's gift is presumably given wholly for the sake of the other, it also declares his independence from others in a way that is perhaps inherently self-aggrandizing.

Indeed, stories involving self-sacrifice, which are touted as paradigmatic examples of selflessness—and which even seem to materialize this selflessness through visceral images of self-mutilation—are consistently characterized by an underlying assertion-of-self through which the bodhisattva is depicted (and perceives himself) as a completely unique and autonomous being, capable of doing what no one else can do, and who gives a unique and unprecedented gift, a gift that surpasses all other gifts. This is a common conceit in these stories: the bodhisattva frequently prides himself on giving the "excellent gift never given before,"[15] and often contrasts himself with other, more lackluster givers. "Ah, how good is this, my gift of an eye!" (*Jātakaṭṭhavaṇṇanā* 499 [Fausboll iv, 407]), King Śibi thinks to himself, while Prince Mahāsattva notes that he is giving up his body, "which is so difficult for others to sacrifice" (*Suvarṇabhāsottama Sūtra* Ch. 18 [Nobel 212]). The elephant Ṣaḍdanta calls himself a "prince of generosity" (*Kalpanāmaṇḍitikā* 69 [Huber 410]), while King Puṇyabala proudly notes that only eight other bodhisattvas in the whole of time have made such a gift as he has.[16] In addition to asserting a strong sense of himself,

15. For example: "Today I will give a gift that has never been given by me before" (*Jātakaṭṭhavaṇṇanā* 316 [Fausboll iii, 54]); "Today I will give you an excellent gift that has never been given before" (*Cariyāpiṭaka* 1.10 [Jayawickrama Pt. 2, 12, v. 12]); "I will give a gift that has never been given before" (*Jātakaṭṭhavaṇṇanā* 499 [Fausboll iv, 403]); "Today I will give to a supplicant an excellent gift never given before" (*Cariyāpiṭaka* 1.8 [Jayawickrama Pt. 2, 6, v. 12]).

16. "Good Son, I will tell you in brief of the perfection of generosity. [I will tell you] how, as I was practicing the bodhisattva conduct, I sacrificed the sacrifice of a gift, [and how] no other bodhisattva previously sacrificed the sacrifice of such a gift, [and how] there will be no bodhisattva [in the future] who, as he practices the conduct leading to awakening, will

moreover, the "selfless" bodhisattva also evinces a certain repugnance at the idea of reciprocity with others. Far be it from him to ask anyone else to share in his compassionate works or to help him in any manner whatsoever. Totally self-sufficient and self-dependent, the bodhisattva *must do it alone*. "You alone . . . are called to be the savior of all," King Śibi reprimands himself (*Kalpanāmaṇḍitikā* 64 [Huber 336]), while King Maṇicūḍa resolves: "For the sake of all beings, I will endure all suffering by myself alone!" (*Maṇicūḍāvadāna* [Handurukande 84]). Within such statements, the bodhisattva aggressively asserts his autonomy and independence from others—even in the very act of self-sacrifice on their behalf.

This paradoxical self-aggrandizement and aggressiveness toward others, which is perhaps an inherent element of the act of self-sacrifice, is not simply my own (rather uncharitable) view of the bodhisattva's generosity; rather, it is a danger well recognized within Buddhist literature itself. In fact, we often find warnings against precisely this danger in manuals and treatises on the bodhisattva path. The *Bodhisattvabhūmi*, for example, pointedly reminds its readers that the "pure gift" of the bodhisattva should be an "unarrogant gift" (S. *anunnata-dāna*), meaning that the bodhisattva "has a humble mind when he gives," "does not give out of rivalry with others," and "does not think that because of that gift, he alone is a giver and a master of generosity, while others are not" (Dutt 94)—a statement that seems almost as if it might be addressed to the heroes of many gift-of-the-body *jātakas*. Arrogance, pride, self-aggrandizement, and contempt for others were thus well-recognized dangers that might arise in the very midst of the bodhisattva's selfless generosity and compassion.[17]

Thus we see that the act of self-sacrifice for the welfare of others—though praised and celebrated as an ideal act—remains highly fraught, and its distinction from the delusion of suicide is not as clear as we might like it to be: is it really about the other, or is it, like suicide, all about the self? We will see something of the same ambivalence in regard to notions of the body expressed within these tales.

---

sacrifice the sacrifice of such a gift, as I sacrificed [such a gift], when I was practicing the bodhisattva conduct—except for [the following] eight good men " (*Karuṇāpuṇḍarīka Sūtra* Ch. 5 [Yamada ii, 355]).

17. As Jan Nattier (135) has noted: "The potential for arrogance on the part of the practitioner who is striving for such a glorious goal [as buddhahood] is a theme that pervades the earliest bodhisattva literature, and various coping tactics are recommended in order to aid the bodhisattva in dealing with this threat."

To Extract the Essence from this Essenceless Body

Jātakas involving the bodhisattva's self-sacrifice exhibit at least two traditional lines of Buddhist thinking about the ordinary human body.[18] We might refer to one line of thinking as the worthlessness of the body: the body is impure, foul, and disgusting (commonly described as a "wound," a "boil with nine openings," and a "bag of excrement"); the body is afflicted by old age, disease, suffering, and death; the body is transient and impermanent (like a "bubble" or "foam")—yet the body's deceptive wholeness leads to delusions of selfhood, sexual passion for others, and other undesirable consequences that entrap one in the repeated rounds of rebirth. Negative views of the body thus center around its impurity, its impermanence, its fragility, and its significant role in reinforcing one's passions and delusions. Given these negative qualities, attachment to the body is worthless and futile, and the Buddhist monk is encouraged to overcome such attachment through a variety of body-focused meditations (although not to the point of committing suicide, as we have seen), such as meditation on the thirty-two loathsome parts of the body or on the nine stages of decomposition undergone by a corpse. These practices, and the notions that underlie them, both suggest the body's inherent worthlessness.

In contrast to this worthlessness, however, we might refer to the second line of thinking as the worth of the body. First and foremost, the body is a necessary locus of awakening; as Bernard Faure has said: "Despite its transcendental claims, awakening is always localized: it needs a locus to 'take place,' and this locus is the body" (Faure 212). More than just a passive locus where awakening "takes place," however, the body is also a necessary instrument for the attainment of awakening. Without the physical body, one could not engage in religious practice of any sort; meditation, worship, ritual, and acts of devotion and merit-making would all be impossible to perform. Thus, the human body, as both the vehicle for one's spiritual progress and the locus of its ultimate goal, should be adequately cared for and maintained. This second line of thinking finds expression in many different contexts. In the Buddha's own life story, for example, true spiritual progress was made only when he renounced severe mortification of the body and came to understand that the body needed adequate food and maintenance. Proper care for the body was thus an essential element of the Middle Way propounded by the

18. Buddhist views of the body have been summarized by many scholars; see, for example, Kajiyama; Hamilton; Wilson 41–76; Collins; and Williams.

Buddha, and distinguished the Buddha's teaching from some of the other religious movements of his time period that engaged overzealously in asceticism. Similarly, the human body is often celebrated for the rare opportunity it provides to engage in religious practice; food is recommended in moderation; health and physical vitality are extolled; and the bodily pleasures of meditation are praised. In a variety of such ways, the essential worth of the human body and the necessity of caring for it properly are clearly recognized and lauded.

The perceived worthlessness and worth of the body may appear, on the surface, to be contradictory, but it is relatively easy to reconcile them with each other. We can see this in a discussion from the *Milindapañha,* in which King Milinda asks the monk Nāgasena why Buddhist monks "cherish and take pride in" the body (through monastic etiquette, for example) if it is not "dear" to them. Nāgasena answers by comparing the body to a wound received in battle: although it is not "dear" to the one who receives it, it is nevertheless "rubbed with ointment, smeared with oil, and wrapped in a fine cloth bandage" so that the person can continue to function. In just the same way, the body is not "dear" to monks, but they care for it "for the benefit of the religious life" (Trenckner 73–74). Thus, the worthlessness of the body as a "wound" and its worth in practicing the dharma are not necessarily in conflict. Nevertheless, the two attitudes must be held in a careful balance.

Stories involving the bodhisattva's self-sacrifice express both lines of thinking, but relate them to each other in a more paradoxical manner, with the body's worth being derived directly from one's realization of its worthlessness. In many such stories, we follow the bodhisattva's thoughts as he proceeds through the following chain of reasoning:

(1) Because my body is worthless, I may as well abandon it for others.
(2) Yet my abandoning of the body (because it is worthless) is also a particular use of the body.
(3) This use of the body (when done in the proper manner and with the proper motivation) is positive in nature and results in desirable rewards.
(4) These rewards paradoxically turn my worthless body into something of incalculable worth.

We can see this chain of reasoning in, for example, *Jātakamālā* 6, in which the bodhisattva is a hare who encounters a brahmin supplicant in the forest. Pondering what food he might offer to this guest, the hare begins by berating the absolute worthlessness of his body in procuring adequate food for a guest, and then—in a kind of "a-ha!" moment—has a sudden realization of its worth:

> There is no possible way I can give to a guest the very bitter blades of grass I nibble off with the tips of my teeth. What a curse is my helplessness! What use do I have for such a weak and miserable life, when a guest who should bring me joy thus becomes a matter of sorrow? When will this wretched body—worthless in its ability to attend on a guest—be of use to someone by being abandoned? . . . I've got it! Indeed, I myself possess something that is suitable for honoring a guest, blameless, easy to obtain, and at my own disposal—the treasure of my body! So why should I despair? I have found something that is proper for a guest. Therefore, heart, let go of your despair and misery! I will honor the requests of guests as they arise with this wretched body! (Vaidya, *Jātakamālā* 32)

Here, the body's worth derives directly from the hare's realization of its worthlessness. That is, it is only because the hare realizes how worthless his body is that he is willing to abandon it for others out of compassion, which then leads him to see that it might, in fact, derive some worth in the very act of being abandoned—enough worth, in fact, so that the "worthless" and "miserable" body is paradoxically transformed into a "treasure." In that moment of sudden realization, the negative worth involved in merely abandoning the body is transformed into the positive worth involved in using the worthless body in a religious act, one which paradoxically transforms the body into a precious "treasure."

The same line of reasoning can be seen in a more compressed form in the *Suvarṇabhāsottama Sūtra.* Here, the bodhisattva is a prince who encounters a starving tigress ready to devour her own young and then thinks to himself:

> There is no use to this [body] because it is nothing but piss, [so] I will now employ it in a virtuous act. Thus, it will be like a boat carrying me across the ocean of birth and death. (Nobel 211)

Once again, we move from the worthlessness of the body (which is "nothing but piss"), to the use of the worthless body in the performance of "a virtuous act," which then paradoxically transforms the worthless body into a "boat carrying me across the ocean of birth and death"—all within the confines of a single brief passage.

The fact that such passages are either more or less explicit in their enumeration of the reasoning that links worthlessness to worth also points to the possibility of another option available to the authors of these tales—that of painting the worthlessness and worth of the body in starkly contradictory terms and celebrating the paradox between them without clarifying how they might be related. This is perhaps a more poetic strategy, one of reveling in the paradox instead of resolving it. In *Jātakamālā* 8, for example, King Maitrībala, in a single verse, refers to his body as "a noxious sore" and a "corpse" that is "perpetually ill and the cause of disease," but also notes that he will use this corpse in "an extraordinary deed" and thus exact upon it an "exceedingly sweet revenge" (Vaidya, *Jātakamālā* 47). In the *Maṇicūḍāvadāna,* Maṇicūḍa exclaims that his "putrid body" is, at one and the same time, a "requirement for [attaining] unsurpassed, perfect, full awakening" (Handurukande, *Maṇicūḍāvadāna* 32). And in *Jātakamālā* 30, the bodhisattva (as an elephant) refers to his body as an "asylum for many hundreds of diseases" but also "a raft for crossing [the ocean of] misfortune" (Vaidya, *Jātakamālā* 211). Within such passages, we leave the realm of doctrine behind and enter a more aesthetic and emotional realm, one in which the foul and loathsome body is suddenly—almost alchemically—transformed into a precious and highly valued object.

The paradoxical relationship I have posited between the "worthlessness" and "worth" of the body is further reinforced within these stories through the use of a particular cliché repeated over and over again. In many such stories, it is said that the bodhisattva, by giving away his body, will "extract the essence from this essenceless body." This statement is usually spoken by the bodhisattva and often addressed to the recipient of his gift:

> I will now extract the essence from my body. (*Jātakamālā* 8 [Vaidya 49])
>
> Today, having met you, I wish to extract the essence from this essenceless body. (*Avadānasārasamuccaya* 3 [Handurukande, *Five Buddhist Legends* 76, v.53])
>
> Today, having gained you as my friend, I am ready to extract the essence from this putrid corpse, destined to decay. (*Maṇicūḍāvadāna* [Handurukande 32])
>
> I must extract the essence from this crumbling, essenceless body, as if I were plucking a piece of fruit from a tree hanging on to a river bank, just as its roots are being torn by the current and giving way. (*Jātakamālā* [of Haribhaṭṭa] 6 [Hahn 54, v. 19])

In all of these passages, the words used for "essence" and "essenceless" are *sāra* and its negative, *asāra*. The term *sāra* has a wide range of related meanings; it refers to the "core," "pith," "sap," "heart," or "essence" of something and, by extension, its "essential part," "best part," "value," or "worth."[19] Thus, the terms *sāra* and *asāra* could legitimately be translated as "worth" and "worthless," and the bodhisattva described as one who "extracts the worth from this worthless body." The cliché thus encapsulates the two major lines of Buddhist thinking about the body I have discussed above within the confines of a single phrase: to "extract the essence from this essenceless body" is to realize the body's worthlessness and thus abandon the body in pursuit of higher religious goals, thus creating the body's worth.

The delicate balance here achieved between the worthlessness and worth of the body is reminiscent of the delicate balance between self-interest and other-interest that I addressed above. Just as we saw that the act of self-sacrifice paradoxically merges self-interest and other-interest together, so also it clarifies the relationship between the body's worthlessness and its worth. In both cases, opposing forces are balanced in a way that protects the celebrated status of self-sacrifice as an ideal and exemplary act.

The Ideal Body Achieved

Once again, however, the question of maintaining the proper balance soon rears its head: just as we saw above that the "self-interest" involved in attaining buddhahood can easily morph into arrogance, pride, and egoism, so too can the limited "worth" of the ordinary body—that is, its ability to be used for religious practice—quickly grow into the dream of a different kind of body altogether: one that is already perfect and ideal, and one that paradoxically overcomes all of the "worthlessness" whose realization is precisely what brings it about. Susanne Mrozik writes of this as yet another "productive paradox" lying at the heart of Buddhist conceptions of the body. She describes this paradox in the following terms:

> The person who cultivates detachment from his body, even to the point of sacrificing his body and life for the sake of others, is the very person who gets the best body of all—the irresistibly beautiful body of a Buddha. Paradoxically, the realization that one's body is inherently

19. See Monier-Williams, s.v. *sāra*.

> disgusting, impermanent, and without abiding essence creates an altogether different kind of body. Likewise, the ability to regard all bodies as alike in their foulness, impermanence, and lack of abiding essence produces a body that is quite different from all others. (Mrozik, *Morality and the Body*, 78–79)

This paradox is fully evident in the *jātakas* involving self-sacrifice, for in spite of their frequent condemnation of the ordinary body's worthlessness, these stories share with other genres of Buddhist literature a tendency to celebrate various types of "ideal bodies" that stand in stark contrast to the ordinary body and overcome all of its deficiencies and limitations. These statements move beyond the mere "worth" of the ordinary body to celebrate—often in literal and concretely physical terms—a body that is already perfect and beautiful to behold. Let me enumerate four different contexts in which the conception of such an "ideal body" occurs.

The first and most prevalent context consists of statements made about the bodhisattva's body by others—for despite the bodhisattva's own tendency to dwell on his body's impurity and repulsiveness, this same body is almost always described by others (and by the authorial voice itself) as one that is already ideal. Thus, in *Avadānasārasamuccaya* 3, King Sarvaṃdada describes his own body as "a parade of decay, disease, and death," yet this same body is hyperbolically extolled by the narrative voice of the text as "having the gait of an elephant in rut, shiny as gold, tall as Mount Sumeru, with brilliant jewel-like features" (Handurukande, *Five Buddhist Legends* 74, v. 50; 74, v. 52; 78, v. 63). In fact, not even the gory act of mutilation can make this body unattractive. For even when his body is cut open and "his blood [is] being lapped up by the demons," King Maitrībala (of *Jātakamālā* 8) is still described as having "a body shining like gold, as if Mount Meru were being embraced by clouds heavy with the weight of rain and reddened by twilight" (Vaidya, *Jātakamālā* 50). In addition to physical beauty, moreover, these bodies are often characterized by supernatural powers that belie the weak and fragile image often painted by the bodhisattva himself—such as the elephant whose tusks emit six-colored rays of light (*Jātakaṭṭhavaṇṇanā* 514 [Fausboll 5, 37, and 53]), or the king whose body emits a powerful halo "like rays from the disk of the moon" (*Divyāvadāna* 22 [Cowell and Neil 316]). In numerous such ways, then, these stories indicate that—at least according to those around him—the bodhisattva's body, far from sharing the foul nature that is supposed to be characteristic of all bodies, is already perfect and ideal.

Secondly, in those stories in which the bodhisattva dies, much the same can be said of the corpse he leaves behind. Because these stories often involve descriptions of the body's impermanence and its mutilation and dumping in the cremation ground, they strongly evoke the meditative practice of *aśubha-bhāvanā,* in which one meditates on dead, rotting, and mutilated corpses in order to foster detachment. Therefore, we might expect the bodhisattva's mutilated corpse to be evaluated in negative terms, and perhaps used as a meditative object illustrating the foul and transient nature of the body for those he leaves behind. Yet this is just the opposite of the reaction to the corpse that occurs in story after story. In the first place, the bodhisattva's lifeless corpse—even when headless, bloody, or mutilated—is still described as an object of great beauty. In *Jātakamālā* 30, even after an elephant has thrown himself off a mountain, the weary travelers who find his corpse extol its great beauty at length, comparing its various parts to lotus-stalks, moonbeams, the graceful curve of a bow, and other poetic images (vv. 34–36 [Vaidya, *Jātakamālā* 214])—just as in *Jātakamālā* 6, a hare's corpse, even after being burnt in a fire, is still "as beautiful as lotus petals and adorned with radiant jewels" (Vaidya, *Jātakamālā* 35). In *Avadānasārasamuccaya* 2, a dead man's corpse is described as being "pleasing although devoid of life," with a "beautiful complexion like polished gold." Even as a dead corpse, it is contrasted with the living bodies of ordinary beings, which are "immersed in the filth and excrement of birth, full of large, quivering worms of affliction" (Handurukande, *Five Buddhist Legends* 54, vv. 56, 58). Rather than being meditated on or allowed to rot further, moreover, the bodhisattva's corpse is almost always made the object of elaborate ritual treatment—for example, cremated on a pile of fragrant wood, interred in a *stūpa* at a great crossroads, adorned with flags and banners, and worshipped with all kinds of offerings (as happens to a king's corpse in *Divyāvadāna* 22 [Cowell and Neil 327]). The holy sites resulting from such ritual treatment are sometimes depicted as having a lasting—almost permanent—duration, such as we find in the *Suvarṇabhāsottama Sūtra,* where the *stūpa* commemorating Prince Mahāsattva's lifeless corpse lasts throughout the eons and is later made to reemerge from the earth by the Buddha himself.

Thirdly, a similar process occurs on a smaller scale in those stories in which the bodhisattva survives—for one of the standard features of such stories is that the bodhisattva restores his injured body to perfect health by performing an "Act of Truth" attesting to his sincere willingness to give his body away (which is, of course, an inherently contradictory act). In the *Maṇicūḍāvadāna,* for example, King Maṇicūḍa, who speaks so eloquently of the "putrid body" before giving away his flesh and blood, later performs an Act of Truth asking for his "perfectly beautiful" body to be restored (Handurukande, *Maṇicūḍāvadāna* 32, 45). Moreover, many such stories manifest a bizarre brand of bodily alchemy wherein the limb offered as gift is not only restored, but becomes greater and more powerful than before. Thus, in *Jātakaṭṭhavaṇṇanā* 499, King Sivi's restored eyes can see through walls, rocks, and mountains, and for a hundred leagues on every side (as he himself states, "I gave away a human eye and obtained one that is supernatural!"; Fausboll iv, 412). Such passages seem to imply that the bodhisattva gives away his impure and "worthless" body in order to acquire one that is better and more powerful.

Finally, most explicit of all are those statements in which the bodhisattva himself declares what type of "ideal body" he is aiming for in exchange for the one he gives away. In *Divyāvadāna* 22, King Candraprabha, as he willingly offers up his own head, hopes that his corpse will leave behind "relics the size of mustard seeds" and be commemorated by "a great *stūpa,* more excellent than any other *stūpa*" (Cowell and Neil 326). This competitive desire for the very best body takes on a particularly grotesque form in those stories involving the theme of the "flesh-mountain." In the story of King Ambara found in the *Karuṇāpuṇḍarīka Sūtra,* King Ambara vows, as he is giving away his body:

> May this body of mine become a mountain of flesh! May whatever beings have flesh for food and blood for drink come eat my flesh and drink my blood! And, by the power of my vow, may my body grow enough [to accommodate] as many beings as may eat my flesh and drink my blood, until it is a hundred thousand *yojanas* in height and five thousand *yojanas* in width! (Yamada ii, 381–82)

This physical transformation indeed comes to pass, and he then explains that he satiated the beings there with his flesh and blood for one thousand years and also gave away a huge number of tongues to be devoured by the birds and beasts, "yet by the power of my vow, one after another of them appeared [until] there was a heap of them as big as Vulture Peak Mountain" (Yamada ii, 382). Likewise, in the same text, King Durdhana also becomes a "flesh-mountain" by means of a vow—a mountain that subsequently grows to a thousand times its original size, with "human heads appearing everywhere, with hair, ears, eyes, noses, lips, teeth, tongues, and many hundreds of thousands of mouths" (Yamada ii, 364). On the one hand, these bodhisattvas wish to become "flesh-mountains" out of sincere compassion for others; on the other hand, there is also an unabashed desire to have the biggest body ever and the largest mountain of tongues. The balance between self-interest and other-interest seems to be lost in the bodhisattva's longing to possess the best body.

In yet other cases, the ideal body the bodhisattva wishes to attain is the very special physical body of a buddha. Thus, in the *Karuṇāpuṇḍarīka Sūtra,* King Ambara gives away his genitals in the hope of acquiring the "mark of hidden genitals," and his flesh and blood in the hope of acquiring the "mark of a golden complexion" (Yamada ii, 380)—which are two of the thirty-two marks characteristic of the physical body of a buddha (the so-called *mahāpuruṣalakṣaṇa*) that make a buddha irresistibly attractive and beautiful. Again, this suggests that the bodhisattva gives away his body not only out of compassion for others, but also to acquire a better body in return.

All of this makes perfect sense, of course, when we remember the total interpenetration of the moral and physical orders characteristic of the Buddhist worldview. In a worldview dominated by the theory of karma, moral virtues such as compassion or wisdom are not exclusively "mental" or "spiritual" in nature, but also have concrete physical embodiments such as a golden complexion or a mellifluous voice. Characters in Buddhist literature (as Susanne Mrozik has noted) "literally reek with sin or are made fragrant with virtue . . . are disfigured by vice and adorned with morality" (Mrozik 31). Thus, cultivating the wisdom that realizes the worthlessness of the body—and the compassion that is willing to give it away—must necessarily result in a pleasing physical form. My discussion is not intended, then, to malign the bodhisattva or to accuse him of impure or ulterior motives. Instead, I have only attempted to show that the act of self-sacrifice out of compassion for others—though justly praised and celebrated in Buddhist texts and consistent with Buddhist thought as a whole—retains a certain showiness, that is, a certain ostentatious veneer, that seems to result in embarrassment. The pure, altruistic act of self-sacrifice often seems just a hair's breadth away from the most flagrant display of self-absorption. Perhaps this is true of all such forms of elective death—which always involve a disturbing collision between the assertion of self and its denial.

Self-Immolation as Ritual Offering

A second variety of elective death that is praised and celebrated in Buddhist sources (primarily Mahāyāna sources) is the self-immolation performed out of devotion and as a ritual offering. Perhaps the most famous example occurs in the "Medicine King" chapter of the *Lotus Sūtra,* in which the bodhisattva

"Seen With Joy By All Living Beings" sets his own body on fire as a devotional offering to the buddha "Pure and Bright Excellence of Sun and Moon," and—in his subsequent rebirth—burns both of his forearms for seventy-two thousand years as a devotional offering to this same buddha's relics (Hurvitz 293–302). Similarly, in other Mahāyāna *sūtras,* bodhisattvas, in a frenzy of Buddhist devotion, write out the *sūtras* using their skin as parchment, their bones as pens, and their blood or marrow as ink.[20] What type of elective death is this?

One way of approaching these self-immolations is to try to relate them to the acts of self-sacrifice discussed above. One of the basic features of the *jātakas* involving self-sacrifice is that they all take place in a long-ago age, when there is no "Buddhism" in the world. In a sense, this is precisely why the bodhisattva must demonstrate his generosity in such an extreme manner—by giving away his very body or life. For buddhas, bodhisattvas, Buddhist monks, and anything having to do with Buddhism are all understood to be powerful "fields of merit" (S. *puṇya-kṣetra*); in other words, gifts bestowed upon them are especially productive of merit, because the merit derived from a gift depends, in part, upon the quality of the "field" in which it is sowed—with gifts directed toward Buddhism being the most "productive" gifts of all. Without any "Buddhism" in the world, the bodhisattva in a long-ago age was deprived of this powerful "field of merit," and therefore had to manifest his generosity in a particularly extreme form. By subsequently becoming a buddha and establishing "Buddhism" in the world, however, he made it possible for others to acquire merit in a much more efficient manner. Part of the message conveyed by the *jātakas* of self-sacrifice, therefore, is that although we should admire the bodhisattva for making such extreme gifts, such gifts are perhaps no longer necessary now that Buddhism exists. Whereas King Śibi had to gouge out his eyes, and Prince Mahāsattva had to be devoured by a starving tigress, the ordinary Buddhist can engage in mundane ritual offerings—such as giving alms to Buddhist monks or offering flowers to an image of the Buddha—and perhaps earn just as much merit as those earlier figures, due to the power of Buddhism. Extreme moral deeds in a buddha-less age can be replaced, in other words, by ordinary ritual offerings in an age characterized by Buddhism.

Another way of saying this is to invoke the tension between using and not using a substitute: As Hubert and Mauss so clearly discerned, every sacrifice is

20. See citations in Lamotte i, 143–45, n. 1, and ii, 975, n. 1.

really a sacrifice of oneself[21]—just as every ritual offering is really an offering of oneself. Ordinarily, however, one does not literally sacrifice or offer oneself, but instead makes use of a substitute—a sacrificial victim or a ritual offering that stands in for and symbolizes oneself. Thus, the ordinary Buddhist who makes a ritual offering to an icon of the buddha is really committing himself to the values represented by the icon—but rather than literally offering himself, he makes use of a ritual substitute. From this perspective, we can delineate what is unique about the stories of self-immolation: all such acts take place within a Buddhist devotional context, and the devotees who perform them have full access to Buddhism as a powerful "field of merit." Nevertheless, they refuse to make use of any substitute, choosing instead to turn themselves into the offering—just as the Buddha once did. The message suggested by such episodes, perhaps, is that once one recognizes the profound debt of gratitude owed to the Buddha for making the mechanism of substitution possible, one realizes that the best way to pay honor to this debt is by returning to the Buddha's example and forgoing the mechanism itself. In the *Lotus Sūtra,* this is celebrated as the best type of offering:

> Excellent! Excellent! Good man, this is true perseverance in vigor! This is called a true Dharma-offering to the Thus Come One. If with floral scent, necklaces, burnt incense . . . and a variety of such things one were to make offerings, still they could not equal this former [act of yours]. Even if one were to give realm and walled cities, wife and children, they would still be no match for it. Good man, this is called the prime gift. Among the various gifts, it is the most honorable, the supreme. For it constitutes an offering of Dharma to the Thus Come Ones. (Hurvitz 295).

The highest form of worship, then, is one that rejects the mechanism of substitution upon which all worship presumably depends. We thus move in a dialectical manner from the immediacy characteristic of the Buddha, to the mediation made available to the ordinary Buddhist follower, and back once again to the immediacy freely chosen by the fervent Buddhist devotee.

---

21. The partial or complete identification of the sacrificer with the sacrificial offering was recognized already by Hubert and Mauss, in their classic 1898 study of sacrifice. Basing themselves on Vedic sources, they posited this identification as a fundamental feature of all sacrifice: "Indeed, it is not enough to say that [the victim] represents [the sacrificer]; it is merged in him. The two personalities are fused together"—and in Vedic sources, this identification becomes "complete" (1964, 32).

Nevertheless, it is perhaps inevitable that pure immediacy is impossible to sustain and must inevitably give way to mediation. This is apparent even in the "Medicine King" chapter itself, if we pay careful attention to its sequence of events; for it is significant, I believe, that in his first life, the bodhisattva "Seen With Joy" burns his entire body as an offering and suffers death as a result, whereas in his second life, he burns only his forearms and then restores them through an Act of Truth. We thus move from the entire body to the major limbs, from death to survival, and from permanent loss to restoration. The pure immediacy of the offering is thus gradually domesticated—and by the time we get to the end of the chapter and its recommendations for the ordinary Buddhist follower, we are down to a single finger or toe:

> If there is one who, opening up his thought, wishes to attain [unsurpassed, perfect, full awakening], if he can burn a finger or even a toe as an offering to a Buddhastūpa, he shall exceed one who uses realm or walled city, wife or children, or even all the lands, mountains, forests, rivers, ponds, and sundry precious objects in the whole thousand-millionfold world as offerings. (Hurvitz 298)

The immediacy that is characteristic of exalted buddhas and bodhisattvas is thus domesticated just enough to become a viable possibility for the ordinary Buddhist devotee. Perhaps we might locate the ultimate endpoint of this process of "domestication" in the common East Asian Buddhist practice of burning incense, or moxa, on the crown of the head (or the forearm) at the time of Buddhist monastic ordination.[22] Here, the practice of self-immolation has been thoroughly ritualized, routinized, and institutionalized. It stands at the beginning of the Buddhist path rather than its end, and becomes a standard procedure that applies to everyone, rather than an option freely chosen by the heroic few. The grotesque display of self-immolation thus gives way to something milder, more comfortable, and more familiar.

In conclusion, while ordinary suicide and ascetic self-torture are both condemned, and martyrdom seems irrelevant as a category, there are several forms of elective death that are legitimated in Buddhist sources from India. Nevertheless, while elective death in the form of either self-sacrifice or self-immolation can be rationalized and even celebrated, its acceptance is never an easy matter; instead, it is forever surrounded by ambivalence, anxiety, and

---

22. The development of this practice on the basis of two Chinese apocryphal *sūtras* and its relationship to more dramatic deeds of autocremation are discussed in Benn 1998.

a constant desire to snatch some bit of life from the jaws of a voluntary death. While serving as a vivid instantiation of such positive moral qualities as generosity, compassion, devotion, and religious commitment, the act of voluntarily taking one's own life remains a disturbing spectacle—and one against which human nature recoils.

14

Reflections on Self-Immolation in Chinese Buddhist and Daoist Traditions

Jimmy Yu

RELIGIOUS SUICIDE HAS developed into a robust field of research in religious studies since 9/11. While much has been written in the context of modern religious terrorist attacks,[1] relatively little attention has been given to just how integral religious suicide was doctrinally, ritually, historically, and socially to premodern religious traditions. While religious suicide naturally relates to the irreducibility of death as a biological fact, premodern people imagined and experienced it within a specific cultural and historical framework. Like many religious traditions, Buddhism and Daoism understood religious suicide as a form of sanctified death. They formulated such sanctity on their own terms and provided distinct justifications, even a model, of religious practice.

The Buddhist doctrine mandates non-injury to all living things and rejects extreme asceticism and bodily injury. Chinese traditions tend to value the integrity of the physical body and to prohibit self-harm. In these traditions, the central moral prescription affirms life and prefers to prevent death. Hence, technologies of mastering death become means for transforming

1. Suicide bombers aim to transform themselves into lethal weapons of warfare to kill as many people as possible. In this respect, they embody a distinctive type of mass murder that is markedly different than religious suicide as discussed in this chapter. For more on terrorist suicides, see for example Kelsay; Hashmi; Khosrokhavar.

death's negative implications into productive power. The technologies of and discourses on the power of transcending mortality may differ, but the basic existential concern is the same. In this chapter I explore one particular kind of religious suicide, self-immolation, in the premodern Chinese Buddhist and Daoist historical milieus. I place this ritual within the wider Chinese (and by extension, East Asian) imagination of religious sanctity and mastery over death.

Ambivalence in the Prescriptive and Descriptive Divide

Prescriptive Buddhist monastic codes (*vinaya*) explicitly condemn the killing of living beings, as well as suicide, and consider such an act as a major offense (*pārājika*) which results in expulsion from the Buddhist order, even though there appears to be an ambivalence regarding suicide committed by an arhat, or a liberated saint.[2] One way to read this ambivalence is to recognize the conflicting attitudes of śramaṇas, or renunciants in ancient India, toward the act of religious suicide. In early Buddhist scriptures and the commentary of the vinaya canon, it is noted that the Buddha instituted a monastic rule against suicide because, in the villages of Vṛjis, a mass number of monks killed themselves and each other after having practiced the "contemplation of the impurity of the body" (Sk. *aśubha-bhāvanā*).[3] Repulsed by their own bodies after practicing this contemplation, some sixty monks[4] jumped off of high boulders, took poisons, hung themselves with ropes, or used knives to take their own lives. Some even convinced a son of a Brahman, Mṛgadaṇḍika, to

2. There is one exceptional case wherein an arhat, Chandaka, took his own life due to extreme bodily pain from illness. When Śariputra, another arhat, questioned the Buddha about this, the Buddha explained that, because Chandaka was an arhat who had ended the rebirth cycle, his action did not constitute a major offense, in contrast to someone who commits suicide and would be reborn again in another life; see story 1266 in the *Saṃyukta-āgama* (*Za Ahan jing*) T no. 99, 2:347b14–348b1. Different vinaya traditions generally agree on not killing, but in the Sarvāstivāda's *Daśabhāṇavāra vinaya*, there is one case which states that suicide is not considered an offense; see T no. 1435, 23:382a2.

3. See story 809 in *Saṃyukta-āgama* (*Za Ahan jing*) T no. 99, 2:207b21–208a08. A variation in this tale occurs also within the textual corpus of the *Mūlasarvāstivāda-vinaya*, where the story can be found twice: once in the *Vinayavibhaṅga* for *bhikṣus* (monks), and again in the *Vinayavibhaṅga* for *bhikṣuṇīs* (nuns).

4. According to the *Samantapāsādikā*, which is a commentary on the Theravāda vinaya, Migalaṇḍika killed five hundred monks in total; see Bhikkhu Anālayo 11–55.

kill them,[5] while others encouraged their fellow monks to kill them. To redress this phenomenon, the Buddha is said to have established the injunction against killing, and he taught the remaining monks in that village the method of mindfulness of the breath (Sk. *ānāpāna-smṛti*) to reach liberation. Whatever we may think of this story, it is important to recognize that apparently, in the ancient Indian ascetic milieu, it was not uncommon for renunciants, whether Buddhist or not, to commit suicide to end their lives.[6]

We know for a fact that Jains who lived at the time of the Buddha regularly practiced sallekhanā, or fasting to death, as a form of release from karmic bondage.[7] Interestingly, the Jain monastic codes prohibit burning, drowning, poisoning, and jumping from high places to commit suicide.[8] However, sallekhanā was acceptable as long as it did not conflict with the principle of *ahiṃsā*, or nonviolence, and it was performed for the sake of ending negative karma. As Vallely shows in Chapter 10, the discourse of sallekhanā continues in the early twenty-first century, and the Jains do not consider sallekhanā as "suicide," but rather, as a triumph of the soul over corporeality. In this light, it is possible to entertain the idea that perhaps early Buddhist vinaya and scriptures, at least those that reject religious suicide, banned all forms of suicide to distinguish Buddhism from non-Buddhist renunciant traditions.

Be that as it may, acceptance of sallekhanā still does not help us to understand the curious prohibition against other forms of suicide. Note that while fasting to death was permissible, other acts such as taking poison and jumping off mountains were not. Yet, the very fact that the Jain monastic codes list these illegitimate forms of self-annihilation—which are not so dissimilar to the ways in which the Buddhist monks from Vṛjis took their own lives—strongly suggests that at least some Jains and other renunciants at the time engaged in these very acts.

If we consider the *jātaka*, with its many stories of self-sacrifice and the heroic bodily offerings of the Buddha in his past lives, as a possible source for understanding the ancient Indian milieu, then we would have to accept the fact that killing oneself to gain release was not an unimaginable or uncommon practice among renunciants. It is, of course, problematic to treat *jātaka* tales, whether fictional or not, as mere reflections of social reality. Yet

5. Theravāda vinaya in the Pāli reports that the monks were killed by Migalaṇḍika.

6. See Oberlies; Olivelle.

7. See Olson 87; Laidlaw; Bronkhorst 31–36.

8. See Schubring 182.

it is important to recognize that, from a literary angle, prescriptive texts generally convey the dominant or mainstream imagination of the time. In most circumstances, such writing tells us what would be familiar to, and thereby accepted by, contemporary readers. In other words, the themes were, at the very least, socially recognizable and imaginable to the intended audience.

Reiko Ohnuma points out a special subgenre within the *jātaka* called "gift-of-the-body *jātakas,*" which feature the bodhisattva as hero, and bodily sacrifice as gift.[9] There are too many examples of such tales to recount here; suffice it to say that an important theme in these *jātaka* tales is the notion of *dāna*, or generosity or offering for the benefit of others. For example, these accounts of self-annihilation as an offering to feed a hungry tigress or living beings aim to inspire belief, veneration, and emulation. They are both descriptions of and prescriptions for religious practice.

Mahāyāna Buddhist scriptures also abound with stories of bodhisattvas or enlightened beings sacrificing themselves through religious suicides. A prime example can be found in Chapter 23 of the *Lotus Sūtra*, in which the Medicine King Bodhisattva swallows various perfumes, sandalwood, aloes, liquidambar gum, and other substances as a preparatory ritual before setting himself on fire as an offering to the Buddha Sun Moon Pure Bright Virtue.[10] The *Avataṃsaka Sūtra* also details Vairocana Buddha's former lives as a bodhisattva, wherein he offered his own body lifetime after lifetime to the buddhas, who praised him for his acts.[11] This practice is said to be the reason for his eventual buddhahood as Vairocana. These scriptures clearly promote a form of sanctity based on self-inflicted violence.

Prescriptive monastic codes and scriptures are not historical accounts, but they are nevertheless useful because they help us reconstruct their authors' values and observations. The narratives in these texts often reveal the stereotypes of the people of the time and their likely reactions to the circumstances in which the authors place them. Even the most extreme fictional stereotype can take on a life of its own as a literary discourse and can influence social practice. Thus, when a Buddhist scripture depicts a bodhisattva engaging in self-immolation as an offering to a buddha, and the text goes on to describe the cosmic reward of future buddhahood for that bodhisattva or the miracles surrounding such an act, this offers us with a window into the

9. See Ohnuma 50.

10. See Benn 54–70.

11. See Yu 43.

understandings and expectations of those who have actually emulated this practice and their contemporary witnesses.

Texts such as these are merely remnant records or tales of the imaginable. "Imagination" here is not intended as a dismissal of ancient practices as something unreal or made-up. Rather, what I refer to is the culturally instituted imagination that people of a certain time and place share in the creation of norms, values, methods, and practices. Religious suicide is a privileged practice through which social meanings are embodied, performed, and reproduced. It was something imaginable, created in the ancient Indian ascetic milieu, communicated through the Buddhist scriptures, the vinaya codes, and the *jātaka* tales. Below, we will examine how this ascetic imagination continued to reproduce and shape—but not ultimately determine—the imagination of Chinese practitioners. Instead of understanding Chinese Buddhist performances of religious suicide as merely reifications of Indian Buddhist norms, however, we will review a selection of cases that illuminate Chinese social agency and creativity.

From Buddhist Texts to Indigenous Chinese Practices

Ancient Buddhist texts portray a rich culture of imaginable and acceptable religious suicidal practices. One of these is ritual self-immolation, as exemplified by the Medicine King Bodhisattva in the *Lotus Sūtra*, to create merit and express devotion. After this scripture was translated into Chinese, beginning in the fifth century CE there emerged numerous historical documents of Chinese Buddhists practicing different methods of religious suicides. In these hagiographies, performers are presented as newly minted Chinese bodhisattvas capable of transferring merit to other beings, or even empowering the state by their willful deaths. However, close examination of them reveals that the Chinese performed self-immolation for a wide range of intended goals beyond Indian notions of generosity or merit-making.

The practice of self-immolation actually predates Buddhism's arrival in China. It was originally associated with rainmaking and self-sacrifice for the greater good, supporting the biocosmic power of the body to affect the cosmos as understood by indigenous worldviews. In non-Buddhists traditions, the practice of self-immolation sometimes became part of the Daoist ritual repertoire of sanctity, and then continued and evolved in other ways. Naturally the Chinese Buddhist ritual of self-immolation in later periods was often inscribed with these competing views. Thus, self-immolation was not a unitary practice, but a multilayered one, and its meanings changed and evolved in different contexts.

In his excellent study, James Benn, for example, has detailed many cases of Chinese Buddhist self-immolation (or "auto-cremation," as he calls it) from the medieval period to the modern era.[12] In my own work, I have placed this ritual in the larger Chinese cultural and religious context of pre-Buddhist understanding of the universe.[13] I argue that it is important to view such "Buddhist" practices in China as an opportunity through which Chinese performers asserted their agency and grafted their own understandings onto this Buddhist ritual.

The Sympathetic Homology Between Body and the Universe

There are numerous examples of self-immolation in official histories of its biocosmological power in association with the rainmaking ritual. For example, the sage-king, King Tang, founder of the Shang Dynasty (ca. 1600–1046 BCE), burned himself as a sacrifice to heaven during a drought to alleviate the suffering of his people. It was said that just as the fire was taking hold, a great downpour of rain fell.[14] Also, in a famous great drought of 90 CE, a Han Dynasty official Dai Feng, who occupied a central political position, "prayed [for rain] fervently without result, so he piled up firewood and sat in the middle to self-immolate. When the flames arose, heavy rain came down violently and he was uninjured. People far and near were all in awe." He was later appointed by the imperial state to be in charge of all matters pertaining to magic and divination, with shamans staffing his department.

It was the benevolent acts of sage-kings and virtuous officials that justified self-immolation. Their altruism trumps over filial piety—the received Chinese view that one should not harm the body because it was given by one's parents. In the workings of the moral universe, if self-immolation was performed for the greater good it would move the heaven to benefit more people.[15] I shall return to this motif of a sympathetic understanding of the universe. For now,

12. See Benn 33.

13. See Yu 115–39.

14. See Birrell 86.

15. See Yu 38–39.

it is important to recognize that official historical records justify the discourse of self-sacrifice, self-inflicted violence, and the resultant sanctity over and above individual devotion to parents. Such an officially institutionalized discourse became a pattern for later records of self-immolation, regardless of whether the performers were literati, Buddhists, or Daoists. A few examples of how this discourse persisted into later periods should suffice to unpack this discourse of sympathetic homology.

In the official history, there is a case of a mid-fifteenth-century official named An Yu, who was a constable in Pujiang County in Sichuan province. During a drought one year and after repeated failures on his part to bring rain, An Yu fasted, bathed, and went to the Daoist Temple of Purple Ultimate. He gathered firewood, piled it up, and made an oath: "If it does not rain, I will burn myself." Before he set himself aflame on the appointed day, heavy rain came down.[16]

We also see the same discourse of heaven responding to self-inflicted violence in Buddhist hagiographical literature. In the sixteenth century there lived a Buddhist cleric by the name of Zhoufu. Despite his Buddhist affiliation, local people referred to him as "Zhou the Transcendent" or "Master Zhou the Perfected Man."[17] Zhoufu was an esoteric practitioner who specialized in *maṇḍala* offerings, recitation of *vaipulya sūtras*, and the employment of incantatory spells, or *dhāraṇīs*. At the end of his life, he is said to have told his followers that the time had come for him to "follow the example of the Buddha and join the bath of fire." He then stacked up firewood, sat down on top of the pile, and started chanting *dhāraṇīs*. Flames suddenly burst from his body. He then said to his followers that, "If there is ever a drought in the future, call my name and rain will fall heavily!" It is said that, from the Wanli period of the late Ming Dynasty onward, when villagers prayed for rain, they simply called out his name, "Zhou the Transcendent!" and rain would pour down—and when it did, it would be accompanied by the sound of *dhāraṇīs*.[18]

The Miscellaneous Record of the Ming details a Buddhist ascetic monk named Yonglong (1359–1392), who bartered with Emperor Taizu to exchange

16. See Menglei (b. 1651) et al., "Human Relationships" ("Minglun huibian"), *juan* 659, 307 CE, 50; the story is also repeated in *Mingchen liezhuan* as noted by Schafer 140.

17. Both appellations have, for lack of a better word, "Daoist" connotations, but the fact that these terms were used in a Buddhist hagiographical text suggests that the author had no qualms about them. Below I discuss the meaning of "transcendent" and the Daoist critique and practice of self-immolation.

18. See Daojie (1866–1934) and Yu Qian (d.u.), *Xinxu gaoseng zhuan* 39:1197; Benn 177–78.

his self-immolation for the freedom of thousands of monks from conscription into the army. Because these monks had failed the basic exam for monkhood and had shown their ignorance of scriptures in their own tradition, Taizu wanted to draft them; nevertheless, he accepted Yonglong's offer, who supposedly gave a plaque to certain officials that read "the wind and rain will be favorable" and urged them to present it to Taizu in times of drought. When Yonglong immolated himself, Taizu freed the monks. That Taizu believed in Yonglong's spiritual power suggests the spiritual efficacy of expiatory rites. Some time later, when a drought occurred, Taizu remembered Yonglong's predictions and used the plaque to pray for rain. We are told that the region was rewarded with a heavy downfall that very evening. Delighted, Taizu exclaimed, "This is the rain from Yonglong!" Because of Yonglong's meteorological mastery, the emperor publicly eulogized him by writing a poem entitled "The Monk Who Shed His Soul."

In all cases of self-immolation, the body was central for negotiating meteorological effects in nature. The main logic behind the body's biocosmological power rests on the indigenous Chinese notion of sympathetic resonance, or "stimulus-response" (*ganying*), which assumes the interpenetration of the unseen and the seen worlds, the presence of the supernatural in the natural.[19] Simply put, when someone performs acts of sanctity in the human realm for the greater good, heaven responds. This discourse is so pervasive that it runs through many Chinese literatures, including miracle tales, hagiographies, and medicinal, astronomical, calendrical, fictional, and even statecraft texts. Naturally, these sources, be they Buddhist or not, had no qualms about connecting self-immolation and rainmaking. The authors of these records felt no need to justify the connection between self-immolation and rainmaking, and their readers did not see this as out of the ordinary. The discourse of sympathetic resonance embodied in this literature not only legitimizes the numerous cases of self-immolation, but also justifies self-immolation to procure rain as a culturally, morally, ritually, and institutionally accepted paradigm.

While Buddhist and literati self-immolation practices were pervasive, this is not to say that they were accepted uncritically by all members of society. Some members of the educated elite, for example, were particularly vociferous in criticizing popular practices of self-immolation by Buddhists and Daoists. What is interesting is that the notion of sympathetic resonance was never questioned. For examples of dissenting voices, let us turn to the

19. See Yu 12–17.

late Ming Dynasty official Tang Shunzhi (1507–1560), who provides a list of essentially ineffective means of bringing rain in his *Discourse on Rain Ritual*:

> Recently, people pray for rain but do not know the [method of] utilizing *yin* to beseech *yin* . . . They only ask Buddhist monks and Daoist clerics to write talismans, perform sacrifice, and hold incense to burn candles and talismans. They do not know that the ancients, in order to relieve drought, had to employ female shamans. Today Buddhist monks and Daoist clerics are used [to alleviate drought]. Even if their [rainmaking] technique is conducted to its perfection, if the person employed is overbearingly *yang*, rain will not come. People of later generations privilege Buddhist monks and Daoist clerics, but in ancient times Buddhist monks and Daoist clerics were nonexistent [in China]. Today ritual prayers for people should be performed by female shamans. If there are counties and cities that seek to quickly relieve drought, but cannot obtain a female shaman, then a female Daoist cleric or a Buddhist *bhikṣuṇī* [i.e., nun] can be used. This is to use *yin* to beseech *yin*.[20]

Tang Shunzhi's argument rests on the efficacy of burning female shamans to procure rain, which reifies the logic of sympathetic response between things in the natural world: female shamans are the epitome of *yin*, and rain is considered *yin*. Burning a female shaman as sacrifice would then procure rain. Thus, in this passage we see that he insisted that female shamans (or Buddhist nuns, if the former cannot be found), rather than monks and clerics, should be employed in this ritual. He advocates a materialist means of bringing rain through the *yin* principle. Elsewhere I have discussed the premodern conception of the body extensively, so I will not repeat it here, but suffice it to say that in premodern China, the body was believed to be efficaciously connected to the cosmos. Its positive and negative powers included the ability to influence heaven and bring rain, as well as a host of other social and cosmological phenomena. In this light, it is understandable why Tang Shunzhi would argue for the right (*yin*) body to burn to procure rain.

---

20. Yu 126–27. For other literati critics, see Yu Zhengxie's (1775–1840) criticism of ritual exposure and self-immolation, "Qiuyu shuo," in *Huangchao jingshi wenxubian* 26a–27b.

Critics of Self-Immolation

Criticisms of self-immolation are also found in certain Daoist sources. Unlike the previous discussion on self-immolation as a means of causing rain to fall, some Daoists perceived this ritual as a threat to the possibility of eternal life and the corporeal body needed to achieve it. Even though some Daoists themselves also engaged in self-immolation, as we will see shortly, their practice took on a very different meaning. For now, let us examine one particular text: the eighth-century *Scripture of Jade Purity of the Great Dao of Most High* (hereafter the *Jade Purity*), which connects self-immolation with heretical "barbarian religions" of the West.

The basic narrative of *Jade Purity* is set in a mythic, apocalyptic time when people of this world follow heretical forms of "austerities"[21] modeled on mountain spirits who disguise themselves as humans or outer-path practitioners who indoctrinate innocent people; in this world, the Daoist divine beings will be those who save humanity. While it does not mention exactly which religion(s) the text is attacking, its xenophobic assertions are undeniable. Eskildsen contends that the text is criticizing a mixture of Buddhism and Zoroastrianism,[22] and I believe there is truth to this claim. However, the use of Buddhist terminology and its association with heresy is quite clear. I have italicized specific Buddhist terms and ideas in the translation below.
In Chapter 1, it states that:

> Some call themselves transcendents, or Brahma; they meditate in empty rooms, or annihilate themselves by *burning their bodies*; some *jump off high cliffs* . . . they *seek extinction* . . . these teachings are deluded. Even though there are scriptures [that justify these teachings], there is no genuine teaching in them. Mixing perverse practices with truth, these people will not attain the Way.[23] [Emphasis added.]

Elsewhere, Fascicle 9 states:

> A mountain spirit in the barbaric region disguised himself in human form, possessing *various marks* [of sanctity] . . . he acquired a following

21. The term used for "austerities" is *kuxing*, the Chinese Buddhist translation for *dhūtaguṇa*. For a discussion of this, see Yu 9–10; 155 n. 22; Benn 33; Eskildsen 8–11.

22. See Eskildsen 139; Lagerway's entry on this text in Schipper and Verellen 525–27.

23. See *Jade Purity* DZ no. 1312, 33, 1:291a.

> of 80,000 people and taught them to worship fire . . . [his disciples] in unison wish to die; each of them entered the piles of hay with folded palms, either sitting or kneeling, and had a hired hand set fire to the hay. The flame consumed them . . . At that time the mountain spirit snapped his finger and praised them, saying that "The body of *vexations*[24] is the dwelling place of a hundred poisons. Quickly distance yourself from it and seek liberation; you must annihilate this body and thereby seek the *Dharma Body*".[25] . . . Such is the austerities of outer path practitioners. They build large bonfires and claim that, "If good men and good women are able to enter this fire, burn their bodies, then they are called '*foremost among great bodhisattvas*'[26] who attain the state beyond vexations and realize the *unsurpassable fruition*; they will also realize the '*bhūmi free from defilement*' in perpetual bliss;[27] or the '*unmovable bhūmi*' "[28] . . . foolish people hearing this would eagerly burn their bodies. . . even within the practice of the Great Way [i.e., Daoism] there are people who subscribe to this.[29] [Emphasis added.]

The text makes further allusions to Buddhism:

> At one time there was an outer path named *Fotuoli*,[30] who came to greet the king with a cauldron . . . the king left the householder's life and became his disciple to seek for the Way . . . on the *eighth of April*[31]

24. "Vexations" here refer to *fannao*, a Chinese rendering for the Buddhist term, *kleśa*.

25. See DZ 1312, 33, 9:365c–366a. "Dharma Body" here is also a Buddhist term that appears frequently in this Daoist text.

26. The term "great bodhisattvas" is *dashi*, which is a Chinese rendering of the technical term, *mahāpuruṣa*. In early Buddhism, this term is reserved for the Buddha; see Mochizuki 10: 581a.

27. This stage is actually a technical Buddhist term, *vimalābhūmiḥ*, for bodhisattva of the second of the ten *bhūmi* stages; see Mochizuki 3: 2299b.

28. The stage of unmovable *bhūmi* is the eighth bodhisattva stage of realization, *acalābhūmiḥ*; see Mochizuki 3: 2299c.

29. See DZ 1312, 33, 9:366c.

30. *Fotuo* is a transliteration for "buddha" in Chinese. The addition of *li* makes this name foreign.

31. In the Chinese Buddhist festival calendar, the eighth of April is typically the celebration for Śākyamuni Buddha's birthday.

he and his vassals made a vow to roast their bodies on that day in order to seek the Way.[32] [Emphasis added.]

The *Jade Purity* represents the crowning phase of Buddho-Daoist interaction.[33] What seems clear in these passages is the polemical attack on austerities and self-immolation, which the author saw as a foreign, perverse practice. It also states that such perversion has infiltrated the "Great Way"—that is, Daoism. While I generally avoid using terms that would suggest these "isms" as discrete, independent traditions, at least in this text it seems clear that the author uses the numerous Buddhist terms and ideas (e.g., seeking extinction, vexations, Dharma Body, bodhisattvahood, etc.) to register in the readers a very specific foreign religious tradition of Buddhism, and characterizes it as a pessimistic tradition that views the body negatively.

The message in the above narrative is simple: the Buddhist promotion of self-immolation is a disguised teaching by inferior mountain spirits meant to delude people. What they advocate is the destruction of life. Only Daoist divinities are able to bring true salvation to humanity.

Everlasting life has always been a cherished goal among those seekers who wish to become transcendents, or *xian*,[34] even though there may be other reasons why becoming a transcendent was attractive.[35] Much has been written about the ascetic ways through which practitioners aim to achieve this state of *xian*, but an undeniable element in this process is the value of the human body. For example, in hagiographical literature, the transcendents ascend to heaven—that is, gain liberation—with their bodies intact. The highest ideal for them is not to leave a corpse behind when their earthly life comes to a conclusion. This suggests that the ideal is actually not to die at all.[36] In this light, the body remains essential because it is needed to engage in various types

32. See DZ 1312, 33, 9:367c.

33. During this phase, from Six Dynasties through to the Tang and Five Dynasty periods (roughly fifth through the tenth centuries), not only did Daoist scriptures borrow Buddhist terms; apocryphal Buddhist scriptures also incorporated Daoist terms and practices; see Mollier.

34. Here, I follow Campany's choice of transcendent over the mistranslation of "immortal"; see Campany, *Making Transcendents*.

35. According to Campany, the sociocosmic implications of which are: 1) the opting out of the ancestral cult; 2) evasion of the horrific bureaucratic underworld; 3) and qualification to take up a post in the celestial administration to become a supergod; see Campany, *Making Transcendents* 57–58.

36. The category of the "transcendent" here is very similar to, for comparative purposes, the Nyingma Tibetan ideal of attaining a "rainbow body," where the physical body of the adept

of corporeal practices, including dietary restraints, macrobiotic exercises, breathing techniques, meditation and visualization, alchemical procedures, sexual disciplines, and various ritual and liturgical practices.

Dying for Everlasting Life

Despite this focus on the integrity of the body, there were, however, alchemical traditions within Daoism that concocted "elixirs" of immortality for ingestion, which ultimately led to voluntary suicides.[37] Another unique Daoist soteriological technique, which is essentially religious suicide, is called *shijie* or "liberation by simulated corpse," and is accomplished through self-immolation.[38] The *Traditions of Exemplary Transcendents*, which comprises seventy stories of hagiographies of transcendents,[39] details one such case involving Ning Fengzi, or "the master who was put in possession of Ning":

> Ning Fengzi was a man who lived during the time of Yellow Thearch.[40] He served him as his supervisor of pottery. One day a [divine] being visited him and showed Fengzi the skill of manipulating fire to emit five colored smoke [in his kiln]. This man taught Fengzi how to do it. Later, Fengzi collected firewood and self-immolated, and was able to rise and descend with that [five-colored] smoke. His body turned to ash, yet his bones remained. The folks at the time burned [the bones]

vanishes into rainbow light at the time of death, usually with no residue remaining; see Cuevas 338.

37. For a complete study of Daoist elixir alchemy, see Pregadio, *Great Clarity*.

38. See Robinet 62; Seidel 230–32. Seidel cites the origin of this practice as dating to the first century, in the works of Wang Chun (27–97) 230.

39. The *Traditions of Exemplary Transcendents* or *Liexian zhuan* is traditionally attributed to the Western Han courtier Liu Xiang (79–78 BCE). However, most scholars now believe that at the extant version of the text was written sometime during the Eastern Han (25–220 CE) era. For a discussion of this work, see Kaltenmark 1–8.

40. Different early mythical traditions about the Yellow Thearch or Huangdi were combined and reinterpreted after the unification of the empire under the Han dynasty. This mythology is complex, but as far as its role in Daoism is concerned, three essential traditions may be distinguished. According to Wolfram Eberhard, there was a cult tradition in the northwest of the empire that was centered on a heavenly god Huangdi. In the myths of the eastern provinces, Huangdi was featured as the ideal ruler of ancient times and the first practitioner of Dao. At the time of the Han dynasty, these two mythical traditions merged and were complemented by the tradition of Huangdi as patron of the "masters of methods." See Eberhard 158–61; citation from Pregadio, *The Encyclopedia of Taoism*, 504.

in a mountain north of Ning. For this reason, he was called Ning Fengzi.[41]

In this case of "liberation" through self-immolation, the prescriptive Daoist explanation would be that Ning Fengzi demonstrated his mastery of death by "feigning" his death. In reality, he was on his way to realize the deathless state of becoming a transcendent. In the above text, Ning Fengzi demonstrated his thaumaturgical power to die masterfully and ascend and descend at will with the smoke from the flame. Tradition also attributes Ning Fengzi as becoming the *xian* of Five Marchmounts.[42]

Yet, despite such mastery, "liberation by simulated corpse" was not the highest method of gaining liberation. In the Daoist imagination, the preferred way of "dying" was actually to ascend to heaven and forego death altogether. Only less advanced adepts had to settle for (feigned) death like other mortals, before moving on to purify their body by a smelting process in the Extreme Yin palace, in the high north of the universe. This is described in the earliest authoritative commentary on the *Way and Its Power* or *Daode jing*:

> The [virtuous] actions of the man of the Dao are perfect and the spirit of the Dao gathers about him. When he retires from the world, he *simulates* death and passes over into the realm of the Extreme Yin. There he revives, goes forth anew and thus does not perish. This is what is meant by "longevity" [in the *Daode jing*]. The profane, however, those who have no virtuous deeds [to their credit], when they die, they come under the jurisdiction of the netherworld administration. They indeed perish.[43] [Emphasis added.]

Ning Fengzi's self-immolation can be understood as the purification process of his biospiritual organisms, so that his mortal elements can be removed before achieving the state where he would never "perish" again. In Ning Fengzi's case, he ascended through smoke. Scholars have noted that Daoist records detail other ways of ascension for those who engage in self-immolation to attain liberation by simulated corpse, such as becoming birds that fly away.

41. See DZ no. 294, 5, 1: 64b.

42. See Zhiting et al., *Daojiao da cidian* 419; for the Five Marchmounts, see Robson's entry in Pregadio, *The Encyclopedia of Taoism* 1072.

43. See *Xianger Commentary* to the *Daode jing*, Chapter 33; citation, with minor adjustments, from Seidel 230.

In other cases, sometimes the performers were able to generate internal flames strong enough for self-immolation.[44] What determines their ability to accomplish liberation through self-immolation is none other than austere self-cultivation.

While the raison d'être and the supposed accomplishments of Daoist self-immolation may seem very different than the literatis' or the Buddhists' meteorological mastery, the basic ingredient of sympathetic resonance is still the same. In the sympathetic universe of premodern China, extraordinary feats of rainmaking or transcendence are possible through sanctified deaths.

Mastering Death

Two issues are at the heart of all of the ritual suicides discussed above. The first is mastery of death; the second is legitimation of this mastery. They work in tandem with each other, making religious suicide an accepted part of the Chinese cultural imagination. The records of self-immolation in China examined above are imbued with the normative discourse of sanctity, moral efficacy, and transcendence. Doctrinally, self-immolation was understood as an act of virtue and altruism; cosmologically, it supported the Chinese sympathetic workings of heaven and nature; socially, it was not necessarily perceived as an act of violence, aggression, or disruption. Instead, self-immolation cemented cosmic relationships, produced order, secured the ontological status of performers, and through the circulation of their stories, instituted the moral imagination of conjuring death.

In premodern times, the Chinese viewed death as a horrifying experience. They imagined that at the time of death, register-keeping spirits, much like the bureaucrats in life, would come to summon them to the netherworld. After judgment by trial, the person proceeded to the "underground prison," or *diyu*, the indigenous conception of hell, where the person must endure endless suffering. There are a number of good studies on the Chinese conception of the afterlife. They show in part that the Chinese imagination of death is connected with the two aspects of Chinese social organization, the kinship system and the imperial bureaucracy: the former requires that the dead be venerated as ancestors; the latter that they be registered and kept in line by subterranean register-keeping bureaucrats.[45]

---

44. See Kaltenmark 40, 45, 89.

45. For studies of the afterlife, see Teiser.

Death is the epitome of *saṃsāra* for Buddhists; it also exemplifies the antithesis of everlasting life for Daoists. Buddhism stresses that the end of one's life span is not a single occasion, but rather, a recurring suffering that one must go through endlessly in the round of transmigration. This notions of suffering and *saṃsāra* exacerbated the indigenous Chinese understanding of death. For the Daoist transcendent, the hallmark of his status and all of his ascetic efforts in preparation during life can be understood as preparation to transcend death.[46] Thus, the attractiveness of religious traditions such as Buddhism and Daoism is that they both provide ways to avoid death.

In the case of Ning Fengzi, his death is depicted as a form of self-mastery when he "ascends and descends" with the smoke from his self-immolation. He is depicted, in fact, as not really "dead" because he has become a transcendent. As exemplified by the cases of Zhoufu and Yonglong, religious traditions in China usually conflate practitioners' deaths with spiritual attainment of bodhisattvahood, or more precisely, depict their exit from self-immolation not as death, but as conquest over death. In all cases, the word "death" is never used. In Zhoufu's case, for example, his presence and meteorological power continue to be felt even after his self-immolation. Whenever there was a drought and people called his name, rain would come down. Like the bodhisattva Medicine King, he was a local bodhisattva who worked for the welfare of all those who prayed to him.

These Buddhist and Daoist hagiographical records depict the sanctity of these practitioners in concrete, visible terms. They also grant credibility to their lives with detailed descriptions of the performers' composure at the face of death, their virtuous deeds, their spiritual practice, and their worldly and world-transcending accomplishments, indicating that the performers have transcended the finality of death itself. Outward signs included meteorological mastery of procuring rain or otherwise changing the weather. For literati performers, often they were rewarded with high imperial officialdom, which testifies to heaven's approval. These accounts are not isolated cases, but instead form a sizable part of the repertoire of Chinese Buddhist and Daoist miracle tales, which in turn create a discourse of "eminent Buddhist monastics" and "Daoist transcendents." Their self-immolations became socially recognized markers of sanctity.

46. For samples of Daoist efforts in becoming the ranks of transcendents, see Campany, *To Live as Long as Heaven and Earth*.

15

Relinquishing the Body to Reach the Pure Land

BUDDHIST ASCETIC SUICIDE IN PREMODERN JAPAN

Jacqueline I. Stone

RELIGIOUS SUICIDE IN premodern Japan was commonly framed in Buddhist terms. Following Buddhism's introduction to the archipelago in the sixth century, its death rites and concepts of the afterlife steadily took root, first among elites and then across other social levels. During Japan's early medieval period—roughly the late tenth through early fourteenth centuries—growing numbers of people aspired to be born, after their death, in one of the pure realms of the buddhas or bodhisattvas (J. *ōjō*). The most sought-after postmortem destination was the Pure Land of Utmost Bliss (Skt. Sukhāvatī, J. Gokuraku; hereafter, "the Pure Land"), the realm of the Buddha Amida (Skt. Amitābha, Amitāyus), said to lie countless world systems away to the west. Once born in Amida's Pure Land, it was thought, one would never again fall back into saṃsāra, the cycle of deluded rebirth; rather, one was certain to achieve buddhahood. Persons who took their own lives in hopes of reaching a pure land (*jigai ōjō*) sought to expedite this liberative process. This chapter will investigate *jigai ōjō*, or *ōjō*-suicide,[1] in early medieval Japan, with attention to who performed it and how, the controversy surrounding it, its place within the larger repertoire of Buddhist ascetic practices, and its intersections with other traditions of heroic suicide. It will also explore how the theme of suicide to reach the Pure Land was

1. I borrow the term "*ōjō*-suicide" from Blum (153).

developed in early and later medieval literature, giving particular attention to the element of gender. First, let us briefly consider the background of this tradition on the Asian continent.

Continental Precedents

As discussed in Chapter 13 in this volume, "elective death" has been controversial in the Buddhist tradition. Ordinary suicide committed to escape the miseries of one's present existence was condemned as a deluded act that would bring painful karmic consequences in future rebirths. But when performed by spiritual adepts due to lofty motives—as a compassionate self-sacrifice to benefit others, or as an offering to the Buddha or his dharma—it could be seen as admirable, even heroic. Tales of the Buddha's past lifetimes (Skt. *jātaka*s) recount how, again and again, he sacrificed body parts, and even life itself, for the sake of living beings, for example, by giving his flesh to feed a starving tigress or stripping the skin from his body on which to record sacred teachings. Similar stories in the Mahāyāna sūtras (scriptures) celebrate bodhisattva heroes who relinquish their lives in sacrifice. These include the famous instance in the *Lotus Sūtra* of Bodhisattva Medicine King (Skt. Bhaiṣajyarāja, J. Yakuō), who in a past life turned his body into a living torch in offering to the buddha of his age, an act praised in the text as "a true Dharma offering" and "the prime gift . . . the most honorable, the supreme" (*Miaofa lianhua jing, T* 262, 9:53b; Hurvitz 271).

Ascetically inclined Buddhist practitioners have sometimes emulated such acts. Hagiographies of eminent Chinese monks and nuns include several examples. Those who performed auto-cremation—self-immolation by fire—seem initially to have been the most numerous, but they were later joined by others who undertook terminal fasts, offered their bodies to wild beasts, or leapt to their deaths from cliffs.[2] Liang-, Tang-, and Song-dynasty collections of monastic biographies group such acts under the rubrics of "relinquishing the body" (Ch. *sheshen*), "discarding the body" (*yishen*), or "being oblivious of the body" (*wangshen*)—broader categories including not only suicide, but less drastic forms of ascetic practice such as allowing mosquitoes, gnats, or leeches to feed on one's flesh; drawing one's

2. Yoshida 191–96; Kieschnick 35–50. See Benn 2007 for a detailed study of Chinese auto-cremation. While "self-immolation" has been used in the media to describe suicides by fire carried out in protest by Buddhists in Vietnam and Tibet, Benn prefers the more precise "auto-cremation," using "self-immolation" to denote self-sacrifice more broadly (8).

own blood to inscribe sūtras; and a spectrum of acts involving burning or cutting the flesh, such as burning the head or forearms with incense or moxa (dried mugwort burned on the skin, usually as a therapy) to seal one's ordination vows or branding or incinerating fingers and limbs as dharma offerings. Acts of terminal self-sacrifice were rooted not only in Buddhist canonical sources such as the *Lotus Sūtra*, but also in apocryphal scriptures composed in China, such as the *Sūtra of Brahmā's Net* (*Fanwang jing*), and the *Sūtra of the Samādhi of the Heroic March* (*Shoulengyan jing*), which extol the merit of extreme ascetic practices, including self-immolation by fire (*T* 1484, 24:1006a, and *T* 945, 19:132b), and in local, non-Buddhist ascetic traditions, such as auto-cremation and branding of the body in connection with prayers for rain (Benn 1998).[3] The legitimacy of ascetic suicide was often questioned by external critics and by Buddhists themselves, giving rise to a body of argument both denouncing and defending its practice.

One Chinese innovation in Buddhist ascetic practice was the idea that sacrificing one's body could lead to birth in a pure land, a development possibly influenced by Daoist notions that auto-cremation would provide the purification necessary to achieve the realm of the immortals (Kieschnick 43, 163, n. 166). "Pure lands," a distinctively Mahāyāna concept, are realms created by the vows of a buddha or bodhisattva; they are "pure" in being free of greed, anger, ignorance and other obstructions that hinder practice. Birth in a pure land was thus considered a shortcut on the bodhisattva path that would otherwise take innumerable kalpas (aeons) to complete. By the fifth century, with the rise of Amidist devotion in China, cases of ascetic suicide aimed at birth in Amida's Pure Land of Utmost Bliss began to be recorded. According to the earliest biography of the Pure Land teacher Shandao (613–681), once, when the master preached to an audience of lay people that they could achieve birth in the Pure Land simply by chanting Amida's name, one of his auditors, deeply moved, promptly climbed a tall tree, uttered the name of Amida, and leapt to his death. In a later version of the story, however, it was Shandao himself who flung himself from a tree in his fervent aspiration for the Pure Land (*Xu gaoseng zhan* 27, *T* 2060, 50:684a; *Jingtu wangsheng zhuan* 2, *T* 2071, 51:119b). Though apocryphal, the story of Shandao's *ōjō*-suicide proved influential in Japan.

3. See also Chapter 14 in this volume.

Forms of Ascetic Suicide in Premodern Japan

Buddhist ascetic suicide appears in the Japanese historical record early on. Regulations governing monastics (*sōniryō*) issued by the court in the eighth century forbade monks and nuns from burning their bodies or committing suicide.[4] While these prohibitions may have been leveled at contemporaneous practices, accounts of specific individuals "relinquishing the body" for explicitly Buddhist reasons appear only rarely before the late tenth century. Yoshida Yasuo[5] has examined fifty-one "acts of relinquishing the body" (J. *shashingyō*), including thirty-four suicides, between 796 and 1183, as recorded in diaries, chronicles, and hagiographical collections, and found that no fewer than thirty of the practitioners involved, including nineteen of the suicides, were said to have been prompted by aspiration for birth in a pure realm, whether the bodhisattva Kannon's Mt. Fudaraku, the Heaven of Satisfaction (Skt. Tuṣita), where the bodhisattva Miroku (Maitreya) dwells, or—overwhelmingly—Amida Buddha's Pure Land of Utmost Bliss (Yoshida 208–17). This section surveys the major forms of Buddhist ascetic suicide attested in the latter part of the Heian (795–1185) and Kamakura (1185–1333) periods, while showing the predominance of birth in a pure land as a stated motive.

The most widely attested method of religious suicide in late-Heian Japan was self-immolation by fire, often inspired by the *Lotus Sūtra* story of Bodhisattva Medicine King. Chronicles and courtier diaries record public acts of auto-cremation in the vicinity of Heian (the royal capital, today's Kyoto) from the tenth through twelfth centuries. For example:

> Fifteenth day, [ninth month, 995]. Kakushin, a monk of Rokuharamitsuji, immolated himself in the fire on the north side of the memorial chapel, while Retired Emperor Kazan and other nobles bowed in reverence. (*Nihon kiryaku* 10, Chōtoku 1 [Kuroita 11:183])[6]

---

4. *Sōniryō* article 27. For this article and its interpretation in an 834 legal commentary, see *Ryō no gige* 2 (Kuroita part 2, 24B:89). For discussion see Yoshida 202–05. A translation of the *Sōniryō* is available at https://dornsife.usc.edu/assets/sites/63/docs/Ritsuryo_Soniryo-Piggott.pdf.

5. Japanese names are given in traditional order, with the surname first.

6. Here and subsequently, years have been converted to the Western calendar, while months and days are given according to the Japanese lunar calendar.

> Sixteenth day, [ninth month, 995]. An ascetic (J. *shōnin*) immolated himself in the fire on Amida Peak. Persons high and low gathered like clouds to watch. In recent years, eleven people in several provinces have immolated themselves. (*Hyakurenshō* 4, Chōtoku 1 [Kuroita 11:9])

> Fifteenth day, [seventh month, 1026]. Clear skies. Early this morning, a nun immolated herself in the fire at Toribeno. (People are calling her the nun of the "Medicine King" chapter.) While her body burned, her mind was not distracted; she faced west until consumed [by the flames]. (*Sakeiki*, Manju 3 [*ST* 6:182])[7]

> Fifteenth day, [fifth month, 1066]. At midday the monk Mongō, who lived at the Shakadō temple in Shijō, immolated himself in the fire at Toribeno. Monastics and laity gathered as though at a marketplace. (*Fusō ryakki* 29, Jiryaku 2 [Kuroita 12:303])

> Fifteenth day, [seventh month, 1174]. An ascetic immolated himself in the field at Funaoka, and high and low gathered. (*Hyakurenshō* 8, Shōan 4 [*ST* 11:90])

Short as they are, these notices offer significant information. The principals are monastics, often ascetics. The "nun" who burned herself at Toribeno would most likely have been a privately ordained "lay nun" (*ama nyūdō*), given that official ordination for women had lapsed by this time. Still, like the male practitioners mentioned, she would not have been an ordinary lay devotee. One notes also the frequent choice of the fifteenth day of the month for these undertakings. The fifteenth was Amida Buddha's *ennichi* ("affinity day"), a day deemed especially favorable for forming a connection with a particular buddha or bodhisattva. And the places chosen were all on the outskirts of the capital that were associated with death. "Amida Peak" overlooked Toribeno, a cremation ground in the eastern, Higashiyama area; the temple Rokuharamitsuji stood adjacent to Toribeno. The "field at Funaoka," to the city's north, was also a cremation ground. It is as though these practitioners reversed the common order of things and cremated themselves before actually dying. Their acts were highly public and drew many spectators. Witnessing the death of an *ōjōnin*—a person deemed to have achieved, or certain to achieve, birth in a pure land—was thought to establish a favorable karmic connection (*kechien*) that would assist one's own birth there as well. Those bent on religious suicide sometimes announced

7. Also mentioned in *Nihon kiryaku* [*gohen*] 13, Kuroita 11:183.

their intentions in advance in order to give others this opportunity, and crowds assembled to watch.

These brief notices tell us little about the intentions of the persons involved. For the motives underlying acts of ascetic suicide—or, more precisely, the motives presumed or expected to underlie such acts—we must turn to didactic tales (*setsuwa*) and hagiographies, especially those known as *ōjōden*, or "accounts of persons born in the Pure Land." The eleventh-century *Stories of Wondrous Manifestations of the Efficacy of the Lotus Sūtra in Japan* recounts the suicide of the ascetic Ōshō (n.d.), said to have been the first auto-cremation in Japan. A *Lotus Sūtra* reciter (*jikyōsha*), Ōshō acts in imitation of the bodhisattva described in the "Medicine King" chapter of the *Lotus*, offering up his body in sacrifice to the sūtra, the buddhas of the ten directions, and all living beings (*Hokke genki* 1:15 [Inoue and Ōsone 72; trans. Dykstra 38–39]).

More commonly, however, auto-cremation is depicted as undertaken in order to achieve birth in the Pure Land, as in the *ōjōden* biography of the monk Nenkaku (n.d.) of Echizen, who grows weary of life. First he faces west and performs a thousand prostrations; then he chants the *nenbutsu*—Amida Buddha's name—in a melodic cadence (*gassatsu*); his fellow practitioners and the visiting monks who have come for the occasion all join in. After mounting the pyre, Nenkaku forms a mudrā (ritual hand gesture), still chanting the *nenbutsu*. When the fire burns down and the smoke has cleared, purple clouds gather in the skies (*Sange ōjōki* 45 [Inoue and Ōsone 680]). Purple or other colored clouds, a staple feature of Pure Land art and literature, were said to indicate Amida's descent, together with his holy retinue, to welcome the dying and escort them to his western Pure Land. They numbered among the extraordinary signs said invariably to appear when a newly deceased person had achieved birth in the Pure Land, such as mysterious fragrance, divine music heard in the air, or auspicious dreams had by survivors.

Non-canonical forms of ascetic suicide also made their appearance during the Heian period, such as self-drownings (*jusui*). A preferred spot was in the sea off the temple Shitennōji, or simply Tennōji, on the coast at Naniwa (today's Osaka), an important pilgrimage site. Popular tradition held that Tennōji's west gate, which faced the sea, communicated directly with the east gate of Amida's Pure Land. *Ōjōnin* would sometimes row out from the west gate and throw themselves into the sea. Again, people gathered to watch, and wondrous signs were recorded (Kubota). Like auto-cremations, self-drownings were sometimes conducted in highly dramatic fashion and witnessed by spectators wishing to establish favorable karmic ties. In one *ōjōden* example, an unnamed *hijiri* ("holy man") bent on drowning himself sets out by boat from Mitsu Harbor on Lake Biwa. Monks from the great Tendai temple on Mt. Hiei along with local villagers follow him in no fewer than fifty to sixty boats. The *hijiri* dons a clean robe and chants the *nenbutsu*, and all the other monks join in. He announces, "After I sink beneath the water, if I achieve birth in the Pure Land of Utmost Bliss, my body will not decay but will reach the west shore. If, however, I should fall into the evil paths, it will drift up on the east shore." The next day, his body is found on the west shore, sitting in the lotus position with its hands placed together in reverence (*Sange ōjōki* 26 [Inoue and Ōsone 676]). Acts of self-drowning were not always individual affairs. A courtier diary entry for the eighth month of 1176 notes: "Fifteenth day. Eleven ascetics drowned themselves. Among them, the one called Rengejō Shōnin was the initiator" (*Hyakurenshō* 8, Angen 2 [Kuroita 11:92]).

Ascetic suicide also included the practice of "crossing the sea to Mt. Fudaraku" (*Fudarakusen tokai*), in which practitioners known as "sea-crossing monks" or "sea-crossing holy men" (*tokaisō, tokai shōnin*) set out in small boats on one-way journeys bound for the pure realm of the bodhisattva Kannon (Skt. Avalokiteśvara), the mountain island of Fudaraku (Potalaka) said to lie in the southern sea. Ascetics boarded small boats and embarked from Nachi in Kumano, a site closely associated with Kannon, or from other points along the southern coast of western Japan, hoping to reach Kannon's realm (Moerman 271). Unlike Amida's Pure Land, far away to the west across innumerable worlds, Fudaraku was said to lie within this world. Nonetheless, those who set sail for it clearly did not expect to sail there in the same way that one might sail, say, to the Korean peninsula or the coast of China. Some *tokaisha* made no attempt to steer or navigate, but instead entrusted their boats solely to Kannon's guiding compassion. One twelfth-century courtier diary tells of a certain ascetic who vowed to reach Fudaraku. He made a thousand-armed image of Kannon and positioned it so as to hold the helm of a small boat. After worshipping the bodhisattva for three years, he embarked, availing himself of a steady wind from the north, and people said that his vow had been fulfilled (*Taiki* 2, Kōji 1 [1142], 8/18 [*ST* 23:72]). In a somewhat later account, one Chijō-bō, a *Lotus Sūtra* reciter at Nachi who set out for Fudaraku, provisioned his boat with only a month's supply of food and lamp oil and had the cabin nailed shut once he had entered it, with not even a chink for light to enter (*Azuma kagami*, Tenpuku 1 [1233], 5/27 [Kuroita 32:130]).[8] Like the *hijiri* described above who drowns himself in Lake Biwa, *tokaisha* were often accompanied at least part way by "fellow

8. Sealed boats of this kind are depicted on Nachi shrine mandalas of the later medieval and early modern periods (Moerman 279–84).

practitioners" who traveled in open boats in order to form karmic ties with them and to share, to some extent, in the merit of their act. Including chronicles, diaries, inscriptions, and literary sources, there are more than fifty notices of individuals who set out for Fudaraku between the ninth and twentieth centuries (Nei 768–69).[9]

A less frequent method of ascetic suicide was self-burial. A courtier diary entry records that on 7/18/1160, southeast of the temple Zenrinji in Higashiyama, an ascetic had himself immured alive in a westward-facing tomb identified as a "side door" to the Pure Land, and spectators, both clergy and laity, gathered at the spot (*Sankiki*, Eiryaku 1 [*ST* 26:119]). A particularly intriguing instance is that of Sainen (d. 1142). In 1906, excavation near Kenninji in Kyoto unearthed a record made by this monk of his preparations for *ōjō*-suicide. It includes Sainen's list of the meritorious deeds he had performed in his lifetime—vast numbers of Buddhist sūtras copied, images commissioned, rituals sponsored, and amounts of food and clothing donated to monasteries—along with forty-eight *waka* poems that he had composed on the theme of birth in the Pure Land, one for each of Amida Buddha's salvific vows.[10] Sainen had first tried, and failed, to drown himself in the sea; his second attempt, by self-burial in a hole dug at his residence, was successful.

Terminal fasts (*danjiki ōjō*) represented yet another method. In his *ōjōden* biography, the holy man Enkū (d. 1039) becomes ill and, though not in pain, over a period of two or three years repeatedly refuses food and drink for five, six, or ten days at a stretch, passing his time in meditation. Urged to take rice gruel, he politely declines, observing that "food nourishes the body bound to deluded birth and death, and prolongs the life of evil deeds." As his flesh melts away, he becomes withered and shrunken. Clerics and laypeople bent on forming karmic ties with him gather at his gate as though at a marketplace. Enkū dies peacefully after chanting the *nenbutsu*, and someone dreams of him seated on a splendid dais and traveling toward the west, escorted by an assembly of monks (*Shūi ōjōden* 3:29 [Inoue and Ōsone 388–89]). Fasting was not always total, nor was it necessarily terminal. In some cases, it was employed in preparation for other acts of religious suicide, as in the case of the ascetic Gyōhan (d. ca. 1128–1131), who fasted for seven days before drowning himself in the sea off Tennōji (*Honchō shinshū ōjōden* 11 [Inoue and Ōsone 685]). It could be used to induce religious visions, as part of one's ongoing religious

9. See also Moerman 271 and 293n20.

10. Sainen's documents appear in Takeuchi, *komonjohen* 64, 67, and 68 (supplementary), 10: 119–25, 129–34.

discipline, or to hasten a death seen as inevitable. It was also linked to other ascetic traditions, such as the Daoist practice of abstaining from grains. Fasting and self-burial together suggest themselves as forerunners of the "self-mummification" practiced by a small group of ascetics of Mt. Yudono in northeastern Japan during the early modern period (1603–1868). These men offered up their lives on behalf of others by eating only pine needles and other tree products (*mokujiki*) for two or three years, thus reducing their body mass as much as possible, and then had themselves buried alive or immured themselves in underground chambers, seated in the posture of meditation, with the notion that, if their bodies mummified, that would signify their spiritual attainment (Hori).

While acknowledging that suicide to reach the Pure Land as practiced in Heian Japan could entail a resolve to advance on the bodhisattva path, Yoshida sees it as a departure from the paradigmatic forms of bodhisattva self-sacrifice described in the sūtras—such as offering one's flesh to wild beasts—in that it aimed chiefly at furthering one's own salvation rather than benefitting others (Yoshida 208, 212–13, 218).[11] However, the distinction is by no means clearcut, as one's own aspiration for the Pure Land could also entail a resolve to promote others' welfare. In the examples above, Sainen, just before his attempted self-drowning at Tennōji, wrote that he dedicated the merit of his act to his deceased parents, his Fujiwara ancestors, and to all living beings, that he and they might together achieve birth in the Pure Land and realize buddhahood (Takeuchi, *komonjohen* 64 [supplementary], 10:124), while the biography of Enkū notes that in the weeks before his death, he daily performed the transfer of merit, directing the benefit of his practices to the enlightenment of all living beings. Yoshida's distinction would seem to be a modern one; medieval commentators, while concerned in other ways about the attitudes underlying religious suicide, do not seem to have inquired whether it aimed at one's own liberation or that of others. Collections of Japanese monastic biographies, like those compiled earlier in China, group together persons who fast to death or perform auto-cremation, whether to reach a pure land or for other soteriologically motivated reasons, along with those engaging in other forms of painful bodily self-sacrifice such as stripping off skin, burning fingers or toes, or offering one's flesh to

11. In fairness, Yoshida tries to approach *ōjō*-suicide in Heian Japan on its own terms, contra earlier Japanese scholarship that had dismissed it as a degenerate practice.

mosquitoes. The interpretive category for *ōjō*-suicide, in short, was ascetic practice.[12]

A Question of Intent

While celebrated in hagiographies, acts of religious suicide were not universally approved. In 1174, learning of an ascetic's plans to immolate himself in the fire at the Funaoka cremation grounds, the courtier Nakayama Tadachika (1131–1195) condemned such acts as heretical, no different from the self-mortification of non-Buddhist ascetics. Bodhisattva Medicine King, whose celebrated act of auto-cremation is described in the *Lotus Sūtra,* had already freed himself from attachments, Tadachika said. "But when deluded ordinary worldlings of the past or present have done this, they must surely have experienced [evil] karmic recompense. And if we go by what is written in the legal codes, monks and nuns ought not to immolate themselves or mutilate their bodies" (*Kirei mondō* 139 [Hanawa 9:450]).[13] Bracketing the issue of legality, which would have been difficult to enforce, Tadachika's criticism hinges on the issue of one's intent or underlying mental state, fundamental to Buddhist karma theory. Ordinary persons, he argues, are simply not capable of the resolve and self-detachment that self-immolation requires, and their attempts to emulate heroic bodhisattvas in the sūtras can only result in painful karmic retribution.

A contrasting view appears in the *Tales of Religious Aspiration* compiled by the literary recluse Kamo no Chōmei (1153/1155–1216). Chōmei had ties to circles of *hijiri*, that is, monks practicing outside formal temple organizations, often living in semi-reclusion and engaged in austere disciplines. Chōmei offers his views on religious suicide in his editorial comment on an account of a *Lotus Sūtra* reciter (*jikyōsha*) of Mt. Shosha in Harima province, a major site for ascetic practice. The story is worth examining in some detail for the light it sheds on contemporaneous attitudes toward "relinquishing the body." In the narrative, the *jikyōsha* confides to a senior monk: "My deep wish is to meet death with right mindfulness and so achieve birth in the [land of] Utmost Bliss, but it is impossible to know how one will die. So I am resolved to cast

12. See the biographies of ascetic practitioners in *Genkō shakusho* by Kokan Shiren (1278–1346) (*DBNZ* 62:133–34) and in *Honchō kōsōden* by Mangen Shiban (1626–1710; *DNBZ* 63:368–70), which reproduces several of Shiren's examples.

13. Tadachika's criticism may have been prompted by the auto-cremation mentioned last in the list of chronicle and diaries entries given on page 284, above.

aside this body now, while no particular deluded thoughts are troubling me and I am free from bodily illness. But to burn my body or drown in the sea would be too ostentatious, and the pain would be severe. So I have decided to make an end quietly, by fasting" (*Hosshinshū* 3:7 [Miki 143]). He also vows to maintain silence when not actually reciting the sūtra.

The *jikyōsha*'s concerns reflect the importance assigned to underlying mental states. On one hand, he is concerned with "meeting death with right mindfulness" (*rinjū shōnen*), an issue of considerable anxiety not only for ascetics, but for premodern Japanese Buddhists in general. One's last thought at the liminal moment of death was held to exert a determinative influence on one's rebirth destination, exceeding even the cumulative acts of a lifetime. By dying with one's mind fixed calmly on Amida Buddha, it was said, even a sinful person might obtain birth in the Pure Land. Yet by the same token, the most devout practitioner, by a single stray desultory or misguided thought at the end, might in effect negate a lifetime of meritorious deeds and tumble down into the evil realms. Hence preparatory practice was deemed essential, and anxieties over whether or not one would be able to focus one's mind correctly at the end prompted many persons, clerics and lay devotees alike, to enlist the service of adepts who could chant Amida's name or other salvific mantras together with them at the end and help guide their dying thoughts appropriately.[14] The *jikyōsha*'s intended suicide, then, is motivated by a desire to direct the circumstances of his death to soteriological advantage by taking his own life before illness or senility might interfere with his mental concentration at the crucial last moment. At the same time, given the fact that spectators often gathered to witness acts of self-drowning and self-burning, he is aware of the danger that, in undertaking such an act, one might become preoccupied with one's performance and the desire to be seen as holy, an egocentric consideration that in itself would obstruct birth in the Pure Land. Thus he decides to die quietly by fasting and entreats his mentor to tell no one.

After a week, the senior monk visits the *jikyōsha* in his small hermitage and finds him reciting the sūtra. "How you must be weakened and suffering!" he exclaims. The *jikyōsha* responds in writing that at first he suffered terribly and feared that his determination would waver, but for the last two or three days, divine boys have appeared in his dreams and moistened his mouth with water so that he feels refreshed and confident that he can die with a focused mind. Trouble starts, however, when the elder monk, deeply impressed,

14. For an extended discussion of this topic see Stone, from which substantial sections of this chapter have been drawn.

decides there can be no harm in telling his close disciples about the *jikyōsha*'s experience. Soon reports spread of the *jikyōsha*'s extraordinary resolve; first monks of the mountain start visiting him to form auspicious karmic ties, and then laypeople begin arriving from throughout the district. Night and day they gather to venerate the *jikyōsha* or throw rice (to ward off malign spirits); bound by his vow of silence, he is unable to object. Driven beyond endurance, he eventually disappears and is never seen again (*Hosshinshū* 3:7 [Miki 142–46]).

Possibly angry at being cheated, as they saw it, of the opportunity to form a superior karmic connection with this holy man, some people evidently began to circulate rumors that his presumed death by starvation was a punishment for having denied food to others in a previous life. Here Chōmei launches a passionate defense. All ascetic practices, he says, are based on restraining desire, mortifying the body, and subduing the mind. Are they all to be dismissed as painful retribution for evil deeds? Buddhas and bodhisattvas, in order to attain awakening, have carried out such austerities because they value the dharma but hold their own lives lightly. Our inability to follow their example is due to the baseness of our minds, Chōmei argues. Simply because we cannot emulate them, there is no need to slander those rare individuals who can. Shandao, he adds, flung himself to his death, and surely Shandao's *ōjō* cannot be in doubt. Chōmei then cites a passage from the "Medicine King" chapter of the *Lotus Sūtra* to the effect that burning a finger or toe in offering to the Buddha surpasses the giving of realms, cities, wives, children, or countless precious objects (*Miaofa lianhua jing*, *T* 9:54a; Hurvitz 273). He comments that burning one's body or peeling off one's skin might appear to be of less use to the Buddha than offering a single flower or pinch of incense, but because relinquishing the body demands profound resolve and endurance of suffering, it constitutes a noble offering and eradicates the sins of prior lifetimes. Whether by fasting, auto-cremation, or drowning, the few persons capable of it are sure to achieve the Pure Land. The legitimacy of their sacrifice, Chōmei continues, is borne out by the appearance, even in the present, degenerate age, of wondrous confirmatory signs, such as mysterious fragrance or purple clouds. Weren't the Mt. Shosha ascetic's repeated dreams of divine youths who moistened his mouth just such a proof? "We should reverently believe [that he attained the Pure Land]," Chōmei concludes (*Hosshinshū* 3:7 [Miki 146–48]). Here Chōmei invokes the power of auspicious signs, widely accepted at the time, to establish that any particular individual had indeed achieved *ōjō*.

Chōmei did not uncritically endorse religious suicide, a point made clear in the very next tale in his collection, which offers the negative example of a *hijiri* named Rengejō (*Hosshinshū* 3:8 [Miki 148–53]).[15] Like the Mt. Shosha ascetic, Rengejō initially decides upon suicide to ensure correct mental focus at the time of death. He confides in the monk Tōren: "With the passage of years, I feel myself growing weaker, and there is no doubt that death approaches. Since my greatest hope is to die with right mindfulness, I intend to drown myself [now,] while my mind is clear." Tōren is shocked. "Such a thing is not to be done. You should rather seek to accumulate the merit of chanting the *nenbutsu*, even by a single day. Such acts are the conduct of foolish people." One imagines that Tōren's reaction represented a common argument against religious suicide. But his admonitions have no effect, and when he sees that Rengejō is determined, Tōren promises to help with the arrangements. At length, Rengejō stands on the bank by a deep place in the Katsura River. He chants the *nenbutsu* in a loud voice and, after a moment, plunges into the water. Learning in advance of his act, a crowd has gathered to witness the *ōjō* of this holy man; their admiration knows no bounds. But sometime afterward, Tōren falls ill with symptoms that suggest possession. The possessing spirit appears and announces itself as Rengejō. He explains that he had changed his mind at the last moment but had been ashamed to back out in front of so many spectators. In his last thoughts of regret and resentment, he fell into the demonic realm. Chōmei comments:

> This is a warning to people of this latter age. The human mind is hard to fathom; pure and honest thoughts will not necessarily arise [at the end]. One may desire to be thought superior to others or, out of pride or jealousy, foolishly make a lamp of one's body or enter the sea on the assumption that one can thus be born in the Pure Land, performing such acts on a whim. This is no different from the painful austerities of [non-Buddhist] heretics and represents a great false view. The pain of entering fire or water is no ordinary thing, and if one's resolve is not deep enough, how can it be endured? When one is in pain, the mind will not be settled. Without the Buddha's aid, it will be impossible to maintain right mindfulness [in this situation]. (*Hosshinshū* 3:8 [Miki 151])

15. *Hosshinshū* 3:8 (Miki 148–53). This could be the same Rengejō mentioned as one of eleven ascetics who drowned themselves in the 1176 entry from *Hyakurenshō* cited on page 286, above.

Medieval didactic tales contain several examples like Tōren's about suicides carried out to reach the Pure Land that fail due to a wrong attitude at the final moment.[16] Sometimes they are paired with stories of practitioners who "get it right" by carefully testing their physical limits in advance. In one such case, an unnamed monk bent on drowning himself to reach the Pure Land worries that, under the stress of drowning, delusive thoughts may arise and impede his salvation. He prevails on a companion to row out with him on a lake and tie a rope to him, instructing that he will jerk on it if he changes his mind. Once in the water, his resolve wavers; he tugs on the line and is hauled out, dripping. On subsequent days, he makes a second and even a third unsuccessful attempt. Finally the day arrives when he leaps in and does not tug on the rope. "In the sky, celestial music was heard and a purple cloud trailed over the waves. When his friend beheld these auspicious signs, tears of gratitude fell with the water dripping from the oars." Here, dignity of performance is humbly sacrificed to achieving correct mental focus, and the monk achieves the Pure Land (*Shasekishū* 4:8 [*NKBT* 85:192–93; trans. Morrell 149–50]).[17]

Chōmei, in his defense of ascetic suicide, also inveighs against the common view of "foolish people" who think that drowning is less painful than autocremation. He quotes "a certain *hijiri*" who reported, "When I was drowning in the water and on the point of death, I was rescued and barely survived. At the time, I thought the suffering of the hells could hardly be worse than the pain of the water forcing itself in through my nose and mouth. Those who think drowning is an easy death just don't know what it's like!" (*Hosshinshū* 3:8 [Miki 151–52]). In contrast to Tadachika, Chōmei clearly believed that, even in a latter age, some people were still capable of achieving liberation through ascetic self-sacrifice and were worthy of reverence. But he fully agreed that, unless rooted in proper intent, such acts could only be delusive.

This ambivalent potential of religious suicide is succinctly stated by Ippen (1239–1289), founder of a mendicant order known as the Jishū. According to his biography, three weeks before his death, Ippen admonished:

> After I die, there will surely be some [among my followers] who fling their bodies [into the sea to follow me to the Pure Land]. If their minds are firmly established [in faith], then no matter what, there can be no impediment [to their *ōjō*]. But when one has not exhausted

16. See for example *Uji shūi monogatari* 133 (*NKBT* 27:323–25; trans. Mills 349–50) and *Shasekishū* 4:7 (*NKBT* 85:190–92; trans. Morell 148–49).

17. For a similar case, see *Hosshinshū* 3:5 (Miki 137–38).

> ego-attachments, [suicide] is something that should not be done. To discard in vain the body of a human being, difficult to obtain, [with which one practices] the Buddhist Way, is a wretched business indeed. (*Ippen hijiri-e* 11 [Tachibana and Umetani 107–08; trans. Brown 58, modified])[18]

Here Ippen makes clear that the very same act can be either liberative or delusive, depending upon one's mental state. Performed with firm faith and a complete lack of self-attachment, ascetic suicide cannot obstruct one's birth in the Pure Land; by implication, it would hasten that attainment. But if undertaken with any lingering egoistical concerns, it would entail, not only wrong thoughts at the determinative final moment, but the sin of vainly discarding the rare conjuncture of opportunities that makes escape from saṃsāra possible: birth as a human being and a connection with the Buddhadharma. As Mark Blum has noted, "The problem lies not in the morality of the act but in the ability of the actor to complete it in the proper frame of mind" (156).

Half a dozen Jishū monks and lay followers did indeed drown themselves after Ippen's death in their desire quickly to rejoin him in the Pure Land.[19] Strikingly, however, after the Jishū became institutionalized, these acts, which had been praised in hagiographies of Ippen, were condemned by the sectarian leadership on doctrinal grounds. According to mainstream understanding, birth in the Pure Land might be achieved via any number of good practices—chanting *nenbutsu* or other mantras, performing esoteric rites, reciting sūtras, commissioning buddha images, and performing charitable acts—and directing the merit of those practices toward *ōjō*. Jishū teachings, however, drew on the exclusive *nenbutsu* doctrine first articulated by the monk Hōnen (1133–1212), who had taught that people of this degenerate age are too ignorant and sinful to achieve liberation through traditional practices that depend upon one's own efforts (*jiriki*, literally, "self-power"). Rather, he said, they should single-mindedly chant the *nenbutsu*, entrusting themselves to "the power that is Other" (*tariki*), that is, the salvific workings of Amida's original vow to welcome to his Pure Land all who place faith in him. From this perspective, committing suicide to reach the Pure Land reflected an egoistic reliance on *jiriki*, the power of one's own acts, to bring about one's salvation.

---

18. See also Brown 58–59.

19. *Ippen hijiri-e* 12 numbers these individuals at seven; *Yugyō Shōnin engi-e* says there were six (Tachibana and Umetani 118, 142).

Jishū leadership a century later accordingly condemned those bereaved disciples of Ippen who had drowned themselves and denied that they had reached the Pure Land (*Yugyō jūrokudai Shikoku kaishinki*, cited in Ōhashi 113). Although articulated in the particular doctrinal terms of "self-power" versus "Other-power," this polemic, too, ultimately centered on one's mental stance.

The Expansion of Ōjō-Suicide

Up until now we have considered suicide carried out to reach the Pure Land within the context of ascetic practice. From around the thirteenth century, however, we find intersections with other traditions of heroic suicide, as well as novel developments of the *ōjō*-suicide theme in literature. As a result, the category expanded to include actors other than ascetic practitioners and, especially in literature, motives quite different from those legitimated by Buddhist orthodoxy. This section surveys some of those developments.

Dying to Rejoin Others

According to the Pure Land sūtras, people are born into Amida's land without the mediation of parents. Rather, one appears there spontaneously, seated inside a lotus blossom; when the lotus unfolds, one finds oneself in the Buddha's presence. By scriptural account, inhabitants of Amida's realm are uniformly gold in color, identical in their physical splendor. Presumably they are of a single gender or no gender at all; being free from desire, they do not have sexuality, nor do they reproduce.[20] They would seem to be undifferentiated, perhaps representing the impartial wisdom and compassion of enlightenment. Yet wherever Pure Land teachings have spread, practitioners have assumed that, in Amida's realm, they would be reunited with specific persons: their deceased teachers, relatives, or friends. Prayers for reunion in the Pure Land were often expressed as a desire to be born with another "on the same lotus pedestal" (*rendai*, or lotus calyx). Ideas of the Pure Land as a place of reunion facilitated a confluence of notions of *ōjō*-suicide with taking one's life to accompany or rejoin someone who had died before.

Loyalty suicide (Ch. *xunsi*, J. *junshi*) as a heroic display of fealty to one's lord was practiced in China and is also attested in Japan from early on. The third-century *Book of Wei* records of Himiko, a shamanic ruler in the ancient

---

20. Scholastic orthodoxy held that there are no women in Amida's realm; female practitioners are born there as men. This pronouncement was often ignored on the ground (Stone 102–04).

Japanese principality of Yamatai, that more than a hundred male and female attendants accompanied her in death (Chen 3:858).[21] A 646 edict issued by Emperor Kōtoku forbade people from following a deceased person by hanging themselves or strangling others that they might follow him (*Nihon shoki* 25 [*NKBT* 68:294]). As these examples indicate, *junshi* could include the sacrifice of others on the death of a powerful person, and whether such deaths were truly "voluntary" or dictated by social expectation remains ambiguous. *Junshi* could also refer to a woman's suicide following the death of her husband. During Japan's medieval period, the *junshi* ideal was incorporated into the warrior ethos.

In some cases, loyalty suicide merged with suicide to reach the Pure Land. We have already mentioned the half dozen followers of Ippen who, after his death, drowned themselves in order to realize quickly "their aspiration to follow their *chishiki* [that is, their spiritual leader], their pledge to share a seat [i.e., a lotus calyx] with him, and the karmic affinity [that would allow them] to be born with him [in the Pure Land]" (*Ippen hijiri-e* 12; *Yugyō Shōnin engi-e* [Tachibana and Umetani 117–18, 142; trans. Brown 50]).[22] One of Hōnen's followers, Saburō Tamemori, a warrior turned lay monk, is said to have committed *seppuku* in the hopes of rejoining his deceased teacher Hōnen and his feudal lord, Minamoto no Sanetomo.[23] Following the death of the Honganji leader Jitsunyo (1458–1525) of the Jōdo Shinshū or True Pure Land sect, some thirty-three people slit open their bellies or drowned themselves in a river or the sea.[24]

In literature, suicide to reach the Pure Land expands to include persons who take their own lives in hopes of rejoining deceased lovers. The war epic *Tale of the Heike* tells how, when the Echizen governor Taira no Michimori is killed fighting against the Minamoto, his widow, the lady Kozaishō (d. 1184), resolves to follow him in death. Kozaishō's former wet nurse and companion urges her instead to take Buddhist vows and devote herself to prayers for her deceased husband: "You must long to share one lotus throne with him [in the Pure Land], but you cannot know where in the six realms and four modes of birth your own rebirth will take you. Drowning yourself would mean

21. Blum gives further examples (148–49).

22. Brown quips, "Presumably the calyx of a religious celebrity like Ippen would have been quite crowded with clerical disciples, lay followers, and assorted beneficiaries and hangers on" (50 n. 6).

23. For discussion of this episode see Blum 154–57.

24. For discussion see Blum *passim*.

nothing, since you cannot count on reunion with him." But the lady will not be dissuaded; she chants the *nenbutsu* a hundred times and, before casting herself into the sea, implores Amida,

> O honor your Original Vow,
> lead me hence to your Pure Land,
> restore to me the love I lost,
> seat us both on one lotus throne! (*Heike monogatari* 9 [*NKBT* 33:231; trans. Tyler 513]).

Cases like Kozaishō's prefigure the theme, found in the early modern theater, of double suicides (*shinjū*), in which the Pure Land is envisioned as a place where lovers, unable to be united in this world, finally can be together (Heine).

As Lori Meeks has noted in examining the Kozaishō episode, the nurse's argument was supported by Buddhist thinking: Michimori's death in the heat of battle would hardly have been conducive to a Pure Land birth, and Kozaishō, not being a religious adept, would have likely found it hard during the ordeal of drowning to maintain the mental focus needed for her self-destruction to result in *ōjō*. The memoirs of a contemporary, one Lady Daibu, far from praising Kozaishō's act, describe it as "an unparalleled tragedy" born of her excessive love for Michimori (*Kenreimon'in Ukyō no Daibu shū* [Itoga 79–80; trans. Harries 167–69]). But with the growth of warrior influence, over the century and more between the historical Kozaishō's death and the compilation of extant versions of the *Heike*, her act came to be seen as a female equivalent of a warrior's loyalty suicide. *Heike* praises her in terms drawn from Chinese classics as a chaste wife who does not serve two husbands (Meeks 152–54).

Mothers who Drown

Kozaishō's drowning is thematically related to several stories about women who drown themselves in order to reach the Pure Land following the loss of a child. An early example, again from Chōmei's *Tales of Religious Aspiration*, concerns a noblewoman and her daughter, who serve together at the court of Emperor Toba (r. 1107–1123). The daughter dies, and the mother is inconsolable, weeping continually even after a year or two has passed. Eventually, people lose sympathy and reproach her, saying, "You are not the first person to lose a child!" In the third year after her daughter's death, without telling anyone, the lady sets out for Tennōji—as we have seen, a major pilgrimage site for *nenbutsu* practitioners. She rents lodgings nearby and engages in intense *nenbutsu* recitation for twenty-one days. Gradually her mind clears. Telling her landlord that she wishes to see the famous coast at Naniwa, she persuades him to row her out to sea, where she faces west, chants the *nenbutsu*, and flings herself into the waves. "Ah, how dreadful!" her companion cries. He tries to pull her from the water, but she sinks like a stone.

Chōmei includes this tale, together with those discussed above, in a section of his collection devoted to religious suicide. The woman's choice of Tennōji, a favorite location for *ōjō*-suicide, together with her focused *nenbutsu* chanting just prior to ending her life, are indeed consistent with this practice. But the narrative suggests that this woman's act could well have been rooted in grief—a valid motive, from a normative perspective, to renounce the world, but not to take one's own life. Buddhist orthodoxy maintains that "relinquishing the body" is liberating only when prompted by religious aspiration; to kill oneself out of sorrow or emotional attachment can only be seen as sinful. Up until the point in the narrative when the woman leaps into the sea, there is little to separate her act from the tragic suicide of a mother unhinged by grief over the loss of a beloved child. But then, at that very moment, purple clouds appear in the sky, witnessed by people on the beach, and fragrance envelops the boat. These incontrovertible signs alert the reader that, however deluded this woman's conduct might outwardly appear, the appearance is misleading; in reality, hers is a case of *ōjō*. Subsequent discovery of her dream diary confirms this verdict, revealing that she had dreamt of being welcomed into the Pure Land by the bodhisattvas Jizō (Skt. Kṣitigarbha), Ryūju (Nāgārjuna), Fugen (Samantabhadra), Monju (Mañjuśrī), and finally, by Amida Buddha himself (*Hosshinshū* 3:6 [Miki 139–42]).

Birth in the Pure Land was believed to depend on right mindfulness in one's final moments, but the content of a dying person's mind was not something others could know. For survivors, the positive determination that a teacher, fellow practitioner, relative, or friend had indeed reached the Pure Land could only be made through the appearance of signs, such as purple clouds massing in the west or mysterious lights or fragrance. Dying with Amida's name or some other holy invocation on one's lips was similarly deemed a proof of *ōjō*. Where no positive indications were in evidence, they were sometimes produced, often in the form of auspicious dreams revealing someone to have achieved the Pure Land. The fortuitous "discovery" of auspicious signs seems to have occurred particularly with deaths that were tragic or untimely, thus encompassing them within the rubric of "*ōjō*" to give them a salvific closure (Stone 211–18). Chōmei's story suggests how the use of purple clouds or similar signs as a narrative device might, from the perspective of the living, transform a suicide prompted by grief into a soteriological achievement.[25]

A similar story occurs in a biography of Hōnen relating his encounter in Harima province with a female entertainer called Tokurai, who is grieving over the death of her young son. With his spiritual insight, Hōnen perceives that the boy is suffering in hell for the sins of a prior life, and he encourages Tokurai quickly to achieve *ōjō* herself so that she can save him. Unlike Kozaishō's nurse, Hōnen does not urge her to offer memorial prayers for the boy's sake. His advice as given here would seem to presume a strict reading of "Other Power" that differentiated his doctrine from the Buddhist mainstream. Because salvation, Hōnen taught, is achieved solely through reliance on Amida and not by one's own good deeds, as a deluded ordinary worldling one cannot assist others' liberation through rites of merit transfer but can aid them only by achieving birth in the Pure Land oneself and then returning from that realm as a bodhisattva. The sorrowing mother, however, takes Hōnen's words more literally than he intended:

> "How sad what you have told me, that my child is in hell. But how happy I am to learn that I will be able to save him by saying the *nenbutsu* at the time of my death [and thereby going to the Pure Land]!" So saying, she left his presence and boarded a boat; she had her women board as well and row her far into the offing. She chanted "*Namu Amida-butsu*" just ten times.[26] Then exclaiming, "May my child and the one buddha [Amida] meet me in the Pure Land!," Tokurai, age thirty-one, leapt into the depths of the sea. At that time, purple clouds gathered in the west. Her body was never recovered, just as though it had been taken up by [Amida's] welcoming host. (*Hōnen Shōnin hiden* 3 [*JZ* 17:312–33])

---

25. This can be also be seen in the *Genpei seisuiki* 47 episode of the "nun with the skull" (*dokuro no ama*) (Kondō 33:665–73). A Taira noblewoman, crazed with grief after the victorious Minamoto have beheaded her young son, is persuaded to take religious vows but refuses to relinquish her son's head, which she wears in a bag around her neck. She becomes a ragged mendicant and eventually drowns herself in the sea off Tennōji. Where most versions of the text depict her death as the tragic suicide of a distraught mother, one recension, the Chōmonbon, undercuts that impression by the addition of purple clouds, music, and fragrance that manifest at her drowning, firmly establishing her as an *ōjōnin* (673).

26. Ten earnest recitations of Amida's name at the moment of death were considered sufficient to reach the Pure Land.

Tokurai's example illustrates a recurring trope in Pure Land literature of an exceptionally pure-hearted individual who, on being told but once of the promise Amida's Pure Land, immediately discards bodily life in the resolve to go there.[27] Here, too, as in Chōmei's narrative, the gathering of purple clouds in the west is deemed incontrovertible proof that the woman has not been dragged down by delusive emotional attachment, but has indeed achieved *ōjō*. These stories suggest how a discursive veil of "birth in the Pure Land" may have been drawn over suicides that, being prompted by grief, would otherwise have been seen as tragic or even sinful. Tales of this kind push back, as it were, against doctrinal orthodoxy by assimilating the proofs of *ōjō* to acts driven by deep human emotion, which is thereby valorized, undercutting normative soteriological demands for non-attachment.

At the same time, these stories undeniably reflect a gendered ethos of maternal self-sacrifice. As seen in the diary entry, cited above, about the "nun of the 'Medicine King' chapter" who immolated herself in the fire at Toribeno in 1026, female practitioners sometimes did commit suicide as an ascetic act, if not as frequently as their male counterparts. In literature, however, this rarely happens. Men perform religious suicide either to reach the Pure Land themselves, or for abstract universal principles: as an offering to the dharma or to benefit living beings. For women, suicide to reach the Pure Land is an extension of devotion to a particular person, usually a husband or child. The ideal grief suicide is female.

Ōjō-Suicide and War Tales

The thirteenth through sixteenth centuries saw the production of war tales (*gunki monogatari*) celebrating the heroic exploits and noble deaths of warriors who fought in the many local insurrections and widespread civil strife of Japan's medieval period. In these tales, heroic death on the battlefield—including the practice of warrior suicide to erase the shame of defeat and avoid capture by the enemy—merge with elements of suicide aimed at reaching the Pure Land. In an account of the 1391 Meitoku uprising, the warrior Namera Hyōgo, fighting to the point of collapse in defense of his lord,

---

27. Examples include the layman in *Xu gaoseng zhan* 27, mentioned above, who flings himself from a tree following Shandao's sermon, and the warrior Ajisaka Nyūdō, who drowns himself in aspiration for the Pure Land after hearing Ippen's teaching (*Ippen hijiri-e* 6 and *Yugyō Shōnin engi-e* 2 [Tachibana and Umetani 50–51, 128–29]).

fends off his assailants and calls out, "I'm exhausted with fighting; let me lie down in peace! I entrust myself to Amida's welcome. People, watch me achieve *ōjō*!" And turning west, he places his palms together and dies on the spot, while foes and allies alike marvel (*Meitokuki* [Tomikura 79]). "Watch the self-destruction of a man of courage!" Satō Tadanobu, ally of the doomed Yoshitsune, calls out to his enemies. He then calmly chants the *nenbutsu* thirty times and recites a prayer transferring the merit he has generated to others; then he slashes open his belly and continues chanting *nenbutsu* as he waits for death (*Gikeiki* [*NKBT* 37:251; McCullough 1971, 205]). In a narrative of the fall of Sasako castle in Kazusa, the lord, Tsurumi Nobunaka, seeing that the battle has turned against him, seeks out the monk Chōyo, who is in service to his family. Chōyo confers on him the ten *nenbutsu*—usually recited by a dying person but here ritually bestowed upon a warrior headed for battle. Chōyo also counsels Tsurumi that he should envision Amida's name as a sharp sword to sever the bonds of birth and death and regard the enemy as ignorance (*mumyō*), which he now has the opportunity of a lifetime to dispel. "In the space of a moment, you will realize supreme awakening. And I shall not be long [behind you]. Together we shall be born on a lotus blossom in the Pure Land." Tsurumi returns to the battle and fights bravely, but the outlook is hopeless. Just as he faces west and draws his dagger, ready to commit *seppuku,* an enemy warrior bears down on him. Tsurumi bursts into laughter. "Take my head quickly!" he cries. His voice continues chanting the *nenbutsu* even after his head is severed, and all who witness or hear of his death praise him ("Sasako ochi no sōshi" [Chiba-ken Kyōdo Shiryō Kankōkai 1:142–43]).

Heroic death by *seppuku* or in doomed resistance, aimed at winning honor and leaving one's name to posterity, represents a vastly different ethos from ascetic suicide aimed at achieving birth in a pure land. Nonetheless, they share notable similarities. Both idealize mental control in one's final moments over physical pain and the fear of death. And, especially as celebrated in literary accounts, the adept's sacrifice of his body to reach the Pure Land and the glorious suicide of a warrior choosing death over defeat were in effect both public performances that might be judged by specific criteria and be told and retold by admiring survivors; both offered admission to a transcendent community, whether of *ōjōnin* in the Pure Land or of great heroes of military tradition.

A gendered distinction also plays out in war tales. In these epics, women take their own lives, and sometimes those of their children, to avoid capture, rape, or murder by the enemy. Drowning is the most commonly employed method, and the female suicides in these narratives are often thematically related to the tales of women who fling themselves into the sea to rejoin a lost husband or child in the Pure Land. The most famous of such episodes is the *Heike* account of the Nun of the Second Rank (Lady Nii, 1126–1185) or Taira no Tokiko, grandmother of Emperor Antoku, who drowns herself together with the eight-year-old sovereign when the Taira ships are overtaken by their enemies, the Minamoto, at the battle of Dan-no-ura. This was of course a real historical incident; Tokiko did indeed drown herself with the child emperor and several attendants. But in the *Heike*'s literary retelling, she is going to Amida's land:

> For some time Lady Nii had expected what she now saw.
> She threw her two gray nun's robes over her head,
> lifted high her beaten silk trouser-skirts . . .
> and lifted the Emperor in her arms.
> "I may be a woman," she said, "but I will not let the enemy take me.
> No, Your Majesty, I shall accompany you.
> All those loyal to our sovereign, follow me!" . . .
> "First, Your Majesty, if you please,
> Face east and say goodbye to the Grand Shrine of Ise[28];
> then, trusting Amida to welcome you into his Western Paradise,
> face west and call his Name.
> This land of ours . . . is not a nice place,
> I am taking you now to a much happier one, the Pure Land of [Utmost] Bliss." (*Heike monogatari* 11 [*NKBD* 33:336; trans. Tyler 610]).[29]

In the *Heike* narrative, Lady Nii's resolute act unites to the rhetoric of *ōjō*-suicide both loyalty to a doomed sovereign, and a resolve not to fall into enemy hands.

Similar episodes involve less exalted personages. The fourteenth-century *Chronicle of the Great Peace* tells of the warrior Aikawa Tokiharu, sent to Echizen to put down an uprising. When it becomes clear that Tokiharu's forces are outnumbered and cannot hold out, he sends for a monk to tonsure himself, his wife, and their two sons. (It was common to administer the

28. Shrine of the sun goddess, the divine imperial ancestor.

29. See also Meeks 156–61.

tonsure to adults just before death, so that one might die as a monk or nun.) Since the boys are certain to be killed by the enemy, Tokiharu resolves that they should accompany him in death. He urges his wife to live on and remarry, but she refuses. "Were our prayers to be united for a thousand lifetimes in vain? . . . Rather I will die with the one I love and be true to our vow to share the same moss-covered grave." Tokiharu then orders that the boys be drowned in the Kamakura River. Their mother escorts them to the riverbank, together with their two nursemaids, and tells them: "This river is called the lake of eight virtues in the Pure Land of Utmost Bliss, a place where children are born to play. Say the *nenbutsu* just as I do, and then let's go into the river." The boys sit facing west, joining their palms together like their mother, and loudly chant Amida's name. The two nursemaids each take one of the boys in her arms and jump with them into the green depths, and their mother flings herself in after them (*Taiheiki* 11 [*NKBT* 34:378–80; see also McCullough 328–30]).

"Going to the Pure Land" is clearly not the driving motivation for this woman's suicide. Her story conveys a complex mixture of grief, loyalty, honor, and the harsh demands of a military culture in time of war. Episodes like hers represent a female parallel to the male warrior's defiant self-disembowelment in the face of defeat. We have already seen how the rhetoric of *ōjō* may have been deployed to soften the tragedy of suicides committed out of despair, as in stories of women who drown themselves to rejoin deceased husbands or children in the Pure Land. Episodes in war tales such as that of Tokiharu's wife suggest that notions of "going to the Pure Land" may have similarly been extended to aestheticize and legitimate other violent and untimely deaths, thus domesticating the horror of war.

Conclusion

In Japan, taking one's life to reach a pure land initially developed in a Buddhist renunciatory context and was performed chiefly by monastics, especially *hijiri* or other practitioners of an ascetic bent. Debates over its propriety centered, not on the morality of the act itself, but on whether the actors were capable of the requisite detachment and resolve. As an idealized model of noble death, *ōjō*-suicide eventually overlapped other, non-Buddhist traditions of heroic self-destruction, such as suicide to accompany one's lord in death or a warrior's act of *seppuku* to avoid disgrace in defeat. In literature, especially, it assumes a gendered dimension, constructing as "*ōjō*" the suicides of women following the loss of children or to avoid capture by the enemy in wartime. These stories suggest how rhetoric of "going to the Pure Land" may have been deployed to recast in a salvific light suicides that would otherwise be seen as sinful or unbearably tragic. In so doing, they ironically open the category of *ōjō*-suicide to include actors whose intense emotional bonds of obligation and affection would have been seen, from a purely doctrinal perspective, as insurmountable hindrances to salvation.

Works Cited

CHAPTER 1

Afsarrudin, Asma. "Martyrdom in Islamic Thought and Praxis." *Martyrdom and Terrorism: Premodern to Contemporary Perspectives*, edited by Dominic Janes and Alex Houen, Oxford UP, 2014, pp. 1–24. DOI:10.1093/acprof:oso/9780199959853.003.0003.

———. *Striving in the Path of God: Jihad and Martyrdom in Islamic Thought*. Oxford UP, 2013.

Aijmer, Goran. "Introduction: The Idiom of Violence in Imagery and Discourse." *Meanings of Violence: A Cross-Cultural Perspective*, edited by Goran Aijmer and Jon Abbink, Oxford UP, 2000, pp. 1–21.

Assman, Jan. "Martyrdom, Violence, and Immortality: The Origins of a Religious Complex." *Dying for the Faith, Killing for the Faith: Old-Testament Faith-Warriors (1 and 2 Maccabees) in Historical Perspective*, edited by Gabriela Signori, Brill, 2011, pp. 39–60.

Baudrillard, Jean. *The Spirit of Terrorism*, translated by Chris Turner, Verso, 2002.

Beekes, Robert S. P. with the assistance of Lucien van Beek. *Etymological Dictionary of Greek*. Brill, 2010.

Behrend, Heike. *Resurrecting Cannibals: The Catholic Church, Witch-Hunts and the Production of Pagans in Western Uganda*. James Currey, 2011.

Bell, Vikki. "The Scenography of Suicide: Terror, Politics, and the Humiliated Witness." *Economy and Society*, vol. 34, no. 2, 2005, pp. 241–60.

Benn, James A. *Burning for the Buddha*. U of Hawai'i P, 2007.

Black, Max. "Metaphor." *Proceedings of the Aristotelian Society*, New Series, vol. 55, 1954–1955, pp. 273–94, www.jstor.org/stable/4544549.

Bloom, Mia. *Dying to Kill: The Allure of Suicide Terror*. Columbia UP, 2005.

Bowersock, Glen W. *Martyrdom and Rome*. Cambridge UP, 1995.

Boyarin, Daniel. *Dying for God: Martyrdom and the Making of Judaism and Christianity*. Stanford UP, 1999.

———. "Martyrdom and the Making of Judaism and Christianity." *Journal of Early Christian Studies*, vol. 6, no. 4, 1998, pp. 557–627.

Burkert, Walter. "Sacrificial Violence: A Problem in Ancient Religions." *Oxford Handbook of Religion and Violence*, edited by Mark Juergensmeyer, Margo Kitts, and Michael Jerryson, Oxford UP, 2013, pp. 437–54.

Castelli, Elizabeth A. *Martyrdom and Memory: Early Christian Culture Making*. Columbia UP, 2004.

Coleman, K. M. "Fatal Charades: Roman Executions Staged as Mythological Enactments." *Journal of Roman Studies*, vol. 80, 1990, pp. 44–73.

Collon, Dominique. "Dance in Ancient Mesopotamia." *Near Eastern Archaeology*, vol. 66, no. 3, 2003, pp. 96–102.

Cox Miller, Patricia. *The Corporeal Imagination: Signifying the Holy in Late Ancient Christianity*. U of Pennsylvania P, 2009.

———. "Desert Asceticism and 'The Body from Nowhere.'" *Journal of Early Christian Studies*, vol. 2, no. 2, 1994, pp. 137–53.

Crane, Susan A. "Choosing Not to Look: Representation, Repatriation, and Holocaust Atrocity Photography." *History and Theory*, vol. 47, 2008, pp. 309–30.

Csordas, Thomas J. "Embodiment as a Paradigm for Anthropology." *Ethos*, vol. 18, no. 1, 1990, pp. 5–47.

De Ste. Croix, D. E. M. "Voluntary Martyrdom in the Early Church." *Christian Persecution, Martyrdom, and Orthodoxy*, edited by Geoffrey de Ste. Croix, Michael Whitby, and Joseph Streeter, Oxford Scholarship Online, 2007. DOI:10.1093/acprof:oso/9780199278121.003.0004.

Durkheim, Émile. *Elementary Forms of the Religious Life*, translated by Joseph Ward Swain, Cengage Learning, 1965, pp. 224–25.

Frankfurter, David. "Egyptian Religion and the Problem of the Category 'Sacrifice.'" *Ancient Mediterranean Sacrifice*, edited by Jennifer Wright Knust and Zsuzsanna Varhelyi, Oxford UP, 2011/2012. DOI:10.1093/acprof:oso/9780199738960.003.0003.

Friedson, Steven M. *Dancing Prophets: Musical Experience in Tumbuka Healing*. U of Chicago P, 1996.

———. *Remains of Ritual: Northern Gods in a Southern Land*. U of Chicago P, 2009.

Girard, René. *Violence and the Sacred*, translated by Patrick Gregory, Johns Hopkins UP, 1977.

Giroux, Henry A. "Disturbing Pleasures." *Third Text*, vol. 26, no. 3, 2012, pp. 259–73. DOI: dx.doi.org/ 10.1080/ 09528822.2012.679036.

Hafez, Mohammed M. "Rationality, Structure, and Culture in the Making of Suicide Bombers: A Preliminary Theoretical Synthesis and Illustrative Case Study." *Studies in Conflict and Terrorism*, vol. 29, 2006, pp. 165–85.

———. "The Alchemy of Martyrdom: Jihadi Salafism and Debates over Suicide Bombings in the Muslim World." *Asian Journal of Social Science*, vol. 38, 2010, pp. 364–78.

Hassan, Riaz. "Suicide Bombings: Homicidal Killing or a Weapon of War?" *Asian Journal of Social Sciences*, vol. 38, 2010, pp. 462–80.

Innis, Robert E. "The Tacit Logic of Ritual Embodiments: Rappaport and Polanyi between Thick and Thin." *Ritual in its own Right*, edited by Don Handelman and Galina Lindquist, Berghahn Books, 2005, pp. 197–212.

Janzen, David. *The Social Meanings of Sacrifice in the Hebrew Bible*. De Gruyter, 2004.

Johnson, Mark. *The Meaning of the Body*. U of Chicago, 2007.

Juergensmeyer, Mark, and Margo Kitts, editors. *Princeton Readings in Religion and Violence*. Princeton UP, 2011.

Juergensmeyer, Mark, Margo Kitts, and Michael Jerryson, editors. *Oxford Handbook of Religion and Violence*. Oxford UP, 2013.

Juergensmeyer, Mark. "Cosmic War." *Oxford Research Encyclopedia of Religion*, Oxford UP, 2016. DOI: 10.1093/acrefore/9780199340378.013.65.

———. "Religious Terrorism as Performance Violence." *The Oxford Handbook of Religion and Violence*, edited by Mark Juergensmeyer, Margo Kitts, and Michael Jerryson, Oxford UP, 2013, pp. 280–92.

———. *Terror in the Mind of God*. U of California P, 2000.

Kapferer, Bruce. "Ritual Dynamics and Virtual Practice: Beyond Representation and Meaning." *Ritual in its Own Right*, edited by Don Handelman and Galina Lindquist, Berghahn Books, 2005, pp. 35–54.

Kitts, Margo. *Elements of Ritual and Violence*. Cambridge UP, 2018.

———. "Ancient Near Eastern Perspectives on Evil and Terror." *Cambridge Companion to the Problem of Evil*, edited by Chad Meister and Paul K. Moser, Cambridge UP, 2017, pp. 165–92.

———. "Discursive, Iconic, and Somatic Perspectives on Ritual." *Journal of Ritual Studies*, vol. 31, no. 1, 2017, pp. 11–26.

———. "Anthropology and the Iliad." *Ashgate Research Companion to Anthropology*, edited by Pamela J. Stewart and Andrew J. Strathern, Ashgate Publishing, 2015, pp. 389–410.

———. "Religion and Violence from Literary Perspectives." *Oxford Handbook of Religion and Violence*, edited by Mark Juergensmeyer, Margo Kitts, and Michael Jerryson, Oxford UP, 2013, pp. 410–23.

———. "The Religious Role in Violence." *Princeton Readings in Religion and Violence*, edited by Mark Juergensmeyer and Margo Kitts, Princeton UP, 2011, pp. 93–100.

———. "The Last Night: Ritualized Violence and the Last Instructions of 9/11." *Journal of Religion*, vol. 90, 2010, pp. 283–312.

———. *Sanctified Violence in Homeric Society*. Cambridge UP, 2005.

Klawans, Jonathan. "Sacrifice and Purity: The Twisted Fortunes of Related Ritual Structures." *Purity, Sacrifice, and the Temple*. Oxford UP, 2005/2007. DOI:10.1093/acprof:oso/9780195162639.003.0001.

Laidlaw, James. "A Well-Disposed Social Anthropologist's Problems with the 'Cognitive Science of Religion.'" *Religion, Anthropology, and Cognitive Science*, edited by Harvey Whitehouse and James Laidlaw, Carolina Academic P, 2007, pp. 211–46.

McClymond, Kathryn. "Don't Cry Over Spilt Blood." *Ancient Mediterranean Sacrifice*, edited by Jennifer Wright Knust and Zsuzsanna Varhelyi, Oxford UP, 2011/2012. DOI: 10.1093/acprof:oso/9780199738960.001.0001.

Mbembé, Stephen Randall J-A. "African Modes of Self-Writing." *Public Culture*, vol. 4, no. 1, 2002, pp. 239–73.

Michelsen, Nicholas. "The Political Subject of Self-Immolation." *Globalizations*, vol. 12, no. 1, 2015, pp. 83–100.

Morgan, David. *The Embodied Eye, Religious Visual Culture and the Social Life of Seeing*. U of California P, 2012.

Muhlestein, Kerry. "Execration Ritual." *UCLA Encyclopedia of Egyptology*, edited by Jacco Dieleman and Willeke Wendrich, e-scholarship U of California, 2008. http://digital2.library.ucla.edu/viewItem.do?ark=21198/zz000s3mqr.

———. "Sacred Violence: When Ancient Near Eastern Punishment was Dressed in Ritual Trappings." *Near Eastern Archaeology*, vol. 78, no., 4, 2015, pp. 244–51.

Murphy, Andrew, editor. *The Blackwell Companion to Religion and Violence*. Wiley-Blackwell, 2011.

Nasrallah, Laura. "The Embarrassment of Blood: Early Christians and Others on Sacrifice, War, and Rational Worship." *Ancient Mediterranean Sacrifice*, edited by Jennifer Wright Knust and Zsuzsanna Varhelyi, Oxford UP, 2011/2012. DOI:10.1093/acprof:oso/9780199738960.003.0007.

Noegel, Scott B. "Corpses, Cannibals, and Commensality: A Literary and Artistic Shaming Convention in the Ancient Near East." *Journal of Religion and Violence*, vol. 4, no. 3, https://www.pdcnet.org/collection-anonymous/browse?fp=jrv.

Olyan, Saul M. "The Instrumental Dimensions of Ritual Violence against Corpses in Biblical Texts." *Ritual Violence in the Hebrew Bible: New Perspectives*, edited by Saul M. Olyan, Oxford UP, 2016, Oxford Scholarship Online 2015. DOI:10.1093/acprof:oso/9780190249588.003.0007.

Perkins, Judith. *The Suffering Self: Pain and Narrative Representation in the Early Christian Era*. Routledge, 1995.

Pongratz-Leisten, Beate. "Sacrifice in the Ancient Near East: Offering and Ritual Killing." *Sacred Killing: The Archaeology of Sacrifice in the Ancient Near East*, edited by Anne Porter and Glenn M. Schwartz, Eisenbrauns, 2012, pp. 291–304.

———. "Ritual Killing and Sacrifice in the Ancient Near East." *Human Sacrifice in Jewish and Christian Tradition*, edited by Karin Finsterbusch, Armin Lange, and K. F. Diethard Römheld, Brill, 2007, pp. 3–33.

Ricoeur, Paul. *Hermeneutics and the Social Sciences*. Cambridge UP, 1981.

Schalk, Peter. "Memorialisation of Martyrs in the Tamil Resistance Movement of Īḻam/Laṃkā." *State, Power, and Violence*, edited by Margo Kitts, et al., Harrassowitz, 2010, pp. 55–74.

Schultz, Celia E. "The Romans and Ritual Murder." *Journal of the American Academy of Religion*, vol. 78, no. 2, 2010, pp. 516–41. DOI:10.1093/jaarel/lfq002.

Schwartz, Glenn M. "Archaeology and Sacrifice." *Sacred Killing: The Archaeology of Sacrifice in the Ancient Near East*, edited by Anne Porter and Glen M. Schwartz, Eisenbrauns, 2012, pp. 1–32.

Shaw, Brent D. "Body/Power/Identity: Passions of the Martyrs." *Journal of Early Christian Studies*, vol. 4, no. 3, 1996, pp. 269–312. DOI: 10.1353/earl.1996.0037.

Shepkaru, Shmuel. "To Die for God: Martyrs' Heaven in Hebrew and Latin Crusade Narratives." *Speculum*, vol. 77, no. 2, 2002, pp. 311–41.

Siebers, Tobin. "The Return to Ritual: Violence and Art in the Media Age." *Journal for Cultural and Religious Theory,* vol. 5, no. 1, 2003, pp. 9–33. http://www.jcrt.org/archives/05.1/siebers.pdf.

Smith, Gregory A. "How Thin Is a Demon?" *Journal of Early Christian Studies*, vol. 16, no. 4, 2008, pp. 479–512.

Somasundaram, Daya. "Suicide Bombers of Sri Lanka." *Asian Journal of Social Sciences*, vol. 38, 2010, pp. 416–41.

Sommerstein, Alan H., and Andrew Bayliss. *Beiträge zur Altertumskunde: Oath and State in Ancient Greece,* De Gruyter, 2013.

Sontag, Susan. *Regarding the Pain of Others*. Farrar, Straus, and Giroux, 2003.

Stewart, Pamela, and Andrew Strathern, editors. *Violence: Theory and Ethnography*. Continuum International Publishing Group, 2002.

Stewart, Pamela. *Ritual: Key Concepts in Religion*. Bloomsbury, 2014.

Strathern, Andrew, and Pamela Stewart. "Introduction: Terror, the Imagination, and Cosmology." *Terror and Violence: Imagination and the Unimaginable*, edited by Andrew Strathern, Pamela Stewart, and Neil L. Whitehead, Pluto P, 2006, pp. 1–39.

Streete, Gail P. *Redeemed Bodies: Women Martyrs in Early Christianity*. Westminster John Knox P, 2009.

Taylor, Charles. "Modern Social Imaginaries." *Public Culture,* vol. 14, no. 1, 2002, pp. 91–124.

Tosini, Domenico. "Calculated, Passionate, Pious Extremism: Beyond a Rational Choice Theory of Suicide Terrorism." *Asian Journal of Social Sciences*, vol. 38, 2010, pp. 394–415.

Turner, Bryan S. *Regulating Bodies: Essays in Medical Sociology*. Routledge, 2002.

Turner, Victor. "Liminal to Liminoid, in Play, Flow, and Ritual: An Essay in Comparative Symbology." *Rice Institute Pamphlet–Rice University Studies,* vol. 60, no. 3, 1974, http://hdl.handle.net/1911/63159.

Van Henten, Jan Willem, and Friedrich Avenmarie. *Martyrdom and Noble Death: Selected Texts from Graeco-Roman, Jewish, and Christian Antiquity*. Routledge, 2002.

Van Hooff, Anton. *From Autothanasia to Suicide: Self-killing in Classical Antiquity*. Routledge, 1990.

Vasquez, Manuel A. *More than Belief.* Oxford UP, 2011.

Watts, James W. "The Rhetoric of Sacrifice." *Ritual and Metaphor: Sacrifice in the Bible*, edited by Christian Eberhart, Society of Biblical Literature, 2011, pp. 3–16.

Wessinger, Catherine, editor. *The Oxford Handbook of Millennialism*. Oxford UP, 2011.
Whitehead, Neil L. *Dark Shamans: Kanaima and the Poetics of Violent Death*. Duke UP, 2002.

CHAPTER 2

Anderson, Hugh. "4 Maccabees (First Century A.D.)." *The Old Testament Pseudepigrapha*, edited by James H. Charlesworth, Doubleday, 1983–85, pp. 2:531–564.
Avishur, Yitzhak. "The Mother and the Seven Sons in Aramaic was Translated from Bagdadian Judeo-Arabic." [Hebrew] *Peamim*, vol. 9, 1981, 125–29.
Baumgarten, Elisheva, and Rella Kushelevsky. "From 'The Mother and Her Sons' to 'The Mother of the Sons' in Medieval Ashkenaz." *Zion*, vol. 7, nos. 1/3, 2006, pp. 301–42.
Berthelot, Katell. "Biblical Conquest of the Promised Land and the Hasmoneaen Wars According to 1 and 2 Maccabees." *The Books of the Maccabees: History, Theology, Ideology*, edited by Géza G. Xeravits and József Zsengellér, Brill, 2007.
Bickerman, Elias J. "The Date of Fourth Maccabees." *Studies in Jewish and Christian History: A New Edition in English Including the God of the Maccabees*, edited by E. J. Bickerman, D. Amram, and D. Tropper, Brill, 2007.
Boustan, Ra'anan S. *From Martyr to Mystic: Rabbinic Martyrology and the Making of Merkavah Mysticism*. Mohr Siebeck, 2005.
Bowersock, Glen W. *Martyrdom and Rome*. Cambridge UP, 1995.
Boyarin, Daniel. *Dying for God: Martyrdom and the Making of Christianity and Judaism*. Stanford UP, 1999.
———. "Martyrdom and the Making of Christianity and Judaism." *Journal of Early Christian Studies*, vol. 6, no. 4, 1998, pp. 577–627.
Brettler, Marc. "Is There Martyrdom in the Hebrew Bible?" *Sacrificing the Self: Perspectives on Martyrdom and Religion*, edited by Margaret Cormack, Oxford UP, 2002, pp. 3–22.
Chazan, Robert. *European Jewry and the First Crusade*. U of California P, 1987.
Cohen, Gershon D. "The Story of Hannah and her Seven Sons in Hebrew Literature." *Mordecai M. Kaplan Jubilee Volume on the Occasion of His 70th Birthday* [Hebrew Section], edited by Mordecai M. Kaplan and Moshe Davis, The Jewish Theological Seminary of America, 1953, pp. 109–22.
Cohen, Jeremy. *Sanctifying the Name of God: Jewish Martyrs and Jewish Memories of the First Crusade*. U of Pennsylvania P, 2004.
Cohen, Shaye. "Masada: Literary Tradition, Archaeological Remains, and the Credibility of Josephus." *Journal of Jewish Studies*, vol. 33, nos. 1–2, 1982, pp. 385–405.
Cobb, Stephanie L. *Dying to be Men: Gender and Language in Early Christian Martyr Texts*. Columbia UP, 2008.

Dan, Joseph. *The Hebrew Story in the Middle Ages* [Hebrew]. Keter Publishing House, 1974.

———. "Hekhalot Rabbati and the Legend of the Ten Martyrs" [Hebrew]. *Eshel Be'er Sheva 2*. 1980, pp. 63–80.

DeSilva, David A. *4 Maccabees*. Sheffield Academic P, 1998.

Doran, Robert. "The Martyr: A Synoptic View of the Mother and Her Seven Sons." *Ideal Figures in Ancient Judaism: Profiles and Paradigms*, edited by J. J. Collins and G. W. E. Nickelsburg, Scholars P, 1980, pp. 189–221.

———. *Temple Propaganda: The Purpose and Character* of *2 Maccabees*. Catholic Biblical Association of America, 1981.

Droge, Arthur J., and James D. Tabor. *A Noble Death: Suicide and Martyrdom Among Christians and Jews in Antiquity*. HarperSanFrancisco, 1992.

Edwards, Catharine. *Death in Ancient Rome*. Yale UP, 2007.

Finkelstein, Louis. "The Ten Martyrs." *Essays and Studies in Memory of Linda R. Miller*, edited by Israel Davidson, Jewish Theological Seminary of America, 1938, pp. 29–55.

Firestone, Reuven. *Holy War in Judaism: The Fall and Rise of a Controversial Idea*. Oxford UP, 2012.

Flavius, Josephus. *Jewish Antiquities*, edited by H. St. J. Thackeray, Ralph Marcus, Louis H. Feldman, and Allen Paul Wikgren, Harvard UP, 1998.

———. *Jewish War*, edited by H. St. J. Thackeray, Harvard UP, 1997.

———. *The Life; Against Apion*, edited by H S. J. Thackeray Apion, Harvard UP, 1926.

Frimer, Dov I. "Masada: In the Light of Halakhah." *Tradition: A Journal of Orthodox Jewish Thought*, vol. 12, no. 1, 1971, pp. 27–43.

Goldin, Simha. *The Ways of Jewish Martyrdom*. Turnhout, 2008.

Goldstein, Sidney. *Suicide in Rabbinic Literature*. Ktav Pub. House, 1989.

Grunewald, Ithamar. "*Qiddush ha-Shem*: An Examination of a Term" [Hebrew]. *Molad*, vol. 24, 1968, pp. 476–484.

Habicht, Christian. *2 Makkabäerbuch*. Güterschoher Verlagshaus Gerd Mohn, 1976.

Hankoff, D. L. "Judaic Origins of the Suicide Prohibition." *Suicide: Theory and Clinical Aspects*, edited by L. D. Hankoff and Bernice Einsidler, PSG Publishing Co., 1979.

Hasan-Rokem, Galit. *Web of Life: Folklore and Midrash in Rabbinic Literature*. Stanford UP, 2000.

Hengel, Martin. *Judaism and Hellenism*. Fortress P, 1974.

Henten, Jan Willem van. *The Maccabean Martyrs As Saviours of the Jewish People: A Study of 2 and 4 Maccabees*. Brill, 1997.

Henten, Jan Willem van, and Friedrich Avemarie. *Martyrdom and Noble Death: Selected Texts from Graeco-Roman, Jewish, and Christian Antiquity*. Routledge, 2002.

Himmelfarb, Martha. "Judaism and Hellenism in 2 Maccabees." *Poetics Today*, vol. 19, no. 1, 1998, pp. 19–40.

———. "The Mother of Seven Sons in Lamentations Rabbah and the Virgin Mary." *Jewish Studies Quarterly*, vol. 22, no. 4, 2015, pp. 325–51.

Hoenig, Sidney B. "Historic Masada and the Halakhah." *Tradition: A Journal of Orthodox Jewish Thought*, vol. 13, no. 2, 1972, pp. 100–15.

Holtz, A. "Kiddush and Hillul Hashem." *Faith and Reason: Essays in Judaism*, edited by R. Gordis and R. B. Waxman, Ktav Publishing House, 1973, pp. 79–86.

Hooff, Anton J. L. *From Autothanasia to Suicide: Self-killing in Classical Antiquity*. Routledge, 1990.

Joslyn-Siemiatkoski, Daniel. *Christian Memories of the Maccabean Martyrs*. Palgrave, 2009.

———. "The Mother and Seven Sons in Late Antique and Medieval Ashkenazi Judaism: Narrative Transformations and Communal Identity." *Dying for the Faith, Killing for the Faith: Old Testament Faith-Warriors (1 and 2 Maccabees)*, edited by Gabriela Signori, Brill, 2012, pp. 127–46.

Kampen, John. *The Hasideans and the Origin of Pharisaism*. Scholars P, 1988.

Kaplan, Kalman J., and Matthew B. Schwartz. *A Psychology of Hope: A Biblical Response to Tragedy and Suicide*. William B. Eerdmans Pub, 2008.

Klawans, Jonathan. *Josephus and the Theologies of Ancient Judaism*. Oxford UP, 2012.

Krauss, Samuel. "Ten Martyrs" (*Asarah Harugei Malkhut*). *Ha-Shiloah*, vol. 44, 1925, pp. 10–22, 106–17, 221–33.

Licht, J. "Taxo or the Apocalyptic Doctrine of Vengeance." *Journal of Jewish Studies*, vol. 12, nos. 3 and 4, 1961, pp. 95–105.

Lieberman, Shaul. "Religious Persecution in Israel." *The Jubilee Book in Honor of Salo W. Baron,* Hebrew Section, edited by Shaul Lieberman, ha-Aḳademyah ha-Ameriḳanit le-Mad'e ha-Yahadut, 1974, pp. 213–46.

Loftus, Francis. "The Martyrdom of the Galilean Troglodytes (B.J. I 312–3; A. Xiv 429–30): A Suggested *Traditionsgeschichte*." *The Jewish Quarterly Review*, New Series, vol. 66, no. 4, 1976, pp. 212–23.

Mantel, Hugo. *The Men of the Great Synagogue* [Hebrew]. Devir, 1983.

Mekhilta de-Rabbi Ishmael, edited by Shaul Horovitz and Israel Abraham Rabin, J. Kauffman, 1931.

Moore, Stephen D., and Janice Capel Anderson. "Taking It Like a Man: Masculinity in 4 Maccabees." *Journal of Biblical Literature*, vol. 117, no. 2, 1998, pp. 249–73.

Neusner, Jacob. *Sifra: An Analytical Translation*. Scholars P, 1988.

Newel, R. "The Suicide Accounts in Josephus: A Form-Critical Study." *SBL 1982 Seminar Papers*, edited by K. Richards, Scholars P, 1982, pp. 351–69.

———. "The Forms and Historical Value of Josephus' Suicide Account." *Josephus, the Bible, and History*, edited by Louis H. Feldman and Gōhei Hata, Wayne State UP, 1989, pp. 278–94.

Nickelsburg, George W. E. *Studies on the Testament of Moses: Seminar Papers*. Society of Biblical Literature, 1973.

Philo of Alexandria. *Philo: In Ten Volumes*, edited by F. H. Colson, and J. W. Earp, Heinemann, 1991.

Rabinowitz, Louis. "The Masada Martyrs According to the Halakhah." *Tradition: A Journal of Orthodox Jewish Thought*, vol. 11, no. 3, 1970, pp. 31–37.

Rajak, Tessa. *The Jewish Dialogue with Greece and Rome: Studies in Cultural and Social Interaction*. Brill, 2002.

———. "The Mother's Role in Maccabaean Martyrology." *Group Identity and Religious Individuality in Late Antiquity*, edited by Éric Rebillard and Jörg Rüpke, Catholic U of America P, 2015.

Reeg, Gottfried. *Die Geschichte von den Zehn Märtyrern: synoptische Edition mit Übersetzung [aus dem Hebräischen] u. Einleitung*. Mohr, 1985.

Renehan, R. "The Greek Philosophical Background of Fourth Maccabees." *Rheinisches Museum f. Philologie*, vol. 115, 1972, pp. 223–38.

Rosner, Fred. "Suicide in Biblical, Talmudic and Rabbinic Writings." *Tradition: A Journal of Orthodox Thought*, vol. 11, no. 3, 1970–1971, pp. 25–40.

Shepkaru, Shmuel. *Jewish Martyrs in the Pagan and Christian Worlds*. Cambridge UP, 2006.

Sievers, Joseph. *The Hasmoneans and Their Supporters: From Mattathias to the Death of John Hyrcanus I*. Scholars P, 1990.

Spero, Shubert. "In Defense of the Defenders of Masada." *Tradition: A Journal of Orthodox Jewish Thought*, vol. 11, no. 1, 1970, pp. 31–43.

Stern, David, and Mark Mirsky. *Rabbinic Fantasies: Imaginative Narratives from Classical Hebrew Literature*. Yale UP, 1998.

———. *Rabbinic Fantasies: Imaginative Narratives from Classical Hebrew Literature*. Jewish Publication Society, 1990.

Stern, Menachem. "The Suicide of Eleazar ben Yair and His Men at Masada, and the Fourth Philosophy." [Hebrew]. *Zion*, vol. 47, 1982, pp. 367–98.

Tromp, Johannes. *The Assumption of Moses*. Brill, 1992.

Tzabar, Yonnah. "The Story of the Mother and the Seven Sons in the Aramaic of the Jews of Kurdistan." [Hebrew]. *Peamim*, vol. 7, 1981, pp. 83–100.

Weigold, Matthias. "Deluge and the Flood of Emotions: The Use of Flood Imagery in 4 Maccabees in its Ancient Jewish Context." *The Books of the Maccabees: History, Theology, Ideology*, edited by Géza G. Xeravits and József Zsengellér, Brill, 2007, pp. 197–210.

Weitzman, Steve. "Josephus on How to Survive Martyrdom." *Journal of Jewish Studies*, vol. 55, no. 2, 2004, pp. 230–45.

Whitters, Mark F. "Taxo and His Seven Sons in the Cave (Assumption of Moses 9–10)." *The Catholic Biblical Quarterly*, vol. 72, no. 4, 2010, pp. 718–31.

Young, Robin D. " 'The Woman with the Soul of Abraham': Traditions about the Mother of the Maccabean Martyrs." *"Women Like This": New Perspectives on Jewish Women in the Greco-Roman World*, edited by Amy-Jill Levine Scholars P, 1991, pp. 67–81.

Zeitlin, Solomon. "The Legend of the Ten Martyrs and Its Apocalyptic Origins." *Jewish Quarterly Review*, vol. 36, 1945–1946, pp. 1–16.

Zsengellér, József. "Maccabees and Temple Propaganda." *The Books of the Maccabees: History, Theology, Ideology*, edited by Géza G. Xeravits and József Zsengellér, Brill, 2007, pp. 181–95.

CHAPTER 3

Castelli, Elizabeth. *Martyrdom and Memory: Early Christian Culture Making*. Columbia UP, 2005.

Corrigan, John, Frederick Dempsey, Carlos M. N. Eire, and Martin S. Joffre, editors. *Jews, Christians, and Muslims: A Comparative Introduction to the World's Religions*, 2nd ed., Routledge, 2012.

Davis, Stephen. *The Cult of St. Thecla: A Tradition of Women's Piety in Late Antiquity*. Oxford UP, 2001.

Dronke, Peter. *Women Writers of the Middle Ages: A Critical Study of Texts from Perpetua (+203) to Marguerite Porête (+1310)*. American Council of Learned Societies Humanities E-Book. Cambridge UP, 1984.

Elliott, Alison Goddard. *Roads to Paradise: Reading the Lives of the Early Saints*. Brown UP, 1987.

Encyclical Epistle of the Church at Smyrna: Concerning the Martyrdom of Polycarp, translated by Alexander Roberts and James Donaldson. https://newadvent.org/fathers/0102.htm.

Pagels, Elaine. *The Gnostic Gospels*. Random House, 1979.

Perkins, Judith. *The Suffering Self: Pain and Narrative Representation in the Early Christian Era*. Routledge, 1995.

Streete, Gail P. C. *Redeemed Bodies: Woman Martyrs in Early Christianity*. Westminster John Knox P, 2009.

Sullivan, Lisa M. "I Responded, 'I Will Not': Christianity as Catalyst for Resistance in the *Passio Perpetuae et Felicitatis*." *Rhetorics of Resistance: A Colloquy on Early Christianity as Rhetorical Formation*, edited by Vincent Wimbush, Scholars P, 1997.

Tite, Philip. "Voluntary Martyrdom and Gnosticism." *Journal of Early Christian Studies*, vol. 23, no. 1, Spring 2015, pp. 27–54.

"Two Homilies Concerning Saint Stephen, Protomartyr." http:www.liturgies.net.

Van Henten, Jan Willem, and Friedrich Avemarie. *Martyrdom and Noble Death: Selected Texts from Graeco-Roman, Jewish and Christian Antiquity*. Routledge, 2002.

Williams, Sam K. *Jesus' Death as Saving Event: The Background and Origin of a Concept*. Harvard Dissertations in Religion. Harvard UP, 1975.

CHAPTER 4

Ashcraft, W. Michael. "Progressive Millennialism." *The Oxford Handbook of Millennialism*, edited by Catherine Wessinger, Oxford UP, 2011, pp. 44–65.

Balch, Robert W. "Waiting for the Ships: Disillusionment and the Revitalization of Faith in Bo and Peep's UFO Cult." *The Gods Have Landed: New Religions from Other Worlds*, edited by James R. Lewis, State U of New York P, 1995, pp. 137–66.

———. "Bo and Peep: A Case Study of the Origins of Messianic Leadership." *Millennialism and Charisma*, edited by Roy Wallis, The Queen's U, 1982, pp. 13–72.

Balch, Robert W., and David Taylor. "Making Sense of the Heaven's Gate Suicides." *Cults, Religion and Violence*, edited by David G. Bromley and J. Gordon Melton, Cambridge UP, 2002, pp. 229–44.

Bearak, Barry. "Eyes on Glory: Pied Pipers of Heaven's Gate." *The New York Times*, 28 April 1997, http://www.nytimes.com/1997/04/28/us/eyes-on-glory-pied-pipers-of-heaven-s-gate.html.

Bromley, David G. "Dramatic Denouements." *Cults, Religion and Violence*, edited by David G. Bromley and J. Gordon Melton, Cambridge UP, 2002, pp. 11–41.

Bromley, David G., and Catherine Wessinger. "Millennial Visions and Conflict with Society." *The Oxford Handbook of Millennialism*, edited by Catherine Wessinger, Oxford UP, 2011, pp. 191–12.

Chrysiddes, George D. "Heaven's Gate." World Religions and Spirituality Project, www.wrldrels.org/profiles/Heaven%27sGate.htm.

DiAngelo, Rio. *Beyond Human Mind: The Soul Evolution of Heaven's Gate*, Rio DiAngelo, 2007.

Do. "Planet about to Be Recycled–Your Only Chance to Survive Is to Leave with Us." Heaven's Gate, 5 October 1996, heavensgate.com/misc/vt100596.htm. Video at www.youtube.com/watch?v=JCotqZfMv34.

———. "Last Chance to Evacuate Earth Before It's Recycled." Heaven's Gate, 29 September 1996, heavensgate.com/misc/vt092996.htm. Video at www.youtube.com/watch?v=m74KOFZYOWM.

———. "Aids in Approaching This Material." *How and When "Heaven's Gate" (The Door to the Physical Kingdom Level Above Human) May Be Entered: An Anthology, by Representatives from the Kingdom of Heaven*, Heaven's Representatives, 1996, pp. iii–iv.

———. "'95 Statement by an E.T. Presently Incarnate." *How and When "Heaven's Gate" (The Door to the Physical Kingdom Level Above Human) May Be Entered: An Anthology, by Representatives from the Kingdom of Heaven*, Heaven's Representatives, 1996, section 1, pp. 5–7.

———. "Undercover 'Jesus' Surfaces before Departure." *How and When "Heaven's Gate" (The Door to the Physical Kingdom Level Above Human) May Be Entered: An Anthology, by Representatives from the Kingdom of Heaven*, Heaven's Representatives, 1996, section 1, pp. 3–4.

Doyle, Clive, with Catherine Wessinger and Matthew D. Wittmer. *A Journey to Waco: Autobiography of a Branch Davidian*. Rowman & Littlefield, 2012.

Federal Bureau of Investigation. "Major Event Log." Lee Hancock Collection, Wittliff Collections, Texas State University, 1993.

Gallagher, Eugene V. "Catastrophic Millennialism." *The Oxford Handbook of Millennialism*, edited by Catherine Wessinger, Oxford UP, 2011, pp. 27–43.

———. "'Theology Is Life and Death': David Koresh on Violence, Persecution, and the Millennium." *Millennialism, Persecution, and Violence: Historical Cases*, edited by Catherine Wessinger, Syracuse UP, 2000, pp. 82–100.

Gifford, Dan, William Gazecki, and Michael McNulty, producers. *Waco: The Rules of Engagement*, Fifth Estate Productions, 1997.

Goodwin, Megan. "Field Notes: Staying after Class: Memory and Materiality beyond Heaven's Gate; Report on the New Religious Movements Group Methods Meeting, 21 November 2014." *Nova Religio*, vol. 20, no. 4, May 2017, pp. 80–93.

Haldeman, Bonnie. *Memories of the Branch Davidians: The Autobiography of David Koresh's Mother*, edited by Catherine Wessinger, Baylor UP, 2007.

Hall, John R., with Philip D. Schuyler and Sylvaine Trinh. *Apocalypse Observed: Religious Movements and Violence in North America, Europe, and Japan*. Routledge, 2000.

Hancock, Lee. "Ex-colonel Says FBI Heard Sect's Fire Plans." *Dallas Morning News*, 8 October 1999.

Hardy, David T., with Rex Kimball. *This Is Not an Assault: Penetrating the Web of Official Lies Regarding the Waco Incident*, Xlibris, 2001.

Hattangadi, Shekhar, director. *Santhara: A Challenge to Indian Secularism?* Shekhar Hattangadi, 2015.

Heaven's Gate. heavensgate.com/.

———. "Our Position against Suicide." Heaven's Gate, heavensgate.com/misc/letter.htm.

——— [Representatives of the Kingdom of Heaven]. *How and When "Heaven's Gate" (The Door to the Physical Kingdom Level Above Human) May Be Entered: An Anthology*, Heaven's Representatives, 1996.

———. "Heaven's Last Mission to This Civilization—To End in '96." 18 August 1995 (unpublished). *How and When "Heaven's Gate" (The Door to the Physical Kingdom Level Above Human) May Be Entered: An Anthology, by Representatives from the Kingdom of Heaven*, Heaven's Representatives, 1996, section 1, 2.

———. 1997. "Student Exit Statements." 8 July 2016, https://www.youtube.com/watch?v=h5IdVndMEr4. Published by Thinker of Thoughts.

———. "'UFO Cult' Resurfaces with Final Offer." 27 May 1993. USA Today Ad/Statement. *How and When "Heaven's Gate" (The Door to the Physical Kingdom Level Above Human) May Be Entered: An Anthology, by Representatives from the Kingdom of Heaven, Heaven's Representatives*, 1996, section 5, 4.

———. "'88 Update—The UFO Two and Their Crew: A Brief Synopsis." 18 October 1988. *How and When "Heaven's Gate" (The Door to the Physical Kingdom Level Above Human) May Be Entered: An Anthology, by Representatives from the Kingdom of Heaven*, Heaven's Representatives, 1996, section 3, 1–17.

———. "HEAVEN'S GATE 'Away Team' Returns to Level above Human in Distant Space." 22 March 1997, http://www.heavensgate.com/misc/pressrel.htm.

Humphry, Derek. *Final Exit: The Practicalities of Self-Deliverance and Assisted Suicide for the Dying*. Dell, 1991.

Jwnody. "Preface." *How and When "Heaven's Gate" (The Door to the Physical Kingdom Level Above Human) May Be Entered: An Anthology, by Representatives from the Kingdom of Heaven, Heaven's Representatives*, 1996, pp. vi–vii.

Kopel, David B., and Paul H. Blackman. *No More Wacos: What's Wrong with Federal Law Enforcement and How to Fix It*. Prometheus Books, 1997.

Koresh, David. "The Seven Seals of the Book of Revelation," unfinished manuscript. *Why Waco? Cults and the Battle for Religious Freedom in America*, by James D. Tabor and Eugene V. Gallagher, U of California P, 1995, pp. 191–203.

———. "Letter to Dick DeGuerin." Letters of Note, 14 April 1993, www.lettersofnote.com/2011/04/we-are-standing-on-threshold-of-great.html.

———. "Audiotape dated 2 March 1993." archive.org/details/david_koresh_radio_sermon_1993.

———. "KRLD Interview." Audiotape dated 28 February 1993.

Lindsay, Hal, with C. C. Carlson. *Late Great Planet Earth*, Zondervan, 1970.

Lvvody. "Ingredients of a Deposit—Becoming a New Creature." *How and When "Heaven's Gate" (The Door to the Physical Kingdom Level Above Human) May Be Entered: An Anthology, by Representatives from the Kingdom of Heaven*, Heaven's Representatives, 1996, Appendix A, 3.

Martin, Sheila. *When They Were Mine: Memoirs of a Branch Davidian Mother*, edited by Catherine Wessinger, Baylor UP, 2009.

Miller, Timothy, editor. *When Prophets Die: The Postcharismatic Fate of New Religious Movements*, State U of New York P, 1991.

Montgomery, Ruth. *Strangers Among Us: Enlightened Beings from a World Beyond*, Putnam, 1979.

Newport, Kenneth G. C. "'A Baptism by Fire': The Branch Davidians and Apocalyptic Self-Destruction." *Nova Religio*, vol. 13, no. 2, November 2009, pp. 61–94.

———. *Branch Davidians of Waco: The History and Beliefs of an Apocalyptic Sect*, Oxford UP, 2006.

Noesner, Gary. *Stalling for Time: My Life as a Hostage Negotiator*, Random House, 2010.

Nrrody. "The Truth Is . . . ." *How and When "Heaven's Gate" (The Door to the Physical Kingdom Level Above Human) May Be Entered: An Anthology, by Representatives from the Kingdom of Heaven*, Heaven's Representatives, 1996, Appendix A, 5.

Pitts, William L., Jr. "SHEkinah: Lois Roden's Quest for Gender Equality." *Nova Religio*, vol. 17, no. 4, February 2013, pp. 37–60.

Reavis, Dick J. *The Ashes of Waco: An Investigation*, Simon & Schuster, 1995.

Richardson, James T. "Minority Religions and the Context of Violence: A Conflict/Interactionist Perspective." *Violence and New Religious Movements*, edited by James R. Lewis, Oxford UP, pp. 31–62.

Roden, Lois. "Baptism by Fire." Audiotape in the Texas Collection, 21 March 1978, Baylor University.

Simpson, Deb. *Closing the Gate*. Piney P, 2012.

Tabor, James D., and Eugene V. Gallagher. *Why Waco? Cults and the Battle for Religious Freedom in America*. U of California P, 1995.

Thomas, Paul Brian. "Revisionism in ET-Inspired Religions." *Nova Religio*, vol. 14, no. 2, November 2010, pp. 61–83.

Walliss, John. *Apocalyptic Trajectories: Millenarianism and Violence in the Contemporary World*, Peter Lang, 2004.

Wessinger, Catherine. "The FBI's 'Cult War' Against the Branch Davidians." *The FBI and Religion: Faith and National Security before and after 9/11*, edited by Sylvester A. Johnson and Steven Weitzman, U of California P, 2017, pp. 203–43.

———. "Notes on Remarks of Mark and Sarah of Heaven's Gate, American Academy of Religion, New Religious Movements Group Methods Meeting, San Diego, 21 November 2014."

———. "Branch Davidians (1981–2006)." *World Religions and Spirituality Project*, 8 January 2013, https://wrldrels.org/2016/02/25/branch-davidians-2/.

———. "Charismatic Leaders in New Religions." *The Cambridge Companion to New Religious Movements*, edited by Olav Hammer and Mikael Rothstein, Cambridge UP, 2012, pp. 80–96.

——— . "Millennialism in Cross Cultural Perspective." *The Oxford Handbook of Millennialism*, edited by Catherine Wessinger, Oxford UP, 2011, pp. 3–24.

———. "Deaths in the Fire at the Branch Davidians' Mount Carmel: Who Bears Responsibility?" *Nova Religio*, vol. 13, no. 2, November 2009, pp. 25–60.

———. *How the Millennium Comes Violently: From Jonestown to Heaven's Gate*, Seven Bridges P, 2000.

———. "The Interacting Dynamics of Millennial Beliefs, Persecution, and Violence." *Millennialism, Persecution, and Violence: Historical Cases*, edited by Catherine Wessinger, Syracuse UP, 2000, pp. 3–39.

——— , ed. *Millennialism, Persecution, and Violence: Historical Cases*, Syracuse UP, 2000.

Wright, Stuart A. "Revisiting the Branch Davidian Mass Suicide Debate." *Nova Religio*, vol. 13, no. 2, November 2009, pp. 4–24.

———. "A Decade after Waco: Reassessing Crisis Negotiations at Mount Carmel in Light of New Government Disclosures," *Nova Religio*, vol. 7, no. 2, November 2003, pp. 101–10.

———. "Anatomy of a Government Massacre: Abuses of Hostage-Barricade Protocols during the Waco Standoff." *Terrorism and Political Violence*, vol. 11, no. 2, 1999, pp. 39–68.

———. "Construction and Escalation of a Cult Threat: Dissecting Moral Panic and Official Reactions to the Branch Davidians." *Armageddon in Waco: Critical Perspectives on the Branch Davidian Conflict*, edited by Stuart A. Wright, U of Chicago P, 1995, pp. 75–94.

Zeller, Benjamin E. *Heaven's Gate: America's UFO Religion*, New York UP, 2014.

———. "The Euphemization of Violence: The Case of Heaven's Gate." *Violence and New Religious Movements*, edited by James R. Lewis, Oxford UP, 2011, pp. 173–89.

———. "Extraterrestrial Biblical Hermeneutics and the Making of Heaven's Gate." *Nova Religio*, vol. 14, no. 2, November 2010, pp. 34–60.

CHAPTER 5

Abd al-Razzaq b. Hammam al-San'ani. *Al-Musannaf*, edited by Ayman Nasr al-Din al-Azhari. Dar al-Kutub al-ʿilmiyya, 2000.

Abu Da'ud al-Sijistani. *Sahih Sunan Abi Da'ud*, edited by Muhammad Nasir al-Din al-Albani. Maktabat al-tarbiya al-'arabiyya li-duwal al-khalij, 1989.

Afsaruddin, Asma. *Striving in the Path of God: Jihad and Martyrdom in Islamic Thought*. Oxford UP, 2013.

Al-'Ayyashi, Muhammad b. Mas'ud. *Kitab al-tafsir*, edited by Hashim al-Rasuli al-Mahallati. Chapkhanah-i 'ilmiyya, 1962.

Al-Bukhari, Muhammad b. Isma'il. *Sahih*, edited by Qasim al-Shamma'i al-Rifa'i. Dar al-qalam, n.d.

Hud b. Muhakkam. *Tafsir kitab allah al-'aziz*, edited by Balhaj b. Sa'id Sharifi. Dar al-gharb al-islami, 1990.

Ibn Abi Shayba. 'Abd allah b. Muhammad. *Al-Kitab al-Musannaf fi 'l-ahadith wa-'l-athar*, edited by Muhammad 'Abd al-Salam Shahin. Dar al-kutub al-ʿilmiyya, 1995.

Ibn Hajar al-'Asqalani. *Tahdhib al-Tahdhib*, edited by Khalil Ma'mum Shiha et al. Dar al-ma'rifa, 1996.

Ibn Maja, Muhammad b. Yazid. *Al-Sunan*, edited by Muhammad Nasir al-Din al-Albani. Maktabat al-ma'arif, 1998.

Ibn al-Mubarak, 'Abd Allah. *Kitab al-jihad*. Al-Maktaba al-'asriyya, 1988.

Jeffrey, Arthur. *The Foreign Vocabulary of the Qur'an*. Oriental Institute, 1938.

Lewinstein, Keith. "The Reevaluation of Martyrdom in Early Islam." *Sacrificing the Self: Perspectives on Martyrdom and Religion*, edited by Margaret Cormack, Oxford UP, 2002, pp. 78–91.

Malik b. Anas. *Al-Muwatta'*, edited by Bashshar 'Awad Ma'ruf and Mahmud Muhammad Khalil. Mu'assasat al-risala, 1994.

Muqatil b. Sulayman. *Tafsir Muqatil b. Sulayman*, edited by 'Abd Allah Mahmud Shihata. Mu'assasat al-ta'rikh al-'arabi, 2002.

Muslim b. Hajjaj. *Sahih*. Dar Ibn Hazm, 1995.

Al-Qurtubi, Muhammad. *Al-Jami' li-ahkam al-Qur'an*, edited by 'Abd al-Razzaq al-Mahdi. Dar al-kitab al-'arabi, 2001.

Al-Razi, Fakhr al-Din. *Al-Tafsir al-kabir*. Dar ihya' al-turath al-'arabi, 1999.

Al-Tabari, Muhammad b. Jarir. *Jami' al-bayan fi tafsir al-qur'an*. Dar al-kutub al-ʿilmiyya, 1997.

Al-Tirmidhi, Abu 'Isa. *Al-Jami' al-sahih*, edited by Kamal Yusuf al-Hut. Dar al-kutub al-ʿilmiyya, 1994.

Al-Wahidi, 'Ali b. Ahmad. *Al-Wasit fi tafsir al-qur'an al-majid*, edited by 'Adil Ahmad 'Abd al-Mawjud, 'Ali Muhammad Mu'awwad, Ahmad Muhammad Sira, and Ahmad 'Abd al-Ghani al-Jamal. Dar al-kutub al-'ilmiyya, 1994.

Wensinck, Arent Jan. "The Oriental Doctrine of the Martyrs." *Semietische Studiën uit de nalatenschap*, edited by Arent Jan Wensinck, Brill, 1941, pp. 91–113.

Al-Zamakhshari, Mahmud b. 'Umar. *Al-Kashshaf 'an haqa'iq ghawamid al-tanzil wa-'uyun al-aqawil fi wujuh al-ta'wil*, edited by 'Adil Ahmad 'Abd al-Mawjud and 'Ali Muhammad Mu'awwad. Maktabat al-'ubaykan, 1998.

CHAPTER 6

Abdulsater, Hussein. *Shi'i Doctrine, Mu'tazili Theology*. Edinburgh UP, 2017.

———. *The Climax of Speculative Theology in Buyid Shī'ism*. Dissertation, Yale University, 2013.

'Alī b. Bilāl. *Al-Maṣābīḥ*, edited by 'Abd Allāh b. 'Abd Allāh b. Aḥmad al-Ḥūthī, Mu'assasat al-Imām Zayd b. 'Alī al-Thaqafiyya, 2002.

Asad, Talal. *On Suicide Bombing*. Columbia UP, 2007.

Baghdādī, 'Abd al-Qāhir b. Ṭāhir al-. *Farq bayn al-firaq*, edited by Muḥammad Fatḥī al-Nādī. Dār al-Salām li-l-Ṭibā wa al-Tawzi' wa al-Tarjama, 2010.

Dakake, Maria. *The Charismatic Community*. State U of New York P, 2007.

Dhahabī, Muḥammad b. Aḥmad al-. *Tārīkh al-islām*, edited by 'Umar 'Abd al-Salam Tadmurī. Dār al-Kitāb al-'Arabī, 1987.

Fyzee, A. A. A. "Ibn Bābawayh (I)." *Encyclopaedia of Islam, Second Edition*, edited by P. Bearman, Th. Bianquis, C. E. Bosworth, E. van Donzel, and W. P. Heinrichs, Brill, 2012, dx.doi.org/10.1163/1573-3912_islam_COM_0318.

Haider, Najam. *The Origins of the Shī'a*. Cambridge UP, 2011.

———. *Shī'ī Islam*. Cambridge UP, 2014.

Ibn Bābawayh, *Amālī al-Ṣadūq*. Maṭba'a al-Haydariyya, 1970.

———. *'Uyūn akhbār al-Riḍā*. Maṭba'a al-Haydariyya, 1970.

Ibn al-Jawzī, 'Abd al-Raḥmān b. 'Alī. *Al-Muntaẓam fi tārīkh al-mulūk wa al-umam*, edited by Muḥammad 'Abd al-Qādir 'Aṭā and Muṣṭafā 'Abd al-Qādir 'Aṭā. Dār al-Kutub al-'Ilmiyya, 2012.

Ibn Kathīr, Ismā'īl b. 'Umar. *Al-Bidāyah wa al-nihāyah*, edited by 'Abd Allāh b. 'Abd al-Muḥsin al-Turkī. Markaz al-Buḥūth wa al-Dirāsāt al-'Arabiyya wa al-Islāmiyya, 1997–98.

Ibn Khallikān, Shams al-Dīn Aḥmad b. Muḥammad. *Wafayāt al-'ayān*, edited by Iḥsān 'Abbās. Dār al-Ṣadr, 2005.

Irbilī, 'Alī b. 'Īsā. *Kashf al-ghumma fi ma'rifat al-a'imma*, edited Ibrāhīm Mīyānjī. Kitābfurūshī-i Islāmiyya, 1962.

Iṣbahānī, Abū al-Faraj al-. *Maqātil al-talibiyyīn*, edited by Sayyid Aḥmad Ṣaqr. Mu'assasat al-A'lamī li-l-Maṭbū'āt, 1998.

Khaṭīb al-Baghdādī, Abū Bakr Aḥmad b. 'Alī al-. *Tārīkh Baghdād*, edited by Muṣṭafā 'Abd al-Qādir 'Aṭā. Dār al-Kutub al-'Ilmiyya, 2011.

Kohlberg, Etan. "Mūsā al-Kāẓim." *Encyclopaedia of Islam, Second Edition*, edited by P. Bearman, Th. Bianquis, C. E. Bosworth, E. van Donzel, and W. P. Heinrichs, Brill, 2012, dx.doi.org/10.1163/1573-3912_islam_SIM_5563.

Kulaynī, Muḥammad b. Ja'far al-. *Al-Uṣūl min al-kāfi*, edited by 'Alī Akbar al-Ghaffārī, Dār al-Kutub al-Islāmiyya, 1983.

Madelung, Wilferd. "al-Kulaynī (or al-Kulīnī), Abū Dja'far Muḥammad." *Encyclopaedia of Islam, Second Edition*, edited by P. Bearman, Th. Bianquis, C. E. Bosworth, E. van Donzel, and W. P. Heinrichs, Brill, 2012, dx.doi.org/10.1163/1573-3912_islam_SIM_4495.

Mas'ūdī, Abū al-Ḥasan 'Alī b. al-Ḥusayn al-. *Murūj al-dhahhab wa ma'ādin al-jawhar*, edited by Charles de Pellat. Manshūrāt al-Jami'a al-Lubnāniyya, 1973.

Modarressi, Hussein. *Crisis and Consolidation in the Formative Period of Shi'ite Islam.* Darwin P, 1993.

Mufīd, Muḥammad b. Muḥammad b. al-Nu'mān al-Shaykh al-. *al-Irshād.* Mu'assasat al-A'lamī li-l-Maṭbū'āt, 1979.

Nawbakhtī, al-Ḥasan b. Mūsā al-. *Kitāb firaq al-Shī'a*, edited by 'Abd al-Mu'nim al-Ḥifnī. Dār al-Rashād, 1992.

Newman, Andrew. *The Formative Period of Twelver Shī'ism.* Curzon, 2000.

Qaradhawi, Yusuf. "Sheik Al Qaradhawi Retracts Fatwa Permitting Palestinian Suicide Bombings; No Need for Them Anymore." www.memri.org/tv/sheikh-al-qaradhawi-retracts-fatwa-permitting-palestinian-suicide-bombings-no-need-them-anymore.

Rosenthal, Franz. "On Suicide in Islam." *Journal of the American Oriental Society*, vol. 66, 1946, pp. 239–59.

Ṣaffār, Abū Ja'far Muḥammad b. al-Ḥasan al-Qummī al-. *Baṣā'ir al-darajāt fī faḍā'il Āl Muḥammad*, edited by Muḥsin Kūchah Bāghī. Mu'assasat al-Nu'mān, 1992.

Ṣāliḥī Najaf'ābādī, Ni'mat Allāh al-. *Shahīd-i jāvīd al-Ḥusayn.* n.p., 1972.

Ṭabarī, Abū Ja'far Muḥammad b. Jarīr al-. *Tarīkh.* Dār al-Kutub al-'Ilmiyya, 1987.

Tottoli, Roberto. "Āṣaf b. Barakhyā." *Encyclopaedia of Islam, THREE*, edited by Kate Fleet, Gudrun Krämer, Denis Matringe, John Nawas, and Everett Rowson, Brill, 2009.

Tustarī, Muḥammad Taqī al-. *Qāmūs al-rijāl.* Mu'assasat al-Nashr al-Islāmī, 1989–.

Wheeler, Brannon. *Prophets in the Quran.* Continuum, 2002.

Ya'qūbī, Aḥmad b. Abī Ya'qūb al-. *Tārīkh al-Ya'qūbī*, edited by 'Abd al-Amīr Muhannā. Mu'assasat al-A'lamī li-l-Maṭbū'āt, 1993.

CHAPTER 7

al-'Amili, Abu Sa'ad. *Martyrdom Operations: The Highest Form of Martyrdom* (Arabic). http://www.tawhed.ws.

al-'Ayiri, Yousuf. *Did Eve Commit Suicide or Martyrdom* (in Arabic). http://www.tawhed.ws.

Ayoub, Shiekh Hassan. *Jihad and Self-Sacrifice in Islam* (Arabic). Dar al-Nadwa al-Jadida, 1983.

al-Azdi, Abu Jandal. *Passages of Jurists about the Rules Concerning Raiding and Human Shields (Bombings and Ambushes)* (Arabic). 20 May 2003, http://www.tawhed.ws.

Bazmool, Muhammad bin Umar bin Salem. *The Precise (muhkam) and Imprecise (mutashabeh) in Takfir and Jihad* (Arabic). Dar El-Mouhcine, 2008.

al-Bukhari, Sahih. *The Book of Funerals*. https://sunnah.com/bukhari/.

———. *The Book of Jihad*. https://sunnah.com/bukhari/.

Cook, David. *Martyrdom in Islam*. Cambridge UP, 2007.

Crone, Patricia. *God's Rule: Government and Islam, Six Centuries of Medieval Islamic Political Thought*. Columbia UP, 2004.

al-Falistini, Abu Qatada. *The Permissibility of Martyrdom Operations: They Are Not Suicide* (Arabic). 6 November 6 1995, http://www.tawed.ws.

Farghal, Yahya Hashim Hasan. *Uncovering the Intentions behind Martyrdom Operations* (Arabic). No date, http://www.tawhed.ws.

Hafez, Mohammed M. "Takfir and Violence against Muslims." *Fault Lines in Global Jihad: Organizational, Strategic, and Ideological Fissures*, edited by Assaf Moghadam and Brian Fishman, Routledge, 2011, pp. 25–46.

———. "The Alchemy of Martyrdom: Jihadi Salafism and Debates over Suicide Bombings in the Muslim World." *Asian Journal of Social Science*, vol. 38, no. 3, 2010, pp. 364–78.

Hatina, Meir. *Martyrdom in Modern Islam: Piety, Power, and Politics*. Cambridge UP, 2014.

Haykal, Muhammad Khair. *Jihad and Combat in Islamic Politics* (Arabic). Dar al-Bayariq, 1993.

Haykel, Bernard. "On the Nature of Salafi Thought and Action." *Global Salafism: Islam's New Religious Movement*, edited by Roel Meijer, Oxford UP, 2013, pp. 33–50.

al-Maqdisi, Abu Muhammad. *Reflections on the Fruits of Jihad: Between the Ignorance of Islamic Law and the Ignorance of Reality* (Arabic). April 2004, http://www.tawhed.ws.

Muhammad, Haitham Abdul Salam. *The Meaning of Terrorism in Islamic Law* (Arabic). Dar al-Kutub al-'Ilmiyya, 2005.

Muslim, Sahih. *The Book of Faith*. https://sunnah.com/muslim/. Accessed 30 November 2016.

———. *The Book on Government*. https://sunnah.com/muslim/.

———. *The Book Pertaining to the Remembrance of Allah, Supplication, Repentance and Seeking Forgiveness*. https://sunnah.com/muslim/.

———. *The Book Pertaining to Piety and Softening of Hearts*. https://sunnah.com/muslim/.

al-Qaradawi, Yusuf. "The (Islamic) Legality of Martyrdom Operations in Occupied Palestine." (Arabic) *al-Mujtama'a*, no. 1204, June 18, 1996, pp. 34–35.

Rosenthal, Franz. "On Suicide in Islam." *Journal of the American Oriental Society*, vol. 66, no. 3, 1946, pp. 239–59.

al-Suhaymee, ‘Abdul Salaam Bin Salem. *Jihad in Islam: Its Meaning, Limits, Forms, and Goals*. Arabic: al-Medina, Saudi Arabia: Dar al-Naseeha, 2008, pp. 112–18.

al-Takrouri, Nawaf Hayel. *Martyrdom Operations in Islamic Jurisprudence* (Arabic). Dar al-Fikr, 2003.

al-Tartousi, Abu Baseer. *The Dangers of Martyrdom or Suicide Bombings*. August 24, 2005. http://www.abubaseer.bizland.com/books/read/b%2055.pdf.

Ibn Taymiyyah, Ahmad bin Abdelhalim. *The Basis of Charging the Enemy: Is It Permissible?* (Arabic). Maktabet Adhwa' al-Salaf, 2002.

CHAPTER 8

Adigal, Prince Ilango. *Shilappadikara. Canto XII, Vettuvavari*, translated by Alain Danielou, New Directions, 1965.

Aguilar, H. *The Sacrifice in the Rgveda*. Bharatiya Vidya Prakashan, 1976.

Alchon, Suzanne Austin. *A Pest in the Land: New World Epidemics in a Global Perspective*. U of New Mexico P, 2003.

Archaeological Survey of India. Annual Reports on Epigraphy (1911–1914), Madras Epigraphical Reports, Archaeological Survey of India, Southern Circle, 1912.

Banerjea, Jitendra Nath. *The Development of Hindu Iconography*. Munshiram Manoharlal, 1985.

Buhler, George, translator and editor. *Laws of Manu. Sacred Books of the East*, Vol. 25, Motilal Banarsidass, 1988.

Colt, George Howe. *The Enigma of Suicide*. Simon and Schuster, 1991.

Daniel Williman, editor. *The Black Death: The Impact of the Fourteenth Century Plague*. Medieval and Renaissance Texts and Studies, 1982.

Dimmitt, Cornelia, and J. A. B. van Buitenen. *Classical Hindu Mythology: A Reader in the Sanskrit Puranas*. Temple UP, 2012.

Durkheim, Émile. *On Suicide*, translated by A. Spaulding and George Simpson, edited by George Simpson, Routledge & Kegan Paul, 1952.

Eggeling, Julius, translator. *Śatapatha Brāhmaṇa*. Motilal Banarsidass, 1988.

Garg, Ganga Ram, editor. *Encyclopedia of the Hindu World*, Vol. 2. Concept Publishing, 1992.

Gottfried, Robert S. *The Black Death: Natural and Human Disaster in Medieval Europe*. The Free P, 1983.

Heesterman, Johannes C. “The Case of the Severed Head.” *Wiener Zeitschrift für die Kunde Süd-und Ostasiens*, vol. 11, 1967, pp. 22–43.

Husain, Mahdi, translator. *The Reḥla of Ibn Baṭṭūṭa: India, Maldive Islands and Ceylon*. Oriental Institute, 1976.

Ilango Adigal. *Shilappadikaram*, Canto XII, Vettuvavari, translated by Alain Danielou, New Directions, 1965.

Kinnsall, Catarina. “Globalization and Religious Nationalism: Self, Identity and the Search for Ontological Security.” *Political Psychology*, vol. 25, no. 5, 2004, pp. 741–67.

Kinsley, David R. *Hindu Goddeses*. U of California P, 1988.

Lorenzen, David N. "New Data on the *Kāpālikas*." *Criminal Gods and Demon Devotees: Essays on the Guardians of Popular Hinduism*, edited by In Alf Hiltebeitel, State U of New York P, 1989.

Lorenzen, David N. *The Kāpālikas and Kālāmukhas: Two Lost Śaivite Sects*. U of California P, 1972.

Miller, Arthur. *After the Fall: A Play in Two Acts*. Penguin Books, 1980.

Minakshi, C. *Administrative and Social Life under the Pallavas*, U of Madras, 1938.

Muller, Max, Ed. "Impurity." *The Laws of Manu: Sacred Books of the East Series*, Vol. 25, translated by Georg Buhler, Motilal Banarsidass, 1988.

Nammalvar. *Hymns for Drowning*. Penguin Books India, 2005.

Narayana Rao, Velcheru, and Gene H. Roghair. *Siva's Warriors: The Basava Purana of Palkuriki Somnatha*. Princeton UP, 1990.

Nathan, Robert. *The Plague in India, 1896, 1897*. Government Central Printing Office, 1898.

Norris, John. "East or West? The Geographic Origin of the Black Death." *Bulletin of the History of Medicine*, vol. 51, no. 1, Spring 1977, pp. 1–24.

Obeyesekere, Grannath. *The Work of Culture: Symbolic Transformation in Psychoanalysis and Anthropology*. U of Chicago P, 1990.

Olivelle, Patrick. *Ascetics and Brahmins: Studies in Ideologies and Institutions*. Anthem Books, 2011.

———. *King, Governance, and Law in Ancient India: Kauṭilya's Arthaśāstra*. Oxford UP, 2013.

———. *The Ashrama System: The History and Hermeneutics of a Religious Institution*. Oxford UP, 1993.

Parpola, Asko. "The 'Fig-Deity Seal' from Mohenjo-Daro: Its Iconography and Inscription." *South Asian Archaeology*, edited by Catherine Jarrige, Prehistory P, 1992, pp. 227–36.

Rao, Rama M. "The Temples of Srisailam." *Journal of the Andhra Historical Research Society*, vol. XVI, 1960, pp. 103–38.

Rao, Velcheru Narayana, and Gene H. Roghair. *Siva's Warriors: The Basava Purana of Palkuriki Somnatha*. Princeton UP, 1990.

Sen, Makhan Lal, translator and editor. *The Ramayana of Valmiki*. Munshiram Manoharlal, 1976.

Shamasastry, R., translator and editor. *Arthaśāstra of Kauṭilya*. 1915. https://archive.org/details/Arthasastra_English_Translation.

Shastri, B. N. translator. *The Kālikāpurāṇa*, Nag Publishers, 1992.

Shastri, Hirananda. "The 'Hamīr-Hath,' or The Obstinacy of Hamīr, the Chauhan Prince of Ranthambhore." *Journal of Indian Art and Industry*, vol. XVII, nos. 129–36, October 1915, pp. 35–40.

Shulman, David. *The Hungry God: Hindu Tales of Filicide and Devotion*. U of Chicago P, 1993.

Sircar, Dineschandra. *Studies in the Religious Life of Ancient and Medieval India.* Motilal Banarsidass, 1971.

Storm, Mary. *Head and Heart: Valour and Self-Sacrifice in The Arts of India.* Routledge, 2013.

———. "An Unusual Group of Hero Stones: Commemorating Self-Sacrifice at Mallam, Andhra Pradesh." *Ars Orientalis,* vol. 44, 2014, pp. 61–84.

Thakur, Upendra. *The History of Suicide in India: An Introduction.* Munshiram Manoharlal, 1963.

Van Buitenen J. A. B, translator and editor. *The Mahābhārata.* U of Chicago, 1973.

Watts, Sheldon. *Epidemics and History: Disease, Power and Imperialism.* Yale UP, 1997.

Wilson, H. H. *The* Vishnu Purana: *A System of Hindu Mythology and Tradition* (Volume 1: Introduction, Book I). Trübner and Co., 1864.

Zydenbos, Robert J. "Virasaivism, Caste, Revolution, Etc." *Journal of the American Oriental Society,* vol. 117, no. 3 (July–September, 1997), 525–35.

CHAPTER 9
Primary Sources

Aparārka. *Commentary on the* Yājñavalkya Smṛti. 2 vols. Ānandāśramasaṃskṛtagranthāvali 46. Ānandāśrama, 1903.

Bhaṭṭa, Devaṇa. *Smṛticandrikā,* 5 vols., edited by L. Srinivasacharya. Bibliotheca Sanskrita 43, 44, 45, 48, 52, 56. Government Branch P, 1914–21.

Bhaṭṭa, Kamalākara. *Nirṇayasindhu,* edited by Nārāyaṇa Rāma Ācārya. Vidyābhavana Prācyavidyā Granthamālā 31. Caukhambā Vidyābhavana, 1991.

Lakṣmīdhara. *Kṛtyakalpataru,* 14 vols., edited by K. V. Rangaswami Aiyangar, Gaekwad's Oriental Series, Oriental Institute, 1941–79.

Madanapāla, *Madanapārijāta* edited by Madhusudana Smritiratana, Bibliotheca Indica 114, Asiatic Society of Bengal, 1893.

Mādhava. *Parāśara-Mādhava, Commentary on the Parāśara Smṛti,* 3 vols., edited by Candrakānta Tarkālaṅkāṛa, The Asiatic Society, 1973–74.

Mahābhārata, edited by V. S. Sukthankar et al., 19 vols., Bhandarkar Oriental Research Institute, 1927–59.

Medhātithi. *Manubhāṣya, Commentary on the* Mānava Dharmaśāstra, edited and translated by Ganganath Jha, 10 vols., Motilal Banarsidass, 1999.

Nīlakaṇṭha. *Śuddhimayūkha,* edited by Anant Yagneshwar Dhupakar, Gujarati P, 1949.

Puṟanāṉūṟu, translated by G. Hart and H. Heifetz, Columbia UP, 1999.

Raghunandana. *Śuddhitattva,* edited by Jīvānanda Vidyāsāgara Bhaṭṭācārya. Siddheśvara P, 1895.

Śatapatha Brāhmaṇa in the Mādhyandina recension, edited by A. Weber. F. Dümmler, 1855.

Upādhyāya, Kāśīnātha. *Dharmasindhu.* Sri Garibdas Oriental Series 14. Sri Satguru Publications, 1986.

Vijñāneśvara. *Mitākṣarā, Commentary on the* Yājñavalkya Smṛti, edited by Nārāyaṇa Rāma Ācārya, Nag Publishers, 1985.
Viṣṇu Smṛti, edited and translated by Patrick Olivelle, Harvard UP, 2009.

Secondary Sources

Brick, David. "The Dharmaśāstric Debate on Widow-Burning." *Journal of the American Oriental Society*, vol. 130, no. 2, 2010, pp. 203–24.
———. "The Widow-Ascetic under Hindu Law." *Indo-Iranian Journal*, vol. 57, no. 4, 2014, pp. 352–83.
Fisch, Joerg. *Burning Women: A Global History of Widow Sacrifice from Ancient Times to the Present*, translated by Rekha Kamath Rajan, Seagull Books, 2006.
Garzilli, Enrica. "First Greek and Latin Documents on *sahagamana* and Some Connected Problems." 2 parts. *Indo-Iranian Journal*, vol. 40, nos. 3–4, 1997, pp. 205–43, 339–65.
Ghose, Jogendra Chunder. *The English Works of Raja Rammohun Roy*, Vol. 2. Srikanta Roy, 1901.
Hall, Fitzgerald. "The Source of Colebrooke's Essay 'On the Duties of a Faithful Hindu Widow.'" *Journal of the Royal Asiatic Society*, vol. 3, 1868, pp. 183–98.
Hart, George L. "Woman and the Sacred in Ancient Tamilnad." *Journal of Asian Studies*, vol. 32, no. 2, 1973, pp. 233-50.
Kane, P. V. *History of Dharmaśāstra*, 5 vols. Bhandarkar Oriental Research Institute, 1962–75.
Lariviere, Richard. "Dharmaśāstra, Custom, 'Real Law' and 'Apocryphal' Sm¨tis." *Recht, Staat und Verwaltung im klassischen Indien*, edited by Bernhard Kölver and Elisabeth Müller-Luckner, R. Oldenbourg Verlag, 1997, pp. 97–110.
Mani, Lata. *Contentious Traditions: The Debate on Sati in Colonial India*. U of California P, 1998.
Nandy, Ashis. "Sati as Profit Versus Sati as a Spectacle: The Public Debate on Roop Kanwar's Death." *Sati, the Blessing and the Curse*, edited by John Stratton Hawley, Oxford UP, 1994, pp. 131–48.
Narasimhan, Sakuntala. *Sati: Widow Burning in India*. Anchar Books, 1992.
Oldenburg, Veena Talwar. "The Roop Kanwar Case: Feminist Responses." *Sati, the Blessing and the Curse*, edited by John Stratton Hawley, Oxford UP, 1994, pp. 101–30.
Olivelle, Patrick. "The Date and Provenance of the *Viṣṇu-Smṛti*: On the Intersection between Text and Iconography." *Indologica Taurinensia* vol. 33, 2007, pp. 149–164.
———. "Dharmaśāstra: A Literary History." *Hinduism and Law: An Introduction*, edited by T. Lubin, D. R. Davis, Jr., and J. K. Krishnan, Cambridge UP, 2010, pp. 28–57.
Potter, Karl H. *Encyclopedia of Indian Philosophies*, vol. 3. Princeton UP, 1981.
Rocher, Ludo, and Rosane Rocher. *The Making of Western Indology: Henry Thomas Colebrooke and the East India Company*. Routledge, 2007.

CHAPTER 10

Amritchandra, Puruṣārthasiddhyupāya. "Sallekhana." http://self.gutenberg.org/articles/sallekhana.

Bharati, Agehananda. "Review of 'Inviting Death: Indian Attitudes toward the Ritual Death' by S. Settar." *Journal of the American Oriental Society*, vol. 119, no. 4, 1990, p. 737.

Bothra, Surendra, *Ahimsa: The Science of Peace*. Prakrit Bharti Academy, 1988.

Cort, John. *Jains in the World: Religious Values and Ideology in India*. Oxford UP, 2001, pp. 137–38.

Dalrymple, William. *Nine Lives: In Search of the Sacred in Modern India*. Knopf Doubleday Publishing, 2009.

Dundas, Paul. *Religion and Violence in South Asia: Theory and Practice*. Routledge, 2006.

———. *The Jains*. Routledge, 2002.

Eliade, Mircea. *Yoga: Immortality and Freedom*. Princeton UP, 1969.

Eplett, Layla. "Rite to Die: Sallekhanā and End of Life." *ScientificAmerican.com*. September 29, 2015. https://blogs.scientificamerican.com/food-matters/rite-to-die-sallekhana-and-end-of-life/.

Granoff, Phyllis. "Fasting or Fighting: Dying the Noble Death in Some Indian Religious Texts." *Heroes and Saints: The Moment of Death in Cross-cultural Perspectives*, edited by Phyllis Granoff and Koichi Shinohara, Cambridge Scholars Publishing, 2007, pp. 73–101.

Hattangadi, Shekar. "Santhara in the Eyes of the Law." *The Hindu*, 23 July 2016. http://www.thehindu.com/opinion/op-ed/santhara-in-the-eyes-of-the-law/article7541803.ece.

Jain, S. Appandai, translator. *Reality*. Jawalamalini Trust, 1992.

Jacobi, Hermann, translator. *The Acāranga Sūtra in Jaina Sutras 1. Sacred Books of the East*. Oxford: The Clarendon P, 1884, http://www.sacred-texts.com/jai/sbe22/sbe2220.htm.

———. *The Sūtrakritanga in Jaina Sutras 2. Sacred Books of the East*. Oxford: The ClarendonP, 1895, http://www.sacred-texts.com/jai/sbe45/index.htm.

Jaini, Padmanabh. *The Jaina Path of Purification*. Motilal Banarisidass, 1979.

Laidlaw, James. *Riches and Renunciation: Religion, Economy, and Society among the Jains*. Clarendon P, 1995.

Luhmann, Niklas. *A Systems Theory of Religion*, translated by David Brenner and Adrian Hermann, Stanford UP, 2013.

Mookerji, Radhakumund. *Chandrapgupta and His Times*. Motilal Banarisidass, 1988.

Pujyapâda, Âcârya. *Sarvârthasiddhi*, translated by S. Appandai Jain as *Reality*. Jawalamalini Trust, 1992.

Samantabhadra Âcârya. *Ratna Karanda Śrāvakāchāra*, translated by Champat Rai Jain as *The Householder's Dharma*. Central Jaina Publishing House, 1917.

Settar, Shadakshari. *Inviting Death: Indian Attitude Towards the Ritual Death*. Brill, 1989.

Soni, Nikhil v. Union of India & Ors. Civil Writ Petition 7414/2006. Public Interest Litigation.

Singh, Jaipat v. Union of India & Ors Special Leave Petition (c) no. 1129 of 2016.

Titze, Kurt. *Jainism: A Pictorial Guide to the Religion of Non-Violence,* 2nd ed. Motilal Banarsidass, 2001.

Tobias, Michael. *Life Force: The World of Jainism*. Jain Publishing Company, 1991.

Tukol, T.K. *Sallekhana is Not Suicide*. L. D. Institute of Indology, 1976.

CHAPTER 11

Ashok, S. S., editor. *Giānī Ditt Siṅgh Rachnāvalī: Śahīdīān*. Bhasha Vibhag Punjab, 1977.

Bedi, T. S., editor. *Sikhān dī Bhagatmālā*. Punjabi UP, 1994.

Bhalla, Sarup Das. *Mahimā Prakāś*, vol. II. Bhasha Vibhag, 2003.

Dhillon, B. S., editor. *Srī Gur-panth Prakāś krit S. Ratan Siṅgh Bhaṅgū*. Singh Brothers, 2004.

Fenech, L. E. *Martyrdom in the Sikh Tradition: Playing the "Game of Love."* Oxford UP, 2000.

———. "Martyrdom and the Execution of Guru Arjan in Early Sikh Sources." *Journal of the American Oriental Society*, vol. 121, no. 1, Jan.–Mar 2001, pp. 20–31.

Fox, Richard. *The Lions of the Punjab: Culture in the Making*. U of California P, 1985.

Garja Singh, editor. *Śahid-bilās (Bhāī Manī Siṅgh) krit Sevā Siṅgh*. Punjabi Sahit Academy, 1961.

Geertz, Clifford. *The Interpretation of Cultures*. Basic Books, 1973.

Gill, R. S. *Drinking from Love's Cup: Surrender and Sacrifice in the Vārs of Bhai Gurdas Bhalla*. Oxford UP, 2017.

Grewal, J. S. *History, Literature and Identity: Four Centuries of Sikh Tradition*. Oxford UP, 2013.

Kang, Mona. *The Concept of Martyrdom in Sikhism and Sikh Martyrs up to the Eighteenth Century*. Dissertation, Panjab University, 1990.

McLeod, W. H. *Who is a Sikh? The Problem of Sikh Identity*. Oxford UP, 1989.

———. *Sikhs of the Khalsa: A History of the Khalsa Rahit*. Oxford UP, 2003

Padam, P. S., editor. *Baṅsāvalīnāmā Dasān Pātśāhīān kā*. Singh Brothers, 1997.

Singh, Pashaura. "Gurmat: The Teachings of the Guru." *The Oxford Handbook of Sikh Studies*, edited by Pashaura Singh and Louis Fenech, Oxford UP, 2014, pp. 225–39.

Singh, Teja. *The Gurdwara Reform Movement and the Sikh Awakening*. N.p., 1922.

Singh, Vir, editor. *Vārān Bhāī Gurdās*. Bhai Vir Singh Sahit Sadan, 1997.

CHAPTER 12

Balasingham, Anton. *War and Peace: Armed Struggle and Peace Efforts of Liberation Tigers*. Fairmax, 2004.

Chandrakanthan, A. J. V. "Eelam Tamil Nationalism: An Insider's View." *Sri Lankan Tamil Nationalism*, edited by A. J. Wilson, U of Washington P, 2000, pp. 157–83.

Hellmann-Rajanayagam, Dagmar. "And Heroes Die: Poetry of the Tamil Liberation Movement in Northern Sri Lanka." *South Asia: Journal of South Asian Studies*, vol. 28, no. 1, 2005, pp. 112–53.

Hoffman, Bruce. "Old Madness New Methods: The Revival of Religious Terrorism begs for Broader US Policy." *The Rand Review*, vol. 22, no. 2, 1998–1999, pp. 12–17.

Kleinfeld, Margo. "Strategic Troping in Sri Lanka: September Eleventh and the Consolidation of Political Position." *Geopolitics*, vol. 8, no. 3, 2003, pp. 105–26.

Liberation Tigers of Tamil Eelam. "Heroes Day Speech (Tamil and English Versions)." www.eelamweb.com/leader/messages/herosday/1998.

Natali, Cristiana. "Building Cemeteries, Constructing Identities." *Contemporary South Asia*, vol. 16, no. 3, 2009, pp. 287–301.

Pape, Robert. *Dying to Win: The Strategic Logic of Suicide Terrorism*. Random House, 2006.

Pfaffenberger, Bryan. *Caste in Tamil Culture: The Religious Foundation of Sudra Domination in Tamil Sri Lanka*. Maxwell School of Citizenship and Public Affairs, 1982.

———. "The Political Construction of Defensive Nationalism: The 1968 Temple-Entry Crisis in Northern Sri Lanka." *The Journal of Asian Studies*, *v*ol. 49, no. 1, 1990, pp. 78–96.

Ramaswamy, Sumathi. *Passions of the Tongue*. U of California P, 1997.

Rao, A. K. "Theologizing the Inaugural Verse: Śleṣa Reading in Rāmāyaṇa Commentary." *Journal of Hindu Studies*, vol. 1, no. 1–2, 2008, pp. 74–92.

Renan, Ernest. "Qu'est-ce qu'une Nation." *The Nationalism Reader*, edited by O. Dabhour and M. Ishay, Humanities P, 1995, pp. 143–55.

Roberts, Michael. "Saivite Symbols, Sacrifice, and Tamil Tiger Rites." *Social Analysis*, vol. 49, no. 1, 2005, pp. 67–93.

———."Tamil Tiger 'Martyrs': Regenerating Divine Potency?" *Studies in Conflict and Terrorism*, vol. 28, 2005, pp. 493–514.

——— . "Pragmatic Action and Enchanted Worlds: A Black Tigers Rite of Commemoration." *Social Analysis*, vol. 51, no. 1, 2006, pp. 73–102.

Schalk, P. "Revival of Martyr Cults among the Ilavar." *Temenos*, vol. 33, no. 1, 1997, pp. 151–90.

——— . "Present Concepts of Secularism Among Ilavar and Lankans." *Zwischen Säkularismus und Hierokratie: Studien zum Verhältnis von Religion und Staat in Süd-Und Ostasien*, edited by P. Schalk, Uppsala UP, 2001, pp. 37–72.

———. "Beyond Hindu Festivals." *Tempel und Tamilen in Zweiter Heimat*, edited by Martin Baumann et al., Ergon Verlag, 2003, pp. 391–420.

Schmitt, Carl. *Political Theology*. U of Chicago P, 2005.

———. *The Concept of the Political*. U of Chicago P, 1996.

Schonthal, Benjamin. "Translating Remembering." *Sri Lanka Reader*, edited by John Holt, Duke UP, 2011.

Smith, Anthony D. *Nations and Nationalism in a Globalized Era*. New York, Polity P, 1995.

Tillich, Paul. *Dynamics of Faith*. Harper Collins, 1957.

CHAPTER 13

Benn, James. "Where Text Meets Flesh: Burning the Body as an Apocryphal Practice in Chinese Buddhism." *History of Religions*, vol. 37, no. 4, 1998, pp. 295–322.

Collins, Steven. "The Body in Theravāda Buddhist Monasticism." *Religion and the Body*, edited by Sarah Coakley, Cambridge UP, 1997, pp. 85–204.

Cowell, Edward B., and Robert A. Neil, editors. *The Divyāvadāna: A Collection of Early Buddhist Legends*, Oriental P, 1970.

Crosby, Kate, and Andrew Skilton, translators. *The Bodhicaryāvatāra*. Oxford World's Classics. Oxford UP, 1998.

Dutt, Nalinaksha, editor. *Bodhisattvabhūmi*. K. P. Jayaswal Research Institute, 1978.

Faure, Bernard. "Substitute Bodies in Chan/Zen Buddhism." *Religious Reflections on the Human Body*, edited by Jane Marie Law, Indiana UP, 1995, pp. 211–29.

Fausboll, V., editor. *The Jātaka Together With Its Commentary, Being Tales of the Anterior Births of Gotama Buddha*. 6 vols. and Index. Trübner, 1875–97.

Hahn, Michael. *Haribhaṭṭa and Gopadatta, Two Authors in the Succession of Āryaśūra: On the Rediscovery of Parts of Their Jātakamālās*. 2nd ed. Studia Philologica Buddhica Occasional Paper 1. International Institute for Buddhist Studies, 1992.

Hamilton, Sue. "From the Buddha to Buddhaghos: Changing Attitudes Toward the Human Body in Theravāda Buddhism." *Religious Reflections on the Human Body*, edited by Jane Marie Law, Indiana UP, 1995, pp. 46–63.

Handurukande, Ratna, editor and translator. *Five Buddhist Legends in the Campū Style From a Collection Named Avadānasārasamuccaya*. Indica et Tibetica Verlag, 1984.

———. *Maṇicūḍāvadāna, Being a Translation and Edition, and Lokānanda, a Transliteration and Synopsis*. Sacred Books of the Buddhists 24. Pali Text Society, 1967.

Horner, I. B., translator. *The Book of the Discipline (Vinaya Piṭaka)*. 6 vols. Sacred Books of the Buddhists, Vols. 10, 11, 13, 14, 20, and 25. H. Milford, Oxford UP, 1938–66.

———. *The Minor Anthologies of the Pali Canon, Part 3: Buddhavaṃsa and Cariyāpiṭaka*. Sacred Books of the Buddhists 31. Pali Text Society, 1975.

Huber, E., translator. *Aśvaghoṣa Sūtrālaṃkāra*. Ernest Leroux, 1908.

Hubert, Henri, and Marcel Mauss. *Sacrifice: Its Nature and Function*, translated by W. D. Halls, U of Chicago P, 1964.

Hurvitz, Leon, translator. *Scripture of the Lotus Blossom of the Fine Dharma (The Lotus Sūtra)*. Columbia UP, 1976.

Jayawickrama, N. A., editor. *Buddhavaṃsa and Cariyāpiṭaka*. Pali Text Society Text Series 166. Pali Text Society, 1974.

Jenkins, Stephen L. "Benefit of Self and Other: The Importance of Persons and their Self-Interest in Buddhist Ethics." *Dharma Drum Journal of Buddhist Studies*, vol. 16, 2015, pp. 141–69.

Kajiyama, Yuichi. "The Body." *Encyclopaedia of Buddhism*, edited by G. P. Malalasekera, Vol. 3, fasc. 4, 616–19, Government of Sri Lanka P, 1972.

Keown, Damien. "Buddhism and Suicide: The Case of Channa." *Journal of Buddhist Ethics*, vol. 3, 1996, pp. 8–31.

Lamotte, Étienne. "Religious Suicide in Early Buddhism." *Buddhist Studies Review*, vol. 4, no. 2, 1987, pp. 105–18.

Lamotte, Étienne, translator. *Le traité de la grande vertu de Sagesse de Nāgārjuna*. 5 vols. Bibliothèque du Muséon 18. Bureaux du Muséon, 1944–80.

Lévi, Sylvain, editor and translator. *Mahāyāna-Sūtrālaṃkāra, exposé de la doctrine du Grand Véhicule selon le système Yogācāra*. 2 vols. H. Champion, 1907–11.

Mahoney, Richard. *Of the Progress of the Bodhisattva: The Bodhisattvamārga in the Śikṣāsamuccaya*. Thesis, University of Canterbury, 2002.

Monier-Williams, Sir Monier. *A Sanskrit-English Dictionary*. New ed. Oxford UP, 1979.

Mrozik, Susanne. *Virtuous Bodies: The Physical Dimensions of Morality in Buddhist Ethics*. Oxford UP, 2007.

———. *The Relationship Between Morality and the Body in Monastic Training According to the Śikṣāsamuccaya*. Dissertation, Harvard University, 1998.

Nattier, Jan. *A Few Good Men: The Bodhisattva Path According to The Inquiry of Ugra (Ugraparipṛcchā)*. U of Hawai'i P, 2003.

Nobel, Johannes, editor. *Suvarṇabhāsottamasūtra: Das Goldglanz-sūtra, Ein Sanskrittext des Mahāyāna-Buddhismus*. Otto Harrassowitz, 1937.

Ohnuma, Reiko. *Head, Eyes, Flesh, and Blood: Giving Away the Body in Indian Buddhist Literature*. Columbia UP, 2007.

Schmidt, I. J., editor and translator. *Der weise und der thor: Aus dem tibetischen uebersetzt und mit dem originaltexte herausgegeben*. Leopold Voss, 1845.

Speyer, J. S., translator. *The Gātakamālā; or, Garland of Birth-Stories by Ārya Sūra*. Sacred Books of the Buddhists 1. Oxford UP, 1895.

Trenckner, Vilhelm, editor. *The Milindapañho: Being Dialogues Between King Milinda and the Buddhist Sage Nāgasena*. Williams and Norgate, 1880.

Vaidya, P. L., editor. *Jātakamālā*. Buddhist Sanskrit Texts 21. Mithila Institute, 1959a.

———. *Avadāna-kalpalatā of Kṣemendra*. 2 vols. Buddhist Sanskrit Texts 22–23. Mithila Institute, 1959b.

Walshe, Maurice, translator. *The Long Discourses of the Buddha: A Translation of the Dīgha Nikāya*. Wisdom Publications, 1995.

Williams, Paul. "Some Mahāyāna Buddhist Perspectives on the Body." *Religion and the Body*, edited by Sarah Coakley, Cambridge UP, 1997, pp. 205–30.

Wilson, Liz. *Charming Cadavers: Figurations of the Feminine in Indian Buddhist Hagiographic Literature*. U of Chicago P, 1996.

Wiltshire, Martin. "The 'Suicide' Problem in the Pāli Canon." *Journal of the International Association of Buddhist Studies* 6, 1983, pp. 124–40.

Yamada, Isshi, Ed. *Karuṇāpuṇḍarīka: The White Lotus of Compassion*, 2 vols. School of Oriental and African Studies, 1968.

CHAPTER 14

Primary

References to the *Taishō shinshū daizōkyō* (85 vols., edited by Takakusu Junjiro, Watanabe Kaigyoku, et al., Taisho Issaikyo Kanko Kai, 1924–1934) are abbreviated as T., followed by the work number, volume number, page number, and the registry column (a, b, or c). A * next to a title of a work indicates that the Sanskrit title is a reconstruction from the Chinese.

References to the *Wanzi xuzangjing* (150 vols., Xinwenfeng chubangongsi, 1968–1970), a reprint of the *Dainihon zokuzōkyō* (150 vols., edited by Nankano Tatsue, Zōkyō shoin, 1905–1912), are abbreviated as X., followed by the work number, volume number, page number, and the registry column (a or b), and line.

References to the Daoist Canon *Daozang* are abbreviated as DZ, followed by index number based on Kristofer Schipper and Franciscus Verellen, *The Taoist Canon: A Historical Companion to the Daozang,* U of Chicago P, 2004. The Daoist works used are from Zhang Jiyu et al., *Zhonghua daozang*, Huaxia chubanshe, 2004.

References to the *Gujin tushu jicheng* by Chen, Menglei (b. 1651) et al. are abbreviated as *GJTSJC*, followed by category, section, *juan*, *ce*, and page number. The *GJTSJC* used for this book is the United Data Banks Digital Publication, Inc., online version as provided by Eastview.com. This database gives page images of the Taipei: Dingwen shuju edition, 1977.

Daojie (1866–1934) and Yu Qian (d.u.). "Xinxu gaoseng zhuan (Continued Biographies of Eminent Monks)." *Gaoseng zhuan heji* (Compilation of Eminent Monks), Shanghai guji chubanshe, 1991.

Shisong lü (Ten Recitations Vinay; Skt. *Daśabhāṇavāra vinaya*). T no. 1435, 23.

Yu Zhengxie (1775–1840). "Qiuyu shuo." *Huangchao jingshi wenxubian*, edited by Ge Shijun (fl. 1888), *juan* 46, "Huangzheng," Wenhai chubanshe, 1972, pp. 26a–27b.

Za Ahan jing (Miscellaneous Āgama Sūtras; Skt. *Saṃyukta-āgama*). T no. 99, 2.

Secondary

Anālayo, Bhikkhu. "The Mass Suicide of Monks in Discourse and Vinaya Literature." *Journal of the Oxford Centre for Buddhist Studies*, vol. 7, 2014, 11–55.

Benn, James. *Burning for the Buddha: Self-Immolation in Chinese Buddhism.* U of Hawai'i P, 2007.

Birrell, Anne. *Chinese Mythology: An Introduction*. John Hopkins UP, 1993.

Bronkhorst, Johannes. *The Two Traditions of Meditation in Ancient India.* Motilal Banarsidass, 1993/2000.

Campany, Robert Ford. *To Live as Long as Heaven and Earth: A Translation and Study of Ge Hong's* Traditions of Divine Transcendents. U of California P, 2002.

———. *Making Transcendents: Ascetics and Social Memory in Early Medieval China.* U of Hawai'i P, 2009.

Cuevas, Bryan. *The All-Pervading Melodious Drumbeat: The Life of Ra Lotsawa*. Penguin Books, 2015.

Eberhard, Wolfram. *Lokalkulturen im alten China*, vol. 1. *Die Lokalkulturen des Nordens und Westens*. Brill, 1942.

Eskildsen, Stephen. *Asceticism in Early Taoist Religion*. State U of New York P, 1998.

Hashmi, Sohail H., editor. *Just Wars, Holy Wars, and Jihads: Christian, Jewish, and Muslim Encounters and Exchanges*. Oxford UP, 2012.

Kelsay, John. *Arguing the Just War in Islam*. Harvard UP, 2007.

Kaltenmark, Maxime. *Le Lie-sien tchouan: Biographies legendaires des immortels taoistes de l'antiquite*. Université de Paris, Centre d'Études Sinologiques de Pekin, 1953.

Khosrokhavar, Farhad. *Suicide Bombers: Allah's New Martyrs*, translated by David Macey, Pluto P, 2005.

Laidlaw, James. "A Life Worth Leaving: Fasting to Death as Telos of a Jain Religious Life." *Economy and Society*, vol. 34, no. 2, 2005, pp. 178–99.

Min, Zhiting, et al. *Daojiao da cidian* (Encyclopedia of Daoist Religion). Huaxia chuban she, 1994.

Mochizuki Shinkō, editor. *Mochizuki Bukkyō daijiten*, 10 vols. Sekai Seiten Kankō Kyōkai, 1954–1963.

Mollier, Christine. *Buddhism and Taoism Face to Face: Scripture, Ritual, and Iconographic Exchange in Medieval China*. U of Hawai'i P, 2008.

Oberlies, Thomas. "Das Sterben 'Lebender Toter': Zur Genese des Instituts des Freitods und Zum Umgang der Indischen Rechtstradition Mit Ihm." *Acta Orientalia*, vol. 67, 2006, pp. 203–28.

Ohnuma, Reiko. *Head, Eyes, Flesh, and Blood*. Columbia U, 2007.

Olivelle, Patrick. "Deconstruction of the Body in Indian Asceticism." *Asceticism*, edited by Vincent L. Wimbush and Richard Valantasis, Oxford UP, 1988, pp. 118–210.

Olson, Carl. *Indian Asceticism: Power, Violence, and Play*. Oxford UP, 2015.

Pregadio, Fabrizio. *Great Clarity: Daoism and Alchemy in Early Medieval China*. Stanford UP, 2006.

———. ed. *The Encyclopedia of Taoism*. Routledge, 2008.

Robinet, Isabelle. "Metamorphosis and Deliverance from the Corpse in Taoism." *History of Religions*, vol. 19, no. 1, Aug. 1979, 37–70.

Schafer, Edward. "Ritual Exposure in Ancient China." *Harvard Journal of Asiatic Studies*, vol. 14, nos. 1/2, June 1951, pp. 130–84.

Schipper, Kristofer, and Franciscus Verellen. *The Taoist Canon: A Historical Companion to the Daozang*. U of Chicago P, 2004.

Schubring, Walter. *Die Lehre der Jains*. Walter De Gruyter & Company, 1935.

Seidel, Anna. "Post-Mortem Immortality or Taoist Resurrection of the Body." *Gilgul: Essays on Transformation, Revolution and Permanence in the History of Religions, Dedicated to R. J. Zwi Werblowsky*, edited by S. Shaked, D. Shulman, and G. G. Stroumsa, Brill, 1987, pp. 223–37.

Teiser, Stephen F. *The Scripture on the Ten Kings and the Making of Purgatory in Medieval Chinese Buddhism*. U of Hawai'i P, 1994.
Yu, Jimmy. *Sanctity and Self-Inflicted Violence in Chinese Religions, 1500–1700*. Oxford UP, 2012.

CHAPTER 15

ABBREVIATIONS

DNBZ *Dai Nihon bukkyō zensho*, 100 vols., edited and published by Suzuki Gakujutsu Zaidan, 1970–1973.
JZ *Jōdoshū zensho*, 23 vols., edited by Jōdoshū Kaishū Happyakunen Kinen Keisan Junbikyoku, Sankibō Busshorin, 1970–1972.
NKBT *Nihon koten bungaku taikei*, 102 vols., edited by Takagi Ichinosuke et al., Iwanami Shoten, 1958–1966.
ST *Zōho shiryō taisei*, 45 vols., edited by Zōho Shiryō Taisei Kankōkai, Rinsen Shobō, 1965.
T *Taishō shinshū daizōkyō*, 85 vols., edited by Takakusu Junjirō and Watanabe Kaigyoku, Taishō Issaikyō Kankōkai, 1924–1932.

Benn, James A. *Burning for the Buddha: Self-Immolation in Chinese Buddhism*. U of Hawai'i P, 2007.
———. "Where Text Meets Flesh: Burning the Body as an Apocryphal Practice in Chinese Buddhism." *History of Religions*, vol. 37, no. 4, 1998, pp. 295–322.
Blum, Mark L. "Collective Suicide at the Funeral of Jitsunyo: Mimesis or Solidarity?" *Death and the Afterlife in Japanese Buddhism*, edited by Jacqueline I. Stone and Mariko Namba Walter, U of Hawai'i P, pp. 37–74.
Brown, Jonathan Todd. *Warrior Patronage, Institutional Change, and Doctrinal Innovation in the Early Jishū*. Dissertation, Princeton U, 1999.
Chen Naiqian, editor. *Sanguo zhi*, 5 vols. Zhonghua Shuju, 1959.
Chiba-ken Kyōdo Shiryō Kankōkai, editor. *Kaitei Bōsō sōsho*, 6 vols. Chiba-shi, 1972.
Dykstra, Yoshiko Kurata, translator. *Miraculous Tales of the Lotus Sutra from Ancient Japan: The* Dainihonkoku Hokekyōkenki *of Priest Chingen*. Intercultural Research Institute, Kansai U of Foreign Studies, 1983.
Hanawa Hokinoichi, editor. *Gunsho ruijū*, 29 vols. Zoku Gunsho Ruijū Kanseikai, 1928–1934.
Harries, Phillip Tudor, translator. *The Poetic Memoirs of Lady Daibu*. Stanford UP, 1980.
Heine, Steven. "Tragedy and Salvation in the Floating World: Chikamatsu's Double Suicide Drama as Millenarian Discourse." *Journal of Asian Studies*, vol. 53, no. 2, 1994, pp. 367–93.
Hori, Ichiro. "Self-Mummified Buddhas in Japan: An Aspect of the Shugen-Dō ('Mountain Asceticism') Sect." *History of Religions*, vol. 1, no. 2, 1962, pp. 222–42.

Hurvitz, Leon, translator. *Scripture of the Lotus Blossom of the Fine Dharma (the Lotus Sūtra)*. Columbia UP, 2009.

Inoue Mitsusada and Ōsone Shōsuke, editors. *Ōjōden, Hokke genki. Zoku Nihon bukkyō no shisō*. Iwanami Shoten, 1995.

Itoga Kimie, editor. *Kenreimon'in Ukyō no Daibu shūū*. Shinchōsha, 1979.

Kieschnick, John. *The Eminent Monk: Buddhist Ideals in Medieval Chinese Hagiography*. U of Hawai'i P, 1997.

Kondō Heijō, editor. *Shiseki shūran*, 33 vols. Kondō Shuppanbu, 1924–1938.

Kubota Jun. "Tennōji to ōjōnin-tachi." *Ronsan setsuwa to setsuwa bungaku*, edited by Mitani Eiichi, Kunisaki Fumimaro, and Kubota Jun. Kasama Shoin, 1979, pp. 215–29.

Kuroita Katsumi et al., editors. *Shintei zōho kokushi taikei*, 66 vols. Yoshikawa Kōbunkan, 1929–1966.

McCullough, Helen Craig, translator. *The Taiheiki: A Chronicle of Medieval Japan*. Columbia UP, 1959.

———, translator. *Yoshitsune: A Fifteenth-Century Japanese Chronicle*. Stanford UP, 1971.

Meeks, Lori. "Survival and Salvation in the *Heike monogatari*: Reassessing the Legacy of Kenreimon'in." *Lovable Losers: The Heike in Action and Memory*, edited by Mikael S. Adolphson and Anne Commons, U of Hawai'i P, 2015, pp. 142–65.

Miki Sumito, editor. *Hōjōki, Hosshinshū*. Shinchōsha, 1976.

Mills, D. E., translator. *A Collection of Tales from Uji: A Study and Translation of Uji Shūi Monogatari*. Cambridge UP, 1970.

Moerman, D. Max. "Passage to Fudaraku: Suicide and Salvation in Premodern Japanese Buddhism." *The Buddhist Dead: Practices, Discourses, Representations*, edited by Bryan J. Cuevas and Jacqueline I. Stone, U of Hawai'i P, 2007, pp. 266–96.

Morrell, Robert E., translator. *Sand and Pebbles (Shasekishū): The Tales of Mujū Ichien, A Voice for Pluralism in Kamakura Buddhism*. State U of New York P, 1985.

Nei Kiyoshi. *Fudaraku tokaishi*. Hōzōkan, 2001.

Ōhashi Shunnō. *Ippen: Sono kōdō to shisō*. Hyōronsha, 1971.

Stone, Jacqueline I. *Right Thoughts at the Last Moment: Buddhism and Deathbed Practices in Early Medieval Japan*. U of Hawai'i P, 2016.

Tachibana Shundō and Umetani Shigeki, editors. *Ippen shōnin zenshū*. Shunjūsha, 1989.

Takeuchi Rizō, editor. *Heian ibun*, 13 vols. Tōkyōdō Shuppan, 1963–1968.

Tomikura Tokujirō, editor. *Meitokuki*. Iwanami Shoten, 1941.

Tyler, Royall, translator. *The Tale of the Heike*. Viking P, 2012.

Yoshida Yasuo. "Shashingyō no tenkai to sono shisō." *Nihon kodai no bosatsu to minshū*, Yoshikawa Kōbunkan, 1988, pp. 187–222.

Index

Lightning Source UK Ltd.
Milton Keynes UK
UKHW011822240622
404918UK00005B/1289

9 780190 656492